THE UN SECRETARY-GENERAL
AND MORAL AUTHORITY

THE UN SECRETARY-GENERAL AND MORAL AUTHORITY

Ethics and Religion in International Leadership

KENT J. KILLE, EDITOR

GEORGETOWN UNIVERSITY PRESS   WASHINGTON, D.C.

Georgetown University Press, Washington, D.C. www.press.georgetown.edu

Library of Congress Cataloging-in-Publication Data

The UN Secretary-General and moral authority : ethics and religion in international leadership / edited by Kent J. Kille.
    p. cm.
    Includes bibliographical references and index.
    ISBN-13: 978-1-58901-180-9 (alk. paper)
    1. International relations—Moral and ethical aspects. 2. Political leadership—Moral and ethical aspects. 3. United Nations. Secretary-General. I. Kille, Kent J.
JZ1306.U55 2007
172'.4—dc22

2007011204

14 13 12 11 10 09 08 07   9 8 7 6 5 4 3 2
First printing

Printed in the United States of America

To the vision of Harold Guetzkow and
In memory of Charles S. McCoy

CONTENTS

ACKNOWLEDGMENTS

The first and most important acknowledgment is to Harold Guetzkow. Dr. Guetzkow initiated the project that produced this volume and ensured generous funding that supported research, travel, and meetings. He stressed the need for a detailed examination of the religious and moral values of the UN secretaries-general while encouraging us to present the study in a manner that would be accessible to a range of interested readers. The authors of this volume hope we have been able to live up to his impressive vision.

The initial guidelines for this study were developed by the editor in conjunction with Dr. Guetzkow and the late Charles McCoy at the Center for Ethics and Social Policy of the Graduate Theological Union in Berkeley, California. We were also assisted at this early juncture by an advisory committee consisting of Edwin Epstein, Mark Juergensmeyer, Jack Sawyer, Courtney Smith, Robert Traer, and William Trampleasure.

The first full meeting of the contributors was held in August 2004 at Seton Hall University's John C. Whitehead School of Diplomacy and International Relations. As the research progressed, follow-up meetings and paper presentations took place at the annual meetings of the International Studies Association–Southern Region in 2004, the International Studies Association in 2005 and 2006, the Academic Council on the United Nations System in 2005 and 2006, and the American Political Science Association in 2006, as well as the Centre for the Study of Religion and Politics at the University of St. Andrews in 2005.

Although they are directly referenced in the relevant chapters, we want to offer our great thanks to those close to the secretaries-general who agreed to be interviewed for this volume—Guri Lie Zeckendorf, Thant Myint-U, Rafee Ahmed, Diego Cordovez, James Jonah, Albert Rohan, Samir Sambar, Paul Wee, Jean-Marc Coicaud, Michael Doyle, Patrick Hayford, Robert Orr, Kieran Prendergast, Lamin Sise, and Gillian Sorensen—as well as those individuals who wished to remain anonymous but who provided important information.

The development of this volume also benefited from discussions with and comments from a wide range of individuals: Mel Dubnick, Nick Nolobof, June Bingham, Sri Chinmoy, Indar Jit Rikhye, Brian Urquhart, Charles Hill, Caroline Lombardo, Michael Barnett, Jacques Baudot, Josef Boehle, Lawrence Finkelstein, Manuel Fröhlich, Leon Gordenker, Mark Graham, Ryan Hendrickson, Ian Johnstone, Robert Jordan, Edward Newman, Henrike Paepcke, Benjamin Rivlin, B. G. Ramcharan, Joel Rosenthal, Michael Schechter, Joseph Schwartzberg, Joe Sills, Winston Sims, and James Sutterlin. An extra thank you to the conference panel discussants who took the time to review and comment on early drafts: Brent Nelsen, Donald Puchala, and Mary Segers. Our deep apologies to anyone whom we have inadvertently failed to acknowledge.

The editor would like to thank his research assistants at The College of Wooster: Emily Hilty, Margaret Ann Stewart, and Stefanie Zaranec. A particular debt of gratitude is owed to Lara Pfaff, who provided invaluable assistance in preparing the book manuscript. The editor would also like to acknowledge the financial support provided by the Henry Luce III Fund for Distinguished Scholarship at The College of Wooster, which aided in the completion of the volume. The support and assistance provided by Richard Brown and the staff of Georgetown University Press is also greatly appreciated.

Finally, we want to express our special gratitude to the secretaries-general who agreed to be interviewed for this volume: Kurt Waldheim, Javier Perez de Cuellar, and Boutros Boutros-Ghali. We greatly appreciate their time and openness in discussing personal views that provided particularly useful insights.

INTRODUCTION

KENT J. KILLE

The office of the UN secretary-general has been described as a needed voice in an international arena where moral principles are often seen as subservient to concerns over power and interest. In fact, because the secretary-generalship is a relatively constrained position lacking in traditional forms of power, those who analyze the position tend to see the moral authority of an officeholder as vital to the operation of the office. Such moral authority is often viewed as dependent on the personal qualities of individual officeholders. As one observer notes, "If it is a moral authority, one may ask, whence does this moral authority derive? It derives from the personality of the Secretary-General himself and not just from the office he holds."[1] It is therefore appropriate to inquire into the religious and moral values of those who hold the office. If a secretary-general's "own morality . . . must forbid him certain policies," and presumably encourage other policies, then one should be able to trace the decision-making implications of these values across the activities of the officeholders.[2]

Past studies examining particular secretaries-general are informative, and analysts have made interesting claims about the importance of the secretary-general's moral authority, but a detailed comparative examination of the moral and religious dimensions of the office has not yet been attempted. Works that discuss the moral or religious basis of the office tend to rely on isolated observations or personalistic evidence. In addition, some of the secretaries-general have been studied along these lines more deeply than others, and even when the religious or moral values of specific secretaries-general have been considered, there has not been a comprehensive analysis. For example, observers have emphasized the importance of the religious values of Dag Hammarskjöld and U Thant, and have implicitly assumed that religion should be an important consideration for understanding the actions of all of the secretaries-general. Yet the religious values of the other officeholders, and their potential impact,

1

have not been examined closely enough to determine whether this is indeed the case.

In exploring whether a secretary-general's religious and moral values affect the handling of the office, this study employs a broader term— *ethical framework*—that encompasses the range of values. Thus all of the case studies in this volume are built around the same central question: Does the ethical framework of an individual officeholder impact the role played by a secretary-general of the United Nations? Although it is generally assumed that the United Nations and the secretary-general are a positive force in the international system, it is equally clear that officeholders and the organization have been placed in compromising positions in international affairs in a manner that calls this assumption into question. We need, therefore, to investigate more closely the personal values that may inform the activities of secretaries-general and to examine how these values operate alongside the institutional norms and political constraints that define the office.

In undertaking such a comprehensive and comparative analysis, the contributors to this volume did not assume at the outset the existence of a relationship between an ethical framework and the decisions of any given secretary-general. The chapters in this volume are also not designed to pass judgment on an individual's personal ethics but rather to assess the ethical framework for each secretary-general and whether this framework had an impact on behavior while in office. Guided by the common research framework established in chapters 1 and 2, the following chapters look closely at each secretary-general in turn. Each chapter establishes the ethical framework of the secretary-general in question, and in the process explores the environmental and experiential factors that influenced the creation of his particular ethical framework. Each case study also examines the ways in which the personal values that made up the ethical framework interacted with external concerns to guide the decisions of the officeholder.

Beyond the specific issues raised in previous analyses of the secretaries-general and the United Nations, this study builds upon and contributes to the increasing recognition of the importance of religion and ethics in international relations. As Jonathan Fox observes, "The assertion that religion can influence our views is not new or in dispute. Religion is often a part of people's worldviews and influences their perception of events and their actions."[3] Yet, despite such acknowledgments of the importance of religion in global affairs and an expanding literature in this area, our understanding of the impact of religious values on the decisions of leaders on the international stage remains limited. Similarly, work on ethics in international affairs has undergone a resurgence and is continuing to grow as an important avenue of inquiry. This study seeks to build on our knowledge of the ethical dimension of international leadership and the potential connections of ethics to diplomacy and international institutions. Our goal is to consider more closely the wider implications of religiously and morally based leadership in the international arena.

Chapter 1 sets out the core arguments and approach underlying the volume. The chapter provides a brief overview of the office of the secretary-general as a moral authority in global affairs and explores the potential connections to officeholders' personal religious and moral values. This discussion is grounded in broader considerations of the place of religion and ethics at the United Nations and international relations. Because the focus of the volume is comparing the officeholders' ethical frameworks and related considerations—including formation of the ethical framework, interaction with external context in formulating decisions, and potential feedback that leads to adjustments in the ethical framework—an overview of these dimensions rounds out the chapter.

Chapter 2, by Dorothy V. Jones, acts in concert with chapter 1 to set the scene for the case studies of the individual officeholders by exploring aspects of the ethical framework and external context. Jones discusses what she labels the secretary-general's "inner code," or "the code within," in conjunction with the "external code" that can provide guidance for officeholders' activities, and she argues that there is likely to be an important interaction between the two. Jones sheds particular light on the deep historical process by which the current external code facing the secretary-general has been established. Her discussion emphasizes the realm of international peace and security, although she also examines issues related to human rights and the administrative duties of the secretary-general.

Chapter 3, on Trygve Lie, is the first of seven case studies. James P. Muldoon Jr. considers whether Lie's evangelical Lutheran faith, and related notions of Pietism, influenced the development of the secretary-general's ethical framework. While Lie's religion may have shaped his "moral vocabulary," Muldoon determines that secular ideals based on social democratic principles lie at the heart of his ethical framework. Muldoon explores this conclusion in relation to Lie's connections with socialism and the labor movement, along with his experiences during World War II, and describes Lie's engagement with a series of peace and security concerns, along with his handling of administrative difficulties and the effort to fight poverty. Muldoon discusses the impact of UN charter principles, the demanding pressures of international politics, and the role expectations of the secretary-generalship on Lie's tenure, but he shows how Lie's values and commitment gave him the strength to persevere in the face of difficult challenges.

In chapter 4 Alynna J. Lyon emphasizes the spiritual core of Dag Hammarskjöld's ethical framework, which was derived from his Lutheran upbringing and beliefs and his interest in medieval mysticism. She also tracks the broader development of his moral values, including the merging of his personal values with the principles set out in the UN charter and how this informed his dynamic ethical framework. Her analysis demonstrates how this ethical framework influenced Hammarskjöld's decision making, from his acceptance of the office to his handling of peacekeeping in the Congo, although she is careful to note that the complexity of the interactions and Hammarskjöld's private nature make it difficult to trace an exact causal relationship.

The importance of U Thant's Buddhist beliefs to his ethical framework, and how they meshed with UN principles and guided his actions while in office, is the subject of chapter 5, by A. Walter Dorn. Dorn also explores Thant's broader spiritual views and moral values—humility, integrity, and equanimity. The analysis of Thant's decisions is built around key ethical dilemmas he faced as secretary-general concerning the use of force, intervention versus nonintervention, impartiality versus neutrality, dependent versus independent office, private versus professional interests, idealism versus realism, and the sacred/secular divide.

In chapter 6 Michael T. Kuchinsky looks at how Kurt Waldheim, a devout Catholic, sought to separate the religious from the political during his tenure as secretary-general. Kuchinsky argues that Waldheim's ethical framework and his decisions in office were based solidly on pragmatism. Kuchinsky examines Waldheim's engagement in addressing difficulties in Cyprus, the Middle East, and Namibia, his handling of human rights, and his Secretariat hiring practices, in connection with a range of pragmatic points. Because of concerns about Waldheim's personal history during World War II and the possible ethical implications of his behavior, Kuchinsky concludes the chapter with a broader consideration of Waldheim as a moral actor.

Javier Perez de Cuellar's conduct in office is the subject of chapter 7, by Barbara Ann Rieffer-Flanagan and David P. Forsythe. Although the authors acknowledge that Perez de Cuellar's personal values could have been informed by his Catholic upbringing, they are unable to find a clear link to particular religious values as a core part of his ethical framework. Instead, their analysis focuses on how Perez de Cuellar's values derived largely from the ethics of liberalism. Their account of his decisions on a range of peace and security issues, his efforts in relation to population control, his handling of UN finances, and his use of delegates emphasizes the importance of contextual factors in understanding his tenure. Rieffer-Flanagan and Forsythe also discuss the difficulty of separating Perez de Cuellar's personal values from the principles of the UN charter, with which they are closely intertwined.

In chapter 8 Anthony F. Lang Jr. looks at how Boutros Boutros-Ghali's ethical framework grew out of his background in a prominent Coptic Christian family in Egypt and his international legal training. Lang highlights five core values that underlie Boutros-Ghali's ethical framework: tolerance, forgiveness/reconciliation, liberal emphasis on human rights, the moral importance and centrality of the sovereign state, and democracy. Lang explores the importance of these values in relation to Boutros-Ghali's involvement with UN intervention in Somalia and Bosnia, UN efforts in Cambodian postconflict peace building, and the administrative reporting mechanism illustrated by his *Agenda for Democratization*. Lang argues that Boutros-Ghali drew on different values in particular situations and that at times external constraints also played an important part in his initiatives.

In chapter 9 Courtney B. Smith examines Kofi Annan's strong spiritual beliefs and moral values to emphasize two key dimensions of his ethical framework: concern for human dignity and commitment to the peaceful resolution of conflict. Smith supplements this with a discussion of Annan's broader personal attributes and emphasizes the core ethical dilemmas that Annan faced in relation to Iraq, Darfur, the Millennium Development Goals, and organizational reform. Smith addresses Annan's focus on balancing his internal code with external constraints and how he sought to design strategies that reconciled the ethical tradeoffs that he made.

Chapter 10 summarizes the key findings of this study and highlights the variation between the ethical frameworks and the vitality of particular religious and moral values of the different secretaries-general. These variations are related to the impact that officeholders' ethical frameworks had on their decisions while in office and how the interaction with external context shaped these decisions. The chapter evaluates the approach employed in this study, the implications for the secretary-general as a moral authority, and prospects for further study of the religious and ethical dimensions of leadership in international affairs.

Notes

1. C. V. Narasimhan, *The United Nations: An Inside View* (New Delhi: Vikas Publishing House, 1988), 274.

2. Leon Gordenker, *The UN Secretary-General and the Maintenance of Peace* (New York: Columbia University Press, 1967), 334.

3. Jonathan Fox, "Religion as an Overlooked Element in International Relations," *International Studies Review* 3 (2001): 59. See also Jonathan Fox and Shmuel Sandler, *Bringing Religion into International Relations* (New York: Palgrave Macmillan, 2004), 57–60.

1

MORAL AUTHORITY AND THE UN SECRETARY-GENERAL'S ETHICAL FRAMEWORK

KENT J. KILLE

In the eyes of Members and non-Members and of people in general, irrespective of their political, philosophical or religious beliefs, the prestige and moral weight of the Office is considerable. . . . Paradoxically, the immense moral capital of the Office contrasts sharply with its limited independent powers.[1]

This chapter begins by considering the place of the UN secretary-general in the international arena. This includes a discussion of the perceived moral authority of the secretary-generalship, along with the personal religious and moral values of officeholders that have been viewed as influencing the handling of the position. Given this emphasis, the chapter places the consideration of a secretary-general's values within the broader context of religion in international relations, as well as specifically in the United Nations, and ethics in international affairs. The chapter concludes with a clarification of the concept of ethical framework and its potential impact on a secretary-general's decisions.

The UN Secretary-General in the International Arena

The UN charter articulates the legal position of the secretary-general.[2] The key articles are in chapter XV of the charter, "The Secretariat," which encompasses articles 97–101. Article 97 states that the secretary-general is appointed by the General Assembly based on the recommendation of the Security Council and establishes the secretary-general as the "chief administrative officer" of the United Nations. The administrative side of the position involves officeholders in a range of tasks that ensure that the affairs of the organization run smoothly. These bureaucratic duties include budgetary and staffing responsibilities. The secretary-general is also responsible for a series of papers and reports.

Many of these reports are issued as part of an officeholder's duties under article 98, where the secretary-general is instructed to perform any functions assigned by other UN organs. Along with the requests for reports that come throughout the year, the secretary-general is required by article 98 to prepare an annual report for the General Assembly that details the activities of the organization. Finally, article 98 outlines a secretary-general's ability to attend meetings of the other organs in the capacity of chief administrative officer as listed under article 97. Obviously it is not possible for an officeholder to be present at all such meetings, but this provision does provide useful access to the discussions occurring in the other organs.

Article 99 specifies that the secretary-general "may bring to the attention of the Security Council any matter which in his opinion may threaten the maintenance of international peace and security." This is an important power, although the right to invoke article 99 directly has very rarely been employed.[3] As Edward Newman observes, however, "The real influence of this article has derived not so much from its formal invocation but from the legal implications that derive from it and the political aura that it stamps upon the Secretaryship-General."[4] Given the need to stay informed regarding threats to international peace and security, the secretary-general may interpret article 99 in an expansive manner well beyond the mechanism of making a request of the Security Council. Related activities can include monitoring and collecting facts regarding conflicts, whether through a personal visit or an intermediary, and independently initiating efforts to resolve breaches of the peace.

Article 100 stresses the "exclusively international character" of the office as separate from the member states. From this independent position, officeholders, as with all members of the Secretariat, are called on to serve "as international officials responsible only to the Organization." The secretary-general is thus expected to spurn instructions from external actors and focus on representing the United Nations. Article 101 details staffing issues for the Secretariat. This article sets out that the secretary-general has control over staff appointments, albeit "under regulations established by the General Assembly." In addition, the article specifies the hiring criteria of "efficiency, competence, and integrity" along with the need to maintain geographical balance in the Secretariat. The important implications of articles 100 and 101 for the secretary-general's independence, integrity, and impartiality are discussed later in this chapter.

Finally, article 7—which lists the Secretariat as one of the principal organs of the United Nations, along with the General Assembly, Security Council, Economic and Social Council, Trusteeship Council, and International Court of Justice—is also often referenced in relation to the secretary-general. With the secretary-general operating as the head of the Secretariat, some observers point to article 7 as underpinning an important leadership position for the office. While article 7 does appear to place the office of the secretary-general on equal footing with the other principal organs of the United Nations, it is important to keep in mind the degree to which this should be emphasized in comparison with the other articles already discussed. For example, article 98 stresses that the other principal organs may assign tasks to the secretary-general, while the secretary-general's capabilities in return are more limited.

As this review reveals, the powers of the secretary-general listed in the charter are relatively restricted. Not mentioned in this legalistic description, however, but stressed in the literature on the secretary-general, are the ways in which the moral stature of officeholders can increase the potential capabilities of the office well beyond basic charter powers. The importance of moral standing to the secretary-generalship has been recognized by the officeholders themselves and is often couched in terms of moral power. Trygve Lie observes in his memoir that the office relies on "a moral power, not a physical one," and Kurt Waldheim stated in a press conference, "All I have is moral power, I have nothing behind me. . . . I have not got the power to force anyone to do anything."[5] More recently, Kofi Annan, commenting in an interview shortly after the 2006 FIFA World Cup, described the secretary-general as "sort of a referee, but without red and yellow cards. He cannot raise them, but he can raise his moral voice."[6]

James Sutterlin cautions, however, that this argument should not be taken too far: "Repeated Secretaries-General have said that the only power they possess is the moral power. . . . This is not quite true. . . . The impact depends not just on the moral principles."[7] While Sutterlin's statement is important to keep in mind, the moral grounding of the office undoubtedly remains a vital area of study. Considerations of moral authority were central in discussions of the selection of Annan's successor, Ban Ki-moon, who took office in January 2007. One of Ban's competitors for the position,

Ashraf Ghani, sought to distinguish himself as best qualified to overcome the "internal problems [that] have undermined the moral authority and effectiveness of the United Nations."[8] Ban has also been directly compared to Annan along moral lines. As James Traub observes, "Ban was explicitly chosen . . . precisely because it seemed he would not seek to be the moral leader or secular pope who Kofi Annan so insistently sought to be."[9]

The Moral Authority of the UN Secretary-General

The notion that the UN secretary-general can operate as a moral authority informs many discussions of the office. As one observer who has written extensively on the secretary-general puts it succinctly, "The United Nations Secretary-General is: the moral voice of the United Nations."[10] Writers on the subject refer to the secretary-general's moral authority,[11] capital,[12] duty,[13] standing,[14] power,[15] stature,[16] courage,[17] and so on. The common theme of the secretary-general as a moral actor at the head of the United Nations emerges clearly.

More broadly, the United Nations as an organization can be viewed as an independent actor that plays a greater role in the international arena than merely representing the interests of its member states.[18] The United Nations can be seen as a "moral power" working on behalf of the peoples of the world and as an organization uniquely suited to tackle issues related to international ethics. In Jacques Baudot's words, "its universality, prestige, traditions of diplomatic restraint, capacity to attract persons of quality from various cultures, and openness to organizations and movements from the non-governmental world make the United Nations the ideal place for debating and deepening the moral and ethical questions that permeate international and global relations."[19] Calls for the creation of a "global ethic" capable of transcending differences between people and encouraging greater cooperation based on shared principles have thus often been directed at the United Nations.[20] The United Nations has incorporated such ideas to some degree—at the UN Educational, Scientific, and Cultural Organization (UNESCO), for instance, which housed the Universal Ethics Project.[21]

Other international civil servants may be held to the same standard as the secretary-general in relation to the call for a global ethic, including the heads of agencies within the UN system.[22] Such officials are perceived as representing the international community in a manner that transcends the interests of the individual member states. For example, the High

Commissioner for Human Rights can be viewed as "a moral authority and voice for human rights victims."[23] The call to promote a global ethic falls most squarely, however, on the shoulders of the secretary-general as the head of the UN system. In fact, the secretary-general is often seen as a living symbol and embodiment of the United Nations. Arthur Rovine writes, "The contemporary Secretary-General symbolizes the Organization, serves as its spokesman, and as defender of its interests and involvement in international politics."[24] As a "defender of its interests," the secretary-general is expected to protect the principles of the charter—not to follow them blindly, but to fashion an ethical stance dictated by and based on the principles.[25] Building on the opening phrase of the charter—"We the peoples of the United Nations"—some have argued that the secretary-general is not simply the chief administrative officer of the United Nations but a representative of all of the world's peoples.[26] Overall, compared to the other actors in the United Nations, "the Secretary-General most clearly speaks for the global interest, beyond the narrow national interest. . . . The Secretary-General has become the closest thing we have to the 'voice' of the world's conscience on the wide range of political, economic, and humanitarian issues."[27]

Of course, not all observers share this view of the secretary-general as a moral voice in the international community.[28] There is a great deal of debate over what role the occupant of the office should play. As Benjamin Rivlin explains, "perceptions as to the proper role of the Secretary-General vary. Some argue that the Secretary-General should be an activist, taking initiatives and providing moral leadership on behalf of the 'UN idea' articulated in the Charter. In contrast, others contend that, at best, the Secretary-General is a marginal player in the international arena, which is primarily the domain of the sovereign states."[29] For example, a report by the United Nations Association of the United States of America argues for a strong secretary-general: "To develop the momentum and sense of direction the world body now lacks, a Secretary-General should act as a forceful and inspiring programmatic leader with a clear conception not only of the U.N. today but also of where he or she would like it to go," and, in presenting the United Nations to the world, "the Secretary-General should be both the U.N.'s most powerful image maker and the world's most prominent spokesperson for multilateral approaches to global problem-solving."[30] At the other end of the spectrum, analysts such as James Barros express the concern that secretaries-general may act too much as moral statesmen for the international community instead of maintaining a lower profile.[31] In Rivlin's view, "the reality lies somewhere in between" the two extremes. Other writers have also emphasized the difficulty of balancing the dual roles of activist executive and servant of sovereign member states.[32]

Whatever one's position, the role of moral leadership lies at the heart of the debate over the secretary-general's proper function. The question of a given officeholder's personal moral and religious views affects this discussion as well. A secretary-general's moral views are often related to an officeholder's integrity, independence, and impartiality.[33] C. V. Narasimhan argues that it is important for an officeholder to possess integrity because "it is the integrity of the Secretary-General that gives moral authority to his office."[34] Integrity is explicitly mentioned in article 101 of the charter: "The paramount consideration in the employment of the staff and in the determination of the condition of service shall be the necessity of securing the highest standards of efficiency, competence, and integrity." James Jonah defines integrity in this context as "implying such rectitude that one is incorruptible or incapable of being false to a trust, to a responsibility or to one's own standards."[35] By specifying the requirement of integrity, the charter links the secretary-general to moral conduct while in office. The expectation is that secretaries-general will adhere closely to an ethical code of behavior and will not allow their standards to be corrupted.

The independence of the secretary-general is also built on the charter, specifically article 100, which emphasizes that the members of the Secretariat "shall not seek or receive instructions from any government or from any other authority external to the organization." A secretary-general's independence thus means freedom from political guidance or control by a particular state's government or by a group of countries acting in consort. By demonstrating that they are making independent decisions without outside influence, officeholders operate with an enhanced level of moral authority. Their decisions are based on what situations require, not on political expediency that reflects the interests of others—in particular the more powerful member states. Jonah emphasizes the importance of this independence, arguing that article 100 contains "cardinal principles which must not be qualified."[36]

Impartiality is also seen as "an asset of enormous importance" that is connected to the "moral standing" of officeholders.[37] Impartiality may be defined as maintaining a nonbiased stance with respect to the particular actors or groups involved in a given issue. When handling disagreements, a secretary-general should be even-handed, without giving preferential treatment to one party or taking the position of one side. But this kind of impartiality also means adhering to the principles and objectives of the United Nations and ensuring that they are not sacrificed when trying to balance the interests of competing parties.[38] When secretaries-general are impartial, then disputants will be more likely to accept their involvement and to see their objective as fidelity to UN ideals rather than to the interests of one side or another.[39] Of course, even when secretaries-general uphold the ideal of impartiality to the best of their ability, they may still be seen as favoring one actor over another.[40]

Observers may insist that stringent demands be made of the secretary-general, that an officeholder maintain an impeccable moral stance at all times and in all circumstances, but this is an unrealistic expectation. A secretary-general is bound to make mistakes. As Leon Gordenker writes, "were it to be otherwise, the Secretary-General would have to be recruited from among the angels."[41] Whether angel or devil, saint or sinner, the secretary-general is on display for the entire world to critique. Therefore, the following section turns to a consideration of what personal values might inform handling the office in such a manner.

The Religious and Moral Values of UN Secretaries-General

As discussed, analyses of the UN secretary-general often emphasize the moral authority of the office. This raises the issue of what related personal values individual officeholders might bring to bear during their tenure. What does it take, in Gordenker's phrase, to be an angel?

To begin with, the religious nature of the metaphor reflects the emphasis that has been placed on the potential importance of officeholders' religious values.[42] For example, interviews carried out at the United Nations for the report *Religion and Public Policy at the UN* found that the religious values of the organization's officials were often very important: "We were surprised by many powerful, personal testimonies in response, both from religious and secular individuals. . . . We see here religion's powerful motivating force, even for individuals who have taken a secular turn in their UN work." In fact, work on this report began with the assumption that the focus would be on religious groups as the primary unit of analysis, but the researchers quickly discovered that individuals and their beliefs were equally important and deserving of study. The report notes that the impact of religious values at the United Nations extends all the way to the top of the organization: "To be sure, the UN has seen its share of great figures with religious sensitivities, if not exclusively spiritual motivations. Secretaries-General Dag Hammarskjöld (1953–1961), a Lutheran, and Kofi Annan (1997–present), an Anglican, are often mentioned in this regard."[43]

This report is far from the first study to acknowledge the importance of Hammarskjöld's spirituality in his service as secretary-general.[44] Similarly, work on U Thant emphasizes the Buddhist values he developed growing up in Burma.[45] As *Religion and Public Policy at the UN* notes, there has also been interest in whether or not Annan's religious values affected his handling of the office.

The religious values of Hammarskjöld, Thant, and (to a lesser degree, to date) Annan have received some attention, then, but the seven secretaries-general represent a variety of religious traditions that provide the basis for an interesting comparative analysis. Like his Swedish successor Hammarskjöld, the Norwegian Lie was raised in the Lutheran tradition. These Lutheran roots differ from the Catholic backgrounds of Waldheim and Javier Perez de Cuellar in Austria and Peru, respectively. Boutros Boutros-Ghali is a member of the Coptic Christian minority in Egypt. Annan is descended from tribal chiefs and grew up surrounded by a mix of faiths, including indigenous beliefs, in Ghana, but personally adheres to the Anglican faith. Clearly these seven men have both religious similarities and differences, but the question of how their religious views and backgrounds affected their handling of the secretary-generalship remains to be explored.

Beyond religion, the broader moral values of the secretaries-general have also been emphasized. The individuals behind the office are viewed as operating under certain "moral precepts" that will affect their policy choices.[46] Hammarskjöld's religious values are generally linked to his broader moral convictions, which are often portrayed as central to how he handled the office. Observers note that Hammarskjöld had a "strongly moral approach to politics" and brought a "sense of religious mission" to the position.[47] In particular, Manuel Fröhlich has examined the "political ethics" of Hammarskjöld and connected them to his political actions.[48]

Analyses of other secretaries-general also highlight their moral dimensions. Shirley Hazzard challenges Lie when she writes, "Crude with forthrightness, devious with astuteness, Lie was above all deficient in ethical perception." Brian Urquhart also considers Thant's moral stance, although he questions its impact on Thant's ability to handle the office. "Of all the secretaries-general," Urquhart writes, "he is the one who has been most unjustly forgotten. It is perhaps not too surprising, since he had a moral view of his office and responsibilities. He was a person of great honesty and courage, but he was not always taken seriously."[49]

Work on Waldheim often concentrates on his moral limitations, particularly on his Nazi-related past in Austria during World War II. In her book on Waldheim, *Countenance of Truth,* Hazzard stresses that "Waldheim speaks incidentally of moral power, as if it were a current of low wattage to be switched on at will. Moral distinction as an inward quality, arduously earned, and unvaunted, eludes him as a concept, let alone as an attainment of moving nations."[50] While in office, Waldheim was described as "a discreet administrator . . . not another moralist," and as not possessing the "moral force" of Hammarskjöld. Another analyst observes, "The incumbent is also expected generally to conform to the highest moral standards. . . . This explains the consternation caused by the disclosure of Waldheim's deliberate falsehoods about his past."[51]

By contrast, Annan has been profiled as an outstanding "moral voice" for the international community.[52] His emphasis on humanitarian ideals in his 1999 speech at the opening of the General Assembly was applauded: "Rather than posing as a bureaucrat protecting organizational turf, his rhetorical question echoed a moral voice. . . . The Secretary-General appreciates that there is no escape from moral reasoning in international politics."[53] At the same time, Annan recognized limits on pressing an ethical stance, in contrast to other secretaries-general, who ignored "warning signs" and "tried to influence the course of events in areas where they felt strongly that they had moral obligations and better policies than those of member states."[54]

Overall, while there is a clear interest in the religious and moral underpinnings of the office, there are gaps in the level of coverage and a lack of systematic or comparative analysis in much of the previous work on the secretary-general. Studies addressing the religious and moral values of the secretary-general generally focus on one individual. In addition, while the values of some of the secretaries-general have been examined in some depth, others have not received this kind of attention. Furthermore, certain aspects of a given officeholder's views tend to be emphasized to the exclusion of others.

Religion in International Relations, Religion in the United Nations

Interest in the religious values of the secretaries-general can be seen within the broader context of an increasing recognition of the importance of religion in international relations. The connection between religion and politics has a long history and remains of great importance on the global stage.[55] In the words of George Moyser, "It is very difficult in the modern world to ignore the presence of religion in public affairs. Virtually on a daily basis, the media provide instances demonstrating that the people, institutions, and ideas that make up the religious sphere have a continuing and important relevance to the political realm."[56] As John Carlson and Erik Owens further emphasize in the introduction to their edited volume *The Sacred and the Sovereign: Religion and International Politics*, "If there is a unifying thesis that this volume's contributors would all affirm, it is that *international politics cannot be fully or properly fathomed without addressing its embedded religious and moral dimensions.*"[57] Despite such recognition of religious factors in international affairs, work on this facet of international relations has received relatively limited scholarly analysis.[58] Recent work, however, indicates that religion shows signs of a "return from exile" in international relations scholarship.[59]

Although religion in international relations remains an understudied area, important considerations arise from the existing literature. One such area of discussion revolves around the question of whether religion plays a positive or negative role in world affairs. Clearly it can do both. Religious issues have led to much bloodshed throughout history, but religious ideals and actors can also promote peace, and much has been written about both faces of religion.[60] Religious organizations are noted for their efforts to defuse international tensions. As David Barash and Charles Webel argue, in the realm of international peace "moral decisions cannot be avoided," and so "religious and ethical considerations must be central to the establishment of peace." Discussions of religion and peace often encompass a hopeful argument that religious ideals can serve as the basis for building a peaceful international community.[61]

Religion and leadership is another important theme. As Marc Gopin stresses, "Religion's visionary capacity and its inculcation of altruistic values has already given birth to extraordinary leaders."[62] Unfortunately, such leadership has been "particularly neglected in the study of international relations," which points to the need for further understanding of the impact of religion on international leadership.[63]

Given the significant place of religion in international relations, and the activities of the United Nations throughout the global arena, the impact of religion within the organization should be an important area of study. Although the United Nations is a secular organization that encompasses all of the world's religions and advocates no particular beliefs, religious views and groups have been an active part of the organization since its inception.[64] However, while the religious beliefs of individual secretaries-general have received some attention, as outlined above, in general the place of religion in the United Nations has rarely been closely examined.[65] The 2002 report by the group Religion Counts emphasizes this point: "When Religion Counts began its research for *Religion and Public Policy at the UN* we were frankly amazed to discover that this would be the first comprehensive analysis of the subject."[66]

The potentially important place of religious values at the United Nations has been stressed in relation to promoting a global ethic. "Envision a world," writes Robert Thurman, "where all the religions really do collaborate to support a United Nations that effectively maintains a humane ethic for a world society!"[67] Such a vision is undermined by conflict between religious groups, however. The Religion Counts report includes an interview with a high-level member of a major UN agency: "'Could the UN be made a better place with the moral values of religions?' he asks rhetorically, and answers: 'Unquestionably.' It is the divisiveness of the religions he finds problematic, a divisiveness he seems to encounter increasingly in policy conversations at UN headquarters."[68]

Religious nongovernmental organizations (NGOs) are a further indication of the presence of religion in the United Nations.[69] The secretary-general faces direct pressure from such NGOs through, for example, declarations and letters to his office.[70] Religious issues also arise at international conferences like the 1995 International Conference on Population and Development, with its "charged religious atmosphere,"[71] and can be seen in UN declarations and resolutions such as the 1981 *Declaration on the Elimination of All Forms of Intolerance and of Discrimination Based on Religion or Belief* and the 2001 General Assembly resolution *Protection of Religious Sites.*[72] An important religious presence operates across the street from UN headquarters in New York at 777 United Nations Plaza. A major meeting among representatives of the world's religions was held at the United Nations during the 2000 Millennium World Peace Summit of Religious and Spiritual Leaders. The summit was not officially sponsored by the United Nations, but the event was scheduled just before the Millennium Summit of Heads of State and Government so that the outcome could influence those deliberations. In addition, the World Council of Religious Leaders, proposed at that meeting, was subsequently established.[73] Although Rivlin's analysis of the event leads him to question the role of religious coordination in the United Nations, Janice Love points to the relevance of this event: "But who cares? . . . For one, we scholars of world politics should care and pay attention. As a discipline we often lack complex understandings of religious actors, belief systems, organizations, and practices. . . . The summit is a powerful symbol for both world politics and for how we study it. This gathering represents a significant trend to which scholars should pay more attention."[74]

Despite the interest in religion at the United Nations, and more broadly in international relations and the influence of religious values on international leaders, the subject has received relatively little scholarly attention. By exploring the religious values of the secretary-general, this volume hopes to add to the understanding of this important dimension of international relations. This research relates more closely to those works that seek to describe, rather than evaluate, the impact of religion. This study's focus is on combining the description of religious values with the moral aspects drawn from other parts of each secretary-general's life, thus producing an ethical framework that can be used to examine officeholders across contexts. Before explaining this concept in more detail, however, let us turn our attention to the study of ethics in international affairs.

Ethics in International Affairs

The possibility that moral principles can guide international action has been much debated. Writers in the field of international relations are often skeptical of normative concerns, and policymakers, focused on national interest, are doubtful about the influence of ethics on foreign policy.[75] Many writers suggest that ethical considerations pale in comparison to the interests of power and that the constraints of the international system make a focus on ethics unlikely.[76] Even those who support the study of ethics in international affairs, such as Jean-Marc Coicaud and Daniel Warner, are careful to acknowledge the limits that still exist in this area, noting, "Ethics has not become a global political reality."[77]

Despite these limits, work on ethics in the international realm has been established as an important avenue of inquiry. It has become increasingly clear that ethical concerns cannot be easily divorced from international affairs, in spite of claims to the contrary.[78] As Ken Booth, Tim Dunne, and Michael Cox put it, "We have to understand ethics *in* world politics and not ethics *and* world politics. Ethics are not separate."[79] This argument has resonated with international relations scholars and, like the study of religion, the study of ethics in international affairs is undergoing a resurgence.[80] Nicholas Rengger concludes that "ethical reflection on international politics has, it would seem, finally come in from the cold. Regarded as something of an Aunt Sally in most discussions of international relations during the Cold War, the last few years have made it obvious to all but the most hidebound (and antiquated) positivist that normative and ethical issues are irrevocably intertwined with all questions of world politics."[81]

This study of the UN secretary-general fits well within the growing call for a better understanding of ethics in international affairs. Given the call for the secretary-general to serve as a moral authority in the international system, studying the officeholders from this standpoint provides new and illuminating perspectives on the place of ethics in international relations.[82] This study also reflects the need to examine morality in international leadership. This premise is at the heart of Cathal Nolan's edited volume, *Ethics and Statecraft: The Moral Dimension of International Affairs,* which sets out "to show that the individual leader is a major conduit by which ethical considerations enter into the decision-making process of states, and thereby affect the course and nature of international politics."[83] Although most of the essays in that volume examine the leaders of states, the collection also includes a chapter on Secretary-General Hammarskjöld, demonstrating that the office deserves close consideration in relation to international moral leadership.[84]

In addition, although some in the diplomatic field might disagree, ethics and diplomacy can be seen as exclusive but linked terms. Unfortunately, given the prevalence of the view that ethics has no place in diplomacy, "the issue of ethics and diplomacy has been less thoroughly explored and in particular has been overlooked" in comparison to ethics in other areas of international relations, such as the ethics of war.[85] In that the secretary-general is a key diplomatic actor in international affairs, examining the relationship between ethics and the office will contribute to this under-explored area.

Finally, this study speaks to the broader issue of ethics and international institutions. One scholar working in this area is Toni Erskine, whose work includes the edited volume *Can Institutions Have Responsibilities? Collective Moral Agency and International Relations.* Erskine looks at international institutions as moral agents, but the arguments and ideas she discusses can be extended to thinking about the secretary-general. For example, Erskine presents the interesting conundrum that individuals can be moral but cannot solve global problems. Collective actors have the potential to solve these problems, but can these actors be considered moral? This line of questioning can be extended to the secretary-general. A given officeholder can be moral in his personal life, but does this translate to his involvement in global affairs? Erskine does not consider the potential impact of an individual on an institution as an ethical actor, but if an international institution can be a moral agent, what, or who, drives the morality of that institution? Would it not be the individual executive head? Erskine advocates "a perspective that would acknowledge the moral agency of institutions without precluding the moral agency of the individual human being"—and it seems that the moral agency of UN leadership can and should be factored into the equation.[86]

A Secretary-General's Ethical Framework and the Handling of the Office

In order to compare the various secretaries-general, this study employs the concept of an *ethical framework* to capture the religious and moral dimensions of leadership in relation to the secretary-general as a moral authority in the international arena. An ethical framework can be defined as the combination of personal values that establish the beliefs, forms of reasoning, and interpretations of the world that guide an individual when making judgments about proper behavior in specific contexts.[87]

Establishing the ethical framework of an officeholder is not an easy task. Ethical leadership "is by its very nature not conducive to 'scientific' study that would please natural scientists and social science quantifiers,"[88] and the contributors to this volume debated long and hard over how to approach this task. The case studies examine the principal components of the ethical framework of individual officeholders and how these relate to their tenure as secretary-general. The moral values can be derived from a wide range of sources, in particular family upbringing, education, culture, and personal history and experience.

As discussed, religious values are also a potentially key part of a secretary-general's ethical framework.[89] But the religious tradition in which a secretary-general was raised is only part of the religious dimension of the ethical framework. Members of a particular faith do not necessarily all behave the same way, and this study focuses on how the different secretaries-general have interpreted their faith traditions and how this has affected their religious views. It would be simplistic to suggest that Waldheim or Perez de Cuellar will act in certain ways just because they are members of the Catholic Church; the aim is to probe more deeply into what aspects of their religion, and of other spiritual influences, informed their actions. In addition, as Jonathan Fox stresses, some policymakers give more "weight" to religion than others.[90] Thus it is necessary to establish not only the religious values of a secretary-general but also the level of devotion.

Ethical framework alone is not likely to explain why a secretary-general makes one decision or another. The actions of officeholders may also be shaped by the external context in which they operate.[91] In considering the secretary-general as a moral authority, a key aspect of this external context is the principles set out in the UN charter. The general principles that operate at the heart of international politics are another external factor that influences decisions. As Dorothy Jones explains in the following chapter, we need to take into account the "external code," along with the "inner code," or "code within," as a guiding factor. Role expectations could also influence the decisions of the secretary-general. While an officeholder possesses a personal commitment to act in a particular manner, the role of secretary-general represents a particular tradition and expectation of authority to which he or she may feel a need to adhere.[92]

As Jones also argues, an individual's ethical framework and the external context in which it operates are likely to interact in important ways. Officeholders may weigh the personal preferences represented in their ethical frameworks against external demands when evaluating a situation and determining how to act. Secretaries-general may seek to balance external demands with their internal ethical frameworks, but such a balance may not be possible and they may need to choose between the two. After all, one cannot assume that the values of the individual officeholders will always mesh with the organizational values.[93] Member states want a secretary-general with values similar to their own, but there is no guarantee that this will be the case.[94] Therefore, neither context nor personal values may be thought of as determining; it is far more likely that there will be a dynamic interaction between the two.

This interaction may have lasting effects on a secretary-general's ethical framework and important implications for an officeholder's policy choices and initiatives. Likewise, a secretary-general's ethical framework may influence changes in the external code of the international arena. Overall, the series of potential relationships to be explored is represented graphically in figure 1.1.

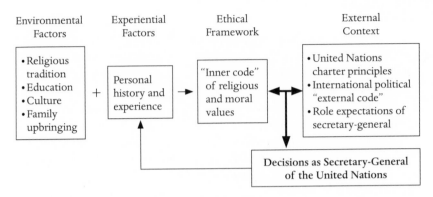

Figure 1.1 Ethical Framework Development and Impact

Tracing the impact of an ethical framework on the decisions of a secretary-general is rarely a simple matter. Ethical decision making revolves around value preferences, but when these preferences are not shared among actors, tensions arise, and difficult choices must be made between what is perceived as "morally right and what is morally wrong."[95] When secretaries-general encounter ethical dilemmas, how do their ethical frameworks guide their conduct? While the specific dilemmas faced may vary across the secretaries-general, possible general dilemmas that could be tracked include: taking a normative stand versus seeking support from states, speaking out strongly versus protecting the office, taking a principled stand versus operating on a pragmatic basis, and accomplishing a mission versus staff security. If a consistent tension between certain ethical choices faced by the different secretaries-general is found, then this provides a good basis for comparison to gauge if and how they handle those choices differently.

The potential role of the secretary-general in promoting a global ethic beyond the national interests of the member states is a recurrent theme in the literature. The tension between a global ethic and multiple national interests lies at the heart of work on ethics in international affairs and the debate over the proper role of the secretary-general and the United Nations. The integration of the peoples of the world, described by one analyst as "perhaps [the] most fundamental . . . of the Secretary-General's tasks in the international arena," can lead a secretary-general to work toward building "shared major values."[96] Nolan makes an interesting distinction between personal and international values that is pertinent here:

The realm of statecraft often raises difficult moral questions and may call for qualities other than those celebrated in the private domain. . . . While it is a *necessary* beginning, it is not a *sufficient* basis for judgment to ask whether leaders remained true to their internal or declared principles once great power was theirs. We should ask as well if they adhered to, and sought to advance, the normative conventions of international society and international law, or of some developed moral theory that reached beyond their personal outlook.[97]

Even when personal values may be inconsistent with the pursuit of a global ethic, will the demands of the office push a secretary-general in that direction? Will the secretary-general hear the call to serve the international community at large, or stand as the chief administrative officer carrying out the instructions of the UN member states?

A broader consideration of ethical dilemmas can be examined in relation to specific issue areas in which the secretaries-general are engaged. Given the range and number of global problems that they are involved in addressing, it is impossible to relate everything that occurs during their tenure to their ethical frameworks. By comparing the different secretaries-general on particular issues, however, we can paint a solid picture of their decisions and how those decisions may or may not be tied to their ethical frameworks. The contributors to this volume were encouraged to focus on three areas: peace and security, social/economic issues, and administrative concerns. The first two categories are of particular interest with regard to religious groups and ethical factors, so their possible connection to a secretary-general's ethical framework is clearly relevant.[98]

Given the emphasis on integrity and independence in articles 100 and 101 of the charter, addressing the administrative dimension also has a place in this discussion. Jonah suggests that this is a particularly important consideration, in that the secretary-general serves as a role model for other members of the Secretariat. The secretary-general can earn the confidence of both staff and member states by showing "moral courage"; the alternative is "a regime of pressure in which the executive heads are under the influence of only the greatest and most audacious powers."[99] Theodor Meron concurs that "it takes an executive head with courage and leadership abilities to set an example for the Secretariat by rejecting political pressure from states and Secretariat employees that conflict with article 101 of the Charter."[100] This includes ensuring that any governmental pressure to influence Secretariat appointments is rebuffed.

Within these issue areas, certain activities, such as the public statements made by officeholders, could be considered. The secretary-generalship can be used as a bully pulpit to press for the acceptance of certain values or actions.[101] James Rosenau argues that this is a vital aspect of the office, in that "the occupant of this post . . . infuses purposes, ideals, and overall strategies into the work of the UN. Thus it matters whether the individual who holds the post has the orientations to contest the paralyzing effects of the sovereignty principle and the bureaucratic resources to do so effectively."[102] Rovine adds that "a positive expression of policy by the Secretary-General . . . can usually be taken as a statement of predominant sentiment among the community of nations, and one that generates an aura of righteousness and legitimacy."[103]

How the secretary-general has sought to develop the office's abilities is another area of consideration. The "ethical autonomy" of a secretary-general can help to evolve a "far broader range of optional procedures for influencing the political organs and individual members" than is set out in the charter.[104] Secretaries-general often carry out activities mandated by the other principal organs of the United Nations, but they may also undertake actions on their own initiative. How secretaries-general interpret mandates, or even seek to influence the formation of a mandate, and how they demonstrate independent initiative, are also important considerations.

Conclusion

There is unquestionably a call for moral leadership at the international level. As the Commission on Global Governance has written, "the world needs leaders made strong by vision, sustained by ethics, and revealed by political courage. . . . Whatever the dimensions of global governance, however renewed and enlarged its machinery, whatever values give it content, the quality of global governance depends ultimately on leadership."[105] The UN secretary-general has long been viewed as a vital source of moral authority who should be able to take on this mantle of leadership. The personal religious and moral values of individual officeholders underpin this endeavor. This volume provides a thorough analysis of the ethical frameworks of the secretaries-general in the hope of providing a clearer understanding of how those frameworks have affected their role in the global arena.

Notes

1. Vratislav Pechota, "The Quiet Approach: A Study of the Good Offices Exercised by the United Nations Secretary-General in the Cause of Peace," in *Dispute Settlement Through the United Nations,* ed. K. Venkata Raman (Dobbs Ferry, NY: UNITAR-Oceana Publications, 1972), 7.

2. For further discussion of the UN charter and the secretary-general, including the basic principles encompassed in the charter that provide part of the external context for officeholders, see chapter 2 of this volume.

3. A. Walter Dorn, "Early and Late Warning by the UN Secretary-General of Threats to the Peace: Article 99 Revisited," in *Conflict Prevention from Rhetoric to Reality,* vol. 1, *Organizations and Institutions,* ed. Albrecht Schnabel and David Carment (Lanham, MD: Lexington Books, 2004), 305–44.

4. Edward Newman, *The UN Secretary-General from the Cold War to the New Era: A Global Peace and Security Mandate?* (New York: St. Martin's Press, 1998), 22.

5. Trygve Lie, *In the Cause of Peace: Seven Years with the United Nations* (New York: Macmillan, 1954), 42; Waldheim quoted in Shirley Hazzard, *Countenance of Truth: The United Nations and the Waldheim Case* (New York: Viking Press, 1990), 97.

6. "We Are a Bit Envious of FIFA," interview with Kofi Annan, *Der Spiegel,* July 18, 2006, http://service.spiegel.de/cache/international/spiegel/0,1518,427239, 00.html.

7. James S. Sutterlin, *The United Nations and the Maintenance of International Security: A Challenge to Be Met,* 2d ed. (Westport, CT: Praeger, 2003), 151. The same point is argued by Andrew W. Cordier, "The Role of the Secretary-General," in *Annual Review of United Nations Affairs, 1960–1961,* ed. Richard N. Swift (Dobbs Ferry, NY: Oceana Publications, 1961), 2.

8. Ashraf Ghani, "Climate of Distrust," *New York Times,* September 28, 2006. Another candidate, Vaira Vike-Freiberga, was also singled out as possessing "all the right qualities. She has moral authority" (Ayca Ariyoruk of the United Nations Association of the United States of America). Olivia Ward, "U of T Grad Hopes To Be First Woman to Lead UN," *Toronto Star,* September 30, 2006.

9. Quoted in Mark Turner, "Annan's Difficult Decade Nears End," *Financial Times,* October 10, 2006. Beyond discussions of Ban's moral leadership potential, questions were also raised regarding whether he bolstered his election chances through indicating that he would appoint individuals from certain countries to important UN posts and target the use of South Korean foreign aid. Ban refuted the accusations, saying, "I'm a man of integrity." Associated Press, "AP Interview: Next U.N. Chief Denies Allegations of Influence Peddling," October 19, 2006. At the same time, in what has been "seen by diplomats as a subtle swipe at Annan and the scandals that have been exposed at U.N. agencies under his watch," Ban stressed in his address to the General Assembly after taking the oath of office,

"I will seek to set the highest ethical standard. . . . I assure you that I will lead by example." Maggie Farley, "Ban Sworn in as U.N. Secretary-General," *Los Angeles Times,* December 15, 2006; UN Document SG/2119 and GA/10558, December 14, 2006.

10. B. G. Ramcharan, "The Secretary-General and Human Security: Good Offices and Preventive Action," in B. G. Ramcharan, *Human Rights and Human Security* (The Hague: M. Nijhoff, 2002), 19. For further work by Ramcharan in the same vein, see "The Office of the United Nations Secretary-General," *Dalhousie Law Journal* 13 (1990): 742–57; "The History, Role and Organization of the 'Cabinet' of the United Nations Secretary-General," *Nordic Journal of International Law* 59 (1990): 103–16; and J. Daniel Livermore and B. G. Ramcharan, "Purposes and Principles: The Secretary-General's Role in Human Rights," in *The Challenging Role of the UN Secretary-General: Making "The Most Impossible Job in the World" Possible,* ed. Benjamin Rivlin and Leon Gordenker (Westport, CT: Praeger, 1993), 233–45.

11. Many scholars have written of the moral authority of the secretary-general, including Cordier, "Role of the Secretary-General"; Leon Gordenker, *The UN Secretary-General and Secretariat* (New York: Routledge, 2005); Jean E. Krasno, Bradd C. Hayes, and Donald C. F. Daniel, *Leveraging for Success in United Nations Peace Operations* (Westport, CT: Praeger, 2003); Nitza Nachmias, "The Role of the Secretary-General in the Israeli-Arab and the Cyprus Dispute," in Rivlin and Gordenker, *Challenging Role of the UN Secretary-General,* 111–32; C. V. Narasimhan, *The United Nations: An Inside View* (New Delhi: Vikas Publishing House, 1988); and James N. Rosenau, *The United Nations in a Turbulent World* (Boulder, CO: Lynne Rienner, 1992).

12. Pechota, "Quiet Approach," 7.

13. Hisako Shimura, "The Role of the UN Secretariat in Organizing Peacekeeping," in *United Nations Peacekeeping Operations: Ad Hoc Missions, Permanent Engagements,* ed. Ramesh Thakur and Albrecht Schnabel (New York: United Nations University Press, 2001), 46.

14. Kjell Skjelsbaek, "The UN Secretary-General and the Mediation of International Disputes," *Journal of Peace Research* 28 (1991): 104.

15. Sutterlin, *United Nations and the Maintenance of International Security,* 151.

16. Brian Urquhart, "The Role of the Secretary-General," in *U.S. Foreign Policy and the United Nations System,* ed. Charles William Maynes and Richard S. Williamson (New York: W. W. Norton, 1996), 218.

17. James O. C. Jonah, "Independence and Integrity of the International Civil Service: The Role of Executive Heads and the Role of States," *New York University Journal of International Law and Politics* 14 (1982): 849; and Brian Urquhart and Erskine Childers, *A World in Need of Leadership: Tomorrow's United Nations, A Fresh Appraisal* (Uppsala, Sweden: Dag Hammarskjöld Foundation, 1996), 23.

18. For a discussion of international organizations as "representative of the community's interests or the defender of the values of the international community,"

and the connection of this to moral authority, see Michael Barnett and Martha Finnemore, *Rules for the World: International Organizations in Global Politics* (Ithaca, NY: Cornell University Press, 2004), 23.

19. Jacques Baudot, "The Moral Power of the United Nations," in *Candles in the Dark: A New Spirit for a Plural World,* ed. Barbara Sundberg Baudot (Seattle: University of Washington Press, 2002), 267. See Baudot for a discussion of the elements of moral power of the United Nations. For a counterpoint, see Falk's discussion in his chapter "The Logic of the Charter," where he questions unrealistic expectations for the United Nations given the Westphalian logic prevalent in the charter, in Richard Falk, *A Study of Future Worlds* (New York: Free Press, 1975), 69–72. Interestingly, at times the member states use moral claims against each other in the context of the United Nations. For example, China has questioned the "moral qualifications" of Japan to serve as a permanent member of the Security Council. Joseph Kahn, "China Is Pushing and Scripting Anti-Japanese Protests," *New York Times,* April 15, 2005.

20. Nancy Hodes and Michael Hays, eds., *The United Nations and the World's Religions: Prospects for a Global Ethic, Proceedings of a Conference Held October 7, 1994, at Columbia University* (Cambridge, MA: Boston Research Center for the 21st Century, 1995); Commission on Global Governance, *Our Global Neighborhood: The Report of the Commission on Global Governance* (Oxford: Oxford University Press, 1995); and World Commission on Culture and Development, "A New Global Ethics," in *Our Creative Diversity: Report of the World Commission on Culture and Development* (Paris: UNESCO, 1995), 34–51. For a further listing of relevant reports, see www.unesco.org/opi2/philosophyandethics/intro.htm, and the discussion in Nitin Desai, "Global Ethics in a Plural World," in Baudot, *Candles in the Dark,* 27–45.

21. UNESCO, "The Universal Ethics Project at a Glance," www.unesco.org/opi2/philosophyandethics/intro.htm; and UNESCO, *Archive of Participant Contributions of the Universal Ethics Project* (Paris: UNESCO, 1998).

22. The ethical dimension of leadership may be traced to executive heads outside the United Nations system as well. For example, the moral arguments and passion that Manfred Woerner, NATO secretary-general from 1988 to 1994, brought to the position can be contrasted with the ethical concerns that undermined the brief tenure of his predecessor, Willy Claes, who ended his time as secretary-general after only thirteen months because of a bribery scandal from his time in Belgian national politics. See Ryan C. Hendrickson, "Leadership at NATO: Secretary-General Manfred Woerner and the Crisis in Bosnia," *Journal of Strategic Studies* 27 (2004): 508–27; and Ryan C. Hendrickson, "NATO's Secretary-General and the Use of Force: Willy Claes and the Air Strikes in Bosnia," *Armed Forces and Society* 31 (2004): 95–117.

23. Charles Norchi, "Human Rights: A Global Common Interest," in *The United Nations: Confronting the Challenges of a Global Society,* ed. Jean E. Krasno (Boulder, CO: Lynne Rienner, 2004), 91.

24. Arthur W. Rovine, *The First Fifty Years: The Secretary-General in World Politics, 1920–1970* (Leyden: A. W. Sijthoff, 1970), 426. Urquhart also stresses the notion of the secretary-general as a "symbol." Brian Urquhart, "The Evolution of the Secretary-General," in *The Dumbarton Oaks Conversations and the United Nations, 1944–1994,* ed. Ernest R. May and Angeliki E. Laiou (Washington, DC: Dumbarton Oaks Research Library and Collection, 1998), 25–33; and Urquhart, "Role of the Secretary-General."

25. See Ian Johnstone, "The Role of the UN Secretary-General: The Power of Persuasion Based on Law," *Global Governance* 9 (2003): 441–58; Howard H. Lentner, "The Diplomacy of the United Nations Secretary-General," *Western Political Quarterly* 18 (1965): 531–50; and Ramcharan, "Office of the UN Secretary-General."

26. For example, Theo van Boven argues that if the Secretariat does not encourage the principles of the United Nations, "it will fail in its responsibilities toward both the Organization and the peoples in whose name the Charter was drafted." Theo van Boven, "The Role of the United Nations Secretariat in the Area of Human Rights," *New York University Journal of International Law and Politics* 24 (1991): 71. Also see Lenter, "Diplomacy of the United Nations Secretary-General," for a discussion of how the secretary-general is an "embodiment, in international politics, of the equivalent of a 'public interest' concept" (534). In addition, see Hazzard, *Countenance of Truth,* and C. S. R. Murthy, "The Role of the UN Secretary-General Since the End of the Cold War," *Indian Journal of International Law* 35 (1995): 181–96. For a further discussion of whom the secretary-general could represent, see chapter 2 in this volume.

27. A. Walter Dorn, "The United Nations in the Twenty-First Century: A Vision for an Evolving World Order," in *World Order for a New Millennium: Political, Cultural, and Spiritual Approaches to Building Peace* (New York: St. Martin's Press, 1999), 128.

28. As Dorothy Jones observes, the officeholder may also interpret this position differently. See chapter 2 in this volume.

29. Benjamin Rivlin, "The Changing International Political Climate and the Secretary-General," in Rivlin and Gordenker, *Challenging Role of the UN Secretary-General,* 5.

30. United Nations Association of the United States of America, *Leadership at the United Nations: The Roles of the Secretary-General and the Member States* (New York: United Nations Association of the United States of America, 1986), 14–15.

31. James Barros, "The Importance of Secretaries-General of the United Nations," in *Dag Hammarskjöld Revisited: The UN Secretary-General as a Force in World Politics,* ed. Robert S. Jordan (Durham, NC: Carolina Academic Press, 1983), 25–37; James Barros, *Office Without Power: Secretary-General Sir Eric Drummond, 1919–1933* (Oxford: Clarendon Press, 1979); and James Barros, "A More Powerful Secretary-General for the United Nations?" *American Journal of International Law* 66 (1972): 81–84.

32. For example, Jakobson describes the dual role pressure as a "double exposure photograph." Max Jakobson, "Filling the World's Most Impossible Job," *World Monitor* 4 (1991): 26. For other examples, see Edward Newman, "The Most Impossible Job in the World: The Secretary-General and Cyprus," in *The Work of the UN in Cyprus: Promoting Peace and Development,* ed. Oliver P. Richmond and James Ker-Lindsay (New York: Palgrave, 2001), 127–53; Howard H. Lentner, "The Political Responsibility and Accountability of the United Nations Secretary-General," *Journal of Politics* 24 (1965): 839–60; Arthur N. Holcombe, *The UN Secretary-General: His Role in World Politics,* Fourteenth Report of the Commission to Study the Organization of Peace (New York, 1962); Skjelsbaek, "UN Secretary-General and the Mediation of International Disputes"; and Narasimhan, *United Nations: An Inside View.*

33. These qualities are also seen as key elements for Secretariat members in general, as established in Staff Regulations 1.4. See Lawrence Ziring, Robert Riggs, and Jack Plano, *The United Nations: International Organization and World Politics* (Belmont, CA: Thomson Wadsworth, 2005).

34. Narasimhan, *United Nations: An Inside View,* 274.

35. Jonah, "Independence and Integrity of the International Civil Service," 849. Jonah discusses the importance of integrity for the UN secretary-general, which he refers to as a "moral obligation."

36. Ibid., 843.

37. Rovine, *First Fifty Years,* 418; Skjelsbaek, "UN Secretary-General and the Mediation of International Disputes," 104. Impartiality has also been linked directly to an officeholder's personality by Newman, who writes, "Another important resource, whose effectiveness is also conditioned by personality, is the impartiality of the office." Newman, *UN Secretary-General from the Cold War to the New Era,* 29.

38. In this sense, the term *impartiality* is being used interchangeably with *neutrality.* The emphasis is placed on the term *integrity* because of the concern of some that "neutrality" indicates a lack of commitment to UN principles that are tied to the moral authority stance. For example, Pechota argues, "Independence and impartiality are perhaps the Secretary-General's strongest weapons. They should not, however, be confused with tolerance and neutrality. The Secretary-General cannot remain indifferent to or tolerate infringement of the Organization's purposes and principles." Pechota, "Quiet Approach," 41. See also van Boven, "Role of the United Nations Secretariat in the Area of Human Rights," 77. For another perspective contrasting the terms *integrity* and *neutrality,* see David P. Forsythe, "UNHCR's Mandate: The Politics of Being Non-Political," Working Paper 33, UNHCR (2001), available at www.unhcr.ch/refworld, which includes the observation, "A widespread view is that neutrality reflects moral bankruptcy. Rather than take a stand for morality and justice, neutrals supposedly sit on the fence. . . . But these views of neutrality do not show a profound understanding of neutral protection as practiced by UNHCR (or really by the ICRC either)" (7).

39. See Jones, chapter 2 in this volume, who traces the ideal of being "non-political" in relation to the secretary-generalship to Sir Eric Drummond at the League of Nations and the subsequent concerns raised regarding the lack of impartiality of his successor, Joseph Avenol. At the same time, see Krain's analysis, which suggests that an impartial approach by the United Nations to intervening in genocide or politicide is ineffective, thus calling into question the potential value of a secretary-general's stressing impartiality in such peace and security situations. Matthew Krain, "International Intervention and the Severity of Genocides and Politicides," *International Studies Quarterly* 39 (2005): 362–87.

40. My thanks to David Forsythe for a conversation that emphasized the importance of considering both the motivation, or attitude, of an officeholder and the impact of actions. See also Forsythe, "UNHCR's Mandate." For a related discussion of the need to distinguish between impartiality in a UN mandate and the implementation of that mandate, see Jane Boulden, "Mandates Matter: An Exploration of Impartiality in United Nations Operations," *Global Governance* 11 (2005): 147–60.

41. Leon Gordenker, *The UN Secretary-General and the Maintenance of Peace* (New York: Columbia University Press, 1967), 334.

42. The image of service to the Secretariat as virtually a religious commitment is seen in an interesting discussion by Townley, who links a seventeenth-century religious dispute to the perception of the international Secretariat. Ralph Townley, *The United Nations: A View from Within* (New York: Charles Scribner's Sons, 1968), 162.

43. Religion Counts, *Religion and Public Policy at the UN* (Washington, DC: Religion Counts, 2002), 33, 36. One of the few detailed studies of religion at the United Nations, the Religion Counts study was drawn together by the Park Ridge Center for the Study of Health, Faith, and Ethics and Catholics for Free Choice. The report incorporates interviews with almost sixty expert informants (see Appendix A, p. 52) carried out in 2000–2001 as part of the effort to better understand the place of religion at the United Nations.

44. See Jan Kerkhofs, *A Horizon of Kindly Light: A Spirituality for Those with Questions* (London: SCM Press, 1999); William O. Paulsell, "Dag Hammarskjöld," in *Tough Minds, Tender Hearts: Six Prophets of Social Justice* (New York: Paulist Press, 1990); Jeffrey G. Sobosan, "Politics and Spirituality: A Study of Dag Hammarskjöld," *Cithara* 14 (1974): 3–12; Gustaf Aulén, *Dag Hammarskjöld's White Book: An Analysis of Markings* (Philadelphia: Fortress Press, 1969); Henry P. Van Dusen, *Dag Hammarskjöld: The Statesman and His Faith* (New York: Harper and Row, 1964); Sven Stolpe, *Dag Hammarskjöld: A Spiritual Portrait* (New York: Charles Scribner's Sons, 1966); and T. S. Settel, *The Light and the Rock: The Vision of Dag Hammarskjöld* (New York: E. P. Dutton, 1966). Hammarskjöld's personal thoughts, often reflecting his religious and moral views, were published posthumously as *Markings*, trans. W. H. Auden and Leif Sjöberg (New York: Knopf, 1964).

45. June Bingham, *U Thant: The Search for Peace* (New York: Knopf, 1966). See especially the chapter "A Faith Takes Hold."

46. Gordenker, *UN Secretary-General and the Maintenance of Peace*, 334.

47. Brian Urquhart, "Dag Hammarskjöld: The Private Person in a Very Public Office," in Jordan, *Dag Hammarskjöld Revisited*, 139; Mark W. Zacher, *Dag Hammarskjöld's United Nations* (New York: Columbia University Press, 1970), 46.

48. Manuel Fröhlich, *Dag Hammarskjöld und die Vereinten Nationen: Die politische Ethik des UNO-Generalsekretärs* (Paderborn: Ferdinand Schöningh, 2002); an English translation is forthcoming as *Dag Hammarskjöld and the United Nations: The Political Ethics of the UN Secretary-General.* For further discussion by Fröhlich of the underpinnings of Hammarskjöld's political philosophy, see Manuel Fröhlich, "The Quest for a Political Philosophy of World Organisation," in *The Adventure of Peace: Dag Hammarskjöld and the Future of the UN,* ed. Sten Ask and Anna Mark-Jungkvist (New York: Palgrave Macmillan, 2005), 130–45.

49. Hazzard, *Countenance of Truth,* 14; Urquhart, "Evolution of the Secretary-General," 31. At the beginning of chapter 3 of this volume, James P. Muldoon Jr. also notes Hazzard's critique but is careful to balance this with alternative views of Lie's "human character."

50. Hazzard, *Countenance of Truth,* 98.

51. Robert E. Herzstein, *Waldheim: The Missing Years* (New York: William Morrow, 1988), 225; Stanley Meisler, *United Nations: The First Fifty Years* (New York: Atlantic Monthly Press, 1995), 188; Skjelsbaek, "UN Secretary-General and the Mediation of International Disputes," 104.

52. Ian Williams, "Kofi Annan: A 'Moral Voice,'" *The Nation,* June 19, 2000, 20–24.

53. Thomas G. Weiss, "The Politics of Humanitarian Ideas," *Security Dialogue* 31 (2000): 11, 20.

54. Barbara Crossette, "U.N. Secretary General Tries to Make His Job Count," *New York Times,* March 7, 1998.

55. As Muldoon explains, "An important element in the evolution of political philosophy is religion. . . . Religious practices were infused in the governance of communities and were instrumental to those who ruled. The admixture of religion and politics remains a potent (and often explosive) force in society." James P. Muldoon Jr., *The Architecture of Global Governance: An Introduction to the Study of International Organizations* (Boulder, CO: Westview Press, 2004), 24. At the same time, it should be noted that a sense of the resurgence of religion on the global scene is reflected by the similar increase in scholarly interest and attention. See Scott M. Thomas, *The Global Resurgence of Religion and the Transformation of International Relations: The Struggle for the Soul of the Twenty-First Century* (New York: Palgrave Macmillan, 2005). See also Hanson's promotion of a "post–Cold War paradigm" that incorporates religion alongside globalization, in Eric O. Hanson,

Religion and Politics in the International System Today (Cambridge: Cambridge University Press, 2006). For a general discussion of different religions and their connection to politics, see Jacob Neusner, ed., *God's Rule: The Politics of World Religions* (Washington, DC: Georgetown University Press, 2003).

56. George Moyser, *Politics and Religion in the Modern World* (New York: Routledge, 1991), 1.

57. John D. Carlson and Erik C. Owens, "Introduction: Reconsidering Westphalia's Legacy for Religion and International Politics," in *The Sacred and the Sovereign: Religion and International Politics,* John D. Carlson and Erik C. Owens, eds. (Washington, DC: Georgetown University Press, 2003), 5. For consideration of the impact of "religious ideas" from the Protestant Reformation on the development of the Westphalian system, see Daniel Philpott, "The Religious Roots of Modern International Relations," *World Politics* 52 (2000): 206–45.

58. In support of this argument, for example, Fox also observes how "religion influences international politics in diverse ways," yet, "with some notable exceptions, the influence of religion has received comparatively little attention in international relations." Jonathan Fox, "Religion as an Overlooked Element in International Relations," *International Studies Review* 3 (2001): 53. For further detailed discussion of why religion has not been a focus of international relations scholarship, see Jonathan Fox and Shmuel Sandler, *Bringing Religion into International Relations* (New York: Palgrave Macmillan, 2004), in particular chapter 2, "The Overlooked Dimension," and McDougall's discussion of reasons for and progress on overcoming "the scarcity of literature on religion and international relations," which opens a special issue of *Orbis* on religion in world affairs, Walter A. McDougall, "Introduction," *Orbis* 42 (1998): 159–70. Johnston also emphasizes that there is a need to "help fill a telling gap in the literature," in Douglas Johnston, "Introduction: Beyond Power Politics," in *Religion, the Missing Element of Statecraft,* ed. Douglas Johnston and Cynthia Sampson (Oxford: Oxford University Press, 1994), 4; see also Douglas Johnston, ed., *Faith-Based Diplomacy: Trumping Realpolitik* (Oxford: Oxford University Press, 2003).

59. Pavlos Hatzopoulos and Fabio Petito, eds., *Religion in International Relations: The Return from Exile* (New York: Palgrave Macmillan, 2003). This volume includes revised versions of many of the articles from a special issue of *Millennium* on religion and international relations, vol. 29, no. 3 (2000).

60. See Marc Gopin, *Between Eden and Armageddon: The Future of World Religions, Violence, and Peacemaking* (Oxford: Oxford University Press, 2000); R. Scott Appleby, *The Ambivalence of the Sacred: Religion, Violence, and Reconciliation* (Boston: Rowman and Littlefield, 1999); Luc Reychler, "Religion and Conflict," *International Journal of Peace Studies* 2 (1997): 19–38; and Chadwick F. Alger, "Religion as a Peace Tool," *Global Review of Ethnopolitics* 1 (2002): 94–109.

61. David P. Barash and Charles P. Webel, *Peace and Conflict Studies* (Thousand Oaks, CA: Sage Publications, 2002), 406. See also Gopin, who argues in *Between*

Eden and Armageddon that religion "will play a critical role in constructing a global community of shared moral commitments and vision" (4).

62. Gopin, *Between Eden and Armageddon,* 4. For a review of studies on spiritual values and the link to leadership, see Laura Reave, "Spiritual Values and Practices Related to Leadership Effectiveness," *Leadership Quarterly* 16 (2005): 655–87; this article is part of a special issue of the journal titled "Toward a Paradigm of Spiritual Leadership."

63. Johnston, "Introduction: Beyond Power Politics," 4.

64. Religion Counts, *Religion and Public Policy at the UN,* 9; and Benjamin Rivlin, "Thoughts on Religious NGOs at the UN: A Component of Global Civil Society," in *Civil Society in the Information Age,* ed. Peter I. Hajnal (Aldershot: Ashgate, 2002), 158–59. For example, see John S. Nurser's account of the role played by religious actors in "Preparing For San Francisco" and "The Charter of the United Nations Organization," in *For All Peoples and All Nations: The Ecumenical Church and Human Rights* (Washington, DC: Georgetown University Press, 2005), 93–125.

65. The role of religion in international organizations in general is a greatly underexamined area. One example of the limited research in this area is an effort to trace the link between religious beliefs of the European public and support for European Union integration. See Brent F. Nelsen, James L. Guth, and Cleveland R. Fraser, "Does Religion Matter? Christianity and Public Support for the European Union," *European Union Politics* 2 (2001): 191–217; and Brent F. Nelsen and James L. Guth, "Religion and Youth Support for the European Union," *Journal of Common Market Studies* 41 (2003): 89–112. For a further discussion of religion in the European Union context, see Peter J. Katzenstein and Timothy A. Byrnes, "Transnational Religion in an Expanding Europe," *Perspectives on Politics* 4 (2006): 679–94.

66. Religion Counts, *Religion and Public Policy at the UN,* 5.

67. Robert A. F. Thurman, "Foreword," in Hodes and Hays, *United Nations and the World's Religions,* vii.

68. Religion Counts, *Religion and Public Policy at the UN,* 39. The religious divisiveness at the United Nations, and in the international arena more generally, can have important implications for a secretary-general considering taking action based on personal religious beliefs. As the head of an organization representing countries that encompass all of the world's religions, an officeholder's perceived impartiality could be compromised if he or she is viewed as biased toward a particular religious group.

69. Rivlin, "Thoughts on Religious NGOs at the UN." Also see United States Institute of Peace, *Faith-Based NGOs and International Peacebuilding,* Special Report 76 (Washington, DC: United States Institute of Peace, 2001), in relation to religious NGO activities.

70. For example, the World Council of Churches issues statements and sends direct letters to the secretary-general calling for action to be taken by the office.

Emilio Castro, the general secretary, wrote in a letter regarding Kuwait, "The churches around the world have affirmed their strong opposition to a war in the Gulf. . . . We are confident that you are actively engaged in efforts to avert a military conflagration. As you intensify those efforts to promote all necessary diplomatic initiatives for a negotiated settlement, we assure you of our highest consideration and our support and prayers for efforts for peace." From Commission of the Churches on International Affairs of the World Council of Churches, *The Churches in International Affairs: Reports 1991–1994* (Geneva: World Council of Churches, 2002), 231. Also see the 1997 call for a Universal Declaration of Human Responsibilities proposed by the InterAction Council and the 1993 Declaration Toward a Global Ethic of the Parliament of the World's Religions, and written response from Secretary-General Kofi Annan, in Hans Kung and Helmut Schmidt, *A Global Ethic and Global Responsibilities: Two Declarations* (London: SCM Press, 1998).

71. Religion Counts, *Religion and Public Policy at the UN*, 5.

72. Cited in Rivlin, "Thoughts on Religious NGOs at the UN," 160.

73. For the goals and activities of the World Council of Religious Leaders, see www.millenniumpeacesummit.com/wc_about.html.

74. "Judging by the unwieldiness and the outcome of the religious summit, a role for religious interfaith activity in pursuit of the goals for world peace and social justice, enunciated as far back as the 1893 World Parliament of Religions, remains a persistent and elusive challenge." Rivlin, "Thoughts on Religious NGOs at the UN," 167. Janice Love, "Religion in Politics: Reflections on the UN's Millennium World Peace Summit of Religious and Spiritual Leaders," *International Studies Perspectives* 2 (2001): 131.

75. See Mervyn Frost, *Ethics in International Relations: A Constitutive Theory* (Cambridge: Cambridge University Press, 1996); and Karen E. Smith and Margot Light, eds., *Ethics and Foreign Policy* (Cambridge: Cambridge University Press, 2001).

76. For a discussion of how ethics have not been incorporated well into international relations theory, and for a counterargument for a "structural ethics" approach, see Ward Thomas, *The Ethics of Destruction: Norms and Force in International Relations* (Ithaca, NY: Cornell University Press, 2001). Also see Raymond's argument that "moral norms are an important, puzzling, and generally neglected element of international relations." Gregory A. Raymond, "The Moral Pulse of International Relations," in *Visions of International Relations: Assessing an Academic Field*, ed. Donald J. Puchala (Columbia: University of South Carolina Press, 2002), 82.

77. Jean-Marc Coicaud and Daniel Warner, "Introduction: Reflections on the Extent and Limits of Contemporary International Ethics," in *Ethics and International Affairs: Extent and Limits*, ed. Jean-Marc Coicaud and Daniel Warner (Tokyo: United Nations University Press, 2001), 6. It can be argued that there is, in fact,

a "global ethic" in place, but not in a positive sense, because "it is an ethic too strongly tilted toward the worship of power, the rule of brute force, the culture of violence," so the focus should be on redefining the global ethic. Thurman, "Foreword," vii. This line of argument reinforces the perspective that one should be careful not to slip into the assumption that "ethics" is the same as an absolutist sense of "good." See Joel Rosenthal, "Introduction: Ethics Through the Cold War and After," in *Ethics and International Affairs: A Reader* (Washington, DC: Georgetown University Press, 1999), 1–7.

78. An important area in this regard, with a range of related literature, is ethics and international security; recent work on this subject includes Iain Atack, *The Ethics of Peace and War: From State Security to World Community* (New York: Palgrave Macmillan, 2005), and John Janzekovic, *The Use of Force in Humanitarian Intervention: Morality and Practicalities* (Aldershot: Ashgate, 2006).

79. Ken Booth, Tim Dunne, and Michael Cox, "How Might We Live? Global Ethics in a New Century: Introduction," in *How Might We Live? Global Ethics in a New Century,* ed. Ken Booth, Tim Dunne, and Michael Cox (Cambridge: Cambridge University Press, 2001), 6. For other arguments stressing that ethics and international politics cannot be artificially separated, see Chris Brown, *Sovereignty, Rights and Justice: International Political Theory Today* (Cambridge, UK: Polity Press, 2002), and Andrew Linklater, *The Transformation of Political Community: Ethical Foundations of a Post-Westphalian Era* (Columbia: University of South Carolina Press, 1998).

80. One aspect driving this resurgence, Amstutz argues, is that it is "clear that the international order has been increasingly challenged because of perceived wrongs and injustices." Mark R. Amstutz, *International Ethics: Concepts, Theories, and Cases in Global Politics* (Lanham, MD: Rowman and Littlefield, 1999), 168.

81. Nicholas Rengger, "Conclusion: The Task(s) of International Ethics," in Coicaud and Warner, *Ethics and International Affairs,* 264.

82. As Religion Counts bluntly states, "Heaven help us if the world's ethical conscience is delegated to governments" instead of handled through the United Nations. Religion Counts, *Religion and Public Policy at the UN,* 49.

83. Cathal J. Nolan, "Introduction," in *Ethics and Statecraft: The Moral Dimension of International Affairs,* 2d ed., ed. Cathal J. Nolan (Westport, CT: Praeger, 2004), 1.

84. Dorothy V. Jones, "The World Outlook of Dag Hammarskjöld," in ibid., 133–46.

85. Roberto Toscano, "The Ethics of Modern Diplomacy," in Coicaud and Warner, *Ethics and International Affairs,* 42.

86. Toni Erskine, "Introduction: Making Sense of 'Responsibility' in International Relations: Key Questions and Concepts," in *Can Institutions Have Responsibilities? Collective Moral Agency and International Relations,* ed. Toni Erskine (New York: Palgrave Macmillan, 2003), 11.

87. My thanks to Anthony Lang for his conceptualization and writing assistance for the material in this chapter on the concept of ethical framework.

88. Joel H. Rosenthal, "Foreword: Biography, Ethics, and Statecraft," in Nolan, *Ethics and Statecraft*, xv.

89. Studies of the secretary-general are hardly alone in this approach. Any discussion of an ethical framework raises considerations of a potential religious basis. Nardin emphasizes this point in the edited volume *The Ethics of War and Peace: Religious and Secular Perspectives*, where he explains, "We have included both religious and secular perspectives in this study because ethical views are often linked with religious beliefs shared by a large number of people, and because these beliefs are a part of the ethical experience that moral and political philosophy must seek to understand." Terry Nardin, "Introduction," in *The Ethics of War and Peace: Religious and Secular Perspectives*, ed. Terry Nardin (Princeton, NJ: Princeton University Press, 1996), 6. This volume includes the perspectives of Judaism, Islam, and Christian pacifism, along with natural law, political realism, and feminism. Other volumes in the Ethikon Series in Comparative Ethics also provide religious alongside secular perspectives on ethical questions. Jewish, Christian, and Islamic ethical commentaries on international society are included in David R. Mapel and Terry Nardin, eds., *International Society: Diverse Ethical Perspectives* (Princeton, NJ: Princeton University Press, 1998); discussions of ethical pluralism from Confucian, Islamic, Jewish, and Christian viewpoints can be found in Richard Madsen and Tracy B. Strong, eds., *The Many and the One: Religious and Secular Perspectives on Ethical Pluralism in the Modern World* (Princeton, NJ: Princeton University Press, 2003); and weapons of mass destruction are considered from both religious and secular viewpoints in Sohail H. Hashmi and Steven P. Lee, eds., *Ethics and Weapons of Mass Destruction: Religious and Secular Perspectives* (Cambridge: Cambridge University Press, 2004). Religion has been acknowledged as a fundamental source of ethical concerns in Robert J. Myers, "After the Cold War," *Society* 28 (1991): 28–34.

90. Fox, "Religion as an Overlooked Element in International Relations," 59; also Fox and Sandler, *Bringing Religion into International Relations*, 57.

91. For further consideration of officeholders' personal qualities and the potential relation of these to the external environment, see Kent J. Kille, *From Manager to Visionary: The Secretary-General of the United Nations* (New York: Palgrave Macmillan, 2006).

92. See Leon Gordenker, "The UN Secretary-Generalship: Limits, Potentials, and Leadership," in Rivlin and Gordenker, *Challenging Role of the UN Secretary-General*, 261–82, for a discussion of the institutional values of the United Nations in relation to the secretary-general. See also chapter 2 in this volume for an examination of the role expectations of the secretary-general.

93. Barros, "Importance of Secretaries-General of the United Nations," 29.

94. Beigbeder emphasizes that member states often hold the perspective that "our candidate should share our objectives and our values." Yves Beigbeder, *The Internal Management of United Nations Organizations: The Long Quest for Reform* (New York: St. Martin's Press, 1997), 15.

95. Coicaud and Warner, "Introduction: Reflections on the Extent and Limits of Contemporary International Ethics," 3.

96. Rovine, *First Fifty Years*, 459. Similarly, Townley views the secretary-general as "furthering the integration and, perhaps, even the preservation of the international community." Townley, *View from Within*, 173.

97. Nolan, "Introduction," 4.

98. For example, Religion Counts stresses that two key concerns of religious groups are social justice and peace. Religion Counts, *Religion and Public Policy at the UN*, 42. The connection of values to the understanding of security is addressed in Alexandra Kent, "Reconfiguring Security: Buddhism and Moral Legitimacy in Cambodia," *Security Dialogue* 37 (2006): 343–61.

99. Jonah, "Independence and Integrity of the International Civil Service," 859.

100. Theodor Meron, "The Role of the Executive Heads," *New York University Journal of International Law and Politics* 14 (1982): 862.

101. Benjamin Rivlin, "The UN Secretary-Generalship at Fifty," in *The United Nations in the New World Order: The World Organization at Fifty*, ed. Dimitris Bourantonis and Jarrod Wiener (New York: St. Martin's Press, 1995), 100.

102. Rosenau, *United Nations in a Turbulent World*, 71.

103. Rovine, *First Fifty Years*, 445. The importance of the ethical standing of the secretary-general in the eyes of the international community in relation to legitimacy can also be seen in Johnstone, "Role of the Secretary-General," and in Danesh Sarooshi, "The Delegation of Powers to the UN Secretary-General," in Danesh Sarooshi, *The United Nations and the Development of Collective Security: The Delegation by the UN Security Council of Its Chapter VII Powers* (Oxford: Clarendon Press, 1999), 50–85. For the linkage of legitimacy with international institutions, see Jean-Marc Coicaud and Veijo Heiskanen, eds., *The Legitimacy of International Organizations* (Tokyo: United Nations University Press, 2001).

104. Thomas M. Franck, "Finding a Voice: How the Secretary-General Makes Himself Heard in the Councils of the United Nations," in *Essays in International Law in Honour of Judge Manfred Lachs*, ed. J. Makarcyzk (The Hague: Martinus Nijhoff, 1984), 31. In a later work, Franck also emphasizes the secretary-general's "unique ethical autonomy" in a section titled "Filling the Void: Action by the Secretary-General in the Face of Inaction by Everyone Else," in *Nation Against Nation: What Happened to the U.N. Dream and What the U.S. Can Do About It* (New York: Oxford University Press, 1985).

105. Commission on Global Governance, *Our Global Neighborhood*, 353.

2

SEEKING BALANCE

The Secretary-General as Normative Negotiator

DOROTHY V. JONES

When the secretary-general of the United Nations looks for guidance in his role as chief administrative officer of the organization, he finds that he stands between two normative codes, each with claims upon his loyalty. On one side is his own code of behavior, the set of personal beliefs and principles that he brings to the office. On the other side is a set of rules and principles that are chiefly concerned with the well-being and protection of the state. Each set of guidelines—the code within and the external code—makes uncompromising demands. It is up to the individual secretary-general to negotiate between the two in order to determine what will guide him as he meets the crises that will invariably occur during his tenure. How this has been done by the seven men who have served as secretary-general is explored in the following chapters. The purpose of this chapter is to provide a contextual framework for the studies of the individual officeholders.

One of the defining features of the context for thought and action by the secretary-general is the Charter of the United Nations. In the preceding chapter, Kent Kille notes that articles 97 through 101 of the charter set out the requirements and duties of the office. As Kille demonstrates, these five articles have generated much scholarly discussion about the powers that they do or do not confer. The charter's influence on the office of the secretary-general does not stop there, however. The charter as a whole reflects the kind of international system within which the secretary-general will have to operate. It expresses the principles of that system and articulates the rules that are supposed to govern behavior there. Finally, it sets out the goal that is the fundamental purpose of the organization and, by extension, the primary objective of actions that the secretary-general might undertake.

This chapter begins, then, with a close examination of the charter, looking first at the goal that is so emphatically stated throughout the document and then at the context that gave this goal such overriding importance. Two contextual aspects are critical in this analysis: the assumptions about the international system that the framers of the charter brought to their task, and the burden of historical memory that weighed on them as they worked. These forces shaped the document that they produced. Without an understanding of the background of the charter, it is difficult to understand the possibilities and limitations that have both empowered and circumscribed the men who have served as secretary-general.

The chapter then considers the seven individual office-holders, portraying them in general terms in order to bring out the commonalities of education, training, and experience that have been thought suitable for holders of this office. It is from this common base that the secretaries-general operate as they seek a workable position between their personal codes and that of the institution and international system they are there to serve. That external code of principles and rules is the authoritative official guide for the secretary-general's actions in office. It is made explicit in the charter, but it did not originate there. It is, rather, the outcome of years of international thought and experience, as both private individuals and leaders of independent states have considered how they might best govern their relations with one another. Because they have also tried to preserve the greatest possible freedom of action for themselves, there is a tension built into this code, and it has been compounded by the late addition of human rights provisions to the code, a subject addressed below.

The chapter moves next to a consideration of some of the complexities of the role of secretary-general. The formal requirements of the office are laid out in the charter, but these do not begin to cover all the areas and situations where a holder of that office must decide on a course of action. Who or what is the secretary-general supposed to serve? The rather vague, general terms of the charter leave open a wide area for choice, or for confusion. Finally, the chapter turns to a discussion of the ways in which the inner code might guide actions taken there. The purpose of this discussion is to suggest possible avenues of research and analysis rather than to specify hard-and-fast rules about the critical transition from private belief to public action.

The Goal Is Peace

A striking assumption underlies the Charter of the United Nations. The founding document of the organization details institutional arrangements and actions for a future that has moved beyond war. This assumption is not a measure of the founders' naïveté. It is instead a reflection of their confidence that they had devised ways to control the interstate violence that had so often erupted into war in the past. The foremost task of the organization, the founders thought, would be to preserve the peace and security that would ensue. The task is given pride of place in chapter I, where the first purpose of the United Nations is set out: "to maintain international peace and security." Throughout the charter, this phrase appears over and over again, as if repetition would ensure its realization. The very word *war* is taboo. It appears once in the preamble as a scourge to be avoided, and then disappears until near the end of the charter in a chapter on interim arrangements to shift from wartime to the predicated peace and security of the future. Should aggression occur in that future, it must, of course, be dealt with, but the charter does not call such aggression an act of war. Rather, it is one of those acts called "breaches of the peace"—that peace so ardently desired by the framers of the charter and so little experienced by subsequent generations.[1]

The framers of the charter may, however, have wrought more than they knew or intended. In their concern for peace and security, they opened the door for the secretary-general of the organization to take a more active role in the pursuit of peace than had been possible for the secretary-general of its predecessor, the League of Nations. The framers had hedged peace around with abundant provisions for its maintenance and safety. As a backup, they added one more. Article 99 of the charter gives the secretary-general the right to step outside the purely administrative functions of that office and call the attention of the Security Council to matters that in his opinion pose a threat to the maintenance of international peace and security. The opening was small, but an active and committed individual might use it to go beyond the formal right of appeal to the Security Council. The possibility for direct involvement in the pursuit of peace was there. Have the seven secretaries-general studied in this volume taken advantage of that possibility? If so, what circumstances allowed them to act when action seemed called for? Given that the secure and peaceful state of international affairs envisioned by the charter has never in fact existed, what have these seven officials done—in the words of Secretary-General Trygve Lie—to "build a firm foundation for the peace of the world"?[2] And, finally, what deeply held religious beliefs, what personal values, have guided their actions in this post? These are some of the questions that are explored in the pages that follow.

Governments have mixed attitudes toward the United Nations and its secretary-general. The organization was founded in a burst of international feeling that has dissipated since the heady days of the San Francisco conference where the charter took final shape in 1945. In the subsequent years of ambivalence, governments have demanded that the secretary-general be active—but not too active; independent—but not too independent; international in outlook—but not too international. When Secretary-General U Thant tried to restore international peace by promoting negotiations to end the Vietnam War, he incurred the lasting enmity of U.S. secretary of state Dean Rusk for this "meddling." Who did the secretary-general think he was, anyway?[3] Who the secretaries-general think they are, as these studies show, has a powerful effect on what they do in their pursuit of peace. A larger question, and one that is still a matter for argument, is this: What does it mean to have an international outlook, given the world as it is? Here, too, these studies may help provide an answer, as the seven men examined here had to answer that question every day they were in office. That office is not a comfortable place to be. The occupant serves as a lightning rod for the storms and tensions of the international system. How well were the storms deflected by these men? Were they able to resolve the tensions and create new opportunities for action? What, in fact, was possible for them? And this is to ask, what is possible through reason and persuasion in a world that responds to power?

A Sort of Second Chance

Two shadows darkened the birth of the United Nations and affected the planners' approach to the future. The first was the experience of war. World War II, still an ongoing conflict as the organization was being planned and the charter written, was so terrible an experience for the generation of the UN founders that they could not bear the thought of another war. They banished the very word from their institutional arrangements, just as they planned to banish war's presence from the world. We know now how quickly their plans were dashed on the political realities of the postwar world, but at the time they believed firmly that this time they had gotten things right. This time they had made arrangements that would allow them to succeed where the League of Nations had failed.

And that was the other shadow that darkened the birth of the United Nations: the political failure of the League. Memory of that failure hovered over the proceedings at Dumbarton Oaks, where the preliminary proposal for a new international organization was drafted; at the summit meeting at Yalta, where membership questions and Security Council voting procedures were hammered out; and in San Francisco, where the charter was put into final form. The prevailing impression was that the League of Nations had been weak. It had been timid. It was the terrible example that must at all costs be avoided. The founders of the United Nations were sure that theirs would be a more muscular organization. Where force was needed, it would be provided, and the peace of the world would be preserved. There would be talk before enforcement at the United Nations, as there had been at the League of Nations, but talk would never be an end in itself. Those who threatened the peace, those who engaged in aggressive action, would know that words were only the first line of the defense of peace. In back of the words lay force.[4]

This confidence about the arrangements to deter aggression carried over into the speeches at the final session of the San Francisco conference where the charter was formally signed and adopted. Voices of self-congratulation rose from the stage of the opera house where the plenary sessions were held. Amid this general chorus of praise was one speech in which praise was tempered by words of warning. The warning was a simple one: To be effective, commitments must not only be made, they must be kept. The subsequent failure to keep the San Francisco commitments regarding aggression was to have a profound effect on the United Nations that the secretaries-general would be called on to serve.

It was Joseph Paul-Boncour who issued the prophetic warning about the central weakness in the deterrence arrangements. This relic of the League of Nations headed the French delegation in San Francisco, but the wielders of power found it difficult to take him seriously. His was a flamboyant public presence, beloved of caricaturists because he was so easily satirized, but his bravura style hid a shrewd appreciation of the realities of power. He regretted, but recognized, the need to move beyond the League of Nations. He had served that organization with devotion, but it had failed in its most basic purpose. That failure lent urgency to the message he brought to the planners in San Francisco, where, as he pointed out, the flaw at the heart of the League's institutional arrangements had been recognized: "Today this flaw has been eliminated. . . . The obligation for all Member States to help in suppressing aggression is plainly established. An international force is to be formed and placed at the disposal of the Security Council." But Paul-Boncour did not stop there. He issued a warning to those who were so sure that they had done better than the founders of the League. With great foresight he focused on the weakness that was to undo their confident arrangements: "But the United Nations, and more especially the great nations with a permanent seat on the Council, must remain truly united. The whole efficacy of the Charter depends on this unity. In the hour when immense hope rises from our hearts, let us swear to remain faithful in peace to this unity which was our strength in war."[5]

The subtext of Paul-Boncour's message was clear: Here is a second chance for peace, a second chance to avoid the terrible destruction of another war. But this is not a chance to begin all over again with a clean slate. The slate is not clean for us any more than it was for the founders of the League of Nations. We must do more than evaluate their weaknesses and feel proud that we are not like them. We must confront our own weakness. And for us, that weakness lies precisely where we are sure we have improved upon the League. It lies with the Great Powers. The success of our innovative arrangements and of this limited second chance depends entirely on a unity of purpose that, even in wartime, has been difficult to maintain.

Paul-Boncour was not the only reminder of the League of Nations in San Francisco—a reminder that was unwelcome to some and to others simply irrelevant. Anthony Eden, Jan Christian Smuts, and V. K. Wellington Koo, all of whom had League associations, by their very presence called to mind a legacy that could not be ignored. The influence of that legacy had been felt from the start of planning for the new organization. A subcommittee in the U.S. State Department that had been appointed as early as June 1942 "began its efforts in July and August with a close examination of each article of the League of Nations covenant."[6] And when the choice was made to create a new organization, the example of the League was still a potent force. Like the League, the United Nations had an assembly, a council, an international court, and a secretariat presided over by a secretary-general. Structurally, then, the United Nations was a child of the League it was to replace.

But the structure of the League was only part of the legacy with which the United Nations—and eventually its secretaries-general—would have to deal. Beyond structure lay a whole host of assumptions about the states of the international system, their relationships to one another, to an international organization, and to their own citizens. This set of assumptions was handed down in its entirety to the new United Nations, and helped to form the context within which the secretaries-general of the organization would operate. Some were more comfortable with it than others, but all had to take account of the assumptions embedded in the legacy of the League. The attitudes of many of those with whom they dealt on a day-to-day basis had been shaped, consciously or unconsciously, by just such assumptions about the place of the state in the international system and thus about the power of the United Nations—or lack of power—to take certain actions at the urging of its secretary-general.

But before the United Nations was well under way, what about the League of Nations? Dispersed and inactive as it had been during World War II, it still had a legal existence. Equally, it still held the hearts of many who had served it and followed its fortunes. Let Emery Kelen and Alois Derso speak for them. These artists of caricature had, they said, "followed the peace junket through Locarno, Rapallo, The Hague, Paris, London, Washington, and New York." Theirs was a clear-eyed, affectionate view of the League. They remembered its slow decline to failure, but they also recalled its high points: "We remember when frail, shaggy Aristide Briand thundered 'Away with the cannons, away with machine guns!' We believed in the men of good will, and were carried away by a passion for peace. There was some grandeur in that fool's paradise."[7]

The United Nations took shape in a much grimmer atmosphere. No one was moved to the flights of rhetorical fancy that had attended the early days of the League. The veteran French diplomat Jules Cambon had regarded these flights with a sarcastic eye. You would think, he said, that the organization was going to bring paradise to earth.[8] The mood for the United Nations was altogether more sober, more a matter of determination: This time we will, we must, succeed. Here, too, Paul-Boncour caught the spirit of the occasion. After the 1945 conference in San Francisco, where the charter was put into final form, he attended the final meeting of the League of Nations Assembly in Geneva the following spring. For many it was a sad occasion, and especially so for Paul-Boncour, who saw how the bright face of hope was being replaced by the set frown of determination. He told the delegates to this last League assembly that in San Francisco there had not been "the enthusiasm and faith which animated our work in the great days of the League of Nations." Pervading the atmosphere in San Francisco was the fear that the United Nations would fail, as the League had done: "The setback suffered by this organization helps to undermine faith in the destinies of the other."[9]

These destinies were passing, even as he spoke, into the hands of the people who would be called upon to serve that "other" organization, the United Nations. The delegates to the General Assembly, the members of the Security Council, and the individual secretaries-general would, in their various ways, take up the tasks that the League of Nations had set down. Inspiration for this task could be found in a comment of the Chilean delegation at the San Francisco conference. The comment was made not as a goal to be pursued but as a statement of fact. Regarding the much-discussed topic of peace, the Chileans said simply: "Peace is the normal life of States."[10] In the years that followed the San Francisco conference, the seven secretaries-general studied here worked with varying degrees of success to make that simple, confident statement come true.

A Family Resemblance

By focusing on the men who have held the post of UN secretary-general, the contributors to this volume have taken the stand that, under certain conditions, individuals matter in international affairs, and their actions can make a difference there. Further, by emphasizing the roles of beliefs and conscience, they have opened a discussion of the place of ethics and religion in international affairs. Abstractions and analytical categories are not the chief methods of the discussion. Instead, careful study is given to the choices made by individual human beings who must think and act in specific contexts of empowerment and restraint. As one student of the subject has said, "There are few more compelling sources for the study of ethics and international affairs than the true stories and historical experiences of statesmen who made hard choices in reconciling principle and power."[11] The secretaries-general were frequently called on to make hard choices. Whether they can be seen as statesmen with the power to take effective international action can be determined only by looking at the record of each individual who has held that office.

Who, then, are these men who have occupied the post of secretary-general of the United Nations? Most obviously, they come from seven different countries. In the order in which they held office, they are Trygve Lie of Norway, Dag Hammarskjöld of Sweden, U Thant of Burma (now Myanmar), Kurt Waldheim of Austria, Javier Perez de Cuellar of Peru,

Boutros Boutros-Ghali of Egypt, and Kofi Annan of Ghana. The experiences of World War II were a strong influence on the first four, as the countries of all but Hammarskjöld were occupied by enemy forces during the war, and Swedish officials walked a hazardous path of neutrality within gunshot of the fighting. But similarity of experience does not stop with wartime events. Despite differences in background, these men have more in common with each other than with many of the citizens of the countries of their birth and upbringing.

Each had the benefit of a university education. Thant attended the University of Rangoon but because of family responsibilities had to leave before taking his degree. The others were able to complete work toward their degrees at the bachelor's or advanced level, five of the six in some branch of law. Six of the men had experience in high-level posts in their national governments before coming to the United Nations. Lie held various positions in the Norwegian government, the most recent, before his UN appointment, as Norwegian foreign minister. At the time of his appointment, Hammarskjöld was a cabinet minister without portfolio, in effect the deputy foreign minister for economic affairs in the Swedish government. The record of public service of these men is impressive, although only selected posts are included here: adviser to the Burmese prime minister (Thant); director-general for political affairs in the Austrian Ministry for Foreign Affairs (Waldheim); ambassador of Peru to Switzerland, the Soviet Union, Poland, and Venezuela (Perez de Cuellar); and deputy prime minister for foreign affairs of Egypt (Boutros-Ghali).

Each of them, before becoming secretary-general, also had experience at some level in the United Nations, either as a delegate to the General Assembly, through work on one of the special UN commissions, or with one of the related UN agencies. This is especially true for Annan, whose service in the UN system goes back to 1962, when he joined the World Health Organization as an administrative and budget officer. Finally, to round off this list of similarities, the ages of all but two of the men, at the time of their appointment, were relatively close. Hammarskjöld was the youngest at forty-seven, Boutros-Ghali the oldest at sixty-nine. The average age of the others when they assumed office was fifty-five. From these comparisons we can get a general picture of the seven men who accepted—and in some cases sought—the post of secretary-general of the United Nations. They were educated, talented, and experienced in public life. They came from elite groups in their respective countries. And they were chosen at ages when they might be expected to be at the height of their powers.[12]

These characteristics put them very much in line with Sir Eric Drummond, the first secretary-general of the League of Nations, whose fourteen-year tenure in that post helped set the pattern for those who occupied a similar post in the United Nations. Drummond had served nineteen years in the British Foreign Office when he was called to service in the League, and his ideal was that of the nonpolitical civil servant. He would never have been chosen if the first idea for a League administrator had been adopted at the Paris Peace Conference where the details of the League Covenant were worked out. But the idea of a well-known political figure holding the office of chancellor was dropped when none could be found to accept the post. The position was changed to that of secretary-general, the head of the administrative staff in the League Secretariat. This was, in theory, a new thing, a nonpolitical international civil service, but although the chief officers were appointed by the organization itself and not by their respective governments, the nonpolitical aspect was hard to maintain even by Drummond. The ideal remained, however, and continued as a goal for the Secretariat of the United Nations and its chief executive officer, the secretary-general. In this there was a strong continuity with the secretary-general of the League. The difference between the two offices, as Drummond himself noted in later years, was the UN official's article 99 right to call the attention of the Security Council to any situation that, in his opinion, threatened international peace and security. This was, said Drummond, "a new and highly responsible duty" that would demand that the post be filled by a person of "high integrity and great courage."[13] Drummond did not add what was also true: Anyone occupying the position of UN secretary-general had to keep in mind the rules and principles that were expected to guide him as he carried out the functions of his office. Because success or failure, as well as continuance in office, depended on how he functioned within this normative framework, it will be useful to examine it in more detail.

The External Code

As Paul-Boncour had noted at the San Francisco conference, the slate was not clean for the new international organization. There were disagreements and pockets of continuing violence to be dealt with. These might have been expected in the aftermath of a war that had been fought throughout much of the world, but the violence and the disagreements did not disappear as memories of the war faded. New grievances simply took the place of the old, and newly independent states brought new demands to an organization they had had no part in creating. This was not the most promising context for the efforts of even dedicated individuals to work toward the condition of peace and security invoked so frequently in the organization's charter. But there were other, more subtle constraints at work. These constraints were embedded in the charter itself. The drafters' earnest attempt to avoid past mistakes and failures, to provide institutional means for a fresh beginning in international affairs, was laced throughout with statements that would have been thoroughly familiar to adherents of the League of Nations.

The founders of the United Nations could not escape this conceptual legacy. It had guided all their efforts, and the arrangements they had made depended on the acceptance of its validity. But they would not have wanted to escape it even if they could. The rules and principles they had set out in the charter were more than just a code of behavior. At a deeper level, the code was also a statement of belief, a kind of creed that both described the world and prescribed the appropriate ways to act in that world. A study of the charter yields nine basic principles and rules that are set out in the document's first chapter, "Purposes and Principles":

1. Sovereign equality of states
2. Territorial integrity and political independence of states
3. Equal rights and self-determination of peoples
4. Nonintervention in the internal affairs of states
5. Peaceful settlement of disputes between states
6. Abstention from the threat or use of force
7. Fulfillment in good faith of international obligations
8. Cooperation with other states
9. Respect for human rights and fundamental freedoms[14]

How this normative framework might function to guide and legitimate the actions of the UN secretaries-general can be seen in the individual case studies. In a very general sense, the framework helps officials determine what international events fall within the domain of possible UN action, and what lies outside the organization's writ. In the Suez crisis of 1956, for example, the invasion of Egypt by the forces of Israel, France, and Great Britain was so clear a breach of the principles regarding peaceful settlement and the nonuse of force that the path to an international response was eased considerably.[15] Similarly, international support for an independent

Namibia was strengthened by reliance on the principle of equal rights and self-determination of peoples.[16] Events do not, however, always fit neatly into the framework. The seventh principle, regarding the carrying out of a promised action, opens the door to disagreement on exactly what a good-faith fulfillment might be, while an effort to maintain the territorial integrity of a state, as required in the second principle, can, under certain conditions, clash with the right to self-determination set out in the third principle. Perhaps the tightest pinch comes when international concern over human rights violations within a state clashes with the proscription against intervention in a state's internal affairs, a situation that presents a particularly difficult dilemma for the incumbent secretary-general.

All of this is only to say that the normative framework set out in the charter is, like other codes of behavior, subject to interpretation. For an international system of independent states, these rules and principles have a very high value as the set of standards that the states have agreed should govern their relations. Further, the agreement has stood the test of time. Adherents of the League of Nations are not the only ones who would have been familiar with most of the elements of this code. The delegates to the Hague conferences of 1899 and 1907 would have been comfortable with most of them as well. The code had been in the making for many years, as the states of the international system asserted their rights, occasionally considered their duties, and gave thought to rules that would give shape and predictability to their relations with one another. These efforts were affected by the work of such private groups as the Institut de Droit International, the American Society of International Law, and the Inter-Parliamentary Union. In the end, though, if the code were to have any official standing, it would have to be acted on by the states themselves. Over the years they had added bits and pieces to the documents through which they signaled their purposes and intentions and tried to guide their behavior: declarations, conventions, treaties, the League Covenant, and, finally, the Charter of the United Nations.

The years following the drafting of the charter saw a steady increase in membership of the United Nations from the fifty-one states whose delegates met for the first session of the General Assembly in 1946. New members, many of them newly independent states from Africa and Asia, began to raise questions about the charter. They pointed out that they had not been involved in its preparation, and that it bore the clear stamp of the developed Western world whose delegates had decided on its final form and content. The more vociferous of the newly independent raised the specter of a kind of legal colonialism, a subtle substitute for the political colonialism from which they had just freed themselves. These concerns were given a thorough airing in a special committee established to examine the charter's principles and their applicability to a post-1945 world. The result, after five years of study, was a resounding endorsement of both the principles and their universality, plus a detailed explication of what each principle was understood to mean, and an affirmation that all were of equal value. The declaration that embodied this gloss was approved by the General Assembly in October 1970. As one noted authority has observed, "The legal significance of the Declaration lies in the fact that it provides evidence of the consensus among Member States of the United Nations on the meaning and elaboration of the principles of the Charter." Although it cannot be seen as an amendment to the charter, it is, nevertheless, "a document of first importance."[17]

And what were the principles that had been given this resounding affirmation? They were the state-centered elements of the code, those concerned with sovereign equality, territorial integrity, nonintervention, and the like. Having achieved the high position of statehood, the newer states were naturally inclined to protect their status, and although the older states might argue the details of the explications, they were not likely to have any basic objections to the state-centered elements of the code. These elements had been affirmed so often that they had taken on the aura of fundamental truths, unchanging and unchangeable. But the code did not stop there. The experiences of World War II had brought to the fore a concern that was focused not on states but on people. The result was the addition of the principle of respect for human rights and fundamental freedoms. Even the newer states, concerned as they were for their own standing, had included in their explication of the charter's principles a reference to the duty of states to "co-operate in the promotion of universal respect for and observance of, human rights and fundamental freedoms for all."[18] It would have been difficult in 1970 for states to ignore entirely the issue of human rights, because by then the simple charter principle of respect for those rights had been expanded and expressed in great detail in such documents as the Universal Declaration of Human Rights, the International Covenant on Civil and Political Rights, and the International Covenant on Economic, Social and Cultural Rights.[19]

All of these could be interpreted as statements of future intent, a reading that preserved the states' freedom of action in domestic affairs. Or they could be interpreted as directives for present action, a reading that had the potential to create tremendous tension in a code that had been gradually devised by states for their own protection and well-being. How this tension might play out in the future was partly in the hands of the successive secretaries-general as they sought to use their office as a force for peace and security.[20] They had, at any rate, been supplied with specific standards by which to judge events and guide their actions, and a specific external code against which to test their own internal codes of values and beliefs.

Whose Servants?

In the first flush of enthusiasm for the United Nations, the poet W. H. Auden and the cellist Pablo Casals collaborated on a musical work they may have hoped would express on an international level the intense loyalties and feelings that had so far been the prerogative of the national anthems of the world. Their international anthem, written for a four-part chorus, was titled *Hymn to the United Nations*. The chorus celebrates music as the perfect paradigm for peace, since peace will grow from peaceful acts, "like music when begotten notes new notes beget." The integrity of this ordered musical progression stood in contrast to the plethora of empty talk about peace: "but song is true, but song is true." The bass section warns, "Let mortals beware of words, for with words we lie," and the tenors continue, "can say peace when we mean war." But the music flows on until the full chorus triumphantly greets the promised day: "Till what it could be, / At last, at last it is." And there is peace.[21]

Even in this abbreviated version, it is clear why Auden and Casals are better known for other works than this one. But beyond that lies a difficulty that the *Hymn to the United Nations* illustrates in a telling and dramatic manner. Peace as a goal, no matter how desired and desirable, is difficult to present in a way that lifts the heart and commands a following. It remains an abstraction that cannot seriously compete with a banner still waving at dawn's early light, or a prayer that God will save our gracious queen. To be effective, peace must appeal to an international outlook—an outlook that is nebulous at best and nonexistent at worst. Yet the secretaries-general of the United Nations are to keep that international outlook in mind in the performance of their duties. The charter is clear in its stipulation that those duties are exclusively international in character.[22] It is considerably less clear on what that stipulation might mean in actual practice. There was an attempt at the San Francisco conference to suggest some of the difficulties that might ensue if national and international loyalties pulled in different directions. In the committee charged with examining the powers of the Secretariat a question arose as to a possible conflict of loyalties. If, for example, a member of the Secretariat were to be involved in plans for UN-authorized military action against a member state, and that state happened to be his own, what then? Wouldn't the Secretariat official be liable to heavy penalty under the laws of his own state for failing to reveal that it was the target of planned military action? The question was raised, but it died in committee without being answered.[23]

It might be thought that the delegates to the first session of the General Assembly would clarify matters when they considered regulations for the Secretariat staff. The regulations, however, simply repeat the charter stipulation about the exclusively international character of the secretary-general's duties, as if its meaning were self-evident. The concern of the delegates, and of the drafters of the charter as well, was in some respects a negative one. They wanted to make sure that "in the performance of their duties the Secretary-General and the staff shall not seek or receive instructions from any government or from any authority external to the Organization," a prohibition that appears both in the charter and in the staff regulations. The General Assembly went further and said that the officials' acceptance of appointment to their positions was a pledge "to discharge their functions and to regulate their conduct with the interests of the United Nations only in view."[24]

The assumption in these strictures seems to be that the "interests" of the United Nations will on any future occasion be collectively agreed on, and be capable of advancement by the secretary-general through appropriate action. But the future is not really at issue here. The past is at issue. What the delegates were trying to guard against was a loss of respect for the new organization because of a loss of confidence in the impartiality of the secretary-general. This had happened to the League of Nations under Joseph Avenol, its second secretary-general. Avenol was widely seen as more a servant of his native France than of the League. Choosing him to succeed Drummond as secretary-general had, however, been more a matter of satisfying national sensitivities than of choosing the best candidate. Drummond was British. France would naturally expect that Drummond's successor would be French. Despite the efforts of Drummond and then the seven secretaries-general of the United Nations to resist this kind of pressure, the parceling out of top-level posts by nationality was, and continues to be, a feature of staffing the Secretariat. It was and is one of the less tractable features with which the secretaries-general have to deal.[25]

Much was left to the initiative and understanding of the individuals who were to occupy the office of secretary-general. The administrative duties of the office were, under ordinary circumstances, not a cause for argument. As chief executive officer, the secretary-general chose the Secretariat staff, supervised its activities, attended meetings of the various bodies of the organization, and made an annual report to the General Assembly. The problems and the opportunities of the office lay in that small opening for an active political role that the founders had provided when they gave the chief executive the right to step outside the bounds of the purely administrative and go directly to the Security Council with political concerns. There were times also when the General Assembly encouraged an active role, as when it asked Hammarskjöld, after the Korean War, to try to secure the release of fifteen American fliers being held by the People's Republic of China, or when, during the tenure of Perez de Cuellar, the assembly stipulated that the secretary-general should become directly involved in the settlement of disputes that might threaten international peace and security. The assembly's stipulation included encouragement for the secretary-general to use his article 99–charter right to take such matters to the Security Council, "at as early a stage as he deems appropriate."[26]

The charter could give the right and the General Assembly could encourage an active role and the use of that right, but the member states could effectively undercut this leadership role by refusing to support or cooperate with a secretary-general who displeased them. Thus the Soviet Union's withdrawal of recognition from Secretary-General Lie, whom they had earlier supported; and thus Secretary-General Boutros-Ghali's failure to win a second term when the United States turned a cold shoulder to his ambition. Whether these actions were in support of the collective interests of the United Nations or the particular interests of the countries involved is an issue that arises time and again as the member states' commitment to the organization fluctuates in response to their domestic concerns. What is clear is that when an internationalist outlook comes up against an opposing national policy, there is usually no way over the obstacle, although there is sometimes a way to go around.

As these examples suggest, one of a secretary-general's primary responsibilities is to keep the member states happy enough—or at least not too unhappy—with the way the duties of the office are carried out that he can continue to function. The charter does not stipulate this, but any secretary-general ignores it at his peril, and this is particularly true in regard to the more powerful states. Part of the problem is that the office is in many ways a diplomatic anomaly. Who or what is the secretary-general supposed to represent? Traditionally, diplomats have represented sovereignty, whether in the form of a city-state, an empire, a monarch, or, as is most customary today, a state. The United Nations is a legal entity, and diplomatic privileges have been extended to certain levels of its employees. But beyond these legalities, what is its standing in a world structured chiefly by power relationships? And when the secretary-general speaks or acts, on what basis can he claim that world's attention?

There are rare occasions when this problem is muted. That state of affairs occurs when the Security Council speaks with one voice. Then the secretary-general can speak and act as if for a sovereign body, with the knowledge that something more than national self-interest, some sense of collective responsibility, might motivate the states to a favorable response. But when the members of the Security Council cannot agree, when council meetings are exercises in endless debate, then, as one diplomat remarked, "It reminds me of slow-motion underwater ballet."[27] Nothing much happens, and it does so at great length, apparently without the need to come up for air. The polite label for the protracted discussions at the United Nations, both on the Security Council and in the General Assembly, is collective diplomacy. But, as one experienced practitioner of modern diplomatic practice has observed, "Collective diplomacy in its various forms is gaining in importance over bilateral diplomacy; but even collective diplomacy takes place largely outside the United Nations. No responsible government, no serious student of international affairs, considers that the conduct of international affairs can be left entirely to the particular part of the modern diplomatic process which is the United Nations as that body operates at present." As for increasing the powers of the secretary-general, as many have suggested, "the greater the powers entrusted to the Secretary-General, the harder it would be for the member states to agree on an individual to wield them."[28]

Agreement is hard enough under current arrangements, as former UN official Brian Urquhart has noted on several occasions.[29] And, having gotten through that often awkward, sometimes demeaning appointment process, the secretary-general has still to wrestle with the question of responsibility. There are the Great Powers, of course, and the Security Council, quarreling and inept as it might sometimes be. And beyond those? What might be due to that "international community" so beloved of orators, so often invoked and so ill defined? It is a question that each secretary-general has had to answer for himself. He has had to decide how broad is the sweep of the international outlook mandated by the charter, and how relevant it is for the performance of his job. From Lie to Annan, the lack of conceptual clarity in the guidelines for the job has presented a problem to be faced or an opportunity to be seized, depending on the personal qualities of the incumbent and the circumstances of the case.

Over time, the opportunities that have been seized have gradually extended the secretary-general's freedom to maneuver. The changes have been small and often little noticed. But they have been incremental. In 1946 questions were raised about Secretary-General Lie's right to bring to the Security Council his views on an Iranian-Soviet dispute then under council consideration.[30] Few would question Secretary-General Annan's right, in the early 2000s, to give his opinion on almost any matter before the council or the assembly. In this respect, the secretary-general has become a spokesperson for a broader responsibility than might be derived from the charter, however that responsibility may be defined now or in the years to come.

The Code Within

The similarities in the lives and experiences of the men who have served as secretary-general of the United Nations were mentioned above. To understand how these men functioned in office, however, it is necessary to come down from that high level of generality and look at individuals. Each will have had different responses to experiences that, in general terms, might seem to be the same, and each will have had different ideas about the best approach to the secretary-general's difficult and demanding job. Even if the goals are the same for everyone in that position, even if they all are keen to advance the common interests of the international community, however defined, the style and manner of operation will differ markedly from one man to another. They will view the organization itself in different ways, and that, too, will affect how they go about their job. For Hammarskjöld the United Nations was an imperfect stage in the development of a true international community, and he spoke in terms of change and growth. Boutros-Ghali, by contrast, spoke of maintenance and balance, terms that reflected his structural view of the organization.[31]

The point is obvious, but it bears repeating: Despite similarities of background and experience, these men came into office with highly developed and markedly different approaches to life and work. They brought with them the administrative styles, communication skills, and personal relationships that had served them well in the past. They brought something else as well, less obvious than the other characteristics but perhaps of greater importance. All brought the set of beliefs and values that had guided them in past actions and that could be expected to guide them as they assumed the functions of their new public role. Few would argue that beliefs and values do not matter in public life, but the connection between inner code and outward action is often obscure. It is rare for someone in public life to be as frank as former U.S. president Jimmy Carter in making explicit the relation between what he believes and what he does. Because Carter is so frank, it is worth looking at how he perceives religious guidance in his affairs and actions. As governor of Georgia and then president of the United States, he faced problems that are different from those faced by the secretary-general of the United Nations, and he had resources at his command, particularly for the carrying out of policy, that are unavailable at the international level. The context for national and international action is obviously not the same. There is, however, a functional similarity that facilitates comparisons. Under the pressures and constraints of his particular office, each incumbent must marshal and sustain enough support to carry out policies while at the same time remaining true to the voice of conscience. A brief look at the interaction between Carter's inner code and his public life can illustrate some of the points that need to be covered in an analysis of the connection between belief and action, and perhaps some of the pitfalls that need to be avoided as well.

Carter's faith is grounded in a biblically based Christianity that would be familiar to millions throughout the U.S. South, where he was born and raised. Central to this set of beliefs is the figure of Jesus Christ as personal guide and savior, and, for Carter, as an example to be followed as well. When he heard his Plains, Georgia, Baptist minister preach a sermon with the title, "If You Were Arrested for Being a Christian, Would There Be Enough Evidence to Convict You?" he was overwhelmed with guilt. "I began to think about the questions the prosecutors might ask me: 'What have you actually done for others in the name of Christ?'" His resolve to do more spurred him to increasing involvement in public service, a response to religious belief that is not limited to Christianity or to the domestic scene. In 1962 Carter was elected to the Georgia state senate. In

1966 he ran for governor of Georgia against Lester Maddox, an avowed segregationist, and lost the election. This loss was almost more than he could bear. In his set of beliefs, God was an active participant in human affairs, and it was up to human beings to discern and help to forward the divine intent. "I could not believe that God would let this person beat me and become the governor of our state." And then the deeply personal griev-ance, the feeling that "God has rejected me through the people's vote."[32]

Here religious belief and public service go hand in hand, each reinforc-ing but also testing the other. Here, too, are illustrated the hazards to the believer when a course of action that seems obviously right and con-sistent with belief goes awry. The ego is, of course, involved: "God has rejected me." But the setback is even worse than that. It raises unsettling questions. What if I am wrong? What if I have not correctly understood the divine intent? There are moments of such self-doubt in *Markings,* the posthumously published diary of Secretary-General Hammarskjöld. This cultivated scion of an elite Swedish family lived worlds apart from Jimmy Carter of Plains, Georgia, but the strains of a God-centered life were as difficult for him as for the farmer from Plains. Like Carter, he was under constant self-examination, and, like Carter, he often found that he did not measure up. "It is not sufficient to place yourself daily under God," Hammarskjöld rebuked himself. "What really matters is to be *only* under God."[33]

When analysis turns outward to action instead of inward to belief, the connection between the two eludes easy explanation. In 1970 Carter became governor of Georgia, and he used his inaugural address to con-demn the South's practice of racial segregation. In 1976 he became presi-dent of the United States, and he used his inaugural address to announce the emphasis on human rights that would become the hallmark of his administration's foreign policy. With his hand on the Bible that his mother had given him, he vowed, "Our commitment to human rights must be absolute."[34] The Bible was open to the verse in Micah in which God calls on believers to do justice, love mercy, and walk humbly before the Lord. For Carter, this was not just an interesting development in the ancient Hebrews' idea of God. It was a divine command.

Some of the complexities at play here are revealed when the views of other southerners are brought into the analysis. Millions throughout the South held beliefs similar to Carter's. Millions had had a similar upbring-ing and similar exposure to sermons that demanded of them reflection on what it meant to be a Christian. And millions had apparently not had the slightest difficulty in wrapping their beliefs around the practice of racial segregation to the point where it could be defended on the basis of divine intent. Similarly, others in high national office were assuredly familiar with the biblical injunction to love mercy and do justice, but even if they attempted that in their personal lives, they had not taken it as a demand that the government should make human rights a pillar of its foreign policy. A critical transition has taken place here. The personal and private has become collective and public. This was a big step for Carter to take, and it caused him no end of difficulties, but for the study of the connection between belief and action it serves a different purpose. It points to questions that can usefully guide analysis. What, for example, are the circumstances in which the personal and private can make this transition into the public realm? What are the collective means chosen for this expression of belief?[35]

When the focus of analysis shifts from the national to the international level, the context for action changes dramatically. Yet religious belief as a subject of inquiry is a constant that allows comparisons to be made. Of the seven men who have held the office of secretary-general of the United Nations, Thant was the most explicit about his faith. He was a devout Buddhist. How that affected his performance as secretary-general is a subject to be explored in the chapter devoted to his time in office. Here it need only be noted that one effect of his faith was a calm demeanor that impressed those who observed or worked with him. When an interviewer suggested that his Buddhist faith might be the source of his apparent tranquility, Thant replied, "It is true that the spiritual and ethical values of Buddhism provide serenity, strength, and humility." He went on to include other faiths as equal sources of strength and stability for their adherents.[36]

Here, then, are two deeply religious men in public life, Carter and Thant. For Carter, religious faith could be unsettling, prompting him to ask if he was doing enough. Was he doing the right thing? Faith was, or could be, an uncomfortable burr in his spiritual center. Thant's faith had the opposite effect. At the core of his spirit were tranquility and calm. The crises that occurred during his tenure could be addressed from a center of strength and stability. Two men. Two faiths. Two different responses to the effect of religious belief in public life.

Obviously, two examples constitute a very small universe from which to draw general conclusions about the connection between belief and action. Just as obviously, neither example is, or is intended to be, a comprehensive look at the world and thought of Thant or Carter, or of the religious traditions to which they adhered.[37] The two examples can, however, suggest some interesting analytical paths. It is clear that choice plays a key role in the movement from belief to action, and that choice continues to be central as obstacles are met along the way, or as external codes, such as that enshrined in the charter, have to be taken into account. An internal code of personal beliefs and values can usefully be thought of as a kind of spiritual filter. The filter helps to determine what is important and what is not, what deserves action and what does not. At that point, considerations of what is possible and what is not also enter in, but before that stage is reached several steps of perception and selection have already taken place, based on this inner code of beliefs and values. Nor is this all of that code's function. During the attempted action, it will often provide strength and spiritual sustenance, and in the aftermath, no matter how the action has turned out, it will guide reflection.

Each of the secretaries-general has had to make the hard choices that the position demands, and each has been guided by the sets of beliefs that are explored in this volume. Theirs has been the task of translating the private into the public, the general into the particular, in circumstances that are relatively new. As Secretary-General Waldheim observed, "Despite the doctrine of peace fundamental to every abiding religion of the world, it has taken humanity a few thousand years to resolve to work collectively to end all-out war and to establish conditions whereby settlements of disputes over ideology or power or territory might be obtained, not by bloodshed, but by discussion and consensus."[38] To a greater or lesser extent, that resolve has been forwarded by the seven men who are the subject of this study.

Conclusion

Reflecting on the proliferation of peace groups and conferences in the nineteenth century, Sir Henry Maine remarked, "War appears to be as old as mankind, but peace is a modern invention."[39] His comment is worth recalling as an aid to understanding the assumptions that underlie the modern quest for peace through the United Nations. At first glance, Maine's comment is puzzling. He could hardly have meant that the general concept of peace was a nineteenth-century invention. Ecclesiastes was not, after all, the only recognition in the ancient world that in the flux of circumstance "there is a time for war and a time for peace." The word *invention* also seems oddly out of place. It implies a deliberate fashioning by human effort. But in this instance, what is being fashioned? Not the condition of peace, for that has rarely been achieved in much of the world. The word must then refer to something else, something that would have been unthinkable in earlier centuries, when wars were taken for granted and peace was the time in between. A different view began to be heard after the Napoleonic Wars, increasingly so as the nineteenth century neared its end. This was the view, expressed in a hundred different ways by peace advocates and conferees, that human society had progressed to the place where peace was no longer the preserve of prophets and visionaries. A universal peace based on justice and equality had at last become *politically* possible. The Covenant of the League of Nations and the Charter of the United Nations were formal expressions of this legacy of thought, a legacy given the bite of urgency by the experiences of two world wars.[40]

If any of the secretaries-general thought that the goal of universal peace was quixotic or impossible, they did not say so in public. Their approaches to the goal varied according to temperament and circumstance, but peace remained the desired end. At the heart of their efforts was the resolution of conflicts in accordance with the means set out in article 33 of the charter: "negotiation, enquiry, mediation, conciliation, arbitration, judicial settlement, resort to regional agencies or arrangements, or other peaceful means of their own choice." Often it was the personal qualities and persistence of the secretary-general that were the key to successful implementation of the chosen means. The charter barely mentions this personal factor, but its prominence during the terms of office of the seven men studied here should put it high in any consideration of the pursuit of peace through the United Nations. Good faith, honesty, truth telling—all the old-fashioned virtues—can become tools of peacemaking in the hands of the secretaries-general, especially if they are perceived as using those qualities in the service of some greater good.

The danger in this approach is that others who could help might rely too heavily on the efforts of the secretary-general. "Leave it to Dag" became a watchword during the term of Hammarskjöld, the second secretary-general.[41] This was a tribute to the impact of his personality, and to his record of pulling the fat from innumerable fires. It also reflects the trend to structure the role of the secretary-general around the traits of the individual holding the office. This personalization of the position was probably far from the founders' minds when they set out the requirements and functions of the office, but, intended or not, the personality of each secretary-general has shaped the office quite as much as the office has shaped the man. That being so, it is important for an understanding of the quest for peace that there be a close study of each of the men who have brought to this office their beliefs and values, and have then, within the constraints of the office and the time, undertaken actions based on their private vision of the right and the good.

So where do things stand in the quest for peace? The endless succession of conflicts around the world calls attention to the fact that the peace and security envisioned in the charter have yet to be attained. This broad failure has, however, stimulated innovative UN approaches that have secured small islands of calm in the midst of violence: the supervision of elections to ensure fairness and transparency; the support and monitoring of ceasefire or peace agreements through the presence of an international peacekeeping force; the establishment of courts where the perpetrators of international crimes might be made to answer for their crimes. As with the personalization of the role of the secretary-general, these initiatives were not foreseen by the founders of the United Nations, but the charter they wrote has proved flexible enough to accommodate innovation.

After surveying fifty years of efforts by the League of Nations and the United Nations to create an organization that could effectively maintain international peace, Raymond Fosdick concluded that the whole undertaking was still in its infancy.[42] Some thirty years on, the conclusion reached by this former official of the League can still be used to describe the international situation. It is as if the eighty years of effort were an extended prologue to the time when the world of the covenant and the charter would come into being: a world of peace and justice, law and plenty—but, above all, a world of peace. Through conflict after conflict, peace is still the desired goal of much international effort. If peace still seems a possible goal, that is due in some measure to the efforts of the seven secretaries-general whose beliefs and actions are explored in this study.

Notes

1. For a copy of the UN charter, as well as a detailed account of the founding of the organization, see Stephen C. Schlesinger, *Act of Creation: The Founding of the United Nations* (Boulder, CO: Westview Press, 2003), 295–321. The admonition to maintain international peace and security occurs twenty-seven times in the

body of the charter and once in the preamble. Charter citations in the text are to the preamble and articles 1.1 and 107.

2. Quoted in Andrew W. Cordier and Wilder Foote, eds., *Public Papers of the Secretaries-General of the United Nations*, vol. 1, *Trygve Lie, 1946–1953* (New York: Columbia University Press, 1969), 35.

3. For the participants' accounts of this conflict of authority, see U Thant, *View from the UN* (Garden City, NY: Doubleday, 1977), 57–84; and Dean Rusk, *As I Saw It, as Told to Richard Rusk* (New York: W. W. Norton, 1990), 462–65.

4. The enforcement provisions of the UN charter are described in chapter VII, articles 39 to 51.

5. *Documents of the United Nations Conference on International Organization, San Francisco, 1945*, vol. 1, *General* (London: United Nations Information Organization, 1945), 667–69.

6. Robert C. Hildebrand, *Dumbarton Oaks, the Origins of the United Nations and the Search for Postwar Security* (Chapel Hill: University of North Carolina Press, 1990), 18. Hildebrand, who has made a close study of the 1944 Dumbarton Oaks conference, points out that the suggestion that the League's four-part structure be retained for the new United Nations was proposed by all the sponsoring powers, not just by the United States. See pp. 93–94. See also Ernest R. May and Angeliki E. Laiou, eds., *The Dumbarton Oaks Conversations and the United Nations, 1944–1994* (Washington, DC: Dumbarton Oaks Research Library and Collection, distributed by Harvard University Press, 1998), for a retrospective evaluation of the Dumbarton Oaks undertakings.

7. Alois Derso and Emery Kelen, *United Nations Sketchbook* (New York: Funk and Wagnalls, with United Nations World, 1950), 9, 11. Like many who had been associated with the League, Derso and Kelen went on to work at the United Nations.

8. Jules Cambon, *Le Diplomate* (Paris: Hachette, 1926), 106.

9. Joseph Paul-Boncour, address to the League of Nations Assembly, April 10, 1946, League of Nations, *Official Journal, 1946, Records of the Twentieth and Twenty-first Sessions of the Assembly, Text of the Debates* (Geneva, 1947), 37.

10. *Documents of the United Nations Conference on International Organization*, vol. 3, *Dumbarton Oaks Proposals, Comments, and Proposed Amendments* (London: United Nations Information Organization, 1945), 293.

11. Joel H. Rosenthal, "Biography, Ethics and Statecraft," foreword to *Ethics and Statecraft: The Moral Dimension in International Affairs*, 2d ed., ed. Cathal J. Nolan (Westport, CT: Praeger, 2004), xv. Useful as background to the studies of individual decision makers is Terry Nardin and David R. Mapel, eds., *Traditions of International Ethics* (Cambridge: Cambridge University Press, 1992). For an example of the difference one individual can make at the United Nations, see Courtney B. Smith, "The Politics of U.S.-UN Reengagement: Achieving Gains in a Hostile Environment," *International Studies Perspectives* 5 (2004): 197–215, especially 204.

12. Information for this group portrait was drawn from the official biographies posted on the UN website, available at www.un.org/sg/formersgs.shtml.

13. Drummond's comments are quoted in Raymond B. Fosdick, *The League and the United Nations After Fifty Years: The Six Secretaries-General* (Newtown, CT: Raymond B. Fosdick, 1972), 46. The standard work on Drummond's tenure as League secretary-general is James Barros, *Office Without Power: Secretary-General Sir Eric Drummond, 1919–1933* (Oxford: Clarendon Press, 1979).

14. The nine principles and rules are drawn from the following charter articles, listed here in the order of their appearance on the list: 2.1, 2.4, 1.2, 2.7, 2.3, 2.4, 2.2, 1.3, and 1.3.

15. Hammarskjöld's response to the Suez crisis is treated in chapter 4 of this volume, by Alynna J. Lyon. The lack of a similar response to the Soviet invasion of Hungary that same year suggests the inadequacy of relying solely on a normative framework as a guide to action.

16. Waldheim's handling of Namibia is discussed in chapter 6 of this volume, by Michael T. Kuchinsky.

17. Ian Brownlie, *Basic Documents in International Law,* 5th ed. (Oxford: Oxford University Press, 2002), 27.

18. Ibid., 31. The cumbersome name of the document is Declaration on Principles of International Law Concerning Friendly Relations and Co-operation Among States in Accordance with the Charter of the United Nations. Brownlie prints the whole document, pp. 27–33. It can also be found in Irving Sarnoff, comp., *International Instruments of the United Nations* (United Nations Publications, E.96.I.15, 1997), 327–30. The declaration is in the annex to General Assembly Resolution 2625 (XXV), October 24, 1970.

19. Ian Brownlie, ed., *Basic Documents on Human Rights,* 2d ed. (Oxford: Clarendon Press, 1982), 21–27, 118–45. Brownlie's prefatory comments provide extensive references to other commentaries and interpretations.

20. The creation of this code of behavior is studied in detail in Dorothy V. Jones, *Code of Peace: Ethics and Security in the World of the Warlord States* (Chicago: University of Chicago Press, 1991). It should be noted that treating the state as a unitary actor, as is done in the text, is a shorthand method of focusing on the outcome of state actions rather than on the complex state decision-making process.

21. Pablo Casals and W. H. Auden, *Hymn to the United Nations,* for four-part chorus of mixed voices with piano (or organ) accompaniment (New York: Tetra Music Corp., 1972). Copy in the Newberry Library, Chicago. An accompaniment for full orchestra was also available from the publisher.

22. Article 100.2 of the charter calls on the members of the United Nations "to respect the exclusively international character of the responsibilities of the Secretary-General and the staff and not to seek to influence them in the discharge of their responsibilities."

23. *Documents of the United Nations Conference on International Organization, San Francisco, 1945,* vol. 7, *Commission 1, General Provisions* (London: United Nations Information Organization, 1945), 557.

24. Article 100.1 of the charter. The Secretariat staff regulations adopted on December 13, 1946, at the first meeting of the General Assembly, are in the Report of the Fifth Committee to the Assembly, Doc A/41, Annex 18, General Assembly, *Official Records,* 604.

25. The standard study of Avenol is James Barros, *Betrayal from Within: Joseph Avenol, Secretary-General of the League of Nations, 1933–1940* (New Haven, CT: Yale University Press, 1969). For an eloquent analysis of the administrative difficulties that appointment by nationality could cause in the Secretariat, see Chester Purves, *The Internal Administration of an International Secretariat* (London: Royal Institute of International Affairs, 1945), 23–26.

26. Article 23 of the 1988 Declaration on the Prevention and Removal of Disputes and Situations Which May Threaten International Peace and Security and on the Role of the United Nations in This Field. The declaration is printed in Sarnoff, *International Instruments,* 62–63. Article 23 is on p. 63. The declaration, A/RES/43/51 in the UN system of citation, was adopted December 5, 1988, at the sixty-eighth plenary meeting of the General Assembly. For the assembly resolution requesting that the secretary-general try to gain the release of the imprisoned American fliers, see General Assembly Resolution 906 (IX), Official Records of the Ninth Session, Resolutions or Annexes, under agenda item 72. For a detailed account of the various policy initiatives, secret messages, and negotiations that eventually resulted in the fliers being freed, see Brian Urquhart, *Hammarskjöld* (New York: Knopf, 1972), 96–131.

27. Charles W. Thayer, *Diplomat* (New York: Harper and Brothers, 1959), 112.

28. Adam Watson, *Diplomacy: The Dialogue Between States* (New York: New Press, 1983), 155, 156.

29. See, for example, Brian Urquhart, "Selecting the World's CEO: Remembering the Secretaries-General," *Foreign Affairs* 74 (1995): 21–26. Urquhart served in the UN Secretariat from 1945 to 1986, the last twelve years as undersecretary-general for special political affairs. He had a ringside seat for observing the selection process and the subsequent relationships of the secretary-general with the states that had supported his appointment.

30. Trygve Lie, *In the Cause of Peace: Seven Years with the United Nations* (New York: Macmillan, 1954), 79–88.

31. Dorothy V. Jones, "The Example of Dag Hammarskjöld: Style and Effectiveness at the UN," *Christian Century* 111 (1994): 1047–50.

32. Jimmy Carter, *Living Faith* (New York: Times Books/Random House, 1996), 202, 208.

33. Dag Hammarskjöld, *Markings,* trans. W. H. Auden and Leif Sjöberg (New York: Knopf, 1964), 99.

34. Jimmy Carter, *Keeping Faith: Memoirs of a President* (Toronto: Bantam Books, 1982), 20.

35. Carter was not always consistent in publicly condemning racial segregation or in privileging human rights over *realpolitik.* This emphasizes the importance of looking at the circumstances that enable or impede a transition from private belief to public action.

36. Andrew W. Cordier and Max Harrelson, eds., *Public Papers of the Secretaries-General of the United Nations,* vol. 6, *U Thant, 1961–1964* (New York: Columbia University Press, 1976), 441.

37. There are numerous studies of the complexities of religious and secular belief systems. For example, see Richard Madsen and Tracy B. Strong, eds., *The Many and the One: Religious and Secular Perspectives on Ethical Pluralism in the Modern World* (Princeton, NJ: Princeton University Press, 2003).

38. Kurt Waldheim, *The Challenge of Peace* (New York: Rawson, Wade, 1980), 3. The work was originally published in France in 1977 under the title *Un métier unique au monde.*

39. Quoted in Michael Howard, *The Invention of Peace* (New Haven, CT: Yale University Press, 2000), 1. Howard's treatment of the subject has influenced mine.

40. There are numerous studies of the peace movements of the nineteenth and early twentieth centuries. An older work that is still useful is A. C. F. Beales, *The History of Peace: A Short Account of the Organized Movements for International Peace* (New York: Dial, 1931; reprint 1971). The essays in Charles Chatfield, ed., *Peace Movements in America* (New York: Schoken, 1973) extend coverage into the 1970s. The focus of Warren F. Kuehl's *Seeking World Order: The United States and International Organization to 1920* (Nashville: Vanderbilt University Press, 1969) is reflected in the title.

41. Dag Hammarskjöld's influence is still strong today. See Kofi Annan, "How Would Hammarskjöld Have Handled This?" *UN Chronicle* No. 4 (2001): 44–47, based on a lecture Annan gave on September 6, 2001, in Uppsala, Sweden.

42. Fosdick, *League and the United Nations,* 1. From 1919 to 1920 Fosdick was undersecretary-general of the League of Nations.

3

THE HOUSE THAT
TRYGVE LIE BUILT

Ethical Challenges as the First UN Secretary-General

JAMES P. MULDOON JR.

> *I am no utopian. I see in the United Nations a practical approach
> to peace and progress—not by any quick and easy formula, but by a
> wise, loyal, and persistent use of its institutions by the Member gov-
> ernments over many years. . . . I see the judgment of history that, in
> this present day and for all the future, world peace is necessary to the
> survival of mankind, and the United Nations, in turn, is necessary
> to the attainment of a world peace that will endure. This is the cause
> I have sought to serve as Secretary-General of the United Nations.
> This is also the cause that will continue to command loyalty in the
> years to come.* —TRYGVE LIE[1]

It is interesting that Trygve Halvdan Lie, who, on February 1, 1946, became
the first elected secretary-general of the United Nations, is all but forgotten.[2] What accounts for the amnesia about this man, a respected labor
lawyer, social democrat, and lifelong politician who toiled for seven long
and difficult years in the service of the international community and
world peace? There are some who argue that Lie was the wrong man for
the job. He had neither the qualifications nor the vision to effectively lead
the new international organization and was too crude and "deficient in
ethical perception."[3] For them, he is best forgotten. Others think he was a
decent man, a "human character" quickly overwhelmed by circumstances,
a casualty of the rapidly deteriorating new world order of the Cold War.[4]
He did the best he could with what he was given. But they, too, see little in
his tenure for which to remember him. Obviously Lie was neither a saint
nor a devil—had he been one or the other, it would probably have assured

him a more prominent place in the history books—but a pragmatic and determined man with limited talents. Perhaps more troubling, though, is not that history has been unkind to Lie, but that it has been simply indifferent.

What has been lost over time is any appreciation of Lie's contribution to the office of secretary-general and to the survival of the United Nations when both were clearly threatened by external forces and events over which he had little if any control. He faced formidable obstacles from the beginning and did his utmost to realize the world's hopes for international peace and security through the United Nations. Lie has much more to his credit in shaping the role of the secretary-general than his detractors seem willing to concede. In fact, his more celebrated successors owe him a great deal for establishing the "implied political prerogatives" of the office, which stem from the language of article 99 of the charter, and for his outspoken advocacy of the "United Nations as an independent political and moral force in the world."[5] Lie pushed hard to gain a foothold for the nascent United Nations amid the turbulence and acrimony of the Cold War, and he achieved a meaningful, albeit limited, role for the organization in the critical issues of the early postwar period. In so doing, he kept the United Nations alive, even as his actions drew the ire of the Great Powers at one time or another, whose interpretation of the role and powers of the United Nations and its secretary-general differed from Lie's. Moreover, his persistence in asserting and exercising the full range of rights—implicit and explicit—that the charter bestowed on the secretary-general never waned. He was indefatigable.

The many trials and tribulations that Lie suffered during his term were less a reflection of his shortcomings as a leader than of the organization's member states, especially the Great Powers, in respecting the charter. The international environment in which Lie had to function was at odds with what the charter expected to emerge after the war and did as much to thwart Lie's efforts to uphold the charter's principles, and to enhance the United Nations' role in the world, as his mistakes did. The political context of the times belied the institutional norms that Lie was mandated to develop, and it could be argued that under such circumstances there was little if anything Lie could do to realize them. In the end, as Alan James points out, "Lie may not have had a very successful term, but the interpretation he stamped on his office was clearly expansionist."[6] But what drove Lie's assertiveness—vanity, power, or simple stubbornness? Was his approach politically naïve and bereft of "ethical perspective"? To what extent did his personal values, religious and/or moral, influence his behavior? These are some of the questions that this chapter tries to answer.

The point of this exercise is to see whether and how Lie's religious and moral values affected his actions as secretary-general. The influence of Lie's personal beliefs and values as opposed to the political and legal norms of the office are not easily separated out. Lie had spent his entire adult life in public office. Like most career politicians of his generation, he aligned his moral convictions with the norms ascribed to public office, since to do otherwise would bring an early end to a political career. The choices he made over the course of seven years as secretary-general reflected the blending of the personal values he had developed throughout his life and the norms of international law that the charter imposed on the office he occupied. His choices were also influenced by the circumstances of postwar international relations—the hard realities of world politics—that circumscribed the leadership role he thought the office was meant to have, which he earnestly sought to play. The confluence of Lie's personal values, his own understanding of the role of secretary-general, and the external context guided his actions.

The first part of this chapter sketches Lie's ethical framework—the religious and moral beliefs that influenced his behavior as a career politician. The values that constitute Lie's ethical framework are fundamentally secular and not religious, reflecting Lie's embrace of socialism as a young man, his training as a labor lawyer, and his association with the Norwegian labor movement. The second part examines some of the challenges Lie confronted as the first secretary-general of the newly minted United Nations. It highlights his approach to the job and the manner in which he sought to realize the principles and ideals of the UN charter. The third part offers some thoughts on how Lie's political decisions and policies reflect the interaction of his ethical framework and his interpretation of the secretary-general's "moral authority" in international affairs.

Ethical Framework

Lie's ethical framework emanated from his childhood experiences. He was born in 1896 to Hulda and Martin Lie in a working-class suburb of Oslo, Norway, but lost his father at an early age. Martin Lie, a carpenter, purportedly packed his bags and tools in 1902 and set sail for the United States, never to be heard from again.[7] The task of raising Lie was left to Hulda

Lie, a strong, broad-minded, independent woman who never remarried. To make ends meet, Hulda Lie converted her home in Grünerlökken, near Oslo, into a boardinghouse, charging residents—many of whom were workers from Sweden, Finland, Poland, Germany, and Russia—twenty cents a day for room and board. Lie was devoted to his mother, whose example instilled in him an appreciation for hard work, self-sacrifice, and service to others.

Evangelical Lutheran Faith and Pietism

Hulda Lie raised her son in the evangelical Lutheran faith and regularly attended services of the state-sponsored Church of Norway. But she did not follow the austere practice of keeping the Christian Sabbath with quiet prayer and reflection—working or indulging other pleasant pastimes was considered inappropriate—as was common among more "devout" Norwegians.[8] She had a boardinghouse to run that required her attention each and every day of the week. Moreover, she was broad-minded on the subject of religion, since her boarders were of various faiths, and she always respected other faiths and expected the same from her son.[9] Modesty and personal rectitude were virtues Lie learned early on in life from both his circumstances and his mother's example.

Lie, like all Norwegian children at that time, received basic religious instruction in school in pietism, or the "personal surrender to God, on the individual plane," which has been at the heart of the evangelical Lutheran faith in Norway since the eighteenth century.[10] It is thus likely that Lie's set of beliefs and values, his "inner code," would have been informed by pietism, if not structured by it. Moreover, pietism, with its emphases on individual morality, service to God and to others, and "living faith," surely gave him a moral vocabulary that he could and would employ throughout his life, personally and professionally.

The adult Lie revealed little of his attitude toward religion, however. He was never outwardly religious, but neither was he hostile toward religion, as he never repudiated his upbringing within the evangelical Lutheran tradition. He was not a churchgoer and was uncomfortable on those occasions when he did attend religious services, especially after he became UN secretary-general, because of the undue attention it attracted. In fact, as a child Lie spent most Sundays playing sports instead of attending church, as he typically worked the other six days of the week. Lie, one could argue, was simply indifferent to the church and religious faith. This is not to say that Lie was devoid of spirituality. He certainly believed in God, and he respected Christian holidays and traditions. He celebrated Christmas and led the family in the Lord's Prayer before meals, and he regularly engaged in silent prayer or meditation in the privacy of his home.[11] Furthermore, Lie recognized the importance others attached to their religion and faith, which goes a long way in explaining his decision, in 1949, to include a "meditation room" in the design of the UN headquarters in New York and to propose to the Special Committee on Methods and Procedure of the General Assembly that each session of the General Assembly open and close with one minute of silent prayer and meditation, in remembrance of those who had died for UN ideals.[12]

Lie was "intensely devoted to his family," and his wife, Hjördis, made certain that their home was a place of refuge and peace for her husband, whether in Grorud during the early years of their marriage, in London during the war, or at Granston Tower in Forest Hills, New York, during Lie's tenure at the United Nations.[13] He took his family responsibilities very seriously, and despite the immense pressures of public office, he made every effort to be with his family for dinner in the evening and to keep within limits any work after hours.[14] The family was clearly an important source of strength and solace for Lie, and he always sought their counsel when confronted with difficult decisions, particularly any decision that would concern his family.[15]

Lie's religious beliefs were a very personal matter. He imposed no religion or religious beliefs on his three daughters but let them choose the church or faith they wished to follow and often admonished them to "always tell the truth," to "always try to do what is right," and to "respect all other religions."[16] Honesty, truthfulness, and right living were core values Lie sought to impart to his children, reflecting the centrality of these values to his own ethical perception. By the time he became UN secretary-general, his religious beliefs had been subsumed in a broader set of secular humanistic values that recognized an individual's right to practice his or her religion and society's obligation to defend religious freedom.

Socialism and the Values of Social Democracy

Another powerful influence on Lie was the growing labor movement and the socialism of the early twentieth century. The residents of the Lie boardinghouse were laborers and workers from throughout northern Europe, and Lie heard about the Russo-Japanese War, the failed 1905 revolution in Russia, and syndicalism and the workers' movement. Not only did the residents of the boardinghouse give Lie a political education, they also helped him get "his first job as a clerk at the Norwegian Labour Party Headquarters in Oslo, marking the beginning of a life-long association with the Norwegian Labor movement."[17] Lie's attraction to socialism was probably the result of his "deprived childhood" and "the industrial milieu in which he was growing up. . . . At best, it was probably a dreary life of constant toil. . . . As Lie stoically noted years later, he 'had never been used to luxury and had had a hard life in his youth.'"[18]

Lie cut his political teeth at an early age in the rough-and-tumble of local Norwegian politics. By age sixteen he had become the president of the Aker branch of the Norwegian Trade Union Youth Organization and "was a practical local politician, driving voters to the polls in a borrowed sledge."[19] Never afraid of hard work or daunted by the immense challenges that his childhood circumstances put before him, Lie made his way through university, earning a law degree from the University of Oslo in 1919, and quickly rose through the ranks of the Norwegian Labor Party. Soon after finishing his studies, he was appointed assistant to the Norwegian Labor Party's secretary. In 1922 Lie took up the position of general counsel to the National Trades Unions Federation, a position he held until he was elected to parliament in 1935. In parliament he rose rapidly in the leadership of the ruling Labor Party, starting out as the head of the Ministry of Justice from 1935 to 1939, then becoming minister of trade, industry, shipping, and fishing in 1939. While serving in the latter post, Lie "ordered 25,000 seamen to avoid Norwegian ports following the Nazi invasion of Norway in 1940," which saved the Norwegian merchant fleet for the Allies during the war.[20]

Lie's early involvement in local politics shaped his character and outlook on life. He strove to be always honest in his dealings with others and was "loyal in his personal relationships."[21] Although he was blunt in speech and thought, and passionate and steadfast in his convictions, he was sociable and had a "fondness for good company and good wine."[22] Ultimately his character was well suited to the life of a politician, and Lie was above all a politician. Socialism and the Norwegian Labor Party provided a framework for his budding dedication to social democratic principles and values, namely, social justice, fairness and equality, human rights and religious freedom, and respect for the law. He developed a deep and abiding faith in what Neil Stammers calls the "strategic pragmatism" of social democracy and the central tenets of the social democratic tradition, characterized by six principles:

1. Social democracy assumes that liberal democracy works: that is, societies with a liberal democratic polity are already democratic in a fundamental sense—even if further democratization is advocated.
2. Social democracy perceives capitalism as both inevitable and also inherently dynamic—the source of growth and wealth creation. Thus, it also necessarily accepts the logical and structural imperatives of a capitalist market economy.
3. Social democracy recognizes that inequalities and deprivation are generated by a capitalist market economy but believes these can be effectively mitigated by some (greater or lesser) form of economic and/or social intervention and regulation.
4. Social democracy is largely wedded to an elitist understanding of the potential relationship between people and political leadership and tends to assume a top-down, hierarchical model of governance.
5. The social democratic tradition has been almost entirely "statist" both internally, in terms of its orientation towards the intervention and regulation referred to above in point 3, and externally, in respect of its approach to foreign policy and international relations.
6. Social democracy has been both united and split by a commitment to methodological nationalism: a privileging of "national" levels of debate, analysis and policy over other possible levels, whether local, regional, or global.[23]

These tenets were as much articles of faith as a political manifesto for Lie. He fully identified with the goals and purposes of the social democratic movement, internalizing its principles and dedicating his life to its success. Essentially, social democratic norms defined Lie's "inner code."

Yet Lie's embrace of socialism was more practical than ideological. He never really read Marx and Engels (though he tried as a youth) and was not known to be among the "leftists" or intellectuals within the Norwegian Labor Party. Lie's rapid rise within the party was due in large part to his political acumen in "sticking with the majority," a "simple device" that helped him "to steer smoothly through the splits of the Norwegian Labor Party when, in 1921, it briefly entered the Communist International."[24] He had an aversion to the more extreme "leftist" elements within the party and strong anticommunist sentiments, which grew stronger as his political career advanced. As he put it in his memoirs:

I had also been an ardent anti-fascist and anti-nazi during all my mature life, at every opportunity condemning the aggressive ideologies of these movements, not least as regards their first victims, the working classes and the Jews. . . . [And] I had fought the Norwegian Communists wherever they appeared in the Norwegian labor movement. As legal consultant to the Federation of Trade Unions I had challenged, in and out of court, the Communists' attempts to take over meeting halls, printing plants, bank accounts, and the like. I had never been popular among Norwegian Communists; in fact, they made me a frequent target for attacks during the twenties and thirties.[25]

Despite claims to the contrary, Lie did have "a solid history of opposition to communism and a strong devotion to Western democratic ideals" throughout his political career. These views were in line with his own beliefs (as well as with the Norwegian Labor Party, in the main) about social democracy and certainly helped him and the party at the polls. Indeed, as Anthony Gaglione points out, "Lie's public record in Norway was marked by conspicuous political success and general respect for his competence and record of achievement."[26]

War, Diplomacy, and Great Power Politics

Lie's introduction to the world of diplomacy came with the invasion of Norway by Nazi Germany in 1940. He accompanied King Haakon VII of Norway throughout much of the arduous flight of the Norwegian government into "exile" in London.[27] He was soon thereafter appointed foreign minister of the government in exile, a considerably different role for Lie, whose "major political interests had been in the domestic field until the war."[28] Despite his lack of experience in the field of diplomacy, Lie discharged his new duties admirably, and by most accounts was impressive in the role.[29] In his capacity as foreign minister, Lie quickly learned just how complex and limited diplomacy can be for a small state. It was particularly difficult to keep Norway and its concerns a priority for the Allies and at the same time protect Norwegian interests from being compromised by the Great Powers during the war.

As a small state strategically situated in northern Europe, Norway had always sought "correct" relations with her powerful Russian neighbor. As James Barros points out, "because of their common boundary line Norway appreciated Russia's interests in northern Europe, especially in the Baltic area; and this appreciation persisted with the wartime Norwegian government sitting in London, whose foreign minister was Lie. Accordingly, Lie had a healthy respect for the Russians."[30] But Lie also recognized the importance of strengthening Norway's relations with Great Britain and the United States, as Norway was within the Anglo-American military theater and relied upon their support and cooperation for its liberation from Nazi occupation, as well as for keeping in check Soviet designs on northern Norway, particularly the Svalbard archipelago. Lie strived to be evenhanded in handling Norway's relations with its wartime allies, knowing that his country's freedom and independence were at stake if he failed to maintain good relations with the so-called Big Three (the United States, Great Britain, and the USSR). Remarking on this balancing act, he wrote in his memoirs:

> In those London years, I dealt with the Big Three equitably, as far as circumstances would permit. Problems were sometimes delicate, as when we had to deal with American generosity, British military red tape, and Russian suspicion during negotiations for Norway's liberation. It was mainly a question of determining when the military should withdraw and yield administrative power, allowing Norwegian civil authorities to take over. But once agreement had been reached among the British, the Americans and ourselves, I informed Soviet Ambassador Alexandre E. Bogomolov that Norway hoped to enter into a similar agreement with the Soviet Union. To our satisfaction, a reply from Moscow came almost at once. On May 16, 1944, I had the pleasure of signing identical agreements covering the liberation of Norway with the United States, the United Kingdom, and the USSR. The other signatory Powers were represented by General Eisenhower, Mr. Eden and Ambassador Bogomolov. Perhaps a mark of the Soviet appreciation of this equal treatment was Soviet evacuation of northern Norway in exemplary style in 1945.[31]

The five years as foreign minister gave Lie a crash course in the realities of power politics and a stark reminder of how fragile relations among the Alliance's biggest players truly were. For Lie there was no better school than the Alliance in which to learn in short order the intricacies of international power and politics, and how to steer a safe course through treacherous diplomatic waters. Lie demonstrated that he was an astute negotiator and a competent representative of his country, earning the respect of Allied diplomats. By the end of the war he had developed a rather interesting reputation as an "affable and forceful . . . direct, unpretentious man, with an energetic, enthusiastic manner; hearty and talkative."[32] *Time* magazine reported that a top U.S. diplomat had "appraised Lie as 'a man with guts; no political or other culture.' . . . Old-style diplomats found him uncouth but impressive, 'a rough diamond.'"[33]

But the stint as foreign minister did not really prepare him for the "unique challenges of conference diplomacy" or for leading a new international organization. The only experience in multilateral diplomacy he had was the short time he spent as the head of the Norwegian delegation to the San Francisco conference on international organization in April 1945, where he "served briefly as chairman of the committee that drafted the articles pertaining to the Security Council in the United Nations Charter" and to the first UN General Assembly in London in January 1946, where he was elected (a month later) secretary-general.[34] Lie was fully aware that he lacked "profound experience in international relations and an expertness in the languages of diplomacy"—qualifications that he and most people thought were essential for any secretary-general of the United Nations.[35] As important as these qualities were considered to be, other essential qualities, of a more personal nature, were also thought significant, namely, moral character and leadership, personal and professional integrity, and progressive views on economic and social issues.[36] In this regard, Lie was probably as well endowed as any other national leader within the Alliance.

No doubt Lie's wartime experience broadened his worldview beyond the narrow confines of Norwegian national politics and interests. Through the personal and professional relationships he developed with the "great war leaders" of America (Roosevelt, Eisenhower, Marshall, Hull, and Stettinius), Britain (Churchill and Eden), and the Soviet Union (Stalin, Molotov, Gromyko, and Vyshinsky), Lie acquired a wider perspective on world politics, particularly the central importance of Great Power hegemony and cooperation in postwar international relations.[37] He also gained a fuller understanding of both the limits and the potential of small states in "making a sincere contribution to the mutual understanding and confidence of the great powers." Lie firmly believed that Allied victory had "only been made possible by the trustful cooperation and understanding between the great powers," and he considered it "imperative that the future peace and security be built on the same foundation. As we stood together in the war, we must stand together in peace." He did not see any "intrinsic conflict of interests between the large and small nations" in privileging the great powers, for "in any new world order the great powers will have to shoulder the main burden of providing the military and material means for maintaining peace."[38]

By the end of the war, Lie and the Norwegian government were fully committed to the creation of a new international organization as "the supreme authority for the maintenance of peace and as the center of international efforts for a new and better world."[39] He stressed in his speech at the charter conference in San Francisco on May 2, 1945, that in forming a new international organization "moral standards should be taken into account":

> To our people who have lived under Axis occupation, it seems essential that this Conference should include among the principles of its organization the aspirations expressed in the United Nations declaration: To defend life, liberty, independence, and religious freedom, to preserve human rights. . . . We hope to bring to the future deliberations and labors of the new Organization the spirit and experience of a community which for centuries has been built on the respect for law and justice. The profound belief in social justice and an unswerving attachment to fundamental human rights and freedom, deeply rooted in our traditions, have been the rock upon which the Nazi attacks upon our convictions have been wrecked.[40]

For Lie, this speech "expressed deeply held personal convictions" and reflected "the real interests of peoples all over the world."[41]

The principles and rules of the UN charter that were thrashed out in San Francisco did indeed reflect the "moral standards" Lie and others called for. The charter affirmed the noble objectives of the Atlantic Charter, and reinforced (even strengthened) the fundamental principles of the Westphalian order—sovereign equality, political independence, and the territorial integrity of nation-states.[42] The United Nations was clearly established to serve and protect the nation-state and the interstate system, hopefully with greater effectiveness than its predecessor the League of Nations, and to be an instrument through which the international cooperation and collective action achieved during the war, especially among the Great Powers, could be sustained. These principles were not "pie in the sky" or "blue-sky thinking" divorced from the ugly realities of power. Like Lie, the founders of the United Nations were practical-minded men and women who clearly saw that the devastation and destruction wrought by two world wars were the result, at least in part, of the breakdown of these moral standards. Although they were acutely aware that power was and would continue to be a fundamental fact of international life, it was also evident that power harnessed to the principles and ideals of the UN charter would bring about a more enduring peace.

Ultimately Lie emerged from the war convinced that politics is a moral act and that politicians are moral actors. Moreover, the war deepened his dedication to the moral standards of Western democratic society—social justice, fairness and equality, human dignity and respect for the law—and increased his resolve to see these principles realized in the world. Lie had a simple motto that captures how his ethical framework worked in both his personal and professional life: When you are convinced that what you believe in is correct and righteous, you have to pursue it and you must never give up.[43]

The Politics of Policy Choice in the United Nations

Lie's ethical framework was severely tested during his tenure as secretary-general. He was frequently confronted with immensely challenging dilemmas on an incredible number of issues in every area in which the United Nations was engaged. In each case he sought practical solutions that were firmly grounded in the UN charter and international law and would "uphold and strengthen the constitutional position of the office of Secretary-General."[44] The policies he devised and the actions he took over the course of his tenure reflected Lie's struggle to position the office of secretary-general "in the front rank of the United Nations attempt to keep the peace."[45] This struggle was most evident in the cases highlighted below.

Finding the "Middle Way" as the Secretary-General's Role

It is well known that the election of Lie as secretary-general was the result of a compromise among the permanent members of the Security Council. He was originally approached by the United States and strongly supported by the USSR for the position of president of the General Assembly but lost to Paul-Henri Spaak, the foreign minister of Belgium, in a rather messy and embarrassing process created in large part by the actions of the Soviets and inaction of the Americans.[46] After losing the election for the presidency, Lie unexpectedly became the only acceptable candidate for the secretary-general position, though not the first choice of any of the Big Three.[47] It was a post that Lie neither sought nor actually wanted, as he noted in his memoirs:

I had been nothing less than catapulted into the Secretary-Generalship of this new international organization, to preserve peace and promote progress in a world beset by unrest, poverty, and great-power rivalry. It was a challenge beyond my wildest dreams; but it was a nightmare as well. I hardly dared to think of the days ahead. Instead, I asked myself again and again, Why had this awesome task fallen to a labor lawyer from Norway? On the surface, the facts were clear and gratifying: my appointment was the product of a meeting of minds in Moscow and Washington and had been ratified by virtual unanimity among the Member states; furthermore, the original suggestion of my name for any United Nations office had come from the United States.[48]

It is no secret that Lie was chosen primarily because the permanent members of the Security Council, particularly the Big Three, thought he was malleable and that they could use him to serve their interests. At the same time, Lie was no "pushover," and he had strong opinions and views that were not always in line with those of the Big Three.

Nevertheless, Lie came into office with high expectations of the organization he was charged to build and confident in his own abilities to realize the promise of the UN charter. In his acceptance speech before the first General Assembly in London, Lie set forth the challenge that he and the member states had taken on:

Those who gave their lives in order that we may be free, those who lost their homes, those who suffered, and still suffer, from the consequences of war have given us a sacred mandate: that is, to build a firm foundation for the peace of the world. We may find difficulties and obstacles ahead of us. But the harder the task, the higher the prize. It is the future of the whole civilized world which is at stake.[49]

Lie recognized almost immediately that the role of secretary-general in meeting this "sacred mandate" was severely constrained by "the hard realities of world politics," which had surfaced in the inaugural meetings of the Security Council in London. Lie wrote in his memoirs:

By the time the delegates left London and I began the final three weeks of preparation for the move to New York I understood much better than before the depth and danger of the split that had been developing between the Soviet Union and the West. I felt that in some respects it was like a crevasse in a glacier which might spread wider beneath the bridge of soft surface snow that was called great-power unity. The confident hopes that I had shared in earlier months with most other statesmen of the smaller powers at least, and certainly with the great masses of people everywhere, were impaired but by no means lost. I saw the dangers more clearly, but I saw also, on the other side, much evidence that the situation was not beyond repair, that the wartime cooperation of the great powers might yet be revived through the United Nations, at least in the most essential things; and I hoped that I might assist in the process.

He was convinced that "the work of the United Nations cannot be advanced without idealism, trust, and faith," but he recognized that the United Nations would never get off the ground in a "paradise of unreality—we must begin by taking things as they are."[50]

Lie had the dubious honor of being the first to balance two conflicting schools of thought on the role of UN secretary-general. On one side were those who wanted the secretary-general to be "a bold leader of international thought and action, as a genuinely international figure stimulating the Member States to rise above their nationalistic dispositions"; on the other side were those who thought that the secretary-general should reflect the "personality" of Sir Eric Drummond, the first secretary-general of the League of Nations, who had "played an important behind-the-scenes role as a conciliator among the Member States."[51] Lie correctly saw that the role envisaged for the UN secretary-general lay somewhere between these two views:

> The Secretary-General unquestionably would be under an obligation to play a great political part; but, I felt, there were limits to the extent of his initiative—the limits of the Charter's text and, even more, the limits imposed by the realities of national and international political life. The Secretary-General might be the symbol of the Organization as a whole—the symbol, in other words, of the international spirit. This, and his strategic situation at the very center of international affairs as confidant of the world's statesmen and as spokesperson to the world's peoples, attached significant influence to his position; but it was a moral power, not a physical one, and moral power in this world is not conclusive. The Secretary-General, it was said, should be more the general than the secretary—but where were his divisions? Thus, I inclined, from the beginning, toward a middle way—a pragmatic and open-minded approach. I would listen to all my advisors and be directed by none. I had no calculated plan for developing the political powers of the office of Secretary-General, but I was determined that the Secretary-General should be a force for peace.[52]

Although the charter is very specific as to the purposes and principles of the organization, foremost being the maintenance of international peace and security through the collective security mechanism of the Security Council, and although the Preparatory Commission set down in considerable detail the operating procedures of the principal organs and the agenda of the first General Assembly session, it was far from clear how much "activism" on the part of the secretary-general in the sensitive area of peace and security would be tolerated. In other words, the practical aspects of the secretary-general's political role were untested in the real world. As Lie put it in his memoirs, "this role, with all its potentialities and its pitfalls for the future, had to be weighed against the hard political realities of a world by no means ready yet to accept either the outlook or the responsibilities of world citizenship. Under the circumstances, how far should the Secretary-General seek to develop his independent political role?"[53] For Lie, this was the central question that the UN founders left unanswered and the core dilemma that he, as well as his successors, faced.

From the outset, Lie's "middle way" was focused on bridging the East-West divide. He felt strongly that the United Nations should and could help reconcile the Great Powers and restore the wartime unity. This path was strewn with innumerable political potholes and shrouded in the darkening gloom of the Cold War. As Gaglione points out:

> Trygve Lie's "middle road" soon became a personal minefield. He attempted to avoid becoming identified with one or the other side in the Cold War, while working to enhance the prestige and influence of the United Nations. In his first annual report to the General Assembly, a document that serves as a yearly "State of the Union" message to the world on the organization, Lie chided the member nations for not doing enough to "capture the imagination and harness the enthusiasm of the peoples of the world" on behalf of the United Nations. He reminded them that the UN was "no stronger than the collective will of the nations that support it." As the prime spokesperson for the new world body, Lie preached his vision in innumerable speeches and press conferences.[54]

The Iranian Complaint

Lie's first run-in with the member states was over the Iranian issue that had been placed on the agenda of the Security Council in March 1946. Iran had lodged a complaint against the Soviet Union over its failure to withdraw its troops from Iranian territory as required by the Tripartite Treaty of 1942. The controversy led to the first Soviet walkout from the Security Council. But the problem was not the Soviet boycott of the council, which lasted less than two weeks; rather, the problem for Lie was the council's decision to keep the issue on its agenda even after the matter was settled between Tehran and Moscow in early April. Lie weighed in on the problem on April 16, 1946, when "he boldly—and correctly—advised by way of legal memorandum, removal of the Iranian issue from the agenda of the Security Council. Since Iran had withdrawn its complaint against the Soviet Union, the secretary-general took the unprecedented step of defying the majority of the council (only the USSR, France, and Poland supported him). Opposing the West for its Cold War attitudes, Lie would later say, 'The United Nations . . . should aim to settle disputes, not inflame them.'"[55]

Lie's intervention in the Iranian issue was, in his view, a matter of "law—of precedent—rather than of influencing the immediate treatment of the Soviet-Iranian request."[56] It established the "right" of the secretary-general, or his deputy acting on his behalf, to intervene in the proceedings of the Security Council, the General Assembly, and the Economic and Social Council at his own discretion. This small victory seemed to embolden Lie, for he interjected himself on a range of issues and matters—the question of Franco's Spain, the Greek question, Palestine, Berlin, the North Atlantic Treaty and the Marshall Plan, the Truman doctrine—and "continued to press his unpopular views concerning the Charter."[57]

As the public record makes abundantly clear, Lie's efforts between 1946 and 1948 to facilitate a "genuinely peaceful and mutually tolerable coexistence between the West and the Communist world"[58] came to naught. Throughout these early years of the fledgling United Nations, the tenor of debate seemed to go from bad to worse as the struggle between Moscow and the West intensified. The Security Council, in particular, "became the scene of bitter combat between the superpowers, with each side seizing every opportunity to embarrass and condemn the other. The Soviet Union was outnumbered and isolated within the United Nations, and the West, at little cost in blood and treasure, used the organization to register its own righteousness and the evil intent of its communist rivals."[59] The cornerstone of the United Nations, cooperation among the permanent members of the Security Council, was crumbling as the deadlock deepened between the Soviets and Britain and the United States. Lie's often clumsy efforts at mediation and conciliation to overcome mounting East–West differences seemed to have little if any effect.

The Berlin crisis in 1948 dashed any hope of Great Power collaboration in the United Nations and "marked a turning point in [Lie's] approach to his role as secretary-general and, ultimately, in his personal fortunes." The Cold War was at a fever pitch, and Lie could see that the Great Powers were well on the way to abandoning the United Nations. The paralysis of the Security Council, which was caused in large part by the Soviet veto, was nearly permanent: "It could neither prevent nor resolve conflicts between the great states or act as a tool of collective coercion against aggression."[60] Lie's role, and that of the United Nations, as the Cold War raged on was increasingly marginal and ineffective. The sense of impotence and irrelevance was accentuated when Truman "unilaterally" launched the Marshall Plan for European economic recovery, circumventing the United Nations and its Economic Commission for Europe, and when the North Atlantic Pact—the Western military alliance—was created.[61] Lie feared that the Soviet Union might quit the organization, which would effectively kill the United Nations and plunge the world into a catastrophic (perhaps even nuclear) war.[62]

The China Question

Lie's belief that the United Nations could be a "force for peace" was thoroughly shaken by several events in 1948—the Communist coup in Czechoslovakia, the invasion of Palestine by Egypt, Jordan, and other members of the Arab League, and the Berlin blockade—and it was to be further tested by developments in the Far East. The Chinese civil war, which had not been a very high priority for Lie, was intensifying, and Mao Zedong's Communist forces had pushed the Nationalist (Kuomintang) forces of Chiang Kai-shek off the mainland onto the island of Formosa (now Taiwan). In October 1949 Mao declared victory and the establishment of the People's Republic of China. It was not long before the question of Chinese representation at the United Nations embroiled the Security Council in a new crisis.

The "cold peace" that followed the Berlin crisis swiftly reverted to the "cold war" in the first days of 1950, when Soviet Ambassador Yakov Malik, armed with a message from Chinese foreign minister Chou En-Lai calling for the expulsion of the "Kuomintang group" from the United Nations, demanded that the Security Council take immediate action to remove the Nationalist Chinese representatives and threatened that it would "not participate in the Security Council until the representative of the Kuomintang group had been removed from membership."[63] Malik made good on this threat after his motion (January 10) to expel the

Chinese Nationalists from the Security Council was defeated. Before his dramatic walkout, which was to last six and a half months, he stated that his country "would neither recognize the legality of any council decision adopted with the participation of the Chinese Nationalist representative nor consider itself bound by such decisions. In the weeks that followed Russian and other communist delegations similarly withdrew from a large number of United Nations bodies."[64]

Lie was once more confronted with an impossible situation. Intent on offering a practical solution, he turned to his legal advisers in the Secretariat for guidance as to what he and the organization could do, while at the same time consulting with the permanent members of the Security Council about the problem. He requested that the UN Legal Department prepare a legal memorandum to review the "juridical aspects" of the question and to determine the principle(s) under the charter that were most relevant and provided the basis for a course of action by the organization and the member states. On the matter of which government should represent China in the United Nations, Lie came to the conclusion that it should be the Communist government in Beijing, as this reflected the reality on the ground:

> Without being happy that the Communists had won the Civil War in China, I did not feel that approval or disapproval of a regime was in question: it was a matter of recognizing the facts of international life. The "Republic of China" to which permanent membership in the United Nations was extended at San Francisco was not a government but a nation of some 475,000,000 people. It was *China*, not Chiang Kai-shek, that belonged to the United Nations. Now the Nationalist Government had been driven from the mainland and controlled only Formosa, an island that had belonged to Japan for half a century and had not yet been finally awarded to China by the peace treaty. How could Chiang Kai-shek speak for China in the United Nations under these circumstances? Another consideration that influenced my judgment was historical. Once before, the world had seen a Communist state—the U.S.S.R.—isolated by the West after a successful revolution. I had always believed that this was a great mistake, and that the West, instead, should have sought every means to fuller intercourse with Russia in the 1920's. Such a policy might well have influenced the development of the Soviet state in a direction other than the one it took. Was the free world now going to cut itself off, in similar fashion, from China and its 475,000,000 people—one-fifth of the world's total population? Finally, the nearest possible approach to universality was a principle

that I always felt to be fundamental to the fulfillment of the purposes of a *world* organization. What chance would the United Nations have of reducing tensions and improving prospects of peace if it were no longer to be the meeting ground between East and West?[65]

He and his legal advisers argued that the "proper principle" to be followed in choosing between the rival governments "could be derived by analogy from Article 4 of the Charter, requiring that an applicant be *able and willing to carry out the obligations for membership*—obligations that could be carried out only by governments which in fact had the power to do so." Hence, if the Communist government "exercises effective authority within the territory of the State and is habitually obeyed by the bulk of the population," then "it would seem appropriate for the United Nations organs, through their collective action, to accord it the right to represent the State in the Organization, even though individual members of the Organization refuse, and may continue to refuse, to accord it recognition as the lawful government, for reasons which are valid under their national policies."[66] In essence, the Chinese representation issue was a matter of credentials and could be settled by securing seven affirmative votes in the Security Council for seating the Beijing government's representatives.

Lie had hoped to secure the seven votes through discreet discussions with all the members of the Security Council, but he lobbied more intensely France, Egypt, Ecuador, and Cuba—members who had not recognized the Beijing government—in that, by his calculations, he only needed two of them to vote yes (Lie assumed that the UK, USSR, Yugoslavia, and India would vote in favor because they had already recognized the Beijing government). He had already been told by the United States that it would abide by any decision with the requisite majority of seven votes of the council on the issue. But Lie's efforts failed to change the member states' policies on the question, and when his strategy became public he was roundly criticized by the Nationalist government and the American "isolationist" press, enduring a stream of personal attacks—a situation to which he had become quite accustomed. At this stage, Lie realized that the China controversy was not responding to his efforts and "that other and new ways had to be found to resolve the crisis."[67] He asked himself if it was still possible to bring the parties together on issues other than that of Chinese representation, and after some reflection "his thoughts turned to what eventually became his ten-point, twenty-year peace program."[68]

Twenty-Year Program for Achieving Peace Through the United Nations

Lie sketched out his ideas for a "broader approach to the East-West deadlock" in a speech to the B'nai B'rith's triennial dinner in Washington, D.C., on March 21, 1950. In that speech, Lie "sought throughout to recall the lasting and central significance of the United Nations to the struggle for peace in all its manifestations—political, economic, and social. He emphasized the long-term nature of the task: 'I do not believe in political miracles. It will take a long series of steps to reduce the tensions of the conflict and bring the great powers together.'" This speech and the ten-point memorandum it inspired, reproduced in Box 3.1,[69] was to be the most ambitious independent political initiative of Lie's tenure, "a personal campaign to convince the superpowers that the United Nations was an indispensable forum for East–West negotiations and to break the deadlock over the issue of Chinese representation."[70]

The memorandum, which was not made public until it had been discussed privately with the leaders of the Big Four—the US, USSR, UK, and France—argued that the "constructive use of United Nations' potentialities could bring to the world a 'real and secure peace.' Such an effort would be attractive to small states that had much to contribute in conciliating the great powers and toward developing constructive and 'mutually advantageous political and economic cooperation.' Lie suggested certain points to be considered in formulating a United Nations peace program, some requiring urgent action, others requiring a twenty-year effort."[71]

From April 20 to May 29, Lie traveled fifteen thousand miles on a carefully planned "peace mission" to Washington, London, Paris, and Moscow, where he discussed his memorandum with Truman, Attlee, Bidault, and Stalin. The "mission was to be in the cause not only of peace, but of reason. . . . This was to be an exploration, not a negotiation," as well as an opportunity "to discuss not only the problem of Chinese representation but other matters of concern to the United Nations."[72] Not surprisingly, the reaction of all of the Big Four leaders to Lie's initiative was cool politeness and far from encouraging. Nevertheless, Lie carried on, "fortified more by the support of the 'man in the street' than of the governments."[73] Upon his return to Lake Success, Lie forwarded to all member states the ten-point memorandum with a cover letter "recounting the reason for my initiative and my visits to the heads of government and Foreign Ministers in the four capitals." He asked for the member states' "earnest attention" to the twenty-year peace program he was proposing (text continues on p. 91)

Box 3.1 Memorandum of Points for Consideration in the Development of a Twenty-Year Program for Achieving Peace Through the United Nations

As Secretary-General, it is my firm belief that a new and great effort must be attempted to end the so-called "cold war" and to set the world once more on a road that will offer greater hope of lasting peace.

The atmosphere of deepening international mistrust can be dissipated and the threat of the universal disaster of another war averted by employing to the full the resources for conciliation and constructive peace-building present in the United Nations Charter. The employment of these resources can secure eventual peace if we accept, believe and act upon the possibility of peaceful coexistence among all Great Powers and the different economic and political systems they represent, and if the Great Powers evidence a readiness to undertake genuine negotiation—not in a spirit of appeasement, but with enlightened self-interest and common sense on all sides.

Measures for collective self-defense and regional remedies of other kinds are at best interim measures, and cannot alone bring any reliable security from the prospect of war. The one common understanding and universal instrument of the great majority of the human race is the United Nations. A patient, constructive long-term use of its potentialities can bring a real and secure peace to the world. I am certain that such an effort will have the active interest and support of the smaller Member States, who have much to contribute in the conciliation of Big Power differences and in the development of constructive and mutually advantageous political and economic cooperation.

I therefore venture to suggest certain points for consideration in the formulation of a twenty-year United Nations Peace Program. Certain of these points call for urgent action. Others are of a long-range nature, requiring continued effort over the next twenty years. I shall not discuss the problems of the peace settlements for Austria, Germany and Japan—because the founders of the United Nations indicated that the peace settlements should be made separately from the United Nations. But I believe that the progress of the United Nations Peace Program such as is here suggested will help bring these settlements far closer to attainment.

1. *Inauguration of periodic meetings of the Security Council, attended by foreign ministers or heads or other members of governments, as provided by the United Nations Charter and the rules of procedure; together with further development and use of other United Nations machinery for negotiation, mediation and conciliation of international disputes.*

The periodic meetings of the Security Council provided for in Article 28 of the Charter have never been held. Such periodic meetings should be held semiannually, beginning with one in 1950. In my opinion, they should be used for a general review at a high level of outstanding issues in the United Nations, particularly those that divide the Great Powers. They should not be expected to produce great decisions every time; they should be used for consultation—much of it in private—for efforts to gain ground toward agreement on questions at issue, to clear up misunderstandings, to prepare for new initiatives that may improve the changes for definite agreement at later meetings. They should be held away from Headquarters as a general rule, in Geneva, the capitals of the Permanent Members and in other regions of the world.

Further development of the resources of the United Nations for mediation and conciliation should be undertaken, including reestablishment of the regular practice of private consultations by the representatives of the five Great Powers, and a renewed effort to secure agreements by all the Great Powers on limitations on the use of the veto power in the pacific settlement procedures of the Security Council.

2. *A new attempt to make progress toward establishing an international control system for atomic energy that will be effective in preventing its use for war and promoting its use for peaceful purposes.*

We cannot hope for any quick or easy solution of this most difficult problem of atomic energy control. The only way to find out what is possible is to resume negotiation in line with the directive of the General Assembly last fall "to explore all possible avenues and examine all concrete suggestions with a view to determining what might lead to an agreement." Various suggestions for finding a basis for a fresh approach have been put forward. One possibility would be for the Security Council to instruct the Secretary-General to call a conference of scientists whose discussions might provide a reservoir of new ideas on the control of weapons of mass destruction and the promotion of peaceful uses of atomic energy that could thereafter be explored in the United Nations Atomic Energy Commission. Or, it may be that an interim agreement could be worked out that would at least be some improvement on the present situation of an unlimited atomic arms race, even though it did not afford full security. There are other possibilities for providing the basis for a new start; every possibility should be explored.

3. *A new approach to the problem of bringing the armaments race under control, not only in the field of atomic weapons, but in other weapons of mass destruction and in conventional armaments.*

Here is another area where it is necessary to reactivate negotiation and to make new efforts at finding some area of common ground. It must be recognized that up to now there has been virtually a complete failure here and that the immediate prospects seem poor indeed. Clearly disarmament requires an atmosphere of confidence in which political disputes are brought nearer to solution. But it is also true that any progress at all towards agreement on the regulation of armaments of any kind would help reduce cold war tensions and thus assist in the adjustment of political disputes. Negotiation on this problem should not be deferred until the other great political problems are solved, but should go hand in hand with any effort to reach political settlements.

4. *A renewal of serious efforts to reach agreement on the armed forces to be made available under the Charter to the Security Council for enforcement of its decisions.*

A new approach should be made towards resolving existing differences on the size, location and composition of the forces to be pledged to the Security Council under Article 43 of the Charter. Basic political difficulties which may delay a final solution should not be permitted to stand in the way of some sort of interim accord for a small force sufficient to prevent or stop localized outbreaks threatening international peace. The mere existence of such a force would greatly enhance the ability of the Security Council to bring about peaceful settlements in most of the cases which are likely to come before it.

5. *Acceptance and application of the principle that it is wise and right to proceed as rapidly as possible toward universality of membership.*

Fourteen nations are now awaiting admission to the United Nations. In the interests of the people of these countries and of the United Nations, I believe they should all be admitted, as well as other countries which will attain their independence in the future. It should be made clear that Germany and Japan would also be admitted as soon as the peace treaties have been completed.

6. *A sound and active program of technical assistance for economic development and encouragement of broadscale capital investment, using all appropriate private, governmental and intergovernmental resources.*

A technical assistance program is in its beginnings, assisted by the strong support of the President of the United States. Its fundamental purpose is to enable the people of the underdeveloped countries to raise their standard of living peacefully by specific and practicable measures. It should be a continuing and expanding program for the next twenty years and beyond, carried forward with the cooperation of all Member Governments, largely through the United Nations and the Specialized Agencies, with mutual beneficial programs planned and executed on a basis of equality rather than on a basis of charity. Through this means the opportunities can be opened up for capital investment on a large and expanding scale. Here lies one of our best hopes for combating the dangers and costs of the cold war.

7. *More vigorous use by all Member Governments of the Specialized Agencies of the United Nations to promote, in the words of the Charter, "higher standards of living, full employment, and conditions of economic and social progress."*

The great potentialities of the Specialized Agencies to participate in a long-range program aimed at drastically reducing the economic and social causes of war, can be realized by more active support from all Governments, including the membership of the Soviet Union in some or all of the Agencies to which it does not now belong. The expansion of world trade which is vital to any long-range effort for world betterment requires the early ratification of the International Trade Organization.

8. *Vigorous and continued development of the work of the United Nations for wider observance and respect for human rights and fundamental freedoms throughout the world.*

It is becoming evident that the Universal Declaration of Human Rights, as adopted by the General Assembly in 1948 without a dissenting vote, is destined to become one of the great documents of history. The United Nations is now engaged on a program that will extend over the next twenty years—and beyond—to secure the extension and wider observance of the political, economic and social rights there set down. Its success needs the active support of all Governments.

9. *Use of the United Nations to promote, by peaceful means instead of by force, the advancement of dependent, colonial or semicolonial peoples, towards a place of equality in the world.*

The great changes which have been taking place since the end of the war among the peoples of Asia and Africa must be kept within peaceful bounds by using the universal framework of the United Nations. The old relationship will have to be replaced with new ones of equality and fraternity. The United Nations is the instrument capable of bringing such a transition to pass without violent upheavals and with the best prospect of bringing long-run economic and political benefits to all nations of the world.

10. *Active and systematic use of all the powers of the Charter and all the machinery of the United Nations to speed up the development of international law towards an eventual enforceable world law for a universal world society.*

These three last points deal with programs already under way to carry out important principles of the United Nations Charter. They respond to basic human desires and aspirations, and coordinated efforts by all Governments to further these programs are indispensable to the eventual peaceful stabilization of international relations. There are many specific steps which need to be taken: for example, under Point 10, ratification of the Genocide Convention, greater use of the International Court of Justice, and systematic development and codification of international law. Important is that Governments should give high priority in their national policies to the continued support and development of these ideals which are at the foundation of all striving of the peoples for a better world.

What is here suggested is only an outline of preliminary proposals for a program; much more development will be needed. It is self-evident that every step mentioned, every proposal made, will require careful and detailed, even laborious preparation, negotiation and administration. It is equally self-evident that the necessary measure of agreement will be hard to realize most of the time, and even impossible some of the time. Yet the world can never accept the thesis of despair—the thesis of irrevocable and irreconcilable conflict.

and indicated that he "might formally submit it to the Security Council at an appropriate time and also place it on the provisional agenda of the next session of the General Assembly."[74] Nineteen days after Lie transmitted and published his memorandum, North Korea invaded the Republic of Korea, abruptly ending "Lie's career as an impartial broker of the cold war."[75]

First Action of the Secretary-General Under Article 99

The unprovoked surprise attack on South Korea by the armed forces of Communist North Korea on the morning of June 25, 1950, was the first "premeditated aggression, swiftly executed" that had occurred since the end of World War II.[76] Lie got word of the invasion from the U.S. assistant secretary of state for international organization, John Hickerson, in a midnight telephone call on June 24. Lie contacted his executive assistant, Andrew Cordier, and instructed him to send a cable to the UN Commission on Korea requesting an immediate report on the situation.[77] He then got in touch with the principal director of Security Council affairs, Dragon Protitch, instructing him to inform the president of the Security Council, Sir Benegal Rau of India, and to make preparations for an "emergency meeting" of the council.[78] Later that night (around three o'clock in the morning), Lie received another call from the United States, this time from Ambassador Ernest Gross, who formally requested that Lie convene the Security Council, which Lie set for two o'clock that afternoon.

When Lie arrived at Lake Success at noon, the cabled report from the UN Commission had arrived, confirming what he had been told by Hickerson and the seriousness of the situation, and suggesting that the secretary-general consider using his powers under the charter (meaning article 99) to bring the breach of the peace to the Security Council's attention. According to Lie, he decided to take up the commission's suggestion, "not only because the United Nations organ most immediately involved so advised, but because this to me was clear-cut aggression—apparently well calculated, meticulously planned, and with all the elements of surprise which reminded me of the Nazi invasion of Norway—because this was aggression against a 'creation' of the United Nations, and because the response of the Security Council would be more certain and more in the spirit of the Organization as a whole were the Secretary-General to take the lead."[79] When the meeting opened, Lie was permitted to speak first by the council president, and although he did not directly invoke article 99, "Lie nevertheless described the military actions of North Korean forces as a 'direct violation' of a resolution in the General Assembly, as well as 'a violation of the principles of the charter.' The Security Council, he continued, had the 'clear duty . . . to take steps necessary to re-establish peace.'"[80] With the Soviet seat still vacant, the council proceeded to consider and adopt an American resolution that declared the armed attack of North Korea a breach of the peace; called for an immediate cessation of hostilities; directed the North Korean armed forces to withdraw to the 38th parallel; and called upon "all Members to render every assistance to the United Nations in the execution of this resolution and to refrain from giving assistance to the North Korean authorities."[81] The North Koreans ignored the Security Council's orders and pressed on with considerable success against the lightly armed South Korean troops, who were in full retreat by June 26.

On June 27, without explicit authorization for the use of force from the Security Council, President Truman ordered U.S. air and sea forces to provide the South Korean troops with cover and support, an action the council endorsed later that evening in a resolution urging all member states to "furnish such assistance as may be necessary to repel the armed attack and to restore international peace and security in the area." Lie sent a cable to all the member states, "drawing attention to the call for assistance to the Republic of Korea and suggesting that, if the governments were in a position to assist, early information on the type of help they could furnish would facilitate the carrying out of the resolution [of June 27]."[82]

Once the responses started coming in, Lie felt that a "coordinating mechanism" was needed for "the United Nations efforts in Korea." He and his advisers accordingly prepared a draft resolution that, as Lie wrote in his memoirs,

> would have requested the government of the United States to assume responsibility for directing such armed forces of Members as might be furnished in pursuance of the resolution of June 27, and recommended to the government of Korea that it place its armed forces under American command. It would further have authorized armed forces acting in accordance with that resolution to fly the United Nations flag and—a key point—would have established a "Committee on Coordination of Assistance for Korea." This committee, I suggested, could be composed of Australia, France, India, New Zealand, Norway, the United Kingdom, and the United States; it might add to its membership states furnishing assistance; it would have a representative of the Republic of Korea; and the Secretary-General would serve as Rapporteur. The explicit purpose was to stimulate and coordinate offers of assistance. Its deeper purpose was to keep the United Nations "in the picture," to promote continuing United Nations participation and supervision of the military security action in Korea of a more intimate and undistracted character than the Security Council could be expected to provide.[83]

The Security Council met on July 7 and "adopted the essence of the draft [Lie] circulated on July 3, less the provision for the Committee on Coordination," creating the Unified Command and enabling President Truman to name U.S. general Douglas MacArthur the United Nations commander.[84]

Although it was clear that the resolutions of June 25 and 27 were orchestrated by the United States (and possible only because of the Soviet boycott of the Security Council), and although the resolution of July 7 removed any doubt as to who was really in control of military operations, Lie did manage to maintain at least the semblance of a UN effort in Korea and, in some respects, to carve out a limited yet meaningful role for the organization in the Korean conflict. Lie's vigorous support of these Security Council decisions, however (and of the General Assembly's resolutions of October 7 and November 3, after the Soviets ended their boycott and resumed their seat in the council on July 27), seemed to indicate that he had "aligned himself with the war aims of one permanent member against the strategic interests of another," undermining "the political understanding on which the principle of collective action rested."[85] Lie, for his part, was quite adamant in defending his position and actions on the Korean conflict:

> Because the Secretary-General had the opportunity and obligation, as spokesman for the interests of the United Nations as a whole, to avoid partisan identification with any particular power or group of powers, some quarters questioned my Korean stand. They said I should have attempted to mediate the war (thus allowing the aggressor to press his attack while I was talking to him and, quite possibly, to occupy all of Korea) rather than directing all my energies toward mobilizing a United Nations army to throw back the aggressor. I rejected this point of view then, and I reject it now. The Secretary-General is not to be "neutral" above all else, "for neutrality implies political abstinence, not political action," and in certain circumstances might well keep him from conscientious fulfillment of his Charter obligations. There is, for example, an "unneutral" predisposition about the Secretary-General's calling the Security Council's attention, under Article 99, to a matter threatening the peace, since it is unlikely that it can ever be in equal interests of the parties to a dispute, in an exact, precisely neutral degree, that a situation in which they are involved be brought before the Council. Rather, the duty of the Secretary-General is to uphold the principles of the Charter and the decisions of the Organization as objectively as he can. This is what I did in Korea.[86]

This steadfast position "earned Lie Moscow's implacable hostility," which led to the "diplomatic and social boycott of Lie by the communist bloc nations" after Lie's term was extended for three years by the General Assembly on November 1, 1950.[87] In many respects, the Korean War was a defining moment for Lie and for the office of the secretary-general. As he later wrote:

> Events between 1951 and 1953—the purgatory of the personnel investigations, the interminable Korean struggle, and the persistent Soviet boycott —made me doubt seriously that I had been right in accepting three more years as Secretary-General. With the Assembly's vote returning me to office, the immediate political objectives had been won: United Nations action in Korea had been reaffirmed, the continuity of United Nations administration had been assured, and the independent position of the Secretary-General had been preserved against the threats and pressures of a great power. But the winning of these objectives—vital as they were—was at a heavy cost to me and to my office. The immediate advantages have to be weighed against the serious impairment in the usefulness of my office that

followed. The Soviet boycott limited my activities to a small part of the political role intended for the Secretary-General by the Charter.[88]

The "middle way" that Lie had worked so hard to develop had foundered on the shoals of the Cold War.

Fighting Poverty

Lie had little time and few resources to devote to what he called "the challenge of our time"—tackling global poverty. The situation was most dire in places ravaged by the war, like Europe, but the problem was and remains much more pervasive throughout the world. Lie, commenting on the situation, noted:

> Today, in the middle of the twentieth century, most human beings still are hungry most of the time; half the world's people have yet to be taught how to read and write, are constantly ill, and expect to die before the age of thirty-five. Calculations show that the per-capita income of almost two-thirds of this total is less than a hundred dollars a year; and other evidence proves that most of the world's population cannot afford decent clothing, housing, and recreation, while hundreds of millions still live in bondage and peonage not far removed from slavery.[89]

Lie correctly saw international economic and social cooperation as a critical element in securing world peace. He considered remedying the gross gap between the rich and the poor, the haves and the have-nots, one of the "most challenging tasks [of the United Nations]—probably the most important, next to maintaining peace, and an essential condition for reaching that highest goal."[90] But he also realized that the modest funds dedicated to this area of work were woefully short of what was needed.

In the initial years of the organization, Lie established a small technical assistance program "through which experts, drawn mainly from the developed nations, were sent to underdeveloped countries to help improve living conditions."[91] But the requests for assistance easily outstripped the program's ability to respond. This led Lie and his economic advisers within the Secretariat to put together a proposal for the UN Expanded Program of Technical Assistance for the Economic Development of Underdeveloped Countries, which was approved by the General Assembly in 1949, the same year that President Truman announced his "Point Four" program of economic aid to developing countries. The expanded program, with an initial commitment of $20 million, marked the beginning of a shift in institutional and political focus of the United Nations from its "excessive preoccupation with the affairs of Europe" to "a host of problems that were largely unconnected to the Cold War."[92] But Lie was unable to convince the major donor countries—namely, the United States and Great Britain—of the real value of channeling their bilateral foreign aid through the United Nations, even when Lie pointed out repeatedly that "more is obtained from the money contributed to the United Nations [technical assistance and economic development] program than from any other similar scheme."[93]

To Lie's disappointment, the modest success of UN aid programs failed to "generate the large transfers of capital required to stimulate economic prosperity in the developing world," or to forestall a new rift in the United Nations between the global North and South emerging out of "Third World demands for the elimination of ignorance, poverty, and disease in what was termed a revolution of 'rising expectations.'"[94] Yet Lie did not lose hope that the member states, particularly those governments that had given generously to economic assistance programs, would see, as he did, what was at stake if the United Nations' work in this field was to stagnate.

> If we fail to act disaster may strike again, and for the following reasons: First, the peoples of the world are today living so close together that they can observe first hand how abundance is the privilege of the relatively few, while poverty remains the curse of the great majority. It would spell bankruptcy for our ethical and moral values for us now merely to ask, "Am I my brother's keeper?" Secondly, we are living in a historical period marked by tremendous progress in science and technology, with means at our disposal which can eradicate poverty from the face of the earth. It would spell bankruptcy for our intellect and our talents for us to waste our energies and let our tools rest idle. Thirdly, with rival ideologies competing for the souls of the hundreds of millions rising in search of a better life, it would spell bankruptcy for all free political thinking for us to permit age-old totalitarianism and international communism to gain new ground and establish violence as the philosophy of humanity.[95]

Although Lie could not focus as closely as he would have liked on developing the United Nations' capacity to help in underdeveloped areas of the world, he did take considerable pride in the many small-scale successes that the United Nations and its specialized agencies had achieved in Latin America, Asia, and Africa. As Gaglione argues, "putting [the Third World's] political agenda [which emphasized decolonization and economic growth over the narrow concerns of the Cold War] aside, it is clear that the United Nations still did much to ease economic and social suffering, and generally improved the level of international cooperation during Lie's tenure."[96]

*Establishing the UN Secretariat and the Pitfalls of
International Administration*

The immediate challenge before Lie after being elected secretary-general in 1946 was not the rising tide of the Cold War but meeting "an almost impossible time schedule" of establishing and staffing the Secretariat. The General Assembly in London had handed him "a table of organization, a set of principles and standards for the recruitment of the Secretariat, and a first temporary budget of $21,500,000 to cover estimated expenses until the end of the year [1946]," estimating that he would need to have in place within the first nine months a staff of 2,450.[97] Drawing from the temporary Secretariat assembled for the London meeting, former League of Nations veterans, and literally tens of thousands of unsolicited applications from around the world, Lie appointed twenty-nine hundred people over the course of 1946, all on a temporary basis, to fill the Secretariat's eight departments—the Department of Security Council Affairs, Department of Economic Affairs, Department of Social Affairs, Department of Trusteeship and Information from Non-Self-Governing Territories, Legal Department, Department of Public Information, Department of Administrative and Financial Services, and Department of Conference and General Services. Out of necessity and under immense time pressures, those appointed were from "areas of the world where persons of the necessary qualifications could be quickly found," a large proportion being American, Canadian, and British nationals.[98]

The problem was not only the enormous scope of the task but also the intrusion of politics on the process. This was most evident in the deal between the permanent members of the Security Council to allocate assistant secretaries-general posts to each—Political and Security Council Affairs to the Soviets, Administrative and Financial Services to the Americans, Economic Affairs to the British, Social Affairs to the French, and Trusteeship and Non-Self-Governing Territories to the Chinese—compromising the prerogative of the secretary-general to appoint *all* posts, though, as Lie remarked in his memoirs, "the Big Five had no right to arrive at any understanding regarding the distribution of the offices of Assistant Secretary-General which was binding upon the Secretary-General. This is not to say, however, that it would have been politic of me to resist the great power accord."[99]

The precedent set by the major powers was quickly picked up by the rest of the UN members, who in turn pressed Lie to appoint their nationals to key posts in the Secretariat staff. The constant pressure from all the member states to hire the minister's protégé or the ambassador's wife's nephew was exacerbated by the charter requirement that the staff be recruited on "as wide a geographical basis as possible," which the member states often invoked to secure the maximum number of posts for their people. It was impossible to accommodate all member states and inevitable that there would be complaints about the uneven distribution of Secretariat positions. In some respects, this problem was of Lie's own making in that he customarily sought nominations for key posts from the member states, which magnified the political nature of what should have been fundamentally an administrative activity. As Barros points out, however, "the problems of the distribution of secretariat staff by nationality and the importance of the functional positions assigned were not peculiar to Lie's secretary-generalship but arose as early as 1919, when Drummond established the League of Nations multinational secretariat."[100]

Staffing problems were compounded further by the difficulties Lie had in establishing the temporary headquarters of the United Nations in New York City, where "there was simply no space to be had" (at least not in Manhattan) for the Security Council, Economic and Social Council, the Trusteeship Council, the General Assembly, and the Secretariat. In the end, Lie was able to get the former municipal auditorium in Flushing Meadows for the General Assembly and to lease half of the Sperry arms factory at Lake Success (Long Island) for the councils, the committees, and the offices of the Secretariat. This interim arrangement was not what the member states or the staff had in mind or truly wanted, but it was the best that was available at the time. Although Lie had been able to ramp up the organization in time for the resumption of meetings of the Security Council, Economic and Social Council, and General Assembly, the operational challenges continued to grow unabated and were to dog Lie throughout his secretary-generalship. Indeed, "the repercussions of this headlong rush to hire, come what may, were still being felt when Hammarskjöld became secretary-general."[101]

The frenetic pace at which Lie was forced to establish a staff and facilities of the organization resulted in a critical shortage of qualified personnel —translators, statisticians, archivists, financial experts, economists, and historians—and an abundance of "officials of mediocre quality." Contributing to the disarray was the "ill-advised introduction of American managerial methods and techniques," which "resulted in over-staffing, inefficiency and a hierarchical system that tied down scores of officials to make sure that staff complied with complex regulations and procedures."[102]

Dissatisfaction with Lie's management inside and outside the UN bureaucracy grew so great that the British pushed for a deputy to take over "most of Lie's administrative tasks and act as a kind of super under-secretary to coordinate many of the secretariat's economic and social activities." But even this practical proposal, which led to the appointment of Australian Robert Jackson as assistant secretary-general for general coordination, did not "remedy the problem" but intensified the divisions and internal bureaucratic politics within the UN Secretariat and contributed to an already complicated and top-heavy management structure.[103] It added neither order to Lie's team nor strength to the office of the secretary-general vis-à-vis the member states.

Obviously, international administration was not Lie's forte, and it did not help matters that the Secretariat, particularly its upper echelon, was from its inception caught up in the Cold War rivalry and eagerly manipulated by the member states. Lie was unable to overcome the member states' abuse of the UN Secretariat's "independence," which had reached its nadir in the fracas caused by Lie's dismissal of U.S. members of the Secretariat who had pleaded the Fifth Amendment before U.S. Senator Patrick McCarran's Internal Security subcommittee of the Senate Judiciary Committee and a federal grand jury investigating the loyalty of Americans employed by the United Nations.[104] Lie's decisions and policies in regard to the Secretariat, particularly during the last six months of his extended term, were devastating to the notion of the UN Secretariat as a nonpolitical, impartial international civil service and to Lie's already low standing with the staff.

Lie, however, considered his actions legitimate and necessary in order to stem the growing attacks on the character and integrity of his office and the Secretariat. He vigorously defended his position in a speech introducing his report on personnel policy to the General Assembly on March 10, 1953, in which he concluded, "I have not yielded one inch on the essential principles I have sought to uphold and defend throughout this time of trial. Some of you may not agree with all the practical steps I have taken to meet the political realities. But there should be no misunderstanding of my intentions in taking each of these practical steps to uphold and defend the international character of the Secretariat and its ability to function in the manner laid down for it in the United Nations Charter."[105] In the end, the General Assembly adopted a resolution that "expressed confidence in the policies pursued" by Lie. But "the difficult situation of the Secretariat, as an island of internationalism in a nationalistic world," was far from resolved. As Lie put it in his memoirs:

> In an international organization that in most respects faithfully reflects the world as it is—a world of sovereign nations, the Secretariat has exclusively international responsibilities. The Secretary-General and his staff have in some respects been placed by the Charter in an advanced—and correspondingly exposed—position. . . . This position, while an honorable one, would have been difficult enough if the first seven years of the United Nations had been lived in a period of comparative world stability and good feeling. . . . We know that the circumstances have, in fact, been quite the reverse. . . . The great conflict of policy and ideology between the Western world and its supporters on the one hand, and the Soviet Union and its associates on the other hand, clearly creates a supreme difficulty for a Secretariat serving an Organization in which both sides are represented.[106]

There is no doubt that the Secretariat's "supreme difficulty" stemmed from the Cold War, but Lie, too, had a hand in the troubles that beset the organization, in that he "seemed to not fully appreciate the need to subordinate his private feelings to his role."[107] His political activities and initiatives were considered too bold, while his actions as an administrator were thought too weak, a near-fatal combination that contributed to the steady loss of confidence of the member states and the staff in his leadership.

Lie knew all too well that his usefulness at the head of the Secretariat had been spent and that it was time for a change, thus his decision to resign in 1952. In his resignation speech, Lie reminded the General Assembly that in 1950 he had agreed to continue in the post only because the Korean war "created circumstances that put me under an obligation to carry on." He also remarked that the policy of the Soviet Union and its allies not to recognize him as secretary-general for nearly three years had made it impossible for him to "exercise the full influence of his office as the universally recognized spokesman of the whole Organization." Of course, there were other considerations as well.

> The Permanent Headquarters, in which I took so much pride and joy, would be completed except for landscaping before the end of 1952. The General Assembly would meet for the first time in that great building to

which so much effort had been given over the years of my service. Then there were the human elements. All who know me are aware that I have my full share of these and am quite open about them—the frailties along with the virtues. I was, to use a good American expression, "fed up." I knew the signs—my irritation at the Soviet needling, my feeling that the Permanent Delegates generally were losing stature, my growing impatience with the Fifth (Administrative and Budgetary) Committee of the General Assembly. I had no doubt there were reciprocal feelings about me from some who had lived too long with my shortcomings. No, the signs were unmistakable. My political experience had taught me that no single person is indispensable. I was dispensable, and should be replaced by a new Secretary-General who could enter the work fresh and with fewer fixed ideas about persons and issues than I.

Once a successor was finally decided upon four months later, Lie had come to the famous conclusion that "the task of the Secretary-General is the most impossible job on earth."[108]

Conclusion

Throughout his secretary-generalship Lie tried to stay true to the goal of world peace as envisaged by the charter as he struggled to build the United Nations on the fractured foundation of the Cold War. Yet, as the discussion above makes clear, neither his dedication to the principles of the charter nor his firm resolve to make the United Nations a "force for peace" was enough to turn the tide of the Cold War or to "move the organization beyond the symbolic stage."[109] Lie's "strategic pragmatism" was insufficient, because "neither the Soviet Union nor the West recognized the United Nations as 'representing a third way,' but instead strove to align the charter with their respective political interests. Thus, when Lie's defense of the charter coincided with Soviet interests, as it did on Iran and Chinese representation, he was applauded for his independence; when it did not, as with Korea, Lie was ostracized politically and socially."[110]

And yet Lie never gave up believing that the moral power of the United Nations would, in the end, triumph. As he told those gathered at the fortieth annual convention of Rotary International in 1949, "In all [the dozen serious crises the United Nations has had to face], the United Nations has not had a single gun at its disposal. A dozen of its representatives, including Count Folke Bernadotte, have died at their posts, literally soldiers of peace whose only weapon was the moral force that could be mobilized by the United Nations. In every instance, this moral force has, in the long run, prevailed."[111] Even when his actions as secretary-general were disparaged and criticized mercilessly, Lie refused to be deterred from doing what he thought was best for the United Nations.

> My eyes were open as I pushed my way into each of the many problems that arose. I did not try to avoid them. I felt it was my duty to enter into them; it was a part of my interpretation of the United Nations Charter and its laws, as well as of the resolutions passed by the General Assemblies. Just as the Secretary-General is the servant of the United Nations and not of any single nation, so he is obligated to risk himself in the interest of a just solution. . . . I probably made many errors as Secretary-General. As the skipper said who suddenly found his ship fast aground: "We all make mistakes." My position was not made more comfortable by my regarding myself as "part" of the United Nations. I felt morally and legally compelled to take what I saw as the "United Nations view," particularly when I felt that the Member states were not living up to their Charter obligations. I did everything in my power to keep the United Nations from sinking or running aground.[112]

Lie certainly faced the many problems and challenges of building and leading the United Nations head on. And guiding him throughout was "his wholehearted commitment to the United Nations and its success in world affairs."[113] The actions he took and the precedents he set during his tenure emanated from that commitment and indicate that Lie's personal values and beliefs, or "inner code," and the "external code" of the UN charter had indeed entwined. In the end, the house that Lie built proved strong enough to withstand the political storms thrown up against it by the Cold War.

Notes

1. From the conclusion of Lie's farewell speech to the UN General Assembly on April 7, 1953, in Trygve Lie, *In the Cause of Peace: Seven Years with the United Nations* (New York: Macmillan, 1954), 417.

2. Technically, Sir Gladwyn Jebb of the United Kingdom was the first secretary-general of the United Nations, but his selection on January 10, 1946, was that of "acting" secretary-general and he served only until the UN General Assembly formally elected Lie on February 1, 1946, to a full five-year term.

3. Shirley Hazzard, *Countenance of Truth: The United Nations and the Kurt Waldheim Case* (New York: Viking Press, 1990), 14.

4. "Interview with A. R. K. MacKenzie," by William Powell, May 31, 1985, UN Oral History Project, ST/DPI/Oral History (02)/G7. See also "Interview with Leland Goodrich," by William Powell, September 16, 1985, UN Oral History Project, ST/DPI/Oral History (02)/G66.

5. Anthony Gaglione, *The United Nations Under Trygve Lie, 1945–1953* (Lanham, MD: Scarecrow Press, 2001), 45.

6. Alan James, "The Secretary-General: A Comparative Analysis," in *Diplomacy at the UN*, ed. G. R. Berridge and A. Jennings (New York: St. Martin's Press, 1985), 40.

7. There is no evidence as to why Lie's father left or any record as to his fate. As an article in *Time* magazine put it, "Driven by the instincts common to migrants of all time in quest of adventure or security or freedom (or simply of wider skies and unfamiliar faces), he sailed toward the west. The hard but hospitable shores received him and he vanished, unknown and untraced, in the fertile chaos of a country's growth. No one ever knew whether he found what he sought. He didn't write home." "Immigrant to What?" *Time*, November 25, 1946.

8. According to Guri Lie Zeckendorf, Lie's daughter, Lie's mother-in-law maintained this Norwegian religious practice until the day she died. Guri remembers that when visiting grandmother Joergensen, she and her sisters would sneak in some needlepoint on Sunday when their grandmother stepped out of the house, and would position themselves near a window in order to be able to quickly hide the needlepoint the moment they spotted their grandmother approaching. Guri Lie Zeckendorf, interview by author, January 19, 2005, New York City.

9. Ibid.

10. For an excellent overview of the history and influence of pietism, see the entry on pietism in *The Dictionary of the History of Ideas*, 3:494–95, available online from the Electronic Text Center at the University of Virginia Library at http://etext.lib.virginia.edu/DicHist/dict.html. Also see Ronald R. Feuerhahn, "The Roots and Fruits of Pietism," Pieper Lectures 1998, Concordia Historical Institute and the Luther Academy, September 17–18, 1998, available at www.issuesetc.org/resource/archives/feuerhhn.htm. According to Erling Bø, the school system was largely the product of the Church of Norway, which backed the establishment of general education in 1739 so as to enable Norwegian youth to study for confirmation. "School started as a school in Christianity—the other two subjects were reading and writing." See Erling Bø, "Christianity in Norway," Odin—Utenriksdepartementet (Ministry of Foreign Affairs), 1995, available at http://odin.dep.no/odin/engelsk/norway/history/032005-990468/index-dok000-b-n-a.html.

11. Zeckendorf, interview. Lie's indifference toward religion was even more pronounced for his wife, Hjördis Joergensen, who was quite adamant in her opposition to the Church of Norway and not favorably disposed toward organized

religion in general. In fact, they were married outside of the Church of Norway in 1921. Lie's trip to Moscow as a junior member of a Labor Party delegation to meet with Lenin, Trotsky, and Grigory Zinoviev that year was their excuse for having a rushed civil wedding, thereby avoiding a run-in with Hjördis's deeply religious mother on the matter.

12. Press conference of May 27, 1949, at Lake Success, New York. In Andrew W. Cordier and Wilder Foote, eds., *Public Papers of the Secretaries-General of the United Nations*, vol. 1, *Trygve Lie, 1946–1953* (New York: Columbia University Press, 1969), 195.

13. Gaglione, *United Nations Under Trygve Lie*, 13.

14. Lie's efforts to balance work and family have been criticized, unfairly in my opinion, as an indication that Lie was uninterested in day-to-day administration and that his "ways of doing things were ineffective and often counterproductive. . . . He was not as hard a worker [at the United Nations] as his Swedish successor Dag Hammarskjöld, in the sense of time spent at the office and at the job, although one could argue that as a family man, which Hammarskjöld was not, Lie had competing obligations for his time." James Barros, *Trygve Lie and the Cold War: The UN Secretary-General Pursues Peace, 1946–1953* (DeKalb, IL: Northern Illinois University Press, 1989), 47.

15. Lie's doubts about either a career move or a personal course of action were often allayed by discussions with his family. A case in point was his decision to accept the nomination by the Americans for the presidency of the first UN General Assembly: "At times like these, members of the Lie family have the habit of coming forward frankly with our own points of view, and now I found myself the most doubtful one present. The others were all but agreed that I could not possibly refuse permission to the American Delegation to suggest my name" (Lie, *In the Cause of Peace*, 4). *Time* magazine reported in the fall of 1946: "In his rather lonely spot among the nations, he is heavily dependent on his family, to which he is undisputed hero. In the United States, Lie lives in a (suburban Norman) house in Forest Hills, L.I. with his wife and two younger daughters Guri and Mette (the eldest, Sissel, is married and lives in Norway). He usually tries to get home for lunch. . . . Lie has iron nerves, can go to bed at the end of a troubled day with a child's placidity and (reports a friend) the pragmatic exclamation: 'I have done all I can—now I might as well sleep.'" "Immigrant to What?"

16. Zeckendorf, interview.

17. Gaglione, *United Nations Under Trygve Lie*, 13.

18. Barros, *Trygve Lie and the Cold War*, 36.

19. "Immigrant to What?"

20. Gaglione, *United Nations Under Trygve Lie*, 13–14.

21. Ibid., 13.

22. "A Man with Guts," *Time*, February 11, 1946.

23. Neil Stammers, "Social Democracy and Global Governance," in *Social Democracy: Global and National Perspectives*, ed. Luke Martell (New York: Palgrave, 2001), 30, 31.

24. "Immigrant to What?"

25. Lie, *In the Cause of Peace*, 19–20.

26. Gaglione, *United Nations Under Trygve Lie*, 13–14.

27. Lie was to develop a strong and close relationship with King Haakon VII during the war and was held in esteem by the monarch as an able government minister. See Tim Greve, *Haakon VII of Norway: The Man and the Monarch*, trans. and ed. Thomas Kingston Derry (London: C. Hurst & Co., 1983).

28. Lie, *In the Cause of Peace*, 3.

29. See the *Time* magazine articles "Immigrant to What?" and "A Man with Guts."

30. Barros, *Trygve Lie and the Cold War*, 36.

31. Lie, *In the Cause of Peace*, 18–19. See also Barros, *Trygve Lie and the Cold War*, 38–42.

32. Barros, *Trygve Lie and the Cold War*, 45.

33. "A Man with Guts."

34. Gaglione, *United Nations Under Trygve Lie*, 14.

35. Lie, *In the Cause of Peace*, 4.

36. According to James Barros, these qualities reflected U.S. views and, to a lesser extent, British and French views, on the United Nations as an organization "for world cooperation and conflict resolution." The Soviet Union, by contrast, saw the "projected world organization as essentially one more bulwark—and a lesser one at that—in protecting and guaranteeing its future security." He goes on to argue that this "largely explains the differences that developed during the wartime negotiations between the Western powers and Moscow over the nature of the secretariat and the secretary-general's office." Barros, *Trygve Lie and the Cold War*, 4.

37. Ibid., 28.

38. Lie, *In the Cause of Peace*, 22–23.

39. Ibid., 23.

40. Cordier and Foote, *Public Papers*, 1:27.

41. Lie, *In the Cause of Peace*, 23–24.

42. The Atlantic Charter articulated the objectives of the United States and the United Kingdom for fighting Nazi Germany, establishing eight "common principles": (1) seek no aggrandizement; (2) desire no territorial changes that do not accord with the wishes of the peoples concerned; (3) respect the right of people to choose their own form of government; and the restoration of sovereign rights and self-government to those who have been forcibly deprived of them; (4) further the enjoyment of all states of equal access to the trade and the raw

materials of the world; (5) desire the fullest economic collaboration between all nations so as to secure improved labor standards, economic advancement, and social security for all; (6) establish a peace that will afford all nations the means of dwelling in safety within their own boundaries and will assure all men in all lands that they may live in freedom from fear and want; (7) establish a peace that guarantees the freedom of the high seas and oceans; (8) believe that all nations, "for realistic as well as spiritual reasons," must abandon the use of force and after "the establishment of a wider and permanent system of general security," the disarmament of nations that threaten, or may threaten aggression, as well as aid and encourage all "practicable measures" toward the reduction of armaments of all nations. See James P. Muldoon Jr., *The Architecture of Global Governance: An Introduction to the Study of International Organizations* (Boulder, CO: Westview Press, 2003), 153–54.

43. Guri Lie Zeckendorf, interview by author, July 6, 2005.

44. Lie, *In the Cause of Peace*, 410.

45. Barros, *Trygve Lie and the Cold War*, 349.

46. See Lie, *In the Cause of Peace*, 1–11; Gaglione, *United Nations Under Trygve Lie*, 12; Barros, *Trygve Lie and the Cold War*, 17–20.

47. Gaglione, *United Nations Under Trygve Lie*, 12.

48. Lie, *In the Cause of Peace*, 17.

49. Cordier and Foote, *Public Papers*, 1:35.

50. Lie, *In the Cause of Peace*, 35.

51. Ibid., 41–42.

52. Ibid., 42.

53. Ibid., 40.

54. Gaglione, *United Nations Under Trygve Lie*, 45.

55. Ibid.

56. Lie, *In the Cause of Peace*, 81.

57. Gaglione, *United Nations Under Trygve Lie*, 46–47.

58. Lie, *In the Cause of Peace*, 89.

59. Gaglione, *United Nations Under Trygve Lie*, 21.

60. Ibid., 43, 42.

61. Lie was initially critical of both the Marshall Plan and the North Atlantic Pact, as he considered them part of a "dangerous tendency, especially in the West, to ignore the UN in the evolution of foreign policy" (ibid., 46) and a direct challenge to the preeminence of the United Nations for collective security. Later he was to praise the contribution of the Marshall Plan for helping to accelerate Europe's postwar recovery, but his concerns about the North Atlantic Pact persisted.

62. His fears were not unfounded, for the obstinacy of the Soviets and its Eastern European satellites in the face of the West's near-automatic voting majority in the Security Council and General Assembly hardened, as reflected in its resort

to the veto (the USSR was the first permanent member to use it) on matters that were clearly no threat to its national interests. The first veto was cast against a resolution settling the Lebanese and Syrian complaints against France and the UK for not withdrawing their troops from their countries at the end of the war, and for walking out of meetings. Throughout Lie's tenure, there were frequent rumors of a Soviet withdrawal from the organization. According to Linda Melvern, "Particularly current were rumours between 1949 and 1952, a period which saw a deterioration in Soviet–UN relations. Indeed, in 1949 the Soviet Union and the satellites began to disengage: the Soviet Union, the Ukraine and Byelorussia left the WHO, Czechoslovakia withdrew from the Food and Agricultural Organization and in 1950 both Poland and Czechoslovakia abandoned UNESCO. By the time of the historic and dramatic walkout of the Soviet Ambassador from the Security Council on 10 January, 1950, over the question of Chinese Communist representation, plans were well underway for the creation of a World Peace Council which was deliberately played as an alternative. . . . The Secretary-General, Trygve Lie, thought Soviet withdrawal almost certain and believed that an alternative UN comprising the Communist states was in preparation. But Stalin stayed, even after he concluded that the UN was an 'instrument of aggressive war', even when the UN waged war against Communists in Korea. Soviet diplomats deny that a complete withdrawal was ever on the cards. . . . Perhaps the Soviets wished it to be known that they might leave; the threat was a way of showing that even though they were in minority, their views should not be ignored." Linda Melvern, *The Ultimate Crime: Who Betrayed the UN and Why* (London: Allison & Busby, 1995), 128–29.

63. Lie, *In the Cause of Peace*, 250.

64. Barros, *Trygve Lie and the Cold War*, 219–20.

65. Lie, *In the Cause of Peace*, 254–57.

66. Ibid., 257.

67. Ibid., 262.

68. Barros, *Trygve Lie and the Cold War*, 236.

69. Lie, *In the Cause of Peace*, 262, 276, 278–82.

70. Gaglione, *United Nations Under Trygve Lie*, 61.

71. Barros, *Trygve Lie and the Cold War*, 239.

72. Lie, *In the Cause of Peace*, 282–83.

73. Ibid., 318.

74. Ibid., 316–17.

75. Gaglione, *United Nations Under Trygve Lie*, 64.

76. The North Korean invasion was not the first armed aggression to occur—the Arab states' invasion of Palestine in 1948 was actually the first—but the magnitude and form of the attack was so reminiscent of the Nazi blitzkrieg in the 1930s that there had to be a military response if the United Nations was to survive. According to Barros, "The fury of the attack, which took everyone by

surprise, reminded Lie of Nazi Germany's invasion of Norway on April 9, 1940. The trauma of the surprise attack was shared by the leaders of the American government who had lived through the Japanese attack on Pearl Harbor. . . . The charter had been blatantly violated, and no amount of sophistry could circumvent that naked fact." *Trygve Lie and the Cold War,* 274.

77. The UN Commission on Korea was established by a 1948 General Assembly resolution to facilitate the peaceful reunification of Korea. Owing to Soviet opposition both to the UN supervised election of Syngman Ree's government of the Republic of Korea in the South and to the commission, the nine-member commission was not allowed to operate north of the thirty-eighth parallel, where a Soviet-sponsored government—the Democratic People's Republic of Korea—was "elected," with Kim Il Sung as its president. There were a number of border skirmishes in the run-up to the invasion, which made the commission uneasy and caused it to expand its observation teams in the area of the thirty-eighth parallel, where South Korean troops were deployed.

78. Technically, there is no such thing as an emergency meeting of the Security Council. All meetings of the council are ad hoc and called to address a specific matter.

79. Lie, *In the Cause of Peace,* 328–29.

80. Gaglione, *United Nations Under Trygve Lie,* 67.

81. Lie, *In the Cause of Peace,* 331.

82. Ibid., 332, 333.

83. Ibid., 333–34.

84. Ibid., 334.

85. Gaglione, *United Nations Under Trygve Lie,* 67. The October 7 resolution authorized UN forces to enter North Korea, and the November 3 resolution, known as the "Uniting for Peace resolution," "engineered a profoundly important shift of emergency power from the veto-ridden Security Council to the veto-less General Assembly" in the event of another Korean-like aggression. Lie, *In the Cause of Peace,* 347.

86. Lie, *In the Cause of Peace,* 342–43. For the discussion about neutrality in this excerpt, Lie directs the reader to Stephen M. Schwebel, *The Secretary-General of the United Nations: His Political Powers and Practice* (Cambridge, MA: 1952), 111.

87. Barros, *Trygve Lie and the Cold War,* 275; Gaglione, *United Nations Under Trygve Lie,* 73.

88. Lie, *In the Cause of Peace,* 385.

89. Ibid., 142.

90. Ibid., 143.

91. Gaglione, *United Nations Under Trygve Lie,* 93.

92. Ibid., 99.

93. Lie, *In the Cause of Peace,* 156.

94. Gaglione, *United Nations Under Trygve Lie,* 93, 95.

95. Lie, *In the Cause of Peace*, 157.

96. Gaglione, *United Nations Under Trygve Lie*, 99.

97. Lie, *In the Cause of Peace*, 52–54.

98. Ibid., 54.

99. Ibid., 45.

100. Barros, *Trygve Lie and the Cold War*, 60.

101. Ibid., 59.

102. Ibid., 58–59; Linda Melvern, *Ultimate Crime*, 28.

103. Barros, *Trygve Lie and the Cold War*, 60–62.

104. Lie has been roundly condemned for his handling of the Fifth Amendment cases and for permitting the U.S. government to conduct its "loyalty investigations" of American Secretariat members on UN premises (see Melvern, *UltimateCrime*, 41–77). But as James Barros points out, "A resolute and less pliant secretary-general might have handled the situation better, but it is doubtful that anyone could have long resisted the enormous pressure felt both from Congress and the American public. Washington's belated decision, after ignoring Lie's earlier prodding, to guarantee the loyalty of Americans employed in the secretariat would have been less shocking and more understandable to well-meaning people, if the myth of a nonpolitical multinational secretariat, first cultivated by Drummond in 1919, had not been oversold. That a nonpolitical secretariat would have been desirable goes without saying; that it could have been obtained, in view of the increasing postwar political, military, and ideological struggle, is clearly unlikely. The tragedy of this period was that, when the myth of an impartial secretariat was exposed to scrutiny, its fragility became obvious. Lie had not decked himself with glory, but the Truman administration, by not vetting Americans being recruited for the secretariat, had failed to give Lie the initial assistance he had requested. Compounded by demagoguery and the impact of the Korean war on American public opinion, events overtook both Lie and the Truman administration." *Trygve Lie and the Cold War*, 320.

105. Lie, *In the Cause of Peace*, 404–5.

106. Ibid., 405, 386, 403.

107. Gaglione, *United Nations Under Trygve Lie*, 123.

108. Lie, *In the Cause of Peace*, 407, 409, 411, 417.

109. Gaglione, *United Nations Under Trygve Lie*, 129.

110. Ibid., 123.

111. Cordier and Foote, *Public Papers*, 1:205.

112. Lie, *In the Cause of Peace*, 418, 421.

113. Barros, *Trygve Lie and the Cold War*, 347.

4

THE UN CHARTER, THE NEW TESTAMENT, AND PSALMS
The Moral Authority of Dag Hammarskjöld

ALYNNA J. LYON

On July 29, 2005, the world celebrated the hundredth anniversary of Dag Hammarskjöld's birth. The anniversary provided an opportunity to reflect on this extraordinary individual and his role in world politics. Hammarskjöld would approve of our contemplation on his birthday, as he himself often noted the day with meditative and reflective writings that he referred to as "roadmarks." These spiritual explorations make Hammarskjöld's moral convictions among the most obvious of all the secretaries-general. We set out in this volume to answer the question, does the ethical framework of an individual officeholder impact the role played by a secretary-general of the United Nations? The answer for Hammarskjöld is a distinct and resounding yes—absolutely. In fact, some argue that it is impossible to understand Hammarskjöld the statesman absent his moral convictions.[1] The exact influence of these convictions may be difficult to distinguish, however, in that it is hard to separate Hammarskjöld's ethical framework from who he was publicly. Thus Hammarskjöld presents a bit of a paradox; he was both a public persona but also a deeply private man.

Fortunately for scholars, Hammarskjöld documented his own relationship with faith and morality as they influenced his life of public service. Published posthumously, *Vagmarken,* or *Markings,* comprises more than six hundred entries by Hammarskjöld on topics ranging from poetry, to biblical references, to nature, as well as confessions and meditations.[2] This collection is full of insight and provides a solid foundation for understanding Hammarskjöld's ethical framework. Hammarskjöld himself described the work as "a sort of white book concerning my negotiations with myself—and with God."[3] At the same time, one must be wary of taking the analysis too far when interpreting and inscribing meaning from the written word. In fact, Hammarskjöld himself once warned against drawing "large conclusions from inconclusive evidence."[4] In this attempt to measure the ethereal world, to find empirical evidence of normative values and faith, we can take Hammarskjöld's own words as our guide:

> That strange moment when a man's features are dissolved into the trembling shimmer on the surface of the wave, through which you peer into the depths without being able to see the bottom. You are tempted to dive in and to grasp—but the water cannot be grasped, and beneath its surface you cannot breathe. One step further and the relation is destroyed, reduced to terror and error: you imagine you are taking possession of a human being, but, in fact, you are losing him. In your attempt to break down the boundaries of a personality, you are building a new prison for yourself.[5]

The analysis in this chapter also incorporates and builds upon the work of many scholars who have written on Hammarskjöld's life, including work on his religious views and spirituality, such as Sven Stolpe's *Dag Hammarskjöld: A Spiritual Portrait,* Gustaf Aulén's *Dag Hammarskjöld's White Book: An Analysis of Markings,* and Henry P. Van Dusen's *Dag Hammarskjöld: The Statesman and His Faith.*[6] Many studies also address Hammarskjöld the statesman, providing detailed personal and political examinations of his role as secretary-general.[7] In fact, Van Dusen systematically traces the entries of *Markings* to the historical and political events of Hammarskjöld's life. At the same time, most sources overlook the forceful influence of Hammarskjöld's faith on his profession. They focus on either the public man as statesman or the private man and his theological reflections; rarely is the nexus between these two roles systematically considered.

In order to consider the connection between Hammarskjöld's ethical framework and the role he played as secretary-general, the chapter first identifies the influence that family, education, religion, and culture had on his ethical framework. The chapter then considers how this framework shaped Hammarskjöld's understanding of his role as secretary-general, the United Nations itself, and the mandates of the institution's charter. Building on this foundation, the final section addresses the question of just how his moral values influenced Hammarskjöld's fulfillment of his duties as secretary-general. This analysis confirms several places where Hammarskjöld drew on his ethical framework and found moral mandates for his actions, his policy agenda, and even his relations with UN member states. With this focus, the chapter establishes that Hammarskjöld's ethical framework influenced his administrative duties (specifically in his reaction to McCarthyism) and his actions in several international crises (the U.S.-Chinese dispute in 1954, the Suez Canal clash, and the peace-keeping mission in the Congo).

Family and Faith: Cornerstones of Public Service

The role of family, and especially of his parents, significantly shaped young Dag's moral constitution. His father, Hjalmar Hammarskjöld, is well remembered as a distinguished descendant of Swedish nobility who served Sweden's King Gustav in several positions, most notably as prime minister from 1914 to 1917. Many of his professional accomplishments were marred by controversy, however, as his time in office corresponded to the intense political turmoil of World War I. When the strain of the war in Europe contributed to a national famine, he was ultimately forced to resign his post. For Hjalmar, virtue was firmly grounded in service, sacrifice, and justice. He was consistently religious and strictly moral, and his strong emphasis on duty reflected his old Swedish Lutheran Christianity. Such reverence for service was willingly adopted by Dag. Yet Dag, the youngest of four, was not the only son to engage enthusiastically in public service; two of his brothers, Bo and Ake, also chose government careers. Dag's own words clearly reflect his family commitment: "From generations of soldiers and government officials on my father's side I inherited a belief that no life was more satisfactory than one of selfless service to your country—or humanity. This service required a sacrifice of all personal interests, but likewise the courage to stand up unflinchingly for your convictions."[8]

The relationship between father and son was a complicated one, however. Dag and his father were not particularly close. Stolpe blames this distance on Hjalmar's personality and describes him as "brilliant . . . but with only meager capacity for making direct and warm contact with his fellowmen." Stolpe also maintains that Dag brooded over the public criticism of his father despite his steadfast pursuit of justice: "From his image and destiny the thoughts of the son turn to Christ, who in greater measure and without guilt was slain for his love and steadfastness."[9] This may have shaped an important moral tension within the younger Dag; he viewed his father's path as right and just, yet his father faced disparagement and public condemnation. A cornerstone of Dag Hammarskjöld's ethical framework emerges from the relationship with his father: a commitment to public service and unwavering faith in one's convictions.

In contrast to the formal distance between the boy and his father, Dag maintained a close relationship with his mother, Agnes Almquist Hammar-skjöld. While her closely held moral and religious convictions, described by one observer as "evangelistic," were also embedded in Lutheranism, her character was distinct from her husband's. She is consistently described as considerate, warm, emotional, and "exuberantly forthcoming . . . with good will and friendliness towards everybody around her. . . . She was a sweet woman and [Dag] Hammarskjöld was very attached to her."[10] Dag's brother Sten wrote about this relationship in *The Boy Who Bowed to God,* "Dag was his mother's gentleman-in-waiting, her page, her faithful and considerate attendant."[11] From his mother Dag inherited quiet warmth and devotion.

In addition to her own influence on the moral fabric of her son, Agnes Hammarskjöld's close friendship with the Lutheran archbishop of Uppsala, Lars Olof Jonathan (Nathan) Söderblom, must have helped form Dag's moral views. Söderblom was affiliated with the "Stockholm Move-ment" and was instrumental in establishing a Christian ecumenical move-ment in theological inquiry and spiritual dialogue. In addition, Söderblom strongly emphasized social ministry. The archbishop was keenly engrossed in rejuvenating faith, personal commitment, social service, and outreach. Söderblom's spiritual quest sought to "bring the spirit of the Gospel to bear upon social, economic and industrial relationships."[12] This commit-ment achieved success in the formation of the World Council of Churches in 1948 and his receipt of the Nobel Peace Prize in 1930. Hammarskjöld wrote of his influence, "From scholars and clergymen on my mother's side, I inherited a belief that, in the very radical sense of the Gospels, all men were equals as children of God, and should be met and treated by us as our masters in God."[13] Thus equality and religious obligation to ser-vice reveal themselves as touchstones of Hammarskjöld's ethical frame-work. We see this also in his respect for Albert Schweitzer (1875–1965). Schweitzer's theological works, as well as his own work in Africa as a phy-sician, prompted Hammarskjöld to describe him as "a living example of the ethics he proclaimed."[14]

Hammarskjöld's education was also filled with moral teachings. He attended Uppsala University, where he earned degrees in law, economics, and humanities. At the time, Uppsala was a religious center as well as an academic hub, "alive with new intellectual currents emanating from the church."[15] Stolpe remarks that, even at an early age, Dag "carried an inner world with him."[16] Yet Hammarskjöld kept his religious side very private during his youth; many associates, including close friends at Uppsala, claimed they never knew the depths of his spirituality.[17] In Hammarskjöld's early journal entries (1925–52), we clearly see inner turmoil and sadness. At one point in 1952 he writes, "Give me something to die for—!" The same entry continues, "Pray that your loneliness may spur you into finding something to live for, great enough to die for."[18] Yet most observers found Hammarskjöld to be a lively and peaceful man. A colleague at Uppsala wrote, "His sense of duty and his industriousness did not weigh heavily on him. On the contrary, he seemed to have a happy nature."[19] From this portrait of Hammarskjöld, public service and sacrifice clearly emerge as elements of his ethical framework.

Neutral Integrity

Another important influence on Hammarskjöld's ethical framework was his Swedish cultural background, which provided, most notably, a strong commitment to neutrality. This view was not one of moral disinterest but reflected instead respect for integrity and a commitment to dialogue in conflict. Neutrality was also cherished by his father, who never declared political allegiance to any group or party; for the elder Hammarskjöld, service was to country, not sect or party. As prime minister, Hjalmar Hammarskjöld pursued a policy of neutrality during World War I. The influence of Osten Undén, the foreign minister of Sweden, also contributed significantly to Hammarskjöld's conception of neutrality. Undén managed to maintain the neutrality of Sweden when there was very little room to maneuver in the political pressures of the postwar years. Hammarskjöld's commitment to neutrality was part of a cultural heritage that became a moral precept. In time he would find that this commitment served him well as he faced the exhausting tasks of a secretary-general seeking progress from a United Nations often paralyzed by Cold War geopolitics.[20]

The values of neutrality and service become operational tools that allowed Dag Hammarskjöld's ethical code to become a mandate for international service. His notions of service, sacrifice, and neutrality took on spiritual tones and became part of his ethical framework. As discussed below, he brought these core values with him into the secretary-generalship, his view of the charter, and his understanding of the United Nations' role.

Hammarskjöld, Lutheranism, and Medieval Mysticism

Hammarskjöld's moral values were intricately interwoven with his spiritual life. It is impossible to appreciate his ethical framework without understanding the role theology played in shaping his moral inclinations. Hammarskjöld closely followed many of the teachings of Swedish Lutheranism. At the same time, he also drew from the writings of other faiths, religious figures, and theologians. Brian Urquhart explains that Hammarskjöld frequently attended many types of services during his tenure in New York, but did so discreetly.[21] Although he accepted many Christian moral tenets, religion for Hammarskjöld was an individual pursuit. In general terms, Christianity provides a range of moral guidelines; in addition to the clear directives of the Ten Commandments, the Old and New Testaments are abundantly focused on morality. Lutheranism in particular also provided Hammarskjöld with certain emphases and directives in relation to ethical beliefs and behaviors, including the belief in righteousness, devotionalism, service to God, and service to man.[22]

Coram Deo: *The Union of God with the Soul*

A central conviction of Hammarskjöld's faith rested on the idea of *coram Deo,* a tenet that characterizes an individual's private and direct relationship with God. This theological assumption is understood by the Lutheran tradition as strongly personal and predicated on faith, receptivity, and acceptance. In Hammarskjöld's own words, "Faith is a state of the mind and the soul. In this sense, we can understand the words of the Spanish mystic St. John of the Cross: 'Faith is the union of God with the soul.' The language of religion is a set of formulas that register a basic spiritual experience. It must not be regarded as describing, in terms to be defined by philosophy, the reality which is accessible to our senses and which we can analyze with the tools of logic."[23]

His words also build on the precept *Deus absconditus,* which teaches that "Christians must look for God under the opposite of what human reason would expect, God's strength under weakness, God's wisdom under folly, God's victory under the cross."[24] This view is consistent with Hammarskjöld's meditations in *Markings,* where he repeatedly refers to not knowing and not expecting to understand the workings of God. Hammarskjöld establishes the significance of his personal relationship with God as well as an understanding of *Deus absconditus:* "God does not die on the day when we cease to believe in a personal deity, but we die on the day when our lives cease to be illuminated by the steady radiance, renewed daily, of a wonder, the source of which is beyond all reason."[25]

Coram Mundo: *Faith and Public Service*

Righteousness, understood as a duality having both external and internal components, is another key Lutheran principle. Purity, piety, and the perfection of inner thoughts are the focus of internal righteousness. Martin Luther, the father of Lutheranism, interpreted the idea of external righteousness as civic righteousness. This teaching calls on the individual to conduct oneself in a manner that is just and to pursue good public acts. A Lutheran lives in a secular world under the rule of civil authority and law, while still governed by God, but also under the gospel in the divine world. Thus the teachings of the church remain relevant to secular life as followers are called upon to engage their faith within the secular world. Thomas Nairn explains that Lutherans hold that "ethics is the study of the implications of faith for the way Christians live."[26] This precept is supported by another distinction: the kingdom before God, *coram Deo*, and the kingdom before the world, *coram mundo*. Hammarskjöld's commentary explores this important dynamic and illustrates its importance to his own life: "Our work for peace must begin within the private world of each one of us. To build for man a world without fear, we must be without fear. To build a world of justice, we must be just. And how can we fight for liberty if we are not free in our own minds? How can we ask others to sacrifice if we are not ready to do so?"[27]

At the same time, morality for Hammarskjöld goes beyond the public-private distinction. It is best explained as a three-way exchange between one's own personal communion with God, God's influence on the mundane world (manifest in public service), and the personal divinity that one applies there as well.[28] Urquhart's insight into Hammarskjöld is helpful here: "Religion for him was a dialogue of his own with God, and faith was the foundation for duty, dedication, and service, qualities that he considered most essential in himself and most admirable in others."[29] This presents a more refined view of Hammarskjöld's moral convictions, as his spirituality is reflected in both his public (*coram mundo*) and private (*coram hominibus*) relationships, as well as in his relationship to God (*coram Deo*).

For Hammarskjöld, religious practice meant more than simply attending services and a cognitive belief in the existence of a deity. The civic component of his ethical framework was his personal sacrifice to public service. Aulén explains, "His faith in God demands realization in action."[30] Indeed, the notion of civil servant and servant to God became blended in Hammarskjöld's writings and speeches. In this case, his piety was brought to fruition in social activism. In *The Freedom of a Christian* Martin Luther describes this conception of service, which builds on the key value of neutral integrity: "A Christian is a perfectly free lord of all, subject to none. A Christian is a perfectly dutiful servant of all, subject to all."[31] In 1956 Hammarskjöld wrote, "thus subordinated, your life will receive from Life all its meaning, irrespective of the conditions given you for its realization."[32] Clearly, Hammarskjöld embraces the charge of personal responsibility, surrender, and service.

Despite his religious foundation in Lutheranism, parts of Hammarskjöld's spiritual convictions were seen by some as notably "un-Lutheran."[33] He was intrigued by medieval Catholic mysticism and was deeply interested in several saints who called for devotional reform of Catholic piety and faith.[34] Figures like St. John of the Cross, St. Teresa of Avila, and Thomas À Kempis had a significant impact on his spiritual development. These individuals called for public service emblemized in Christ's acts, and Hammarskjöld accepted this unquestioningly.[35] For example, Thomas À Kempis wrote an important treatise on Christian devotionalism titled *The Imitation of Christ,* in which he says, "He does much who loves much. He does much who does a thing well. He does well who serves the common good rather than his own interests."[36] Hammarskjöld's own words echo this sentiment:

> The explanation of how man should live a life of active social service in full harmony with himself as a member of the community of the spirit, I found in the writings of those great medieval mystics for whom "self-surrender" had been the way to self-realization, and who in "singleness of mind" and "inwardness" had found strength to say Yes to every demand which the needs of their neighbors made them face, and to say Yes also to every fate life had in store for them.[37]

Urquhart also describes Hammarskjöld's emulation of Christ: "His identification with Christian thought was not messianic, but rather in the old tradition of the imitation of Christ in sacrifice and service to others."[38] Thus it was in the medieval mystics that Hammarskjöld found the guidelines for action in public service.

His family, Lutheranism, and the medieval mystics all influenced and reinforced an essential component of Hammarskjöld's moral convictions—

a deep commitment to social outreach. In an early UN press release Hammarskjöld expressed this commitment: "Only in true surrender to the interest of all can we reach that strength and independence, that unity of purpose, that equity of judgment which are necessary if we are to measure up to our duty to the future, as men of a generation to whom the chance was given to build in time a world of peace."[39] Overall, Hammarskjöld's ethical framework may be mapped as a triangular relationship. Three primary doctrines engage each other to form his value system. The first involves his own spiritual relationship with God (*coram Deo*). Spirituality in his private life (*coram hominibus*) provides the second pillar. Spirituality in his public service (*coram mundo*) provides the third. Within this triad there are several layers, beginning with his personal convictions and broadening out to the public sphere. Faith, receptivity, and acceptance are core principles that set a foundation for all other engagements. His ethical framework, then, holds public service, self-sacrifice, and neutrality as more public manifestations of the first stratum. From here his personal convictions broaden out to include more community-oriented values. Here we find his commitment to the Christian principles of peace, equality, and justice. The final dimension really takes shape through his service as secretary-general. The values of peaceful resolution of conflict, economic opportunity, political equality, and international justice are manifestations of his more personal operational code. Figure 4.1 illustrates the parameters of

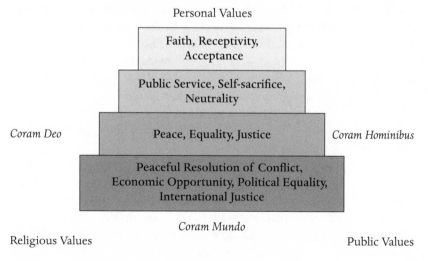

Figure 4.1. Map of Hammarskjöld's Ethical Framework

Hammarskjöld's ethical framework.[40] This figure traces Hammarskjöld's intricate, multidimensional, and intensely reflective ethical framework. We shall see how he incorporates each layer of his ethical framework into the mandates provided by the UN charter.

Let us turn now to the question of how Hammarskjöld's ethical framework was articulated in the political and moral dilemmas he faced during his tenure as secretary-general. The first section examines the synchronization of his ethical framework with the moral mandates of the UN charter, in particular how his principles of receptivity, self-sacrifice, and service were realized in his acceptance of the position of secretary-general. His view of the secretary-general as a "secular pope" and his understanding of the United Nations as an instrument of faith are then detailed.

The Charter, Psalms, and the New Testament

Hammarskjöld came to the United Nations with a wide range of previous experience in public service. He served as secretary of the Royal Commission on Unemployment and moved into the position of chairman of the Riksbank (the National Bank of Sweden). In the international realm, he helped negotiate a significant Swedish–U.S. trade agreement and also served as the Swedish representative to the Organization for European Economic Cooperation and the Marshall Plan. He acted as the undersecretary of the Finance Ministry and later held positions in the Foreign Ministry, including representing Sweden in the UN General Assembly. After Trygve Lie resigned in 1953, Hammarskjöld was selected to serve as the second UN secretary-general.[41] Following his re-election in 1957, he served until 1961, when he was killed in a plane crash during a peace mission in the Congo. Copies of the UN charter, the New Testament, and Psalms were found with Hammarskjöld at the crash site.[42] Indeed, it has been reported that he kept these three documents with him throughout his tenure at the United Nations.[43]

Hammarskjöld's nomination to the office of secretary-general came at a very tense time in international relations. The divide between the United States and the Soviet Union was beginning to cut deep; harsh tones, mutual suspicions, and rigid posturing were felt throughout the United Nations. Even Hammarskjöld's nomination was the result of global power politics. As a candidate from nonaligned Sweden, neutrality was his chief asset in a world body increasingly split along East–West lines.

Before ascending to this post, however, Hammarskjöld was often discontented. Stolpe describes his state of mind as one of persistent turmoil exacerbated by feelings of loneliness, isolation, and, surprisingly, egocentrism.[44] Urquhart observes that before Hammarskjöld became secretary-general, his writings indicated a "nagging discontent." Yet, both Stolpe and Urquhart find that Hammarskjöld's outlook and character were transformed by his appointment as secretary-general. Stolpe offers the explanation that Hammarskjöld's turmoil and constant struggle ended with his appointment as secretary-general. Not having sought the office, he was surprised by the nomination, and initially unsure about serving in such a capacity. He cabled the Security Council president to express his uncertainty: "With a strong feeling of personal insufficiency, I hesitate to accept candidature, but I do not feel I could refuse the task imposed upon me."[45]

His advancement to secretary-general presented Hammarskjöld with a moral dilemma, yet he saw the nomination as a calling. His decision to serve exemplifies the influence of his moral convictions on his life of public service. We can see in the decision a reflection of Luther's concept of the "spiritualization of secular life."[46] This is the reverse of the traditional notion of God calling individuals from their secular life to a spiritual life; one is called to faith and service in *all* vocations. For Hammarskjöld, spiritual and public life were intertwined, and he interpreted his nomination to the secretary-generalship as spiritual remuneration. His value system, which upheld public service guided by morality, found a firm footing in the role of international servant. Two entries in *Markings* provide a glimpse of his jubilation and his belief that his private torments were behind him: "It *did* come—the day when the grief became small. For what had befallen me and seemed so hard to bear became insignificant in the light of the demands which God was now making. But how difficult it is to feel that this was also, and for that very reason, the day when joy became great."[47] Aulén claims that Hammarskjöld was plagued by feelings of loneliness, selfishness and the "meaninglessness of life."[48] In accepting the position of secretary-general, he had found new opportunity and meaning in life. The week he accepted the position he wrote, "For all that has been—Thanks! To all that shall be—Yes!"[49] The acceptance of the office shifted his longing into a spiritual calling with clarity and direction. In this position, Hammarskjöld claimed that he had become a "perfectly happy man" with "ideal preparation."[50] At the same time, this euphoria was combined with a profound sense of duty. We find a similar tone in 1957, when Hammarskjöld renewed his acceptance of the secretary-generalship, writing, "Yes to God: yes to destiny, yes to yourself."[51]

As secretary-general, Hammarskjöld's dedication to the office was complete. Henrik Klackenberg, a close friend and associate, observed, "I remember chiefly his moral stature and incorruptible justice, his integrity and whole-hearted commitment, and his never-failing sense of responsibility vis-à-vis the Task."[52] His concept of service to God and man was operationalized into extreme dedication to his duties as secretary-general. He often worked twenty-hour days, and even chose not to marry, explaining that any such family obligations would disrupt his focus on his work.[53]

The Secretary-General as a Secular Pope

Several virtues in Hammarskjöld's ethical framework overlap with the parameters of the office of the secretary-general. Hammarskjöld's family and cultural upbringing gave him an understanding of service and neutrality that was uniquely conducive to the secretary-generalship. The notion of public obligation that he inherited from his father, Lutheranism, and the medieval saints can be seen in the charter's call for the secretary-general to be a servant to the international community. Hammarskjöld's first impromptu press conference in New York expressed his commitment to serve: "In my new official capacity the private man should disappear and the international public servant takes his place. The public servant is there in order to assist . . . he is active as an instrument, a catalyst, perhaps an inspirer—he serves."[54] Hammarskjöld also used religious metaphors to describe the role of the secretary-general. He once referred to the position of secretary-general as "that of a 'secular pope' and" the United Nations as "a secular 'church' of ideals."[55]

The second driving principle that influenced Hammarskjöld's understanding of his role as secretary-general was the concept of neutral integrity, discussed above, which for Hammarskjöld meant an emphasis on a neutral secretary-general promoting peaceful internationalism as a common goal for all in the international community. His views are expressed in a 1961 lecture:

> He is not requested to be a neuter in the sense that he has to have no sympathies or antipathies, that there are no interests which are close to him in his personal capacity or that he is to have no ideas or ideals that matter to him. However, he is requested to be fully aware of those human reactions

and meticulously to check himself so that they are not permitted to influence his actions. This is nothing unique. Is not every judge professionally under that same obligation?[56]

The United Nations as an Instrument of Faith

In examining Hammarskjöld's understanding of the mission of the United Nations, we find parallels between his conception of faith as a "union with God and the soul," and his view of the UN charter.[57] In fact, his commitment to the dictums of the charter may be characterized as a union with the man and the charter. Andrew W. Cordier observes that Hammarskjöld "had almost a religious respect for the Charter."[58] The charter offered him both a moral mandate and a legal template for solving conflicts in times of international crisis. Hammarskjöld spoke of Saint Paul's idea of a "need for faith, hope, and charity" as forming the foundation for a "United Nations ideology." He saw the United Nations as a symbol of faith, an "instrument of action," and "a framework for acts of charity."[59] He championed the mandates laid out in the preamble to the UN charter, which calls on the institution to "save succeeding generations from the scourge of war . . . to establish conditions under which justice and respect for the obligations arising from treaties and other sources of international law can be maintained . . . to promote social progress and better standards of life . . . to practice tolerance and live together in peace . . . and to unite our strength to maintain international peace and security." Hammarskjöld echoes this mandate in a 1956 address to the Security Council: "He must also be a servant of the principles of the Charter, and its aims must ultimately determine what for him is right and wrong. For that he must stand."[60]

Hammarskjöld's ethical framework was easily married to the values expressed in the UN charter. His personal ethical commitments, grounded in Lutheranism, meshed well with the moral guidelines expressed in the charter's preamble, as well as in the specific mandates of the United Nations to create a framework for his public ethics. Mark Zacher remarks that Hammarskjöld pursued five primary goals as secretary-general: economic opportunity, political equality, the prevention of violence, the preemption of conflict through negotiation, and international justice.[61] He specifically mentions a multifaith quest for peace in a 1953 address to the General Assembly: "We are of different creeds and convictions. Events and ideas which to some of us remain the very basis of our faith are elements of the spiritual heritage of man which are foreign to others. But common to us all, and above all other convictions stands the truth, once expressed by a Swedish poet when he said that the greatest prayer of man does not ask for victory but for peace."[62]

As shown in figure 4.1, Hammarskjöld's commitment to service, neutrality, peace, equality, and justice, once combined with the mandates of the UN charter, became a guiding force. In Zacher's words, Hammarskjöld's moral code actually became "a strong commitment to the ethical principles of the Organization." These operating guidelines set a moral agenda for the prevention of violence and the promotion of economic opportunity, political equality, and international justice. Zacher argues that "these attributions of a certain 'religious' character to United Nations principles reveal in an indirect manner that Hammarskjöld saw the normative bases of the United Nations as an extension of his own philosophical principles into international affairs."[63] In this manner, Hammarskjöld drew upon his ethical framework as a compass with which to stabilize himself, direct his orientation, and provide momentum to this direction when entering the choppy waters of international relations.

By the end of his tenure, his own ethical framework was closely integrated with the founding principles of the UN charter. Thus Hammarskjöld's ethical framework, a product of his upbringing, Swedish culture, Lutheranism, and medieval Catholic mysticism, meshed exceedingly well with the organizational values expressed in the UN charter. Figure 4.2 illustrates how these values combined and overlapped with the charter in several supporting places.

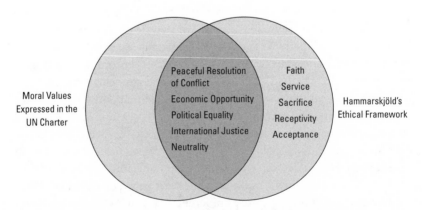

Figure 4.2. Confluence of Hammarskjöld's Ethical Framework and UN Charter Mandates

Neutral Integrity and the Pursuit of Peace and Legal Justice

Let us now examine Hammarskjöld's ethical framework as it influenced his involvement in four cases: the challenges of McCarthyism, the disputes surrounding the 1954 U.S.–Chinese clash over captured U.S. airmen, the crisis over the Suez Canal, and the peacekeeping mission in the Congo.

The Storm of McCarthyism

Almost immediately, Hammarskjöld's view of neutral integrity for the pursuit of a higher goal confronted a challenge in McCarthyism. Lie, Hammarskjöld's predecessor, came to the post of secretary-general as the result of a Big Five agreement, and he faced considerable constraints at the beginning of the long Cold War. Lie, under the pressures of McCarthyism, had allowed agents from the Federal Bureau of Investigation to be stationed inside UN headquarters (legally international territory) to investigate Secretariat staff who were suspected of Communist sympathies. Hammarskjöld began his tenure in the middle of this controversy and was at once faced with the tensions inherent in Great Power servicing. In essence, this was a twofold crisis; both the interrogation of UN officials (American citizens working in the Secretariat's office) and the stationing of FBI agents on the premises of the United Nations were hot-button issues, and the secretary-general risked incurring the wrath of the United States if he prohibited either one. The recently appointed U.S. representative to the United Nations, Henry Cabot Lodge Jr., requested that the FBI scrutinize all U.S. citizens working in the office of the Secretariat. When staff members refused, invoking the Fifth Amendment, Washington requested that they be dismissed. Before Hammarskjöld had even officially taken office, the General Assembly requested a report from the secretary-general on personnel policy with regard to this matter.

After the decision to accept the nomination of the secretary-generalship, this situation was the second moral dilemma Hammarskjöld faced. The presence of the U.S. investigators was a violation of articles 100 and 101 of the UN charter, which obligates member states "not to seek to influence" UN staff, declares that the secretary-general has sole authority over the staff, and ensures the "integrity" of the Secretariat. Hammarskjöld's first act was to remove the FBI agents from the premises. He resoundingly declared, "you can't be here: whatever permission may have been given in the past is withdrawn." In a personal conversation, he described the presence of the agents as "intolerable, absolutely intolerable."[64] Hammarskjöld viewed the American attempt to influence the personnel of the Secretariat as undermining the value of the United Nations as an arbitrator and autonomous actor. The integrity of the institution was in jeopardy.

Hammarskjöld was also faced with the U.S. request for staff dismissal; he responded by creating a judicial structure that allowed for an independent investigation of specific cases. His report on this issue was extensive and focused on the notion of integrity; through it he managed to weave in a reaffirmation of the UN mission. With his notion of neutral integrity guiding the document, he issued a statement requiring that staff not engage in any political activities outside their duties within the United Nations. These provisions, combined with a legal mechanism, managed to keep the Americans at bay without triggering their condemnation of either the institution or the office. Hammarskjöld's approach to the problem was one of honoring the ability of the United Nations to promote international concordance. A core value, neutrality for a greater cause, was intricately woven into the legal parameters of the UN charter. Interestingly, rather than framing his mandate as an expansion of power, he explained it as his fulfilling the duty and responsibility of the administration of the office.[65] In a statement to the U.S. staff in Geneva, he explained, "Why are the standards and the independence of the Secretariat so important? The more I see of the work in the United Nations, the more convinced I feel of this importance. Countries are arming in order to be able to negotiate from a position of strength. The Secretariat too has to negotiate, not only in its interest, but for the cause of peace and a peaceful development of our world."[66] Later, in 1956, this precedent was invoked when Egypt's president Nasser tried to obtain information on Egyptian citizens working within the UN system in order to exercise oversight and potentially fire them. Again Hammarskjöld framed the issue as a question of neutrality and the ability to serve the international community without impunity.

The pressure of McCarthyism clearly presented a moral challenge to Hammarskjöld—one that tested the fragile balance between advocacy and impartiality and between the concerns of Great Power interests and the neutral integrity of the United Nations, including the office of the secretary-general. In avoiding a confrontation with the United States, Hammarskjöld proved to be skillful and adept. At the same time, he clearly incorporated his own notions of neutrality and service into protecting his staff legally. From this point forward, the young UN Secretariat (only eleven years old at the time) became a significant, legitimate, autonomous actor in world politics.

Diplomacy in China

Hammarskjöld's ethical framework also influenced his actions in resolving conflicts between powerful states. One early indication of this can be seen in his handling of a clash between the United States and Communist China. During the Korean War, several downed American pilots were captured and held by the Chinese. The pilots were subsequently convicted of espionage, but the Americans argued that the Chinese needed to return the pilots as prisoners of war according to the Korean Armistice Agreement. During these exchanges, domestic factions within the United States (specifically the hardliners, including Senator Joseph McCarthy) pushed Eisenhower to respond aggressively. As tensions escalated, the UN General Assembly, responding to an American request, asked Hammarskjöld to use "continuing and unremitting efforts" to secure the safe release of the pilots "by the means most appropriate in his judgment."[67]

Hammarskjöld was faced with two key problems. The first involved serving as an instrument for the United States. The second concerned whether it was appropriate for the secretary-general to involve himself personally, and Hammarskjöld initially contemplated sending a neutral intermediary on his behalf. In the end, much to the surprise of many, he determined that he would personally engage the Chinese and that the task was the responsibility of the United Nations, as the airmen had been captured under the flag of a UN operation. He viewed his engagement as an action independent of any superpower influence, one that would bolster both the power of the office and the stature of the institution. Thus Hammarskjöld in effect decided to "crash the gate" and requested a personal meeting with the Chinese leadership in Peking. Hammarskjöld knew that the Chinese government's desire for international recognition could be used as leverage at the bargaining table. Only days before traveling to Peking, his entry in *Markings* reflects how Hammarskjöld sought spiritual support: "To have faith—not to hesitate!"[68]

After six months of meetings between Hammarskjöld and Chou En-Lai, China's prime minister, the airmen were freed.[69] A letter relating the release was couched in religious language: "Today we accomplished something, God and I. That is to say it was God who built while I stood below with paint-pot shouting."[70] Hammarskjöld's efforts in this crisis are significant both in terms of the unprecedented use of the secretary-generalship in international mediation, which speaks to his initiative and courage, and in the level of diplomatic sensitivity he displayed, which underscores his respect for, and faith in, neutrality and legal justice. His direct but judicious response to the crisis earned him admiration for his unique style in negotiation, which was dubbed the "Peking formula." Finally, his handling of the crisis illustrates the interaction between public service, passionate yet nonaligned activism, and institutional innovation within the confines of international law and bureaucratic mandates. He wrote in *Markings*, "He broke fresh ground—because, and only because, he had the courage to go ahead without asking whether others were following or even understood . . . he had been granted a faith which required no confirmation—a contact with reality, light and intense like the touch of a loved hand: a union in self-surrender without destruction, where his heart was lucid and his mind loving."[71]

Peacekeeping in a Tempest: The Suez Crisis

Hammarskjöld once wrote, "Suez was my third child. Its parents arrived here in a state of great perplexity and some fury. God knows how it will go—but the baby isn't screaming much now, and perhaps with good help, I shall be able to teach it to walk."[72] For Hammarskjöld, the prevention of violence included a commitment to reconciliation. This meant going beyond the cessation of hostilities between countries and moving them, very gradually, to a place of dignified communication.[73] Throughout Hammarskjöld's handling of the Suez Canal crisis, a situation that had the potential to escalate into a much broader conflict, his commitment to peaceful resolution of conflict stood fast.

The conflict arose in 1956 when Egyptian president Nasser nationalized the Suez Canal. This was followed by Israel's ground invasion of Egypt's Sinai Peninsula. Fearing the economic consequences of Nasser's controlling the waterway, the French and British issued a statement demanding the withdrawal of both parties and declared that they would place a security force in the canal zone to separate the combatants. Two days later, when Nasser refused to comply with these demands, the French and British began bombing Egypt. In an effort to defuse the crisis, the Americans in the Security Council proposed a ceasefire that called for an Israeli withdrawal, but France and Britain vetoed the measure and subsequently rebuffed a resolution proposed by the USSR.

Hammarskjöld responded to this diplomatic posturing in a measured but powerful address to the Security Council. The statement followed the legal framework of the charter and demonstrated his commitment to international justice and peace. In it, Hammarskjöld confirmed the transnational goals of the United Nations and his role as secretary-general.

> The principles of the Charter are, by far, greater than the Organization in which they are embodied, and the aims which they are to safeguard are holier than the policies of any single nation or people. As a servant of the Organization, the Secretary-General has the duty to maintain his usefulness by avoiding public stands on conflicts between Member Nations unless and until such an action might help to resolve the conflict. However, the discretion and impartiality required of the Secretary-General may not degenerate into a policy of expedience. . . . A Secretary-General cannot serve on any other assumption than that within the necessary limits of human frailty and honest differences of opinion—all Member nations honour their pledge to observe all Articles of the Charter. . . . Were the Members to consider that another view of the duties of the Secretary-General than the one here stated would better serve the interests of the Organization, it is their obvious right to act accordingly.[74]

Included in the statement was a bold offer by Hammarskjöld to resign. In response, the members of the Security Council, including the Americans, the French, the Soviets, and the Iranians, issued an immediate declaration of confidence. With his elegant speech, Hammarskjöld gracefully steered bellicose posturing toward an endorsement of international vision and a commitment to peace.

Backed by Hammarskjöld, U.S. secretary of state John Foster Dulles proposed mediation between Egypt, Britain, and France. Following concerted negotiations between the foreign ministers, the canal was reopened. On November 1, 1956, in the face of a deadlocked Security Council, the General Assembly stepped forward to pass Resolution A/3256; this measure included a ceasefire and the removal of Egyptian, Israeli, French, and British troops under the oversight of Hammarskjöld himself. In a *Markings* entry of that date, Hammarskjöld quoted Psalm 37, verses 7–8: "Hold thee still in the Lord. . . . Fret not thyself, else shalt thou be moved to evil."

Hammarskjöld felt that there needed to be strong controls that would take the form of a UN force along the armistice lines. Yet he was very wary of any contributions from the Great Powers that could lead to further escalation. He therefore created a force with an autonomous UN command structure (different in kind from the American-led force in Korea). Hammarskjöld supported a move by Canadian representative Lester Pearson to create a UN presence that would oversee the withdrawal of forces and monitor the ceasefire. The General Assembly authorized Hammarskjöld to create the UN Emergency Force to the Middle East (UNEF), which aided in the de-escalation of fighting in the region. He then assumed the responsibility of clearing the Suez Canal, a task that was completed within four months. The resolution of the Suez Canal crisis introduced the word *peacekeeping* into the lexicon of the United Nations. Hammarskjöld wrote in his journal, "Somebody placed the shuttle in your hand: someone who has already arranged the threads. . . . Your own efforts 'did not bring it to pass,' only God—but rejoice if God found a use for your efforts in his work."[75]

The Congo

Dealing with the conflict in the Congo was a particularly trying time in Hammarskjöld's tenure as secretary-general. As usual, Hammarskjöld put a great amount of effort into preemptive diplomacy and pursued a peaceful resolution to the conflict. As the Congo began the painful task of decolonization, it quickly devolved into chaos as violence erupted between the Belgian military leaders and the Congolese forces they directed. The mutiny was followed by widespread rioting and an intervention by the Belgian colonial power to quell the situation. Sensing imminent catastrophe, Prime Minster Patrice Lumumba and President Joseph Kasavubu implored the United Nations to intervene. In response, Hammarskjöld invoked article 99 for the first time in UN history, placing the situation in the Congo at center stage among international issues and making it of highest priority to the Security Council. In an effort to overcome member states' reluctance to act, Hammarskjöld sought to justify direct UN involvement on moral grounds, declaring, "I wish to say this as an act of justice, necessary if this Organization is to live up to the moral standards it professes and if it is to be able to count in the future on the services of those for whom those standards are a creed which it is their duty to uphold in practical action."[76] His remarks were well received; after just four days (an impressive feat in itself) the Security Council approved a peacekeeping force, Opération des Nations Unies au Congo (ONUC), for deployment to the Congo. Under Hammarskjöld's direction, thirty-five hundred troops entered the Congo to assist in the removal of the Belgian forces.

Further complicating the situation in the Congo were moves toward secession by the country's Katanga region under Moise Tshombe. Lumumba requested ONUC presence there to quell the unrest and remove Tshombe, but as the peacekeepers arrived the Security Council passed Resolution 146, declaring the Katanga problem strictly internal. Under certain provisions, UN involvement in domestic conflicts was expressly prohibited, and ONUC balked at removing Tshombe. Hoping for an invitation to Katanga, Hammarskjöld personally escorted four planeloads of UN peacekeepers to the restive province. After tense radio exchanges with Tshombe, his request to land with the forces was granted. With the ONUC forces in place, he began negotiations between the secessionists and the central government. In response, Lumumba, who was disappointed that the United Nations would not remove Tshombe, appealed for weapons and transportation assistance from the Soviets. As Soviet trucks rolled into the Congo, alarmed American politicians initiated countervailing support for President Kasavubu. Highlighting contrasting views of the United Nations' role, and divergent loyalties, the conflict between Kasavubu and Prime Minister Lumumba ended with the latter's dismissal in September 1960.[77]

These political events presented Hammarskjöld with his greatest personal challenge yet, and even threatened the institutional post of secretary-general. Charging that Hammarskjöld's involvement in the Congo, especially his meeting with Tshombe, compromised Soviet interests, Nikita Khrushchev launched a bombastic tirade against the office of the secretary-general on the floor of the General Assembly. The Soviet plan sought to counter the perceived imperialist and partisan sympathies displayed by Hammarskjöld by proposing an administrative change to the United Nations' highest post. The USSR requested a restructuring of the office into a three-person "troika" that, from the Soviet perspective, would ensure "a genuinely democratic organ" and dilute the powers of the office.[78] This proposal gained currency throughout the Communist world, but Hammarskjöld responded, "I shall remain in my post during the term of my office as a servant of the Organization in the interest of all those other nations, as long as they wish me to do so. In this context the representative of the Soviet Union spoke of courage. It is very easy to resign. It is not so easy to stay on. It is very easy to bow to the wishes of a Big Power. It is another matter to resist."[79] The General Assembly responded to his statement with a standing ovation; Hammarskjöld's successful defense against Soviet ambitions once again strengthened his own position and the overall power of the Secretariat. Hammarskjöld responded to the threat to his own personal integrity, the threat to the secretary-generalship, and potentially to international stability by returning to the core moral values of service and neutral integrity. His strong commitment to personal accountability and service enabled him to confront the Soviets publicly, with Khrushchev looking on in the General Assembly. In one of only a few *Markings* entries in 1960, Hammarskjöld turned again to Psalms on Christmas Eve, when he quoted Psalm 4:9: "I will lay me down in peace, and take my rest; for it is thou, Lord, only that makest me dwell in safety." Hammarskjöld's ethical framework, with its core belief in neutral integrity, and his general commitment to the UN charter, compelled him to remain an advocate for the world's less powerful nations.[80]

Ethical Framework as Secretary-General

From close consideration of his private writings, it is clear that the ethical framework revealed in Hammarskjöld's personal musings deeply influenced his interpretation of the UN charter, the role of the secretary-general, and the pursuits of the United Nations. In fact, it is possible to generalize that Hammarskjöld's ethical framework also influenced both his international political agenda and his method of administration.

Ethics and Agenda

One essential social teaching of Lutheranism is the call to bring peace into God's world; here the parallels to Hammarskjöld's own agenda are very clear. This translates to a public moral agenda, or *coram hominibus*, involving devotion to disinterested yet upright neutrality in the service of equality and peace. This creed was evidenced in numerous applications of world politics, and its values strongly promoted the strengthening of international cooperation.[81] Specific examples include his approach to diplomacy (i.e., the "Peking formula"), conflict resolution (the creation of UNEF), and, finally, a dedication to reconciliation (the Suez crisis). James Barros has called the use of the office for international diplomacy as a neutral model of internationalism the "Hammarskjöld model."[82]

Hammarskjöld's view of the United Nations as a moral actor contributed to his remodeling of the Meditation Room just off the lobby of the General Assembly. He was personally involved in even the minor details of the planning and design of the room; he viewed it as "a place where the doors may be open to the infinite lands of thought and prayer."[83]

Hammarskjöld also wrote, "The United Nations stands outside—necessarily outside—all confessions but it is, nevertheless, an instrument of faith."[84] It is this idea of the institution and the office as moral actors and instruments of God's work that constitutes the most transparent connection between Hammarskjöld's personal values and his work at the United Nations. The ethical framework of Hammarskjöld's upbringing fused with the moral guidelines of the UN charter to reveal a moral frame of reference that he relied upon throughout his tenure. This moral framework revealed itself repeatedly in both crises and mundane administrative tasks.

Ethics and Administration

Hammarskjöld's ethical framework forged a deep respect for duty and accountability and nourished a dogged persistence and optimism that carried over to his administration. Those who believe they are on a "mission from God" tend to exhibit more determination in the face of obstacles and conviction, and more confidence in their program, than those inspired by merely secular values. These traits signify the spiritual blueprint of Hammarskjöld's religious path. Lutherans are portrayed as inclined "to take the long view" insofar as they are patient and not prone to notions of their instrumental utility in an apocalyptic transformation.[85] Lutherans are seen as persistent, and Hammarskjöld embodies this characteristic fortitude, as we can see in his statement in the midst of the China situation: "Apparently easy successes with the public are possible for a juggler, but lasting results are achieved only by the patient builder."[86]

Along with the deep commitment to service, Hammarskjöld's ethical framework also brought to his office an energy and enthusiasm that supported the normative goals of justice, peace, and equality. In a speech to the American Association for the United Nations, he compared the United Nations to the quest of Columbus and the journey of the *Santa Maria* and warned against impatience, cynicism, and a sense of futility.[87] This activism, as one observer put it, manifested itself as "Hammarskjöld explored to the fullest extent the powers and responsibilities vested in the secretary-general."[88] Hammarskjöld saw beyond the partisan squabbles and challenges of the Cold War era to focus on the unique opportunities of the United Nations; his moral vision, specifically, allowed him always to consider the international body as a "collection of possibilities."[89]

His ethical framework, resting on the foundation of duty and service, provided Hammarskjöld with determination, vision, and courage. He effectively stood up to threats to his own office during the FBI incident and boldly confronted overt aggression by the French, British, Chinese, Americans, and Soviets during several international crises. His resolve in these situations helped augment the influence and credibility of the United Nations and its highest post. The ties between faith and moral conviction are key elements in Hammarskjöld's decisiveness. Wilder Foote captured this when he observed that Hammarskjöld "was sustained and inspired by pure and firmly founded beliefs and ideals about life and human relationships to which he was true in word and act."[90] His faith in destiny and righteousness brought Hammarskjöld to an interesting place of clarity and deep conviction concerning his motives and international dealings. He himself identified this as "integrity of action." Much of this was rooted in deep faith; "for the sacrificed—in the hour of sacrifice—only one thing counts: faith—only among enemies and skeptics."[91] At the same time, Hammarskjöld's faith, although it served as a constant guide and was ever present in his private musing, was not obvious in his management. His ethical framework never revealed itself as a public crusade.

The Dynamics of Hammarskjöld's Ethical Framework

Despite its central tenets, the evolution and circumstantial flexibility of Hammarskjöld's ethical framework suggests a kind of dynamism. Through his time at the United Nations he moved closer and then further away from his faith. Periods of angst and questioning were followed by moments of surrender and "unity," as he put it in *Markings*. In fact, over time the sacred became more pronounced in both his thoughts and deeds. As is illustrated in his response to McCarthyism and to the China situation, his activism began tentatively. In these early measures, Hammarskjöld drew strongly from the legal framework of the UN charter. At the same time, his early personal writings, as expressed in *Markings,* are hopeful. In 1956 he wrote, "Do what you can—and the task will rest lightly in your hand, so lightly that you will be able to look forward to more difficult tests which may be awaiting you." "To love life and men as God loves them—for the sake of their infinite possibilities." Generally, biblical references throughout his first term as secretary-general express this optimism, as in his reference to John 3:8: "And the *light* shineth in darkness, and the darkness comprehended it not."[92]

From 1958 to 1961, however, *Markings* entries evince a darker tone, as Hammarskjöld lamented a loss of spiritual resolve. During the final years of his tenure and, sadly, his life, a preoccupation with suffering, blood, even death, was not uncommon. A 1961 entry quotes Psalm 109:25: "Help me, O Lord my God: O save me according to Thy mercy." On August 2, 1961, the day that the constitutional crisis was resolved in the Congo, he quoted Psalm 60:2: "Thou has moved the land, and divided it; heal the sores thereof, for it shaketh." Aulén observes that in the later writing there is a more sullen tendency, and that the *Markings* entries of 1959 are full of references to "faith," while the poems and entries of 1960 and 1961 are ostensibly prayers. In the last three years of his tenure, personal authority and resolve came to guide Hammarskjöld's policy actions. Over time, Hammarskjöld's spiritual quest more readily engaged internationalism, and his skill and moral fortitude grew with each crisis.

Hammarskjöld's words written for the dedication of the UN Meditation Room illustrate the seamless transition his ethical framework made from the world of spirituality to the UN mandate and world politics: "The stone in the middle . . . is a reminder of that cornerstone of endurance and faith on which all human endeavor must be based. The material of the stone leads our thoughts to the necessity for choice between destruction and construction, between war and peace."[93] The combination of Hammarskjöld's moral convictions, his respect for the office, and the mandates found in the UN charter also produced his activism. It seems fair to say that the strength of Hammarskjöld's spiritual calling, while clear, is tempered in his administrative duties.[94] The concept of answering a calling and saying "yes" to a moral obligation to service to others is a clear and guiding principle that took Hammarskjöld all the way into the Congo. But did he, in Gordenker's terms, "consider himself 'recruited from the angels'?"[95] Hammarskjöld addressed this very matter on several occasions, and it is clear that he did not see himself as an "angel" per se, in that he did not claim spiritual power independent of his faith. In his first dated journal entry as secretary-general, he wrote, "God spake once, and twice I have also heard the same: that power belongeth unto God." In another famous edict, he answered Gordenker by paraphrasing Paul's first letter to the Corinthians: "Not I, but God in me."[96]

Conclusion

As we saw in chapter 1 of this volume, the authority of the office of secretary-general can derive from the individual characteristics of the officeholder.

Hammarskjöld's ethical framework clearly influenced his service, and it greatly enhanced the influence of the office. Conor Cruise O'Brien identifies the role of moral principles in Hammarskjöld's statesmanship: "Hammarskjöld more than anyone had given the United Nations a focus of moral authority which would attract an international loyalty, and used it in the cause of peace and justice."[97] In a 1998 interview, when Kofi Annan was asked which secretary-general he admired most, he replied, "Hammarskjöld," explaining, "I liked his fortitude, his vision, his principled and moral stand on issues."[98] Furthermore, Hammarskjöld contributed significantly to the overall power, legitimacy, and mandate of the United Nations. In a 2001 article Annan again discussed the influence of Hammarskjöld's administration and moral convictions:

> His life and his death, his words and his action, have done more to shape public expectations of the office, and indeed of the Organization, than those of any other man or woman in its history. His wisdom and his modesty, his unimpeachable integrity and his single-minded devotion to duty, have set a standard for all servants of the international community—and especially, of course, for his successors—which is simply impossible to live up to. There can be no better rule of thumb for a Secretary-General, as he approaches each new challenge or crisis, than to ask himself: "How would Hammarskjöld have handled this?"[99]

Hammarskjöld was a brilliant diplomat, his actions significantly guided international politics, and his legacy set a clear moral tone that rested firmly on his own principled convictions. At the same time, one should not forget that outside his moral convictions, he possessed many qualities that shaped his leadership and legacy. Many remember him as a brilliant diplomat with a unique combination of legal cunning, personal charisma, and professional grace.

Finding bridges between ethics and leadership is a delicate undertaking in many respects. To establish an individual's primary ethical commitments is in itself challenging. This is further complicated by the fact that human value systems are impermanent and prone to transformation. Another challenge lies in discerning how these private moral convictions may reveal themselves in the very visible administrations of a secretary-general. In addition, Hammarskjöld is a difficult study, for he persistently protected his private life and, as an expert statesman, veiled his personal convictions. Yet, in the case of Hammarskjöld, these convictions are the basis for public service; they charted the path toward his activism as secretary-general and helped pave a moral corridor for the realization of the hopefulness embodied in the United Nations.

Notes

1. Henry P. Van Dusen, *Dag Hammarskjöld: The Statesman and His Faith* (New York: Harper and Row, 1967), xii.

2. There is some controversy over the accuracy of W. H. Auden's translation of *Vagmarken*. Critics assert that Auden took liberties with the text and embellished in several places; they also claim that the title itself should have been translated as "Waymarks," as adopted from Jeremiah 31:21 in the King James Bible. See Warren Hoge, "Swedes Dispute Translation of a U.N. Legend's Book," *New York Times,* May 22, 2005.

3. Hammarskjöld to Leif Belfrage, cited in Sven Stolpe, *Dag Hammarskjöld: A Spiritual Portrait* (New York: Charles Scribner's Sons, 1966), 5.

4. Address at luncheon given by the American Political Science Association, Washington, DC, September 11, 1953, cited in Wilder Foote, ed., *Servant of Peace: A Selection of the Speeches and Statements of Dag Hammarskjöld* (New York: Harper and Row, 1962), 35.

5. Dag Hammarskjöld, *Markings,* trans. W. H. Auden and Leif Sjöberg (New York: Knopf, 1964), 92.

6. Other relevant works include Andrew W. Cordier, "Motivations and Methods of Dag Hammarskjöld," in *Paths to World Order,* ed. Andrew W. Cordier and Kenneth Maxwell (New York: Columbia University Press, 1967); Emery Kelen, ed., *Hammarskjöld: The Political Man* (New York: Funk and Wagnalls, 1968). For a direct discussion of Hammarskjöld's "political ethics," see Manuel Fröhlich, *Dag Hammarskjöld und die Vereinten Nationen: Die politische Ethik des UNO-Generalsekretärs* (Paderborn: Ferdinand Schöningh, 2002); an English translation is forthcoming as *Dag Hammarskjöld and the United Nations: The Political Ethics of the UN Secretary-General.*

7. Examples include Emery Kelen, *Hammarskjöld* (New York: G. P. Putnam's Sons, 1966); Joseph P. Lash, *Dag Hammarskjöld: Custodian of Brush Fire Peace* (Garden City, NY: Doubleday, 1961); Brian Urquhart, *Hammarskjöld* (New York: Knopf, 1972); and Mark W. Zacher, *Dag Hammarskjöld's United Nations* (New York: Columbia University Press, 1970).

8. Written for Edward R. Murrow's radio program *This I Believe,* and published in a book of the same name in 1954 by Simon and Schuster; reprinted in Andrew W. Cordier and Wilder Foote, eds., *Public Papers of the Secretaries-General of the United Nations,* vol. 2, *Dag Hammarskjöld, 1953–1956* (New York: Columbia University Press, 1972); and Foote, *Servant of Peace,* 194.

9. Stolpe, *Dag Hammarskjöld,* 19, 16.

10. Lash, *Dag Hammarskjöld*, 24, 20.

11. Quoted in Stolpe, *Dag Hammarskjöld*, 25.

12. Lash, *Dag Hammarskjöld*, 23.

13. Reprinted in Foote, *Servant of Peace*, 23–24.

14. Quoted in Gustaf Aulén, *Dag Hammarskjöld's White Book: An Analysis of Markings* (Philadelphia: Fortress Press, 1969), 32. Hammarskjöld engaged in a continual dialogue and correspondence with Schweitzer until his death.

15. Lash, *Dag Hammarskjöld*, 23.

16. Stolpe, *Dag Hammarskjöld*, 32.

17. In fact, Hammarskjöld remarked on occasion about the lack of real substance in these early friendships, and their shallow conversations. Ibid., 38.

18. Hammarskjöld, *Markings*, 85.

19. P. O. Ekelöf, quoted in Hammarskjöld, *Markings*, xi.

20. James Barros, "The Importance of Secretaries-General of the United Nations," in *Dag Hammarskjöld Revisited: The Secretary-General as a Force in World Politics*, ed. Robert S. Jordan (Durham, NC: Carolina Academic Press, 1983), 37.

21. Urquhart, *Hammarskjöld*, 24.

22. As discussed in chapter 1 of this volume, there is no assumption that all Lutherans will accept these principles and act in a specific way. This is only to suggest Hammarskjöld's interpretation of such moral guidelines.

23. Hammarskjöld, "Old Creeds in a New World," written for Edward R. Murrow's radio program *This I Believe*, November 1953, cited in Cordier and Foote, *Public Papers*, 2:195.

24. Mark U. Edwards Jr., "Characteristically Lutheran Leanings?" *Dialog: A Journal of Theology* 41 (2002): 50.

25. Hammarskjöld, *Markings*, 56.

26. Thomas A. Nairn, "The Christian Moral Life: Roman Catholic and Lutheran Perspectives," *Let's Talk* 6 (2001), available at www.mcsletstalk.org/v6n23.htm.

27. UN Press Release SG/360, December 22, 1953, cited in Cordier and Foote, *Public Papers*, 2:208.

28. Henry Van Dusen argues that Hammarskjöld's spiritual life is best understood as a trinity of public servant, private man, and inner person. Van Dusen, *Dag Hammarskjöld*, 6.

29. Urquhart, *Hammarskjöld*, 24–25.

30. Aulén, *Dag Hammarskjöld's White Book*, 119.

31. Martin Luther, *The Freedom of a Christian*, in *Luther's Works*, American ed., 55 vols. (Philadelphia: Fortress Press/Concordia Publishing House, 1955), 31:34.

32. Hammarskjöld, *Markings*, 130.

33. See Hjalmar Sundén, *Krsihusmeditationer I Dag Hammarskjöld' Vagmarken* (Stockholm: Verbum, 1966), 73; Aulén, *Dag Hammarskjöld's White Book*, 125; and Van Dusen, *Dag Hammarskjöld*, 179.

34. The question of the influence of mysticism on Hammarskjöld is controversial. Gustaf Aulén points out that religious faith for Hammarskjöld was dialectic. For further discussion on the influence of mysticism, see Aulén, *Dag Hammarskjöld's White Book*, 32–57.

35. This section was greatly enhanced by conversations with Michael Kuchinsky.

36. Thomas À Kempis, *The Imitation of Christ*, trans. Aloysius Croft and Harold Bolton (Milwaukee: Bruce Publishing Company, 1949), 15, available at www.ccel.org/ccel/kempis/imitation.html.

37. Written by Hammarskjöld as part of Edward R. Murrow's *This I Believe* radio program, cited in Hammarskjöld, *Markings*, vii.

38. Urquhart, *Hammarskjöld*, 23.

39. UN Press Release SG/360, December 22, 1953.

40. The figures used in this work, and the related discussion, are adapted from Alynna J. Lyon, "Moral Motives and Policy Actions: The Case of Dag Hammarskjöld at the United Nations," *Public Integrity* 9 (2006–7): 79–95.

41. Several sources indicate that Hammarskjöld was unaware that he was being considered for the position of secretary-general. See Urquhart, *Hammarskjöld*, 13.

42. Reported in Andrew W. Cordier and Wilder Foote, eds. *Public Papers of the Secretaries-General of the United Nations*, vol. 5, *Dag Hammarskjöld, 1960–1961* (New York: Columbia University Press, 1975), 573.

43. Dorothy V. Jones, "The World Outlook of Dag Hammarskjöld," in *Ethics and Statecraft: The Moral Dimension of International Affairs*, 2d ed., ed. Cathal Nolan (Westport, CT: Praeger, 2004), 141.

44. Stolpe, *Dag Hammarskjöld*, 50, 69–79.

45. Urquhart, *Hammarskjöld*, 23, 13.

46. See Edwards, "Characteristically Lutheran Learnings?" 52, for a complete discussion.

47. Hammarskjöld, *Markings*, 90.

48. Aulén, *Dag Hammarskjöld's White Book*, 16–17.

49. Hammarskjöld, *Markings*, 89.

50. Stolpe, *Dag Hammarskjöld*, 80.

51. Hammarskjöld, *Markings*, 157.

52. Quoted in Stolpe, *Dag Hammarskjöld*, 57.

53. Ibid., 55–56.

54. Dag Hammarskjöld, statement to the press on arrival at International Airport, New York, April 9, 1953, UN Press Release SG/287.

55. W. H. Auden, "Foreword," in Hammarskjöld, *Markings*, xvii; address to the American Association for the United Nations, September 14, 1953, in Cordier and Foote, *Public Papers*, 2:94.

56. Lecture delivered to the congregation at Oxford University, May 30, 1961, in Hammarskjöld, *Markings*, xix.

57. Phrase used by Hammarskjöld in his address before the Second Assembly of the World Council of Churches, Evanston, Illinois, August 20, 1954, cited in Foote, *Servant of Peace,* 56.

58. Andrew W. Cordier, "The Political Role of the United Nations Secretary General," speech to the International Fellows Program at Columbia University, April 20, 1964.

59. Dag Hammarskjöld, "The United Nations—Its Ideology and Activities," speech to the Indian Council of World Affairs, February 3, 1956, UN Department of Public Information Pamphlet, April 1956, 659.

60. Security Council Official Records, Eleventh Year, 751st meeting, October 31, 1956.

61. Zacher, *Dag Hammarskjöld's United Nations,* 22.

62. Here he refers to the words of Erik Axel Karlfeldt. Statement before the plenary session of the General Assembly, April 10, 1953, cited in Foote, *Servant of Peace,* 29–30.

63. Zacher, *Dag Hammarskjöld's United Nations,* 13, 23.

64. Lash, *Dag Hammarskjöld,* 49.

65. "Transcript of Background Press Conference on Reports on Personnel Policy and Administrative Tribunal Awards," New York, November 3, 1953, cited in Cordier and Foote, *Public Papers,* 2:147–49.

66. "The Weapons of the Secretariat," message to the United Nations States Day at Geneva, December 4, 1953, in ibid., 2:192–93.

67. United Nations General Assembly Resolution 906, December 10, 1954.

68. Hammarskjöld, *Markings,* 102.

69. It is interesting to note that the Chinese Embassy in Stockholm several times requested information concerning the date of Hammarskjöld's birthday; the American airmen were released within days of that date. In fact, the United Nations claims, "According to Chou En-lai, he timed the release of the remaining eleven prisoners as a way of maintaining his personal friendship with Hammarskjöld and as a 50th birthday gift," www.un.org/depts/dhl/dag/time1955.htm.

70. Cited in Stolpe, *Dag Hammarskjöld,* 36.

71. Hammarskjöld, *Markings,* 110.

72. Hammarskjöld to Bo Beskow, quoted in Stolpe, *Dag Hammarskjöld,* 82.

73. Jones, "World Outlook of Dag Hammarskjöld," 134.

74. Security Council Official Records, Eleventh Year, 751st meeting, October 31, 1956.

75. Hammarskjöld, *Markings,* 141, 143.

76. Dag Hammarskjöld, "Statement of UN Operations in the Congo Before the General Assembly," October 17, 1960, cited in Foote, *Servant of Peace,* 321.

77. Lumumba was later assassinated, and the Congo ultimately fell into the hands of Joseph Mobutu.

78. Nikita Khrushchev, "Speech Delivered at the Fifteenth Session of the General Assembly," September 23, 1960.

79. Address to the United Nations General Assembly, October 3, 1960, in Cordier and Foote, *Public Papers,* 5:200–201.

80. Further research could explore his efforts to calm crises in Guatemala, Jordan, Lebanon, Hungary, Tunisia, as well as Cambodia and Thailand.

81. For an overview of Lutheran ethics, see Nairn, "Christian Moral Life." See also Karen L. Bloomquist and John R. Stumme, eds., *The Promise of Lutheran Ethics* (Minneapolis: Fortress Press, 1998).

82. Barros, "Importance of Secretaries-General of the United Nations," 37.

83. Foote, *Servant of Peace,* 160.

84. Term used by Hammarskjöld in his address before the Second Assembly of the World Council of Churches, in Foote, *Servant of Peace,* 56.

85. Edwards, "Characteristically Lutheran Leanings?" 57.

86. Dag Hammarskjöld, "Statements at Johns Hopkins Commencement Ceremonies," June 1955, in Cordier and Foote, *Public Papers,* 2:507.

87. Address to American Association for the United Nations in cooperation with the New York University Institute for Review of United Nations Affairs, New York, September 14, 1953.

88. Mongi Slim, "Hammarskjöld's Quest for Peace," in *The Quest for Peace: The Dag Hammarskjöld Memorial Lectures,* ed. Andrew W. Cordier and Wilder Foote (New York: Columbia University Press, 1965), 5.

89. Jones, "World Outlook of Dag Hammarskjöld," 143.

90. Foote, *Servant of Peace,* 13.

91. Hammarskjöld, *Markings,* 150–51.

92. Ibid., 124, 127, 128.

93. "A Room of Quiet," in Cordier and Foote, *Public Papers,* 2:711.

94. Zacher, *Dag Hammarskjöld's United Nations,* 46.

95. Leon Gordenker, *The UN Secretary-General and the Maintenance of Peace* (New York: Columbia University Press, 1967), 334.

96. Hammarskjöld, *Markings,* 102, 90.

97. Conor Cruise O'Brien, *To Katanga and Back* (New York: Simon and Schuster, 1962), 14–15.

98. Kofi Annan, "Conversations with History," Institute of International Studies, University of California, Berkeley, April 1998, available at http://globetrotter. berkeley.edu/UN/Annan/annan-con2.html.

99. Kofi Annan, "How Would Hammarskjöld Have Handled This?" *UN Chronicle* No. 4 (2001): 44–47, based on a lecture Annan gave on September 6, 2001, in Uppsala, Sweden.

5

U THANT
Buddhism in Action

A. WALTER DORN

The election of U Thant as secretary-general on November 3, 1961, six weeks after the tragic death of Dag Hammarskjöld, was a novelty in international relations. U Thant (pronounced Oo Thawnt)[1] was the first non-European secretary-general in the United Nations or the League of Nations, and the first from a newly independent or developing nation. His country, Burma, had only gained its independence in 1948, three years after the founding of the United Nations, and the nation's foreign service was little more than a decade old. But, with Thant's active participation, Burma had already made a mark on the international scene as one of the founders of the Non-Aligned Movement in 1955, a new experiment in the Cold War period. Because of both national and personal characteristics, Thant was acceptable to both sides of the Cold War and to the newly emerging states that were about to form a majority in the General Assembly. The U.S. ambassador to the United Nations, Adlai Stevenson, commented at the time that Thant was "the only human being out of a hundred nations represented at the UN who was acceptable to everybody."[2]

For many Westerners, the greatest novelty of the new UN leader was that he was a Buddhist—and a devout one at that. Western newspapers and magazines featured this aspect of his life, as in a cover story in the *New York Times Magazine* titled "The Meditation of U Thant" and a book about his cultural and religious background.[3] Buddhism was an important part of Thant's upbringing, and it strongly shaped his worldview, his ethical principles, and his actions as secretary-general. But because he did not explain his official decisions using religious reasoning, the precise influence of religion in specific situations is sometimes difficult to discern. However, the overall influence is certain. He himself writes in his memoirs, "to understand my conception of the role of the Secretary-General, the nature of my religious and cultural background must be understood."[4]

There are a great many examples to illustrate the influence of religion on Thant's ethics and behavior. This chapter examines his religious and moral values and evaluates the extent to which these influenced him, especially as he dealt with the toughest challenges facing any UN chief: the ethical dilemmas. In particular, seven dilemmas will be considered: (1) use of force, (2) intervention versus nonintervention, (3) impartiality versus neutrality, (4) independent versus dependent office, (5) private versus professional interests, (6) idealism versus realism, and (7) the sacred/secular divide. The chapter will analyze how Thant used his ethical framework to deal with the major challenges he faced in his life and while in office.

East Meets West: A Life Story in Brief

Thant was born in the small town of Pantanaw in British-controlled Burma (then part of India) on January 22, 1909. He was the eldest of four sons of a relatively prosperous rice miller and a very devout Buddhist mother. He attended the National High School in Pantanaw and University College in Rangoon. Like many Burmese youths, he spent some time in a Buddhist monastery, though formal religiosity was not a trait in his studious and independent-minded character. He was an avid reader, and school friends nicknamed him "the Philosopher." Unfortunately, Thant had to cut short his college education because of the death of his father. As the eldest son, he had to take responsibility for the family, a burden increased because a cousin had swindled most of the family's inheritance. He became a schoolteacher.

At age twenty Thant won the All-Burma Translation Competition, and at twenty-two he succeeded his friend U Nu as principal of his old high school. Besides teaching and administration, he translated several English works into Burmese, including a book on the League of Nations. One of his role models was Sir Stafford Cripps, the socialist British politician with strong religious (Christian) convictions, who would later bring unsuccessful independence proposals to neighboring India.[5] Thant also admired the nationalist leaders Eamon de Valera of Ireland, Sun Yat-sen of China, and Mahatma Gandhi of India.[6]

During the Japanese occupation of Burma (1942–45), Thant served as a member of the Pantanaw Administrative Council, though he spent three miserable months in bomb-ridden Rangoon as secretary of the Educational Reorganizing Committee. He commented privately that the Japanese system was much worse than the British one, though many Burmese at first welcomed the Japanese. He was under a Japanese "adviser" who actually "ruled," so he was glad when he could return to Pantanaw. Once there, Thant refused to implement an edict to make Japanese compulsory in schools, and he cooperated with the growing resistance. At one point he was under imminent threat of arrest but avoided this fate after being fore-warned by former students and a friendly Japanese soldier.[7] Though not a major participant in the Burmese resistance, after the war he accepted a request from resistance leaders to write the history of their struggle.

As Burma prepared for independence in 1948, Thant became press director for the government in waiting. He left Pantanaw to join his old friend U Nu, who became Burma's prime minister upon independence. Thant's farewell address as principal to the students of the National High School was remembered fondly: "In this world, try to be both good and able. If you do not become able men, at least try to be good men. The country has no use for able but bad men."[8] To the students and staff, Thant was an example of what he preached: able as well as good.

One of his jobs early in the Cold War was to review and possibly cen-sor superpower propaganda for the Burmese government, an opportunity that led him to observe that both sides were guilty of "vast oversimplifica-tion," falsely stereotyping and dehumanizing the other.[9] China's civil war also encroached upon Burma when elements of the battered Kuomintang army took sanctuary within Burma's borders.

More menacingly, Burma was experiencing a civil war of its own. When the Karen insurgency began in 1948, Thant risked his life to go behind Karen lines in an attempt to negotiate peace. Though he was respected by Karen leaders, nothing came from that mission. In a great personal tragedy, his hometown, including his family properties, was burned to the ground in 1949. He was in Rangoon when the insurgents pushed the front to within four miles of the capital before falling back. This trying experi-ence with secessionist forces was to have a major influence on his thinking and, quite possibly, his later actions as UN secretary-general.

In 1954 he became secretary to Prime Minister U Nu, and in 1955 accompanied him to the Bandung Conference, where the Non-Aligned Movement was formed. In Burma and abroad, Thant acquired a scrupu-lous reputation as someone free from corruption and selfish motives. In 1957 U Nu appointed Thant Burma's permanent representative to the

United Nations. As a new ambassador, he stated earnestly, "It is in the UN that most of us have pinned our only hope for the future."[10] In 1961, as the conflict in the Congo became a quagmire for the United Nations, Thant was named chairman of the Congo Conciliation Commission. After Hammarskjöld died suddenly in a plane crash on September 17, 1961, while trying to negotiate peace in the Congo, Thant (as a leader of the Non-Aligned Movement) became involved in the lengthy selection of a new secretary-general. But when he himself was touted as a candidate, he withdrew from the negotiations.

Thant's activities, achievements, and disappointments as UN secretary-general are described throughout this chapter, so they are not repeated here. The chapter examines his character, ethics, and religious beliefs, before analyzing some of the ethical dilemmas he faced.

Personal and Ethical Character

Virtually all the people who knew and worked closely with Thant in the United Nations laud him as an example, if not an ideal, of an ethical and moral person. Some also speak of him as a spiritual figure, possessing saint-like qualities. For instance, Robert Muller, the executive director of the office of the secretary-general (1970–72), described him as "a master in the art of living," a "modern monk," and a "great ethical statesman."[11] No doubt Thant possessed humility, integrity, equanimity, serenity, and many spiritual qualities in abundant measure. In account after account, his kindness, consideration and understanding for his fellow humans are much in evidence. Muller gave him the epithet "U Thant the Kind," along with "Lie the Robust" and "Hammarskjöld the Magnificent."[12] Apparently Thant never showed anger, almost never complained about people, and only very occasionally showed frustration, though the job was, no doubt, extremely frustrating at times.

Humility

Thant's humility was legendary, and he probably deserves the title of the most humble secretary-general to date. His actions show that he truly pursued neither power nor privilege, placing the common good above self-interest in his work. To begin with, he was reluctant to take the post of secretary-general. When approached, he did not advocate his candidacy or even show interest.[13] Only when he emerged as the only acceptable candidate to all did he finally agree to serve. Accepting reappointment in 1962, he insisted that it be for a term starting in 1961, thus shortening his tenure by a year. Similarly, in 1966, he declared that he would not stand for re-election, frequently repeating, "there is no indispensable man."[14] But under sustained pressure he finally agreed to a second term, to universal acclaim.[15]

Days after first taking office in 1961, the Burmese government offered him the nation's second-highest title, but he declined the honor, and in September 1965, when the Norwegian ambassador visited him to tell him that he was the choice of the Norwegian Nobel Committee for the Nobel Peace Prize, he humbly remarked, "Is not the Secretary-General merely doing his job when he works for peace?"[16] He recorded his pleasure when UNICEF was announced a month later as the award winner, though Thant's undersecretary, Ralph Bunche, himself a Nobel laureate, murmured that it was a "gross injustice to U Thant."[17]

Thant was a simple as well as a humble man, uncomfortable in lavish surroundings and happy in the presence of children. He remarked that he preferred the rustic environment of the countryside to the majestic halls of heads of state, like the "chandeliered Elysée Palace with its resplendent *garde républicain*."[18] He usually avoided the red carpet treatment while traveling. When President Johnson offered Air Force One for an important trip to South Asia in 1965, Thant declined, saying that he "would feel awkward with a party of only five in such a big plane."[19]

Thant did not mind most types of criticism. If it was free from spite, he even appreciated it. He told a biographer, "At the UN we are the regular recipients of an immense flow of criticism and admonition . . . a form of stimulus which we should welcome, although, of course, it can, like all good things, be overdone."[20] Shortly after his retirement, he read an academic paper titled "U Thant and His Critics" that analyzed the main criticisms against him.[21] He asked the author, Alan James, to send him a hundred copies, presumably for sharing with friends and former colleagues.[22]

He usually took criticism in silence. To the frustration of colleagues, he often refused even to defend himself. For instance, when he was accused of being indifferent to the plight of Soviet Jews, he refused to divulge that, in fact, he had quietly helped hundreds of them by passing petitions to the Soviet government.[23] Brian Urquhart observed that he was "remarkably free of the desire to take credit, to justify himself or to blame others when things went wrong."[24] When Thant willingly absorbed unfair criticism from many quarters after the 1967 war, Urquhart regretted his boss's refusal to "pass the buck" to a disunited Security Council or to the parties themselves. Thant "strongly resisted" any efforts to correct the record at the time (though in his memoirs he did so).[25] He allowed himself to be a scapegoat. What he said about the United Nations could also apply to himself personally: The United Nations "provides an invaluable repository and a safe target for blame and criticism which might otherwise be directed elsewhere."[26] He was sometimes called the "human shock absorber."[27]

Apparently he strove to take criticism with total personal detachment. If criticism was fair, he would admit to making a mistake, as he did after publicly (and uncharacteristically) referring to Moise Tshombe and his fellow secessionists as a "bunch of clowns."[28] If criticism was unfair and deliberate, he would try to absorb it. He would remain silent, but insiders knew that it sometimes smouldered within him. Urquhart and Kurt Waldheim even blamed this lack of outer reaction as a source of ill health. After his third year in office, he developed a peptic ulcer, which might have been stress-related. His chef de cabinet C. V. Narasimhan ventures, "His total serenity in his personal relations was no doubt the cause of his ulcers; although his doctors advised him to 'explode' now and again, it was inconceivable that he would, even to save his health."[29] Later in his term, he also began to suffer from acute fatigue.[30] He died on November 15, 1974, after a two-year struggle with cancer, probably related to his regular cigar smoking (he particularly liked the Burmese cheroot).

Thant's main vehicle for dealing with frustrations was meditation. His daily practice included extending "good will towards all living creatures." In Buddhist fashion, he tried to let go of the narrow and tightly held concepts of "me and mine" and establish detachment. The extent to which he achieved this is evident in the remarkable statement, "I do not particularly worry about my own life. . . . I do not particularly distinguish between the lives of my own children and the lives of the children of other people. Nor do I distinguish between Burmese lives and American lives and Russian lives and Chinese lives."[31]

Integrity

Stories of Thant's integrity, like his humility, are abundant, but only one short anecdote will be described here. When the manuscript of June Bingham's biography *U Thant: The Search for Peace* was complete, she offered him the typescript for review. He declined, saying, "if I make a small change, then I would be implicated in writing it." The author retorted, "but no one would know." She reports his stern look as he replied, "I would." His first biography was left unreviewed and uncensored.[32]

Thant's strong moral sense often overrode his political sense, Urquhart wrote, causing Thant "to do what he believed was right, even if it was politically disadvantageous to him." Thant's advisers also said that when he followed advice offered to him, he "took complete responsibility for his actions, regardless of their outcome."[33] He would not blame others for decisions he had made. Thant's goal was simple and to a great extent selfless: "All my faith and all my efforts are unhesitatingly pledged to maintaining and developing this Organization as an indispensable centre for harmonizing the actions of nations in the attainment of our common ends."[34]

Though keenly interested in promoting the common good, Thant did not aspire to political leadership. In Burma he deliberately chose not to become a politician, though many opportunities lay open to him. Close friends like U Nu were leaders in political parties, but he never joined one, neither before nor after independence. U Thaung, Thant's third younger brother, commented that politics "meant cliques, disruptions, power-craze. . . . U Thant detested politics, although it would not be wrong to say that there could not have been more than a handful in Burma who studied as much politics and public affairs as he."[35] Instead of politics, he pursued a life of public service as an educator and civil servant, remaining as far as possible from the grasp of corrupt politics. To his credit, Thant attained the highest positions of civil administration in Burma and arguably the world.

Simplicity and Detachment

Thant's simplicity and detachment were cause for both appreciation and apprehension. He often responded to others with silence, not of the cold and callous type but in a kind and loving manner that the Buddhists sometimes call "noble silence." For this he was known as the "Bronze Buddha" among Secretariat officials.[36] Understandably, this sometimes gave rise to frustration.[37] Ambassador George Ignatieff of Canada admired Thant's "serenity and self-discipline" but wanted more engagement when discussing important and controversial issues like the peacekeeping force in the Sinai prior to the Six-Day War, in which Canada had a substantial number of troops. "When I tried to reason with him, he just smiled in his gentle, enigmatic way, without any indication whether or not I was getting through to him. Being an emotional Slav, I found this attitude exasperating . . . he never showed any reaction, not even impatience, and never said yes or no. For a while it got so bad I could hardly bear to speak to him."[38] That was a serious problem, coming from the ambassador of a country as supportive of the United Nations as Canada.

Despite his propensity to silence, he was an eloquent speaker, a prolific writer, and someone who enjoyed humor in life. He appreciated the "funny stories, wit and good jokes [that] his staff like to pass to him each day."[39] Urquhart, however, complained of Thant's "school-boy jokes," in which he had "laboriously become word perfect." Furthermore, Urquhart writes that Thant was, "by Western standards, in some ways rather simple-minded," especially when compared to the brilliant Hammarskjöld. Certainly Thant's approach to issues was less complicated, less nuanced. He held strong views of right and wrong. Urquhart writes, "His stewardship had none of the flair or high personal style of Hammarskjöld, but his undertakings were just as courageous."[40]

Equanimity

Thant's Buddhist ideal led him to seek equanimity under all circumstances. As an example of this practice, Thant pointed to the sudden death in 1962 of his only son, thrown from a bus in Rangoon, as a tragedy he took with "minimal emotional reaction."[41] His first words on hearing the news were said to have been, "My poor wife!"[42] A similar story arises from another great tragedy in his life. When his home village of Pantanaw was burned to the ground during the height of the Karen insurgency of 1949, his wife lamented, "Oh, my house!" Thant exclaimed, "Oh, my books!"[43]

A colleague in Burma, Dr. Maung Maung, joked about Thant's dispassion by comparing him with U Nu: "When Nu fell in love, he wrote poetry aflame with emotion and dedicated them, one and all, to the dear lady. When Thant fell in love, he wrote letters to the editor, and articles and a new book." U Nu was also a devout Buddhist who wanted to make Buddhism the state religion of Burma (to which Thant and others successfully raised strong objections), but Thant's temperament was obviously quite different from Nu's.[44]

Visitors to Thant's office frequently remarked about his "strength of quiet dignity" and his composure. New York City mayor Abraham Beame wrote, "In stormy times, he was an island of calm in a sea of controversy.

His meditative ways helped him to maintain the neutrality so necessary to sustaining the confidence of differing nations."[45] Thant explains, "I was taught to control my emotions through a process of concentration and meditation. Of course, being human, and not yet having reached the state of *arahant* or *arhat* (one who attains perfect enlightenment), I cannot completely control my emotions, but I must say that I am not easily excited or excitable."[46]

Religious Beliefs: Buddhism and Beyond

Thant described himself as "a spiritual person above all else."[47] To many who knew him, Thant not only lived but exemplified his faith. Some used spiritual words to describe him, such as Indian diplomat Lakhan Mehrotra, who felt a "spiritual glow" around the man: "One had to see him to believe what was preserved of the spiritual strength he carried within him." UN worker France Vacher observed "holiness surrounding him."[48] Canadian ambassador Ignatieff wrote, "My experience led me to the conclusion that I was communing with a mystic, who by constant self-discipline had attained a degree of self-control rarely encountered."[49] Thant cared deeply about his religion, Buddhism, but he also held to a wider set of spiritual beliefs about the human condition that were entirely compatible with his faith.

Buddhism

Thant was not ostentatious or proselytizing about his faith, but on direct questioning he would share his beliefs frankly. UN official Robert Muller was a Christian whose close contact with Thant led him to a growing appreciation of Buddhism and spirituality. Thant was pleased to share his ideas with Muller, who later wrote several books describing and praising Thant's faith and philosophy of life.[50]

Publicly, it was difficult to get Thant to speak about Buddhism, but in one instance, at an international teach-in at the University of Toronto, he made a short and succinct statement about his faith and its application to international affairs.[51] Thant was surprisingly strident, almost fundamentalist, in introducing Buddhism. He conveyed none of the subtlety and searching mystical quality that were characteristic of Hammarskjöld. Buddhism, Thant stated, was "the supreme way to spiritual perfection."

It offered the world "absolute truth" (*Dhamma*) and was a "rational explanation of the mysteries of life." These bold remarks echoed an earlier statement: "I believe that Buddhism as a religion is superior to other religions." With humility, he continued, "but this conviction does not blind me to the fact that there are hundreds of millions of people who believe otherwise."[52]

His description of Buddhist principles at the Toronto teach-in and in his memoirs is clear, unequivocal, and inspired: "Buddhism teaches, above all, a universal compassion to be extended to all living beings, irrespective of their status, race or creed." He explained that all beings deserve compassion because they all suffer, and that wrong actions are the result of human ignorance. All beings are interdependent because *Dhamma* applies to everything. Thant so firmly believed in *karma*, the principle of reciprocal action (cause and effect), that he regarded doing harm to another as folly. "Whatsoever he does to another he does in effect to himself." Furthermore, if "each of us were to realize" the principle of *karma*, he claimed, the world would become free of crime, war, and injustice.[53]

Buddhism advocates the practice of compassion (*karuna*) and good will (*metta*) to all. The practice should be done "impartially and spontaneously, expecting nothing in return, not even appreciation," wrote Thant.[54] A true Buddhist is "expected to pray for the happiness of all human beings." This he did on a daily basis.

Violence to any living creature was to be renounced in thought as well as deed.[55] So should the three cardinal vices in Buddhism: craving or greed, hatred or anger, and illusion or ignorance.[56] They are to be replaced with the four cardinal virtues: *metta* (including charity), *karuna, mudita* (sympathetic joy), and *upekka* (equanimity or equilibrium).[57] The *Dhammapada*, the most widely cited Buddhist scripture, states: "Never in the world is hate appeased by hatred; it is appeased by love—this is an eternal law."

Another Buddhist goal, he declared, is to become selfless and unattached in one's meditation and action. Avoiding egotism is necessary, or in time it will inevitably beget "the twin sins of pride and prestige." Like material objects, such things are "transitory and even illusory."

Though a devout Buddhist with a simple and straightforward approach to his faith, Thant was not a fundamentalist, despite the way he described his religion in Toronto. He saw the dangers of fundamentalism and the problems that arise from religions. At a meeting on the Middle East he said, "As an Asian, let me confess that a major weakness of Asia is religion employed as a weapon for political ends. . . . History records numerous examples of wars waged by religious zealots, whether they be Christians or Jews, Moslems or Hindus, Buddhists or Confucianists."[58] Thant was unimpressed by formal ritual and "not attuned to religiosity." He compared his form of Buddhism to that of a Unitarian in a predominantly Protestant America.[59]

Although Buddhist thought does not explicitly include the concept of a God, Thant was ready to accept it. "There is one God, hidden in all things, all pervading, the inner soul of all things," Thant quoted Dr. Sarvepalli Radhakrishnan, the president of India, as saying. "We tear asunder this invisible bond and break the body of humanity if we use violence against one another."[60] When Ambassador Stevenson concluded his address to the newly installed secretary-general with the remark "God bless you!" Thant would have appreciated it. Narasimhan, Thant's Hindu chef de cabinet remarked, "U Thant was a Buddhist, but not a fanatic. Indeed one could not conceive of his being fanatical on any subject, except perhaps in respect of his total commitment to the Charter of the United Nations."[61]

Meditator as Well as Mediator

Thant practiced meditation every morning shortly after arising, usually at 6:00 A.M. He said his goal was to empty or quiet the mind, "to separate oneself from the conflicts outside," and to prepare himself for the day with detachment. The regularity of his practice is revealed in his description of an incident in 1967. In the opening hours of the Six-Day War, on June 5, 1967, Thant was awakened at 3:00 A.M. by a distress call from his under-secretary, Ralph Bunche. Thant writes that he "left for the UN at 3:45 A.M., without, for the first time in my memory, my morning meditation."[62]

During the Cuban missile crisis, one of the most fearsome conflicts in world history, Thant went to Havana for discussions with Castro. He writes that, as he tried to meditate at 6:30 A.M., scenes of U.S. warships, Cuban anti-aircraft emplacements, and an unsmiling Castro "flitted across my mind's eye. It was difficult to shut off my senses, even for a brief moment, and feel inner peace. In any case, I managed to practice metta (good will) and karuna (compassion) to all."[63]

From Individual to Global

The Buddhist solution to all problems is to raise the state of consciousness of the individual using simple moral precepts and strict spiritual practices.

Do these principles apply to nations as well? Thant's answer was undoubtedly yes. For Thant, the charter embodied many of the Buddha's teachings. "Tolerance is the principal foundation on which the UN Charter rests," he said at the Toronto teach-in.[64] Furthermore, the charter dictum to "practice tolerance and live together as good neighbours is the practical application of the principle of reciprocity." The UN goal to be a "centre for harmonizing the actions of nations" is the same as that of a compassionate, nonviolent person.[65] In his inaugural address to the General Assembly he vowed to pursue "the ideal of universal friendship" with an "attitude of objectivity."[66]

No doubt, the harmony he perceived between the UN charter and his Buddhist faith was a source of tremendous strength for him in his work. Table 5.1 further illustrates the close correspondence of many principles of Buddhism and of the charter. Buddhist nonviolence can be paired with the charter's nonuse of force. The principle of unity in diversity informs both. A potential parallel between international law and cosmic law sees humans attempting to duplicate the natural order. Buddhist nonegoism is matched by the charter's call to transcend national interests and, in the words of Thant, to work for a "larger goal: the common interest of all countries."

Unlike Buddhism, however, the charter (chapter VII) includes important provisions for armed international action against threats to the peace. Thant found this to be a difficult dilemma, especially when he was called upon to use force in the Congo. At that time a verse of the *Dhammapada* clung to his conscience: "He who guides others by a procedure that is non-violent and equitable, he is said to be a guardian of the law, wise and righteous."[67] As we shall see later, he was only partly able to reconcile his beliefs and his actions.

A Broader View

Thant also found inspiration in the works of great spiritual thinkers of other religious and cultural backgrounds. He deeply appreciated Albert Schweitzer and his ethic of "reverence for life," because, as Thant wrote, "I had trained all my life to regard human life as sacred." Thant also embraced the concepts of Pierre Teilhard de Chardin, a Jesuit priest, such as the unifying power of love, an orderly universe, and the world community —"a common soul in the vast body."[68]

Table 5.1 Comparison of the Principles of Buddhism and Those of the UN Charter

Buddhist Concept	UN Charter Provisions
Metta (good will or kindness) practiced "to all, without distinction"	• "to practice tolerance and live together in peace with one another as good neighbours" (Preamble) • "to develop friendly relations among nations" (art. 1.2) • "promoting and encouraging respect for human rights and for fundamental freedoms for all without distinction as to race, sex, language, or religion" (art. 1.3)
Karuna (compassion) the "duty to mitigate the suffering of others"	• "to save succeeding generations from the scourge of war, which twice in our lifetime has brought untold sorrow to mankind" (Preamble) • "to unite our strength to maintain international peace and security" (Preamble and art. 1.1) • "to employ international machinery for the promotion of the economic and social advancement of all peoples" (Preamble) • "to achieve international cooperation in solving international problems of an economic, social, cultural, or humanitarian character" (art. 1.3) • "the interests of the inhabitants of [non-self-governing] territories are paramount, and [administering nations] accept as a sacred trust the obligation to promote to the utmost [...] the well-being of the inhabitants of these territories" (art. 73)
Ahimsa (nonviolence) respect for all	• "all Members shall refrain in their international relations from the threat or use of force against the territorial integrity or political independence of any state" (art. 2.4) • "to ensure . . . armed force shall not be used, save in the common interest" (Preamble) • "to reaffirm faith in fundamental human rights, in the dignity and worth of the human person, in the equal rights of men and women and of nations large and small" (Preamble) • "respect for the principle of equal rights and self-determination of peoples" (art. 1.2) • encouraging respect for human rights and for fundamental freedoms for all without distinction as to race, sex, language, or religion (art. 1.3)
Karma (law of cause and effect) "law of reciprocal action" cosmic justice "as you sow so you reap" (Christian equivalent) consequently, "hurt not others in ways that you yourself would find hurtful," hence practice *metta, karuna, ahimsa*	• "all Members shall settle their international disputes by peaceful means in such a manner that international peace and security, and justice, are not endangered" (art. 2.3) • "to establish conditions under which justice and respect for the obligations arising from treaties and other sources of international law can be maintained" (Preamble)

In 1965, at a time of war, Thant visited Sarvepalli Radhakrishnan, the Hindu president of India, but much of their conversation was about religion and spirituality. Dr. Radhakrishnan, as an Oxford professor, had produced one of the most authoritative translations of the *Dhammapada,* an important Buddhist scripture. Thant heartily agreed with his view that the essence of all religions is the same and that "religion is not a creed or code, but an insight into reality." This 1965 meeting, called in the wake of the Indo-Pakistan war, was more than a political meeting; it was a "spiritual experience," wrote Thant.[69]

Thant took the unprecedented step of inviting Pope Paul VI to the United Nations. When cautioned that it might be advisable to obtain prior approval from the General Assembly, Thant responded: "No impartial observer would accuse a Buddhist Secretary-General of prejudice in inviting the head of the Roman Catholic Church to the United Nations."[70] This first-ever visit of a pontiff to the United Nations (or to the United States for that matter) brought great satisfaction to Thant. Together the two visited the UN Meditation Room, designed by Thant's predecessor Hammarskjöld. The words the pope spoke from the podium of the General Assembly were music to Thant's ears: "The edifice of modern civilization must be built on spiritual principles, the only principles capable not only of supporting it but also of enlightening and animating it."[71]

Thant bemoaned the fact that, apart from an occasional visit by a religious figure, the spiritual dimension was not visible in the activities of the world organization. It was for this reason that he took great delight in the creation of the UN Meditation Group in 1970.[72] Its leader was (and remains) Sri Chinmoy, a spiritual teacher who preaches the essential unity of religions, the spiritual significance of the United Nations, and the value of meditation for inner and outer peace. After viewing a performance of Sri Chinmoy's play *Siddhartha Becomes the Buddha,* Thant spoke about spirituality:

> Sri Chinmoy has drawn a very vivid picture of the identity between God and Truth, soul and inner Light, which I hope will create an abiding interest in these two religions—Hinduism and Buddhism—which in many ways constitute the key to all great religions. I feel very strongly, as some of my friends know, that only by the practical application of the teachings of great religious leaders, particularly the development of the moral and spiritual aspects of life, as Sri Chinmoy has stressed in the play—love, compassion, tolerance, the philosophy of live-and-let-live, modesty and even humility—that only with this approach, only with this method, will we be

able to fashion the kind of society we want: a truly moral society, a decent society, a livable society, which is the goal of all great religions.[73]

Toward a Global Ethic

Thant wanted to write a book to be titled *Ethics for Our Time* to blend "the virtues of the Oriental wisdom with the merits of Western dynamism."[74] While his illness and death prevented him from even starting this book, he did include much of this type of thinking in his memoirs. His aim in writing the memoirs, as he told Sri Chinmoy, was "to show how spirituality and philosophy can lead and guide politics."[75]

In his memoirs, he applied his belief system to shine a light on the problems of the day, pointing the way to ethical and spiritual solutions. He declared with considerable foresight that the division between rich and poor nations is "more real, more lasting and ultimately more explosive" than that between communists and capitalists. Furthermore, it was "no longer morally acceptable or politically expedient for the more advanced nations to ignore the backwardness and poverty of others." He decried the "huge resources wasted on armaments," which he regarded as senseless spending on potential "destruction and death" instead of "construction and life."[76]

To solve these problems, a "global mentality" was needed to replace narrow-minded nationalism, though he acknowledged that patriotism had its place. Thant hoped that the notion of "world citizenship" or "planetary citizenship" would become accepted alongside national citizenship. The second to the last sentence of his memoirs is: "Perhaps my own Buddhist upbringing has helped me more than anything else to realize and to express in my speeches and writings the concept of world citizenship."[77]

Ethical Dilemmas

The real test of an individual's ethical framework is its application in practice. As secretary-general, Thant had to make many difficult decisions, some involving life and death, where answers were not obvious or easy. The great challenges of his office covered issues of peace (including nuclear confrontation in the Cuban missile crisis, the quagmire in the Congo, and the Vietnam War), social friction (including decolonization), and administrative tasks (such as saving the United Nations from financial bankruptcy). For a moral person like Thant, decisions involving ethical dilemmas were the hardest, so these are analyzed in detail here.

The Use of Force

Thant abhorred all forms of violence. This attitude was, he wrote, "embedded in my inner self."[78] As a young man, he had admired Gandhi's nonviolent campaign in India. He wanted his country, Burma, also to throw off the British yoke without violence. He later heaped praise on the UK for granting "genuine independence—without bloodshed, without resentment, without ill-feeling."[79] His instrument in the Burmese national struggle was the pen and not the sword. Yet as secretary-general he was given a sword, and he did use it. This made him an unlikely proponent of military force, as will be seen.

Buddhist philosophy internalizes the concept of conflict ("an inner struggle") and calls upon adherents to reject all forms of violence. Buddhism exhorts individuals to neutralize violence by changing themselves and to overcome negative and destructive forces through compassion and love. Echoing Buddhist thought, Thant wrote that "violence erodes the spirit of law, order and international morality."[80] Some Buddhists believe that force may be used for self-defense, but the religion does not provide much guidance on how to use it. There is no development of a "just war" theory comparable to the one that evolved in Christian thought from St. Augustine onward.

Like all other secretaries-general, Thant frequently deplored the use of force by states. He criticized the Soviet invasion of Czechoslovakia (1968), the American invasion of the Dominican Republic (1965), and U.S. bombing campaigns in the Vietnam War. He made himself unpopular with the White House and the State Department for his frequent assertions that "military methods will not bring about a peaceful solution to the Vietnamese problem." And when an American politician suggested that nuclear weapons might need to be used in Vietnam, he was particularly blunt: "I am against the use of atomic weapons for destructive purposes anywhere, under any circumstances—and anybody who proposes the use of atomic weapons for destructive purposes is, in my view, out of his mind." More generally, in 1968, he boldly claimed, "I have consistently—indeed, necessarily—deplored any and every resort to force as a means of settling international differences since such action is in contravention of the Charter."[81]

On the other hand, he recognized that international force is needed to uphold international law, as evidenced by the League of Nations experience: "The League system, to be effective, needed the *power to compel compliance* with the law. Without this power it could not persuade; but, given the power, the use of force could have become unnecessary and persuasion would have proved practicable. Unfortunately the League had neither the will nor the means to organize such *overwhelming force.*"[82] Thant strongly believed in the Wilsonian concept of collective security, though it was foreign to Buddhist thought. He even suggested that a permanent UN force, while "not a practical proposition at this point in time," would "eventually and surely emerge."[83]

As soon as Thant became secretary-general in 1961, he had to transform theoretical notions on the use of force into practical ones. In the Congo during the previous year, Hammarskjöld had assembled the largest UN peacekeeping force up to that time—indeed, at almost twenty thousand troops, it was the largest such force created until the end of the Cold War. In February 1961 the Security Council had authorized Hammarskjöld to use force "in the last resort" to prevent civil war. But it was left to Thant to oversee the implementation of what would today be called "peace enforcement" measures. As it turned out, the Buddhist Thant was less averse than the Christian Hammarskjöld to using force in the Congo. In part, this was because Hammarskjöld's own difficult experiences and untimely death in the region had fostered international support for more robust peacekeeping in the conflict-ridden country. Both the United States and the Soviet Union approved of the United Nations' use of force to end the secession of the Katanga province, though the UK, France, and Belgium advocated a milder approach.

THE CONGO CASE: FROM SELF-DEFENSE TO OFFENSE

Thant received a baptism by fire in the Congo: Eight days after his appointment as secretary-general on November 11, 1961, thirteen Italian airmen working in the Opération des Nations Unies au Congo (ONUC) were murdered by mutinous Congolese troops.[84] UN peacekeepers were also targeted by mercenaries working for the secession of the mineral-rich Katanga province. The Security Council, on November 24, instructed ONUC to remove all foreign military and paramilitary personnel (i.e., mercenaries), using the "requisite measure of force, if necessary." The secretary-general was also authorized to "take all necessary measures to prevent entry or return of such elements."[85] The rambunctious Katangan leader Tshombe responded with an inflammatory speech in the Elizabethville stadium, declaring that "U Thant will launch a war on our territory. . . . You cannot all have automatic weapons or rifles. But we still have our poisoned arrows, our spears, our axes . . . not one United Nations mercenary must feel safe in any place whatever."[86]

Tshombe's speech had the anticipated repercussions: Some UN officials in Katanga, including Urquhart, were kidnapped and assaulted a few days later. Thant responded forcefully, declaring that indiscriminate arrest or molestation of UN civilians must be "resisted by all possible means including use of force, offensive and defensive, as necessary."[87]

The United Nations also had under its protection some thirty-five thousand anti-Tshombe Baluba in a refugee camp that was under frequent attack by Katangan paramilitary forces—similar in situation to the UN-protected areas in Bosnia thirty years later (though without the tragic results). Thant negotiated continuously with Tshombe, but he soon realized that the Katangan leader was acting in bad faith. When a secret Katangan plan for a full-scale attack on ONUC was seized in early December 1961, Thant authorized a UN action "to assure freedom of movement."[88] Fighting from December 2 to 19 ended when Tshombe agreed in the Kitona Declaration to renounce the secession of the province. But in the months that followed, Tshombe predictably reneged and UN troops were repeatedly attacked. The United Nations refrained from launching an offensive. Then, beginning on December 24, 1962, the United Nations suffered a sustained four-day attack on its positions in the Katangan capital. This allowed Thant to authorize the final and most forceful round of engagement with Katangan forces, dubbed "Operation Grand Slam" by officials in the field, who were well prepared for it. The declared objective was to "gain complete freedom of movement for ONUC all over Katanga."[89]

Operation Grand Slam proceeded well from the start. At one point, however, Thant ordered the UN advance to stop at the Lufira River. The UK government was calling for an immediate ceasefire in the face of threats from Katangan fighters that any attempt to take the strategic minefields beyond the river would result in these resources being blown up. But the troops in the field, seeing no resistance, proceeded to the minefields, finding that all the mercenaries had fled. It was a pleasant surprise for Thant. When Bunche came back from the Congo with letters of apology from troop leaders for the "initial breakdown in communications," Thant was contrite: "I felt that it was I, not they, who should have apologized for my miscalculation and apprehension based on scare reports from London and Brussels."[90] The Katangan secession was now over. Tshombe's military potential and foreign support disintegrated and he was obliged to accept a peaceful settlement.[91]

The casualties suffered by ONUC during its three rounds of action in 1961–62 were forty-two killed and two hundred wounded. Several hundred Katangan forces and perhaps fifty civilians were also killed.[92] Overall, ONUC (1960–64) suffered the most fatalities of any UN mission, even more than the post–Cold War missions in Bosnia and Somalia.[93]

ANALYSIS AND JUSTIFICATION

Ironically, in the Congo Thant proved to be a determined fighter, and he supported the troops in the field. Later Thant would write, somewhat proudly, that ONUC proved to be the "first experience, under combat conditions in the field, of an armed force composed strictly of international units and strictly under UN command."[94] The UN force was robust, even by today's standards. It acquired artillery, tanks, and fighter jets. It dropped bombs (including inadvertently on a hospital, something not often mentioned). It developed a sophisticated intelligence-gathering system and it did take offensive action, despite claims that it was acting in self-defense only.[95]

What could justify Thant's resort to such force? The answer is provided not in Buddhist scripture but in the just war theory that arose out of the Christian tradition. Though he himself did not refer to it, a look at Thant's explanations at the time and in his memoirs shows that all the elements for a just war existed in his thinking: just cause, right intention, right authority, last resort, proportionality, and minimum use of force.

The *justice of the cause* generated controversy in Thant's day. In fact, Katanga supporters argued that the province's secession was a legitimate exercise in self-determination. Thant takes pains to refute this argument in his memoirs.[96] The Congo had been admitted to the United Nations as a "unified state," with the written agreement of Tshombe in 1960. Furthermore, "no sovereign state in the world ever recognized the independence of Katanga," and Tshombe's government was "never able to exercise effective control" over the whole province.

Thant may have had deeper reasons for his aversion to Katangan secession and civil war. For one, his native Burma (and Thant himself) had suffered enormously from secessionist attempts (the Karen insurgency) shortly after independence. He had also seen at close hand the devastating effects of the 1947 partition of India. As secretary-general during a period of widespread decolonization, Thant was also keenly aware of the precarious state of many Afro-Asian territories. Should secession be recognized or encouraged in one country, it could easily spread to others. Thant, the United Nations, and almost all members of the international community strongly supported the territorial integrity of former colonies and emerging states. Thant expressed antisecessionist sentiments strongly in February 1970: The United Nations "has never accepted and does not accept, and I do not believe it will ever accept, the principle of secession of a part of its Member State."[97] The United Nations' acceptance of some twenty secessions in the former Communist bloc in the 1990s was to prove his prediction wrong, though the principle of territorial integrity remains strong in the international community.

The other criteria for a just war were also applicable. Thant, the United Nations, and ONUC could not reasonably be accused of selfish or undeclared motives; therefore the *right intent* criterion was implicitly satisfied, at least in Thant's mind. The *right authority* provision was also easily met because the UN charter permitted the Security Council to authorize force, which it did in two resolutions on the Congo. This was a key to Thant's belief that the use of force was legitimate.

The *last resort* criterion was also very much on Thant's mind. Indeed, the first Security Council resolution, adopted during Hammarskjöld's tenure, urged the United Nations to prevent civil war, using force "if necessary, in the last resort."[98] Thant learned from many experiences that Tshombe could not be trusted; he "always went back on his promises, assurances and declarations."[99] Therefore Thant would rightfully claim that "it was only after all other efforts failed" that the order for armed action was given. The final UN operation in late 1962 was provoked by a sustained Katangan attack, which some soldiers in the field considered a blessing because it gave the United Nations reason to respond forcefully.

Proportionality was also present. That is, the extent of force was proportional to the threat. The Katangan military included fighter jets, extensive weapons holdings, an organized *gendarmerie,* and a cadre of toughened mercenaries who disregarded the rules of warfare (for instance, using vehicles with red cross markings to transport weapons).[100] The UN actions could not, as a whole, be considered excessive.

The "minimum of casualties" from Operation Grand Slam brought great relief for Thant and his advisers at UN headquarters. He sent a congratulatory message to ONUC forces, declaring that the fighting had been "forced upon us" and that "it was only after all other efforts failed that the order was given to undertake defensive action of removing the hostile gendarmerie roadblocks which has now been completed so successfully and fortunately with a minimum of casualties."[101]

Though Thant claimed that UN troops used their arms only "in self-defence under attack," not all actions were in self-defense. For instance, one of Thant's orders had wider objectives and permitted offensive actions: ONUC was to take "all counteractions—ground and aerial—deemed necessary to restore complete freedom of movement in the area."[102] Although the Security Council authorization allowed for more than self-defense, Thant justified his actions using the universally accepted principle of self-defense. The concept was stretched significantly but not unreasonably. Given the current practice of UN intervention in civil conflicts, Thant's politically correct declaration that ONUC was not an intervention into internal affairs rings hollow today, but it must be considered in the restrictive environment of the day.

Although Thant justified his actions to others and to himself, he felt his conscience "pricking" him for using force. As a Buddhist, he was saddened by violence toward any human being, be it a UN soldier, a Congolese rebel, or a foreign mercenary. "Every morning I prayed for the sparing of lives. In the course of my meditation, I practiced *metta* (good will) and *karuna* (compassion) to all in the Congo, without distinction as to race, religion or colour. I realized, however, that the moral principles of my religion had to be adjusted to the practical responsibilities of my office." Thant viewed the United Nations' actions in the Congo "as a battle for peace, not as a war; to me war—all war—is folly and insanity."[103] He recognized the practical necessity of international force under international authority. Though not a Buddhist concept, it was an ethical one as long as it satisfied the commonsense criteria described in just war theory.

In Thant's mind, international force could be justified, and at times force was a practical necessity. Later Thant would deplore "the failure of the Security Council to enforce some of its decisions" in the Middle East and would ask the council to consider applying chapter VII to order India and Pakistan to cease fighting in 1965.[104] Fortunately for Thant and his conscience, the Congo was the only operation in which he had to give orders to UN soldiers to apply force against a determined opponent. Throughout the rest of his tenure, he would call for utmost restraint over the use of force and plead for the sparing of innocent lives. Apart from the Congo, his interventions, including peacekeeping, did not go beyond self-defense.

To Intervene or Not to Intervene?

The dilemma of intervention challenged Thant throughout his entire term, as it does all secretaries-general. On the one hand, many dire situations morally demanded UN mediation or even stronger intervention to prevent conflict and save lives. On the other hand, there are many restrictions on the secretary-general, including ones laid out in the UN charter. The limitations in the founding document had been included expressly because history had shown that outside interference in internal matters was the cause of countless wars. Most nations harbored some fear that an outside power, perhaps even the United Nations, would intrude uninvited into their domains. Hence the UN charter emphasized respect for national sovereignty, and article 2 (7) specifically prohibits UN intervention in matters "essentially within the domestic jurisdiction of any state," though enforcement actions under chapter VII are exempted from this rule.[105]

Given the sensitivities of the day, Thant was very careful not to intervene uninvited. For example, in the absence of an invitation from the government of Nigeria, he refused requests to mediate the Biafra conflict. Though mass killing and starvation were shown frequently on television in 1968–70, there was little he could do apart from limited humanitarian work. When Canadian prime minister Pierre Trudeau pressed him for UN action, Thant responded that the appropriate forum for dealing with the dispute was the Organization for African Unity (OAU), whose involvement the Nigerian government endorsed (and controlled). The secretary-general further pointed out that if the United Nations became involved in this civil war, it could be seen as encouragement for secession, a threat faced by many newly independent African states.[106] So the conflict ran its awful course, with more than a million dead by the time the Nigerian government won its final military victory in 1970. This conflict was no doubt a source of sadness and frustration for Thant.

His good offices were also declined in the civil conflict in Northern Ireland. Ireland sought Thant's help, but Britain adamantly refused any "outside intervention."[107] Similarly, the principle of consent meant that when President Nasser asked Thant to pull UN peacekeepers out of Egypt, Thant felt obliged to comply, though he made a valiant attempt to change Nasser's mind. During the Vietnam War Thant received mixed signals from both sides, and his statements on the prerequisites for peace at times offended the parties, who sought military victory on the battlefield. Still, he felt obliged to speak out, and he dauntlessly investigated ways to bring the parties together, with limited success.

He was outspoken on the internal situations in Northern Rhodesia and South Africa because these involved racism and because the Security Council had not only discussed them but had invoked chapter VII to recommend that states apply sanctions. On Rhodesia, his statements were in line with his rather militant stand against colonialism.[108] Thant was a strong spokesman for decolonization, an important international issue of the day, noting that "the United Nations stands for the self-government and independence of all peoples, and the abolition of racial discrimination without reservations. It can never afford to compromise on these basic principles," and "self-determination remains the most sacred right of all people who still find themselves subjugated."[109]

Thant did sometimes intervene without prior invitation, but he did so cautiously. On such occasions his preferred technique was to send identical appeals to both parties to a conflict. This would ensure that he was treating them impartially. He did this in the Cuban missile crisis to good effect. After some forty-five countries requested his intervention to prevent global catastrophe, he sent President Kennedy and Chairman Khrushchev identical letters requesting that they freeze the situation so talks could take place, possibly with his help. Both Kennedy and Khrushchev sent high-level negotiators to the United Nations to supplement the efforts of their UN ambassadors. Thant's efforts there were rewarded with success. President Kennedy would later say, "U Thant has put the whole world in his debt."[110]

In the final analysis, Thant's concept of intervention was consistent with Buddhist principles as well as with the UN charter. He tried to show compassion and concern for all. "The Secretary-General has the duty to do whatever he can, in whatever way seems most appropriate, so long as his action does not violate the Charter."[111] Many times he offered his "good offices" to help resolve a conflict situation. But when his offers were declined, he remained respectful and tolerant of those he was dealing with, realizing that the secretary-general cannot intervene without the consent of the parties. It was a philosophy of live and let live.

Impartiality Versus Neutrality

Thant strove for "impartiality" but rejected "neutrality." He felt that on moral issues it was impossible and immoral to be neutral because neutrality implied a lack of concern. When Ambassador Stevenson interviewed him on television five days before his election as secretary-general, Thant explained that, like a judge, the UN secretary-general must be impartial toward all people but not neutral about a crime that has been committed.[112]

As a Buddhist, he believed that the welfare of all people was his concern. The same Buddhist attitude also meant that he should not discriminate among people: He should instead respect all individuals, though still take action to prevent wrongdoing. His meditation practice of viewing the world selflessly helped him gain an impartial perspective. Thus the legal and the religious views of impartiality coincided in Thant's case.

In practice, too, Thant was impartial. He was never accused of being partial toward Asians, Buddhists, or newly emerging states, though he had deep affinities with all three groups. He also managed to overcome potential personal prejudices in his life: against the British for colonialism, the Japanese for occupation, the Karens for civil war, and the cold warriors for trying to divide the world carelessly. He lived by the motto "to make the world safe for diversity." Diversity, for him, meant upholding respect for all human beings, and for the rule of law.

The tendency to take sides in national or international disputes was foreign to him, though he was constantly pressured to do so. He preferred to judge actions, not people or countries. He said in a U.S. media interview, "Within a civilized and orderly society, a criminal act is judged for its criminal character and not for its political significance. In your country, a Democrat does not applaud a robber because he has robbed a Republican and vice versa. But internationally, this is exactly what all too frequently happens."[113] His impartial attitude gained him sustained respect in the Cold War. This saved him from the ill fate suffered by his two predecessors. He left the office in 1972 on good terms with both superpowers.

When it came to identifying aggression, however, Thant was bold and outspoken. He brazenly criticized the superpowers for their respective military actions in the Dominican Republic, Vietnam, and Czechoslovakia. Though such criticism could have repercussions for his re-election chances, Thant clearly was not concerned. Thant did express sympathy with Western-style democracy but felt that patience was needed with new nations to allow them to grow naturally. In the matter of capitalist versus socialist economic principles, he advocated a balance of the two.

One international act that he found "despicable" was airplane hijackings, which rose in frequency in his last years in office. When Algeria asked him to secure the release of captured Arab guerrillas in Israel in return for release of Israeli passengers on a hijacked plane in Algiers, he "categorically refused." He viewed hijacking as an international crime that should in no instance be rewarded.[114] Still, he gained the respect of both sides for his mediation in that crisis.

As a mediator between opponents, Thant had to preserve his impartiality, while suggesting solutions that both sides could accept. "Reaching a compromise is an art, not a formula," he said. "You have to take the rights and wrongs of both sides into consideration and feel your way to a solution that is fair to them and all the other people affected by the decision. There are rarely only two sides to any problem."[115]

Hans Morgenthau, the *realpolitik* theorist who favored direct confrontation with the Soviet bloc, criticized Thant for overstating the value of compromise and accused him of elevating it to "a universal principle of foreign policy" rather than keeping it as one of many possibilities.[116] For Morgenthau, it was unethical not to align with the United States in the Cold War struggle, but Thant considered nonalignment, the "attitude of objectivity," and "the ideal of universal friendship" to be essential for his work as secretary-general.[117]

Independent Versus Dependent Office

The secretary-general is primarily a servant of the UN membership, but the officeholders have also developed an independent voice and role. Thant felt that he was "at the service not only of all Member governments but of the peoples of the United Nations."[118] A natural tension exists for any secretary-general with respect to how independently he can speak and act in that larger cause.

Thant accepted certain constraints. First, of course, he sought to always abide by the UN charter and devoted himself to its implementation. The secretary-general "must tread his way though this jungle of conflicting national policies with the Charter as his only compass." Second, Thant felt that "any Secretary-General, irrespective of his personal views on any issue, is obliged to stand by every resolution or decision of the main deliberative organs of the Organization."[119] This team-spirit attitude sometimes meant defending and accepting views that were contrary to his own. As a former ambassador, Thant was accustomed to confining his public statements "within the four corners of my government's set policy and statements."[120]

As secretary-general, Thant sometimes dealt with this dilemma of conflicting personal and professional views by using the concept of "two U Thants." In 1964, for example, Thant was asked whether Communist China should be admitted to the United Nations. The vote for admission had not carried in the General Assembly, though the resolution was gaining ground each year. Thant replied at a press conference, "Please try to remember that there are two U Thants—the U Thant who represented Burma before 1961 and the U Thant of post-1961 as the Secretary-General of the United Nations. The 1964 U Thant is not supposed to have views in that capacity on such matters."[121] Around 1970, however, Thant started speaking openly and strongly in favor of China's admittance. The vote finally swung in China's favor in October 1971. The next month Thant was delighted to personally welcome the newly arrived representatives from the People's Republic of China.

When the press asked Thant for his opinion about the 1962 coup in Burma by General Ne Win, Thant also gave a "two U Thants" reply but added, "One of them is temporary."[122] It was generally known that Thant opposed the military overthrow of his long-standing friend and former boss Prime Minister U Nu.

Thant was not a passive secretary-general in voice or action. In the spirit of his predecessor, Dag Hammarskjöld, he sought to push the limits of the office. Before being elected in 1961, for instance, Thant asserted that he alone would appoint his senior officials, despite initial Soviet insistence on Security Council review for appointments. Perhaps as a sop or compromise, Thant let it be known that he would include a Soviet national among his top advisers.

Unlike any secretary-general before or after, Thant created two new peacekeeping missions on his own authority, without prior Security Council authorization. The establishment of the United Nations Yemen Observer Mission (UNYOM) and the United Nations Security Force in West Irian (UNSF) was, he felt, well within his purview because the parties had approached him, not the council, and after negotiations they had arrived at a mission mandate and agreed to pay the full costs of the mission. This circumvention of the council, however, brought strong criticism from the Soviets. Though other countries came to Thant's defense, resolutions were passed in the UN organs that authorized the missions *ex post facto.*

In 1967 Thant decided on his own authority to withdraw the United Nations Emergency Force (UNEF) after Egypt had so requested. Some member states claimed that the decision properly belonged to the General Assembly, which had created the force, or the Security Council, which had primary responsibility for international peace and security. Nonetheless, Thant only notified the troop-contributing nations of his decision without seeking their approval or that of any UN body. The complaining nations, including Canada, did not exercise their right to challenge Thant's decision in one of the main organs.

After the Six-Day War, Thant was savagely criticized for his decision, as he himself describes in his memoirs. The *Spectator* of London titled an editorial page "U Thant's War," and an opinion piece in the *New York Times* creatively, though unfairly, accused Thant of using "his international prestige with the objectivity of a spurned love and the dynamism of a noodle."[123] The Israeli government (which had refused a request to station UN peacekeepers on its territory) compared Thant to a firefighter who vanishes at the site of fire. To top it all, Nasser claimed he had not requested the full withdrawal of UNEF.[124] At the time, Thant simply absorbed the blame.

Thant resisted bringing matters to the attention of the Security Council when he knew the council would not be able to deal with them. Though this might have lessened his burden, his team-player approach would not allow him to pass the buck easily (as he could have done in 1967). Unlike his predecessor, Thant never formally invoked article 99 of the charter, which gives the secretary-general the right to add a new issue to the council's agenda. If member states did not raise the issue, Thant figured there must be reason.

In the East Pakistan crisis of 1971, however, he became so frustrated with the lack of action in the Security Council in the face of an impending war that he took the unusual step of publicly releasing a memo he had sent to the council to prod it to consider this emerging "threat to international peace and security." Had he invoked article 99, he could have forced the council to meet to consider the situation, but he avoided this action. Thant strongly relied on the implied powers of article 99. For him, it meant that he had to keep a "watching brief" on situations that could threaten the peace.[125] In East Pakistan, he devoted himself primarily to humanitarian assistance.

Although criticism of the superpowers could come at a heavy price (as his two predecessors had discovered), Thant did not hesitate to blame the United States and the Soviet Union when he saw blatant violations of the charter. He labeled the Soviet invasion of Czechoslovakia a "serious blow to the concepts of international order and morality which form the basis of the Charter."[126] When the Soviet Union accused the United Nations of being a "tool of imperialists" in the Congo, Thant could not help but respond.[127] In 1962, when given the opportunity to address the Soviet people on radio, he boldly declared, "The Russian people do not fully understand the true character of the Congo problem," prefacing his words with the remark that he did not believe in "honeyed words."[128] Similarly, on the Vietnam War, he said at a press conference, "I am sure that the great American people, if only they knew the true facts and background to the developments in South Vietnam, will agree with me that further bloodshed is unnecessary."[129] Quite undiplomatically, he repeated the famous maxim that "in times of war the first casualty is truth."

Thant also criticized the actions of several other nations: Belgium for supporting mercenaries in the Congo (a former colony), South Africa for its racist apartheid policies, Rhodesia for its unilateral declaration of independence, and France and Russia for nuclear testing, which he called "a manifestation of a very dangerous psychosis."[130] Surprisingly, Thant did not receive a strong rebuff from nations for his criticisms. Part of his success lies in the difference between his substance and his style. His sense of morality gave power to his words, but they were spoken with great humility, respect, and sensitivity—"his words often being much stronger than his tone." Though his statements were not "sugar-coated," he never lost his temper.

Private Versus Professional Interests

The work of a secretary-general is intense and demanding. Sometimes it is exhilarating, but more often than not it is frustrating. Though Thant did not agree with the words of Trygve Lie that it was "the most impossible job in the world," he said he thoroughly understood why his predecessor felt that way. Not only does the role present political challenges, it also takes a heavy personal toll.

In Thant's case, the toll included his health and family life. He had to be hospitalized for a brief period near the end of his third year for peptic gastritis, and later in his tenure he suffered from ulcers, acute fatigue, and hemorrhoids. He was diagnosed with cancer shortly after leaving office.[131] As secretary-general, he was committed to ten-hour workdays six days a week, less on Saturdays. He could be interrupted at any time of day or night with news of a serious conflict breaking out somewhere in the world. Furthermore, his wife had not acclimatized to North America: she did not learn to speak English and did not socialize with Thant's colleagues or the diplomatic corps. She wanted to return to Burma. These were some of the personal reasons behind his reluctance to serve a second term in 1966, despite universal demands that he do so. Thant chose to place UN service above personal interest.

In 1972 a much weaker and at times hospitalized Thant determined that, for the sake of the United Nations as well as for himself, he would not run for a third term. In his farewell speech in December 1971, he spoke of his retirement bringing him a "tremendous sense of relief bordering on liberation."[132]

A secretary-general's privacy is also jeopardized. His thoughts, feelings, and actions are constantly questioned on issues ranging from international crises to personal beliefs. Thant tried to keep his religion private, despite strong interest from the media and the public. The teach-in in 1967 was one of the few forums where he addressed the issue directly. He started out by saying, "normally I would be unwilling to discuss in public my religious convictions," but he agreed under "the special circumstances of the Toronto teach-in." He left these circumstances unspecified, but they probably related to the burgeoning interest in Buddhism in that era, and perhaps also to the fact that the organizer was the son of his friend George Ignatieff, the Canadian ambassador to the United Nations.

Thant gave UN duties priority over personal concerns and even over his religious identity. In a meeting with Buddhists, he told them that in his office in Manhattan, "I must forget that I am a Burmese and Buddhist. . . . Most of my visitors have something specific to say to me, I must open myself to them, I must empty myself of myself."[133] Sometimes his visitors brought weighty problems. In some cases, they brought criticism of Thant himself.

The secretary-general was subjected not only to criticism but also to outright slander. U.S. secretary of state Dean Rusk made the outrageous statement that Thant was working to win the Nobel Peace Prize. In response to Thant's criticism of U.S. policies in Vietnam, right-wing groups accused him of "insolent candor" and of being an "apologist and propagandist for Communist aggression in SE Asia."[134] One group even claimed that "by 1963, the UN was headed by avowed Marxists."[135]

Thant seldom lowered himself to the level of his critics and often accepted unfair criticism in silence. He also kept the same humble attitude when he was successful. "The perfect good offices operation is one which is not heard of until it is successfully concluded, or even never heard of at all."[136] Much of Thant's political work was "quiet diplomacy," done away from the glare of media attention and outside the chambers of the United Nations.

Because of Thant's affinity for reporters, however, his staff sometimes had to excuse him from spontaneous "lobby press conferences." Thant was the first to establish daily press conferences with the spokesman of the secretary-general and he is credited by Secretary-General Kofi Annan with "opening up the United Nations to the media."[137] But his affinity for the press rarely interfered with his "good offices" functions, which he carried out with modesty and considerable discretion.

Thant's answer to the personal-professional dilemma can best be summed up in the Buddhist-sounding dictum "service over self."

Idealist Versus Realist

Thant struggled between his idealistic vision of a world at peace, operating in accordance with the UN charter, and a realistic view from close quarters of national behavior during the Cold War. He had to deal daily with the narrow politics of nationalism, the conflict of ideologies, the selfish motives of many politicians, and, all too often, resentment against UN interference. He once commented on politics, "Behind their smooth façade of words, there goes on all the time bitter haggling, accentuated by bland international blackmail and power threats, euphemistically called diplomacy."[138]

In listing qualities necessary for an officeholder, Thant included both idealism and pragmatism: "a sense of obligation to the human community in its broadest sense . . . and an urgent sense of political realism."[139] His general evaluations of the world situation, included in his annual reports, were often critical but realistic: "The unbridled rivalry of nations is the dominant factor in international life"; "the greatest obstacle to the realization of the principles of the Charter is the inescapable fact that power politics still operates." He called for patriotism to "take new and more creative forms than the old concepts of political domination or material power."[140]

Like every secretary-general, Thant also had to reconcile unlimited idealistic objectives with limited means. Knowing the bounds of international progress, he proposed realistic goals that he knew could conceivably be implemented and avoided those that were premature or overly idealistic, however appealing they may have been. It is a testament to his political judgment that most of his proposals eventually saw the light of day. In a remarkable speech to the World Federalists Association in Ottawa in 1970, he advocated seven goals for UN reform, which were, to a large degree, ultimately achieved:

1. "Decisions of the United Nations, particularly the Security Council, must be made enforceable." During Thant's tenure, the Security Council did not apply mandatory sanctions, except in the cases of South Africa and Rhodesia, and did not take military enforcement action under chapter VII of the charter, with the Congo being an arguable exception. After the Cold War, by contrast, sanctions were applied to more than a dozen nations or groups of individuals, and military enforcement was applied in several important cases (e.g., Iraq–Kuwait 1991, Angola, Sierra Leone, Congo 2003). Now, more than ever before—though perhaps still not sufficiently and not with enough impartiality—UN decisions are being enforced.

2. "The unused provisions of the Charter, which can add greatly to international peace and security, should be activated." Specifically, Thant suggested that council meetings be held at the ministerial or head-of-state level (now happening frequently, though only three times at the latter level, the first in 1992),[141] greater use of the International Court of Justice (whose case load increased dramatically after the Cold War),[142] and the establishment of UN fact-finding bodies (which also are much more frequent in modern times).

3. "The International Court of Justice must be empowered to interpret the UN Charter." While there were two examples in Thant's time of ICJ cases involving interpretation of the charter, the practice has increased since then.[143] However, the court has yet to challenge the legality of a Security Council decision.

4. "Universality" should be the goal of the United Nations. This has been achieved.[144] A major step was the inclusion of China in 1971, a year after Thant's Ottawa speech.

5. "Global authorities" should be established "to deal with serious global problems," particularly the environment. A United Nations Environment

Program (UNEP) was created in 1972, as Thant had urged, with head-quarters in Nairobi. Many others followed.

6. An "international regime to administer the resources of the seabed" should be established. The UN Convention on the Law of the Sea, opened for signature in 1982, created the International Seabed Authority.

7. "The United Nations urgently needs a stand-by force." The current UN Standby Arrangements System (UNSAS), created in 1994, allows the United Nations to better choose from potential troop-contributing nations. Furthermore, a Standby High Readiness Brigade for UN Peace Operations (SHIRBRIG) became operational on January 1, 2000, with headquarters near Copenhagen. It has sixteen experienced members who have earmarked troops for UN service. Thant rejected the idea of a standing (as opposed to standby) UN force as premature, preferring to support more realistic measures.

These examples show that Thant was at once a visionary and a practical man, fully cognizant of the realities and limitations of the international community. Between what he called the "two poles" of the United Nations—the charter and "unconcealed selfish nature of national sovereignty"—he sought modest but progressive means to bring the charter dream to reality.[145] Throughout his term of office, he pushed the United Nations to greater goals that were within reach. To summarize Thant's approach, he was an idealist in vision and a realist in action.

The Sacred/Secular Divide

Though religious, there is no reason to believe that Thant was superstitious. But, like many Burmese Buddhists, he did have horoscopes cast on occasion. One was prepared, for instance, for his neighbor and biographer June Bingham when her husband was running for election to the U.S. Congress. It is also quite likely that one of his secretaries, an American woman whom he brought with him to the United Nations from the Burmese mission, was engaged in astrology. Out of respect for Thant, the American press never investigated this practice. When Thant's press officer, Ramses Nassif, asked him if he believed in astrology, he answered adroitly, "I do not believe in it, nor do I reject it—but let me tell you, there are many great people in Asia who would not make a major decision without consulting their horoscope."[146] In fact, Thant was one of those Asians, but he kept this practice private.

His Buddhist upbringing and strong beliefs were no secret, but he did not promote these in his official duties or speeches (with a few exceptions, as noted above). He did make a special "pilgrimage" to sacred Buddhist sites while visiting heads of state in south Asia in 1967, but these visits were for his own benefit, not official functions.[147] He respected the non-religious character of the world organization, though he regretted the exclusion of the spiritual dimension.

The United Nations was founded as a secular institution, despite the religious convictions of many of its founders (including Presidents Franklin Roosevelt and Woodrow Wilson before him) and the close parallels between religious principles and the UN charter. Like the founders, Thant valued religion as a source of inspiration but realized the dangers of "religion employed as a weapon for political ends."[148] He had opposed the adoption of Buddhism as the state religion of Burma, and he would no doubt have opposed any religious favoritism in the United Nations. Still, he felt that by ignoring the religious and spiritual side of life, the United Nations was missing an important part of human existence. These facets were, in his view, essential to lifting the human condition. He took up this issue squarely in his farewell address in 1971:

> I have certain priorities in regard to virtues and human values. An ideal man, or an ideal woman, is one who is endowed with four attributes, four qualities—physical, intellectual, moral and spiritual qualities. . . . I would attach greater importance to intellectual qualities over physical qualities. . . . It is far from my intention to denigrate intellectualism, but I would attach greater importance to moral qualities . . . like love, compassion, understanding, tolerance, the philosophy of "live and let live," the ability to understand the other person's point of view, which are the key to all great religions. And above all I would attach the greatest importance to spiritual values, spiritual qualities. I deliberately avoid using the term "religion." I have in mind the spiritual virtues: faith in oneself, the purity of one's inner self which to me is the greatest virtue of all. With this approach, with this philosophy, with this concept alone, will we be able to fashion the kind of society we want, the society which was envisaged by the founding fathers of the United Nations.[149]

Soon after Muller arrived as director of the secretary-general's office in 1970, he asked Thant if he had any unfulfilled dreams.[150] There were three: the entry of China into the United Nations (realized in 1971), new forms of international education (partly fulfilled with the creation of the United

Nations University in 1973 and the University for Peace in 1980, largely though Muller's efforts), and spirituality at the United Nations. Explaining the last dream, Thant said, "I always listen to political and economic speeches. I never hear a spiritual voice in the United Nations, even though I am a spiritual person above everything else." Fortunately, this dream was realized soon after Thant uttered those words.

As mentioned earlier, in 1970 a UN Meditation Group was formed under the leadership of Sri Chinmoy, an Indian spiritual teacher, who took an approach that Thant fully supported. The group, still in existence today, honors all religions, is open to all, offers silent meditations for delegates, staff, and NGO representatives, and organizes a vigorous program of UN lectures, concerts, and commemorations (including UN charter day walks and annual peace runs). The group later established the U Thant Peace Award, which is offered to individuals who exemplify the aspirations of the former secretary-general. The awardees have included Nelson Mandela, Mikhail Gorbachev, Javier Perez de Cuellar, and Desmond Tutu, among many others. The November 1974 issue of *Meditation at the United Nations,* the monthly bulletin of the group, was dedicated to Thant shortly after he passed away. The bulletin was full of touching tributes, including those given by ambassadors in a special service of commemoration that the group organized the day after Thant's passing. At the commemorative service, Sri Chinmoy's remarks revealed the depth of spiritual appreciation for the late secretary-general: "Beloved Brother, man of silence, man of peace, may the Supreme grant your soul Eternity's Silence, Infinity's Peace."

By embracing spirituality, Thant overcame the problems of narrow sectarianism and religious disharmony. He chose to focus on the commonality of all religions, the spiritual essentials that easily relate to the UN charter and that unite peoples and nations: "How are we to practice tolerance? What states of mind are necessary for all of us to live together in peace with one another as good neighbors? How are we to unite our strength to maintain international peace and security? The answers to these questions lie, it seems to me, in our ability to bring out the best in us and to return to the basic moral and ethical principles of all great religions."[151]

Conclusion

Thant served the United Nations during a tumultuous decade of world history, a period that put to the test his faith in both Buddhism and the UN charter. Fortunately, these two aspects of Thant's thinking were not only compatible but mutually supportive. His reservoir of good will and tolerance, gained through meditation and Buddhist practice, helped him to be an effective UN mediator between the East and West in the Cold War, between the North and South in the age of decolonization, and between emerging nations in the global South. In the world-threatening Cuban missile crisis, he was able to serve as a humble bridge between nuclear-armed superpowers as well as to placate a furious Castro in Havana. Because of his self-effacing style, even his strong criticisms of superpower actions, for example in Vietnam and Czechoslovakia, were tolerated by them. After the Six-Day War he allowed himself to become a convenient scapegoat for international inaction, accepting this unenviable role with as much Buddhist detachment as could be summoned.

His Buddhist-internationalist ethical framework was possible because he took a broad view of his religion and embraced a spiritual view of humanity. He placed the human being at the center of his considerations long before the modern terms "human security" or "sovereignty of the individual" became popular. For him, the differences between North and South, East and West were much less important than the everyday human struggle for dignity and the inherent oneness of humanity. His belief in cosmic law and order (*Dhamma* in Pali, or *Dharma* in Sanskrit) led him naturally to seek the rule of international law and order based on the organized will of the international community as expressed through the United Nations. His Buddhist belief in nonviolence and human equality helped him speak from the depths of conviction about the necessity of peaceful dispute settlement, the nonuse of force, and fundamental human rights.

Ethical dilemmas did arise in his term of office. He ordered UN peacekeepers to use force to prevent the secession of Katanga from the Congo. Though his conscience was troubled by this necessity, he justified this use of force as a last resort, authorized by a legitimate body (the Security Council) and applied at the minimum level necessary to accomplish the aim, as well as other just war criteria. In addition, he stood strongly against secessionism in the Congo as in any other country.

He faced another dilemma when countries ruthlessly suppressed rebel movements but rejected his overtures to play a pacifying or mediating role. In the Biafra-Nigeria conflict, he accepted a minor role in humanitarian relief at a time when many nations were calling for a greater role. Similarly, when Egypt requested the withdrawal of UN peacekeepers from its territory, he dutifully complied after Nasser rebuffed his peace initiative. He accepted the centrality of state sovereignty and respected the right of states to determine the extent of his intervention in their affairs. Again, he humbly placed himself in the background.

When Thant did intervene, he adopted an impartial attitude, using the charter as his compass. He felt that the secretary-general could not pick sides or favorites and should judge only actions, not people. Furthermore, his Buddhist practice was to show good will and compassion to all, without discrimination. He rejected neutrality, as that would mean turning a blind eye to suffering and the wanton destruction of war, and sought to give all a sense of peace, even seeming adversaries like Tshombe.

When his personal convictions conflicted with UN resolutions, he felt obliged to support the UN organs, though sometimes admitting to two views (the "two U Thants"). Here his Buddhist sense of self-effacement came in handy: He could sacrifice his personal views for the larger whole. Though he had a strong conscience, he kept himself humble and as detached as possible.

When conditions allowed, he did push the limits of his independence. He created new peacekeeping operations on his own authority and spoke out on many sensitive matters, all the while keeping within the bounds of UN policy. He did not hesitate to criticize even the great powers if they transgressed the UN charter or the resolutions of the main UN organs. He was outspoken against "colonialism, war, the arms race and unequal distribution of world resources."[152]

He had to find a Buddhist balance ("the middle path") between noble ideals and human realities. He accepted the limitations of office, proposing small but feasible steps while keeping his vision on the larger goal of world peace and social justice. He envisioned and fostered, using his considerable administrative skills, the creation of many new bodies, including the UN Development Program (UNDP) and the United Nations University.

Finally, his dream of a more spiritual United Nations was substantially realized with the creation of the UN Meditation Group in 1970. He wrote the group's leader, Sri Chinmoy, in 1972, "You have instilled in the minds of hundreds of people here the moral and spiritual values which both of us treasure very dearly."[153] Thant felt deeply that "the edifice of modern civilization must be built on spiritual principles,"[154] and that "the ideal of human synthesis has been developed by almost all great religions."[155] He held a holistic view of his religion among other religions and within the greater sphere of human activity and experience.

Thant's life and actions showed that Buddhism is not only a personal voyage with the goal of nirvana, the perfect state of inner meditation, but also a life of service to the world—one committed to the peace between as well as within human beings. He was a novel and rare example of a Buddhist on the international stage, an important political figure who sought to apply good will and compassion in global politics. Thant was a prime example of Buddhism in action.

Notes

1. U Thant is pronounced "Oo Thawnt," though Burmese frequently make the final "t" a silent one. The prefix *U* shows respect and is roughly equivalent to the English word "mister" (literally "uncle"). Like many Burmese, Thant had only one name. In Burma (Myanmar), he is called "Pantanaw Thant" to identify him more clearly.

2. Quoted in June Bingham, *U Thant: The Search for Peace* (New York: Knopf, 1966), 281.

3. Gertrude Samuels, "The Meditation of U Thant," *New York Times Magazine,* December 13, 1964, 32; Bingham, *U Thant.* Bingham and Thant became acquainted when he was still an ambassador. After he became secretary-general she gained his reluctant permission to write his biography. She lived near him in the Riverdale neighborhood of New York City, which gave her the opportunity to meet him occasionally and ask questions. She also made a trip to Burma to interview Thant's relatives and to research the conditions and history of Burma, something that helped gain Thant's approval for the book.

4. U Thant, *View from the UN* (Garden City, NY: Doubleday, 1978), 20.

5. Unfortunately, Cripps's 1942 proposals were rejected by the Indian National Congress, and India began down the painful road of partition.

6. Bingham, *U Thant,* 97, 125.

7. Ibid., 171.

8. Ibid., 190.

9. Ibid., 194.

10. Ibid., 220.

11. Robert Muller, *The Example of a Great Ethical Statesman: U Thant,* special supplement to the United Nations Meditation Group Bulletin, January 1977 (Jamaica, NY: Agni Press, 1977); and Robert Muller, *New Genesis: Shaping a Global Spirituality* (Garden City, NY: Doubleday, 1982), 132.

12. Muller, *Example of a Great Ethical Statesman,* 9.

13. Thant, *View from the UN,* 7.

14. Bingham, *U Thant,* 280. On September 19, 1966, Thant issued an unequivocal statement: "It is my belief, as I have said more than once in the past, that a Secretary-General of the United Nations should not normally serve for more than one term. I have similarly made it known that I do not believe in the concept of indispensability of any particular person for any particular job. In the circumstances the conclusion I have reached will, I hope, be understood by all my friends and colleagues: I have decided not to offer myself for a second term as Secretary-General, and to leave the Security Council unfettered in its recommendation to the General Assembly with regard to the next Secretary-General." UN Press release SG/SM/567, September 19, 1966, quoted in Raymond B. Fosdick, *The League and the United Nations After Fifty Years: The Six Secretaries-General* (Newton, CT: Raymond B. Fosdick, 1972), 159.

15. "With genuine esteem for the Secretary-General himself delegate after delegate took the rostrum and pleaded [with] the Secretary-General to reconsider" his decision not to accept a second term. *Newsweek,* October 1996, quoted in the *Jakarta Post,* "Myanmar's U Thant Steered United Nations During Crisis," January 24, 2000, available at www.globalpolicy.org/secgen/pastsg/uthant00.htm.

16. Bingham, *U Thant,* 259. Thant did accept two dozen honorary degrees from universities around the world. They are listed in Sri Chinmoy, *U Thant: Divinity's Smile, Humanity's Cry* (Jamaica, NY: Agni Press, 1977), 10. He also accepted the Jawaharlal Nehru Award for International Understanding in 1967 from the government of India (Chinmoy, *U Thant: Divinity's Smile,* 14); Thant, *View from the UN,* 23; and C. V. Narasimhan, *United Nations at 50: Recollections* (Delhi: Konark Publishers, 1996), 129.

17. Quoted in Brian Urquhart, *Ralph Bunche: An American Odyssey* (New York: W. W. Norton, 1993), 396.

18. Thant, *View from the UN,* 61.

19. Quoted in Brian Urquhart, *A Life in Peace and War* (New York: Harper and Row, 1987), 203.

20. Quoted in Bingham, *U Thant.*

21. Alan James, "U Thant and His Critics," in *The Year Book of World Affairs, 1972,* ed. G. W. Keeton and G. Schwartzenberger (London: Stevens, 1972), 43–64.

22. U Thant to Alan James, 1972, in UN Archives, New York, Series 0893, box 6, file 41. Professor James and the journal editor wrote back that it was not possible to supply the copies.

23. Thant, *View from the UN,* 352.

24. Urquhart, *Life in Peace and War,* 190.

25. Thant, *View from the UN,* chapter 8. See especially 268–71.

26. U Thant, *Portfolio for Peace: Excerpts from the Writings and Speeches of U Thant, Secretary-General of the United Nations, on Major World Issues, 1961–1968* (New York: United Nations, 1968), 29.

27. Bingham, *U Thant,* 5.

28. Ibid., 7. Many thought Thant's comment was a drastic if not amusing understatement. Tshombe had ordered the harassment and killing of UN peace-keepers in Katanga, and probably had the Congolese prime minister, Patrice Lumumba, killed as well. Thant's full statement was: "Mr. Tshombe is a very unstable man, he is a very unpredictable man. The same can be said of his two colleagues. . . . I have tried to get Mr. Tshombe and the Central [Congolese] government to negotiate, but without any result. I don't know what I can do with such a bunch of clowns." Quoted in Fosdick, *League and the United Nations,* 148.

29. Narasimhan, *United Nations at 50,* 182. In late 1964 Thant was admitted to a New York hospital for treatment of an ulcer. He received a transfusion, prompting colleagues to remark that Thant was now "part American . . . let us hope his neutralism has not been diluted!" Quoted in Bingham, *U Thant,* 15.

30. Urquhart, *Life in Peace and War,* 226.

31. Quoted in Muller, *New Genesis,* 50.

32. Bingham, *U Thant,* 4.

33. Urquhart, *Life in Peace and War,* 190.

34. Thant, *Portfolio for Peace,* 3.

35. Bingham, *U Thant,* 110.

36. Ibid., 5.

37. Muller, *Example of a Great Ethical Statesman,* 2.

38. George Ignatieff, *The Making of a Peacemonger* (Toronto: University of Toronto Press, 1985), 226.

39. "A Visit with U Thant," *New Republic,* January 8, 1966, 11.

40. Urquhart, *Life in Peace and War,* 190.

41. Thant, *View from the UN,* 23.

42. Bingham, *U Thant,* 11; and Narasimhan, *United Nations at 50,* 84. Ramses Nassif, who, along with C. V. Narasimhan, brought the news of the death of his son, recalls that his first words were: "I wonder how my wife will take it." Ramses Nassif, *U Thant in New York, 1961–1971: A Portrait of the Third UN Secretary-General* (London: C. Hurst, 1988), 21. Apparently Thant carried on with his duties at the United Nations that day, but later, when a reporter expressed sympathy, his eyes filled with tears. Samuels, "Meditation of U Thant," 116.

43. Bingham, *U Thant,* 198.

44. Ibid., 121, 232.

45. Quoted in Chinmoy, *U Thant: Divinity's Smile,* 64.

46. Thant, *View from the UN,* 20. Close colleagues like Ralph Bunche were able to detect subtle signs of irritation and nervousness on occasion, such as thumping pencils, bumping knees, and chain-smoking of cigars. Urquhart, *Bunche,* 396.

47. Quoted in Douglas Gillies, *Prophet: The Hatmaker's Son* (Santa Barbara, CA: East Beach Press, 2003), 23.

48. Both men quoted in Chinmoy, *U Thant: Divinity's Smile,* 63, 34.

49. George Ignatieff, "U Thant as Secretary-General: Private Qualities in Public Life," *International Perspectives* (January–February 1975): 35.

50. Robert Muller, *Most of All, They Taught Me Happiness* (Garden City, NY: Doubleday, 1978). See also Muller's *New Genesis* and *Example of a Great Ethical Statesman.*

51. UN Press Release SG/SM/822, October 20, 1967, reprinted as "Statement on the Role of Religious Convictions at the Third International Teach-In, 22 October 1967," in Andrew W. Cordier and Max Harrelson, eds., *Public Papers of the Secretaries-General of the United Nations,* vol. 7, *U Thant, 1965–1967* (New York: Columbia University Press, 1976), 599–602.

52. Thant, *Portfolio for Peace,* 14.

53. Cordier and Harrelson, *Public Papers,* 7:600.

54. Thant, *View from the UN,* 21.

55. The main Buddhist scripture, the *Dhammapada,* does not give exceptions to the rule of nonviolence, but there are references to permitted violence in other Buddhist texts.

56. Bingham, *U Thant,* 74.

57. Thant, *View from the UN,* 21.

58. U Thant, "On Tension in the Middle East," in Thant, *Towards World Peace: Addresses and Public Statements* (New York: Yoseloff), 29.

59. Bingham, *U Thant,* 61.

60. Thant, *Towards World Peace,* 398.

61. C. V. Narasimhan, "U Thant as I Knew Him," *Secretariat News,* December 16, 1964, quoted in Narasimhan, *United Nations at 50,* 184.

62. Thant, *View from the UN,* 254.

63. Ibid., 186.

64. Ibid., 26.

65. UN charter, article 1.4.

66. Fosdick, *League and the United Nations,* 145.

67. Thant, *View from the UN,* 145.

68. Ibid., 24; and Bingham, *U Thant,* 273.

69. Thant, *View from the UN,* 406.

70. Nassif, *U Thant in New York,* 56

71. Quoted in Muller, *New Genesis,* 113. Also available at www.christusrex.org/www1/pope/UN-1965.html.

72. The group at present is called Sri Chinmoy: The Peace Meditation at the United Nations. It meets twice weekly at UN headquarters for silent nondenominational meditation.

73. Chinmoy, *U Thant: Divinity's Smile,* 47. Sri Chinmoy's play is available at www.srichinmoylibrary.com/siddhartha-becomes-buddha.

74. Muller, *Example of a Great Ethical Statesman,* 7.

75. Chinmoy, *U Thant: Divinity's Smile,* 6.

76. Thant, *View from the UN,* 441, 444, 452.

77. Ibid., 454

78. Ibid., 144.

79. Quoted in Bingham, *U Thant,* 185.

80. Thant, *Portfolio for Peace,* 6.

81. Ibid., 49, 42, 72.

82. Thant, *Towards World Peace,* 400 (emphasis added).

83. Ibid., 282.

84. Andrew W. Cordier and Max Harrelson, *Public Papers of the Secretaries-General of the United Nations,* vol. 6, *U Thant, 1961–1964* (New York: Columbia University Press, 1976), 135.

85. Security Council Resolution 169, November 24, 1961, available at www.un.org/documents/sc/res/1961/scres61.htm.

86. Fosdick, *League and the United Nations,* 146–47.

87. Quoted in Trevor Findlay, *The Blue Helmets' First War? Use of Force by the UN in the Congo, 1960–64* (Clementsport, Nova Scotia: Canadian Peacekeeping Press, 1999), 115.

88. Thant, *View from the UN,* 137; and A. Walter Dorn and David Bell, "Intelligence and Peacekeeping: The UN Operation in the Congo, 1960–64," *International Peacekeeping* 2 (1995): 11–33.

89. Thant, *View from the UN,* 143.

90. Ibid., 144.

91. Ironically, after a short exile abroad, Tshombe returned to the Congo and became its prime minister in July 1964 in a coalition government, serving at the helm of the very country he had earlier tried to break up. After corrupt elections, however, he was forced to flee to Spain. On June 30, 1967, his plane was hijacked to Algeria, where he was confined to jail, and he died from heart failure in 1969.

92. Findlay, *Blue Helmets' First War,* 135.

93. Statistics on fatalities in UN peacekeeping operations are provided at www.un.org/Depts/dpko/fatalities/fatal1.htm. The ongoing UN Force in Lebanon (UNIFIL), established in 1978, has the same number of fatalities as ONUC had in its four years of operation (1960–64): 250. The UN forces in the former Yugoslavia (UNPROFOR, UNPF, and UNPREDEP, 1992–95) suffered 228 fatalities over a four-year period.

94. Thant, *View from the UN,* 145.

95. Dorn and Bell, "Intelligence and Peacekeeping."

96. Thant, *View from the UN,* 107.

97. *United Nations Monthly Chronicle,* No. 36 (February 1970): 1.

98. Security Council Resolution 161, February 21, 1961, available at www.un.org/documents/sc/res/1961/scres61.htm.

99. Thant, *View from the UN*, 108.

100. Ibid., 138.

101. Quoted in Findlay, *Blue Helmets' First War*, 131.

102. Ibid., 118. These are words from Thant's authorization for use of force on December 5, 1961.

103. Thant, *View from the UN*, 144–45.

104. Ibid., 328.

105. This provision can be traced back to the insistence of former president Howard Taft in his communications to Woodrow Wilson in Paris to appease conservatives in the U.S. Senate.

106. Ignatieff, *Making of a Peacemonger*, 237–39; and Thant, *View from the UN*, 54.

107. Thant, *View from the UN*, 53.

108. Cordier and Harrelson, *Public Papers*, 6:132.

109. "Statement by Secretary-General U Thant at the Assembly of Heads of State and Government of the Organization of African Unity," UN Press Release SG/112, July 17, 1964, available at www.rfksa.org/documents/5.php#37; Thant, *Portfolio for Peace*, 98.

110. Samuels, "Meditation of U Thant," 115; and quoted by Ambassador Zenon Rossides in Chinmoy, *U Thant: Divinity's Smile*, 17.

111. Thant, *View from the UN*, 44.

112. Bingham, *U Thant*, 253.

113. Thant, *View from the UN*, 343.

114. Ibid., 302–6. Thant was surprised to learn after the hijacking that Italy had secretly worked out a deal for the release of Arab insurgents in Israeli jails.

115. Bingham, *U Thant*, 196.

116. Ibid., 272.

117. Fosdick, *League and the United Nations*, 145.

118. Cordier and Harrelson, *Public Papers*, 6:254.

119. Thant, *View from the UN*, 44, 33.

120. Bingham, *U Thant*, 238.

121. Ibid., 259.

122. Samuels, "Meditation of U Thant," 115.

123. Quoted in Thant, *View from the UN*, 230.

124. Ibid., 268.

125. Ibid., 50.

126. Ibid., 382.

127. Cordier and Harrelson, *Public Papers*, 6:71.

128. Ibid., 222. Bingham believes that the Soviets censored these critical words from his address to the Soviet people.

129. Thant, *View from the UN*, 67; Bingham, *U Thant*, 267.

130. Cordier and Harrelson, *Public Papers*, 6:168.

131. Urquhart, *Life in Peace and War*, 226; and Nassif, *U Thant in New York*, 24.

132. Farewell address to the UN General Assembly, quoted in the *Jakarta Post,* January 24, 2000.

133. Quoted in Muller, *Example of a Great Ethical Statesman,* 6.

134. Bingham, *U Thant,* 277.

135. John A. Stormer, *None Dare Call It Treason* (Florissant, MO: Liberty Bell Press, 1964), quoted in Bingham, *U Thant,* 278.

136. Thant quoted in Urquhart, *Bunche,* 429.

137. Kofi Annan, "Secretary-General's message for the launch of the U Thant Institute," December 5, 2003, available at www.un.org/apps/sg/sgstats .asp?nid=680. The homepage of the institute is www.uthantinstitute.org.

138. Quoted in Bingham, *U Thant,* 238.

139. Nassif, *U Thant in New York,* 16.

140. Thant, *Portfolio for Peace,* 3–5.

141. Security Council meetings at the head of state level occurred on January 31, 1992, September 8, 2000, at the time of the Millennium Summit, and September 14, 2005. However, heads of state gather each year for the opening of a new General Assembly.

142. In the 1960s the International Court of Justice issued only four judgments and one advisory opinion. In the 1990s the ICJ issued thirty-five judgments and three advisory opinions.

143. For example, in the *Certain Expenses* Case of 1962, the ICJ determined that, in accordance with the UN charter, the cost of UN peacekeeping was a regular expense of the organization and hence an obligation of all member states.

144. With the admission of Switzerland in 2002, no major state remains outside the United Nations, unless Taiwan is considered a separate state. Most countries consider Taiwan part of the People's Republic of China.

145. Thant, *View from the UN,* 43.

146. Nassif, *U Thant in New York,* 24.

147. Thant devotes a chapter of his memoirs to his pilgrimages to major Buddhist sites in south Asia in 1967. In Kandi, Sri Lanka, he visited the temple of the Sacred Tooth Relic. In India, newly installed prime minister Indira Gandhi arranged for his visit to Sanchi, the location of *stupas* and other monuments built by the Buddhist emperor Ashoka around 250 B.C. In Pakistan, Foreign Minister Ali Bhutto escorted him on a visit to Taxila, an ancient Buddhist seat of learning under excavation. Thant wrote that he was "speechless with awe and veneration" (*View from the UN,* 405). In Nepal, the king provided his personal helicopter to allow Thant to visit Lumbini, the birthplace of the Buddha. It was "one of the most important days of my life" (ibid., 417). Thant was disappointed, however, by the physical state of the site. He eagerly initiated a joint UNESCO-Nepali project to develop the sacred location that later was declared a "World Heritage Site."

148. Cordier and Harrelson, *Public Papers,* 6:9.

149. Quoted in Muller, *New Genesis,* 8.

150. Gillies, *Prophet,* 23.

151. "Secretary-General's New Year Message," UN Headquarters, December 23, 1966, quoted in "The United Nations and World Peace: A Tribute to U Thant, A Symposium and Commemoration of the Eighty-Fifth Birth Anniversary of the Late Secretary-General," Harvard University, January 21, 1994 (unpublished photo exhibition).

152. Bernard J. Firestone, *The United Nations Under U Thant, 1961–1971* (Lanham, MD: Scarecrow Press, 2001), 108.

153. Chinmoy, *U Thant: Divinity's Smile,* 52.

154. Nassif, *U Thant in New York,* 61.

155. Thant, *View from the UN,* 24.

6

AN ETHICAL ENIGMA
Another Look at Kurt Waldheim

MICHAEL T. KUCHINSKY

Kurt Waldheim, as the fourth secretary-general of the United Nations, in many ways remains an enigma. How can one man represent the world's loftiest principles as grounded in the UN charter, yet fall to the level of a suspected war criminal condemned for the international community's most heinous sins? What adequately explains a man whose role in advancing such causes as peace building, economic development, and human rights made him sought after and welcomed for many years, but later shunned as a blot on the international system?

Enigmas embrace paradoxes, ironies, and multiple explanations. They discomfort us. So, too, does the diplomatic career and life of Secretary-General Waldheim, provoking questions about the relationship between religious and moral values and his policy decisions. A hasty answer—that his deficiencies were an extension of Cold War superpower politics, or the inherent structural weaknesses of the United Nations, or a matter of personal ambition trumping social justice—may be comforting, but they are also inadequate. All of these choices are present in the life and work of the man.

Ethically ambiguous images create tensions or polarizing experiences, becoming symbols that point to larger issues.[1] Examples of this for many Americans might be the concept of abortion, red-and-blue voting maps, Abu Ghraib, or Vietnam, all of which produce tensions and disputed values in the United States.[2] Waldheim is another such symbol, and because his public life spans decades in the global spotlight, he provokes varied responses.[3]

This chapter examines whether and how Waldheim's ethical framework influenced his policy choices while secretary-general. Waldheim's approach to the Cyprus and Middle East conflicts, his efforts in Namibia's quest for national independence, the pursuit of the UN Human Rights

Statement on Religious Tolerance, and his concerns over employment practices in the Secretariat are its focus. At the same time, information concerning Waldheim's World War II service record, specifically the alleged crimes and his defense against the allegations, raise unique (and troubling) moral questions. When one takes into account the different sources for his values, Waldheim's actions across situations suggest that his Roman Catholic religious values do not by themselves explain his actions. Instead, Waldheim's pragmatism provides a better explanation of his conduct in office.

Scholars have identified Cyprus, the Middle East, and Namibia as signature issues of Waldheim's tenure as UN secretary-general. He inherited them from his predecessors, worked on them during his time in office, and passed them on to his successors. Thus they make a suitable lens through which to view his policy choices and practice. In addition, the movement toward a UN Religious Human Rights document, although it began before Waldheim took office, was approved by the General Assembly in the last days of his second term. The administrative challenges of hiring practices in the Secretariat, faced by all secretaries-general, can also contribute to our understanding of Waldheim.[4]

One answer to the question of who we are as individuals and as a species was given in a theological creedal formula—*similar justus et pecator*—which translates roughly as "one who is both justified and sinner." Waldheim was certainly at least this. What follows is an analytical dialogue about Waldheim, his ethical framework, and several cases from his work while secretary-general.

Values and Contexts

Waldheim was born in 1918, in the chaotic years between two world wars and the dissolution of the Austrian empire. The time of his ethical and intellectual formation witnessed a nation searching for its identity and stability amid interparty rivalry, an economy in collapse and an uncoordinated coalition government reeling under reparations debt, the rise of an indigenous Nazi Party and a nationalist militia (the *Heimwehr*), an end to parliamentary government (1933), an attempted coup, a civil war between Christian Socialists and Social Democrats (1934), the growth of fascist movements under Mussolini and Hitler, the assassination of the Austrian chancellor, Engelbert Dollfuss, the debilitating national debate over *Anschluss* (Germany's annexation of Austria), Germany's invasion (1938), and a Vienna that would become a prewar testing ground for German policies against Jews and other minorities.[5] Waldheim commented that "the greatest impetus to my choosing a diplomatic and political career was provided by the circumstances and events of the era in which I grew to manhood," and he pursued this ambitious vocation in spite of his father's hope that he would become a teacher.[6]

The fortunes of Waldheim's family life paralleled the national storms. His father, Walter Waldheim, was a schoolteacher and an active member of the Christian Social Party (CSP), the more conservative party of the day, aligned with the Roman Catholic Church. The family was Roman Catholic (staunchly so, according to some), and Waldheim attended Catholic Mass even during the war years.[7] His father was promoted to the position of school administrator and ultimately superintendent of schools in Tulln, the community where Waldheim and his siblings grew up. Walter Waldheim attended CSP meetings and supported Austrian nationalism and independence, anti-Nazism, and resistance to plans for *Anschluss*— positions that would later lead to his arrest by the Gestapo, followed by the loss of his position and pension. Waldheim supported his father's political and nationalist positions, but he did not officially join any party.

Although Waldheim was raised Roman Catholic, were there any specific indicators of a religious character that would surface in his later work as secretary-general? He commented in *The Challenge of Peace* on the importance of religion:

> I have always held that religion must remain separate from politics. In our family, faith was perceived as a deeply personal commitment that must derive from individual volition. A priest at school had already taken great pains to teach me that religion has more to do with love and humanitarian concern than creed and that all great faiths embody principles akin to the Ten Commandments so fundamental to my own Catholic convictions. Those early lessons have been greatly reinforced by my experiences in the diplomatic service. I have met many peoples and learned much of many cultures other than my own, and these encounters have only expanded my religious outlook. That is why I maintain that the spiritual aspirations of all peoples and all religions must be respected quite apart from other human enterprise, since they are universally directed towards improving our common condition.[8]

What stands out in this passage is not so much Waldheim's Catholic origins but his conviction that all religions strive to improve the human condition.

This is of more interest to Waldheim than any particular religious tradition or notion of transcendence. When asked directly about his religious heritage and its significant values, Waldheim responded by detailing the practices of a Roman Catholic household (such as attending Mass, confirmation, and baptism), and then listed the Ten Commandments as influential for understanding the concepts of tolerance and acceptance among people.[9] Religion may be influential but it is acted upon privately, influences choices indirectly, and becomes less important once removed from concrete applications. Can any of these personal religious values be linked to the teachings of his church?

Papal teaching affirmed the long-standing tradition of Catholic social action for the purposes of achieving human social good, charity, and justice in times of crisis, and this teaching was reaffirmed by Popes Benedict XV and Pius XI between the two world wars.[10] Peace among nations was to be considered the will of God, while war and its consequences were seen as outmoded forms of international relationship.[11] Providing for both social order and human dignity in the household, the economy, the state, and the international system of states was not outside the interests of God or the teachings of the church.[12] The Roman Catholic Church vigorously defended its truth claims against competing ideologies, especially those of liberalism, fascism, and communism, while pointing out the oppressive ill effects of these ideologies on the church. Of particular interest in this series of attacks on other ideologies was one that Pius XI directed specifically at the leaders of the church in Germany and of the German people delivered on March 14, 1937.

> Whoever exalts race, or the people, or the State, or a particular form of State, or the depositories of power, or any other fundamental value of the human community—however necessary and honorable be their function in worldly things—whoever raises these notions above their standard value and divinizes them to an idolatrous level, distorts and perverts an order of the world planned and created by God, he is far from the true faith in God and from the concept of life which that faith upholds. Beware, Venerable Brethren, of that growing abuse in speech as in writing, of the name of God as though it were a meaningless label to be affixed to any creation, more or less arbitrary, of human speculation.[13]

Taken collectively, the interwar encyclicals provided a vision for global order and charitable human relationships in keeping with past church claims of its authority and truth, while bearing witness against false ideologies and the oppression of the church. As Pius XII wrote in *Democracy and a Lasting Peace*, giving voice to the hopes of church leaders for an outcome of World War II:

> It is the duty to do everything to ban once and for all wars of aggression as a legitimate solution of international disputes and as a means towards realizing national aspirations. . . . Many attempts in this direction have been seen in the past. They all failed. And they will all fail always, until the saner section of mankind has the firm determination, the holy obstinacy, like an obligation of conscience, to fulfill the mission which past ages have not undertaken with sufficient gravity and resolution. . . . If ever a generation has had to appreciate in the depths of its conscience the call: "war on war," it is certainly the present generation. . . . The decisions already published by international commissions permit one to conclude that an essential point in any future international arrangement would be the formation of an organ for the maintenance of peace, of an organ invested by common consent with supreme power to whose office it would also pertain to smother in its germinal state any threat of isolated or collective aggression. . . . No one could hail this development with greater joy than he who has long upheld the principle that the idea of war as an apt and proportionate means of solving international conflicts is now out of date.[14]

Waldheim's personal faith converged neatly with such principles. But his religious idealism, if it can be called that, stood side by side with a sort of cultural pragmatism.[15] Several of Waldheim's colleagues interviewed for this chapter referred to the importance of culture in his "Austrian-ness" and to the Austrian characteristic of being able "to make one's way." What they meant by this was an ability to pursue personal goals even in the face of external obstacles, but also a willingness to compromise when necessary, and to put off the achievement of those goals until the circumstances were more propitious. One of Waldheim's colleagues described this as "Waldheim's Austrian realistic and pragmatic instinct for politics."[16]

Classical pragmatists understood that the discovery of truths and ethical choices were intimately related to experience and context, which defined those truths in light of outcomes, utility, and practicality: "Grant an idea or belief to be true . . . what concrete difference will its being true make in any one's actual life? . . . What, in short, is the truth's cash-value in experiential terms?"[17] Put most simply, that which is true is that which proves most useful, especially in relation to the individual.[18] Discovering and acting upon truth and value require responding to problems and challenges by adapting to current conditions, understandings, and beliefs. In order to ascertain truths, "inquiry proceeds from an interruption or dis-equilibrium in experience and is addressed to the solution of particular, concrete problems considered in context."[19] Principles become working hypotheses; truths must be modified as discoveries and outcomes become clear and verifiable; truth contributes to utility and human good, all best achieved within the dialogical community.[20] In essence, "political pragma-tism is a form of instrumentalism geared at emergent ends-in-view . . . it refers knowledge to experience, to the consequences of ideas and action, and to the possibilities inherent in present relationships; it also places con-siderable faith in education and communication as ways of creating the conditions necessary for democratic social change."[21]

There is a significant scientific and experimental quality in the practic-ing pragmatist, but it is not devoid of a moral dimension.[22] Because moral pragmatism insists that value (ethical and otherwise) is achieved in the rational encounter between the personal and social dimensions of self-hood, the individual has an obligation to contribute positively as part of an ongoing self-developmental process that leads to what can or should be.[23] Thus a type of moral imperative and willfulness arises, where nothing of value comes to pass by escaping from the world and allowing its indeter-minacy to take its own course. Not knowing what any final result (and certainly no absolute or guaranteed result) will be, the individual strives to "face life courageously and bring out of it what he can."[24] Although it is unlikely that Waldheim studied the American pragmatists, he certainly studied some of their European roots—Immanuel Kant, G. W. Leibniz, Jeremy Bentham, and Rudolf Lotze.[25]

In addition, Waldheim's colleagues described "Austrian-ness" as an interest in and an awareness of the importance of professional roles, authorities, and protocol. This worked itself out in Waldheim's effort to elevate the office of the secretary-general to be equal to heads of state or government.[26] Waldheim remarked with pride that he had restored respect to the office of secretary-general—a quality lost since the origin of the United Nations—on account of his interest in protocol.[27]

Waldheim and War: Making the Way

The prospect of war stood in the middle of Waldheim's formative years. He spent the years before World War II alternating between academic study and military service. At the end of his formal schooling in 1936 and before attending university, Waldheim enlisted in Austria's compulsory military service, choosing to serve one year in the cavalry followed by reserve duty. In 1937 he was admitted into the Vienna University and the Consular Academy to prepare for his career in diplomacy and law, but Waldheim would lose his academic position a year later with his father's arrest. A fellow student commented that he was known to be an active liberal Catholic and an anti-Nazi.[28] Yet Waldheim became a member of the National Socialist Student League in 1938 and was called to active duty in 1938 in the German army.[29] He returned to the Vienna Academy to complete his consular program and pass basic legal examinations in 1940, before being sent to a military reconnaissance unit in France. From there, Waldheim's active military service continued on the Eastern Front, where he was wounded in battle and medically discharged and repatriated to resume the study of law in 1941. Years later Waldheim reflected on his military service:

> It was impossible to escape military service. . . . I was called up, along with my brother just as World War II began. . . . Actually, at that period, a soldier was better off than a civilian if his politics were questionable. . . . Anti-Nazi literature was circulated under cover and, of course, I read it all. I found men who shared my views, and our long discussions gave us a chance to air our feelings. Sunday Mass was well attended. It provided us with a rallying point and a means of manifesting our opposition to the notoriously anti-religious policies of the regime. . . . The knowledge that I was serving in the German army was hard to bear. Deliverance from my bitter situation finally came when our unit moved into active combat on the Eastern front in 1941. I was wounded in the leg and medically discharged.[30]

Contrary to this assertion that Waldheim was discharged after sustaining the leg wound, military records show that Waldheim was reassigned to Army Group E in the Balkans and became a staff support intelligence officer and translator at the rank of lieutenant, was decorated numerous times for his military service, returned intermittently to Vienna to complete his doctoral studies, and remained in active duty until the end of the war. Portions of Army Group E oversaw the removal of more than forty thousand Jews from Salonika and, in the latter stages of Germany's retreat from the Balkans, engaged in atrocities against nationalist Balkan Serbs.[31]

Questions about Waldheim's military service first surfaced with a Yugoslavian request for extradition (1947) during Waldheim's service in Austria's Foreign Ministry.[32] Various writers, both individual and institutional, have seen differing degrees of political and moral damage to Waldheim's character and reputation as a result of his service in the Nazi army. Waldheim's defenders have tended to argue that his involvement was passive rather than active, and that his guilt is less a personal matter than a matter of Austria's collective guilt. As one of them has written, "After 1986, questions were raised about Waldheim's knowledge of and culpability in war crimes. It now seems clear that Waldheim did not play any active part in the tragedy of the Jewish population of Salonika, where forty thousand were shipped to death camps in Germany between June 1942 and May 1943."[33] Waldheim's defense also emerged from between the lines—he only carried out orders, was never in the vicinity when atrocities were committed, and was unable to recall or halt the trauma. His defenders have argued that no witnesses have been produced to implicate Waldheim personally in Nazi atrocities, or they have explained his participation as simply the result of the chaos of war.

In the 1980s, however, when the extent of Waldheim's service in the Nazi army came to light and became, for a time, an international media event, the voices of his many detractors overwhelmed those of his supporters. A report by the U.S. Department of Justice concluded that, "after a complete review of the available evidentiary materials . . . we have no doubt that during World War II, while serving as a Wehrmacht officer in the Balkans, Kurt Waldheim assisted or otherwise participated in persecution because of race, religion, national origin, or political opinion. Moreover, Mr. Waldheim has failed to rebut the case against him or otherwise demonstrate that he did not engage in activities."[34] The Pennsylvania state legislature passed a resolution requesting "the Honorable Kurt Waldheim, President of Austria, to resign because of his participation in and knowledge of war atrocities. . . . The International Historians' Commission concluded that Austrian President Kurt Waldheim had intimate guilty knowledge of Nazi atrocities."[35] That commission concluded that

> As O1 in Athens, Waldheim was aware of the practice of transporting Italian prisoners/internees to Germany in September 1943. . . . The higher command staffs were aware of these unlawful activities as well as of numerous executions. As O1, Waldheim probably had only limited practical possibilities of influencing the course of such events. His role as O3 in Arsakli in the framework of his function as intelligence officer for reports on the enemy situation can also be characterized in a similar manner. The picture which emerges is one of differing proximity, depending on position, to measures and orders which were incriminating in terms of the laws of war. These

conclusions do not provide a final answer to the question of Waldheim's wartime guilt. In general terms, even the mere knowledge of infringement of human rights near one's place may constitute a certain guilt—if a person, for lack of strength or courage, disregarded a human duty to intervene. . . . The Commission has not noted a single instance in which Waldheim protested or took steps . . . against an order to commit a wrong that he must doubtlessly have recognized as such. . . . One circumstance in Waldheim's favour is the fact that he had only extremely modest possibilities of any sort of opposition to the wrongs being committed. Such actions had highly differential importance depending on the level at which they were undertaken. The practical possibilities for counteraction were very limited for a young member of staff who had no power of command. . . . In all probability, such actions would not have led to any concrete result. . . . This would have appeared as a courageous act, but would hardly have resulted in any kind of practical success. . . . The Commission views its task as one relating to Waldheim's statements and descriptions regarding his military record. . . . Waldheim's own description of his military past does not tally at many points with the findings of the Commission. He attempted to let his military past slip into oblivion and, when that no longer proved possible, to play it down and make it appear innocuous.[36]

And one book that appeared after the revelations argued that "it is far more damaging for the collective conscience of Europe to live through the consequences of the scandal, namely, a victory for silence, despite pious assertions of a willingness for openness. . . . The case of the new President of Austria brutally demonstrates how the Old World has grown senile. The subtle distinctions made by professional war-crimes hunters between 'active' and 'passive' Nazis have proved to be inadequate."[37]

These far-ranging comments testify to the ambivalence we may feel about Waldheim. They ascribe various degrees of damage done by Waldheim to himself, to communities of people (Jews and Serbs), to a nation-state and its identity (Austria), and to the United Nations, or the modern prospect of Europe. In them, culpability is expunged and affirmed, parsed between active and passive acts, or elevated to an omission of guilt by an entire people unable to escape history. One can also recognize Waldheim's defense between the lines—carrying out orders, not in the vicinity, unable to recall, no witnesses, unable to halt the trauma, or the nature of chaotic times. And between accusation and defense there emerge the conflicts between the ideals and realities, the omissions and commissions, the *Zeit* and *Ziel* of Waldheim's very human capabilities.

The Constraining Environment of Public Service

With the end of World War II came a new world order and new international institutions, hope for a new Austria, and a new profession for Waldheim. Waldheim began his foreign-service career in 1945 optimistically: "I was still young enough to want to help to create a world in which oppression and injustice and all the corresponding social ills would no longer be tolerated, one in which my country might regain an honorable place and play a useful role again. . . . I was determined to lend whatever talents I possessed to that endeavor."[38] Waldheim's diplomatic career would move between Europe and North America, the Austrian Foreign Ministry and the United Nations, for nearly forty years.[39]

What was Waldheim's view of the challenges he faced as secretary-general? Some of his reflections about global order appeared in a work published during his campaign to replace U Thant as secretary-general. In *The Austrian Example,* Waldheim recounted the effects of the twentieth century on Austria, presenting his country's story as the pilgrimage of a modern neutral state, and the historical catharsis of Austria's experience:

> It is generally acknowledged that international peace, justice, order and development in the world are prerequisites for the survival and welfare of small countries. It has been Austria's experience that working actively towards these aims while remaining outside big power groups not only strengthens the independence and prosperity of a country but also contributes to a relaxation of tensions and a general improvement in the international climate. It might be an example that can point the way to new approaches to the goal we are all striving to reach: international peace, justice and prosperity.[40]

The Austrian Example analyzed important issues of the day—the relationship between the Soviet Union and the United States, détente and arms control talks, the inclusion of the People's Republic of China as a full member in the United Nations, the increasing interdependence among states, and the ongoing poverty gap for developing states.

Waldheim's wide-ranging agenda reflected his belief that the trauma of the war and the injustice that prevailed around the world needed to be addressed by whatever possible means. At the same time, he understood that this mission would have to be pursued within the prevailing structural constraint on progress—a Cold War order stalemated by two superpowers.

Waldheim saw the United Nations as a global forum in which all states could participate, a negotiating body focused upon the office of the secretary-general, and an institution of universal importance for global order as envisioned by its charter. The value of the United Nations, for Waldheim, lay in its necessary presence in international affairs as a forum of last resort for resolving interstate conflicts. At the same time, Waldheim was well aware of the constraints he would face as secretary-general, both those inherent in the international system and those built into the bureaucratic structure of the United Nations:

> It would have been easy to indulge in exalted romanticism about my new position. After all, I had just become, in a sense, a spokesman for humanity. Alas! The reality, I knew, was different. The lustre of the United Nations had dimmed in the twenty-five years since it had been established. I had seen enough of its day-to-day operations to know that moments of high drama and events of earth-shaking significance were rare. Instead, seen from the inside, the United Nations in 1972 was buffeted by ideological passions, nationalist rivalries, colonial and racial controversies, and conflicting economic and social demands. Its operations were cumbersome, often ineffectual, sometimes even mind-numbing.[41]

This pragmatic assessment of the institution and of his new office is echoed in the comments of others about Waldheim and the skills he brought to the task. Brian Urquhart wrote of Waldheim:

> Under the incessant pressures of his office, he has steadily developed the relationships, the techniques, and the approaches that are required to carry out the tasks with which he is entrusted. In the nature of things, the secretary-general is often given problems which no one else has been able to solve and must improvise as best he can a means of tackling them. . . . It demands above all a dedication to peace and to the principles and objectives of the United Nations Charter strong enough to overcome incessant setbacks, difficulties, and physical and mental fatigue.[42]

Waldheim made a similar point when he wrote:

> The secretary-general of the United Nations is charged with some tasks of extraordinary difficulty. In performing them, he obviously cannot make everybody happy. Each government expects support for its own position and is disappointed when it fails to get it. . . . The job seems impossible because it swings inexorably between frustration and satisfaction. . . . As its principal official, the secretary-general must also be chief administrator, diplomat, and representative of the United Nations. He is generally

held responsible for all that occurs in the Organization, even for resolutions of the General Assembly or other autonomous UN bodies that he has no authority to instruct. . . . The scope open to the secretary-general in the fulfillment of his tasks is both broad and narrow. It is broad in that his functions are defined so vaguely that he can act whenever he considers it in the interests of peace and co-operation to do so. It is narrow, because the secretary-general must be ever mindful of the interplay of forces among governments and of his role as honest broker. . . . Another contradiction in the secretary-general's role is that he is both dependent and autonomous.[43]

Waldheim gives more weight than Urquhart does to the tactical element in the challenges that any secretary-general will face. His sense of caution and awareness of the pitfalls is even more pronounced in the following passage:

At the level of the Secretary General, who must take action in areas of high political volatility, the maintenance of independence and neutrality poses a vexing dilemma. If the Secretary General takes the initiative to move left or right—acts or refrains from acting—on a particular issue, he will probably please some states and antagonize others. The Secretary General who loses the confidence of a permanent member of the Security Council enjoying the veto is in a most difficult position. His effectiveness is gravely impaired and his usefulness therefore jeopardized. He can work productively only if he maintains harmonious relations with United Nations members of all persuasions.[44]

Clearly, Waldheim had a good sense of the need to maneuver in a hostile environment and to be satisfied with incremental achievements.

Toward an Ethical Framework

What was Waldheim's personal code of values as he approached the enormously difficult job of secretary-general? The following passage addresses this question in perhaps one of his most introspective comments on his normative framework:

What had guided me along the lonely path through the undergrowth of ideologies and vested interests? . . . I feel that certain decisive influences can be traced: the history of Europe, my continent, and Austria, my homeland; my bitter experiences of war; my study of law and my diplomatic career; as well as my belief in democracy and the tenets of Christianity. Together they helped me to observe the claims of my conscience amidst all the different and often conflicting advice submitted by my international advisors. It was the tragic involvement of Europe in two world wars that engendered in me, as in so many of its citizens, the hope that national power politics could be overcome, and gave birth to my dream of a supranational world government. It was Austria's indefatigable will to recover, and its active policy of neutrality, which showed me and my countrymen what solidarity and hard work can achieve and how bridges can be built between neighbours, however different their ideological concepts might be. It was the war, with its hecatombs of innocent victims and ravages of minds and material, that convinced me of just how much men and women all over the world cherish one common desire: peace and security for themselves and their children. It was my study of law that brought home to me the degree to which a peaceful family of nations is dependent upon the observance of mutually accepted norms as well as upon an international mechanism for solving conflict. It was [through] my diplomatic career . . . that I learnt to overcome distrust and skepticism through personal contacts and patient dialogue free of all emotions. It was allegiance to democracy, tempered by the experience of fascism, which taught me that in the final analysis nothing is weaker than dictatorship. . . . Nowhere have I found another with a comparable degree of success and respect for human dignity. Finally, it was my Christian faith that led me to recognize and, wherever possible, alleviate the spiritual and material misery of others. At the same time, there is nothing more profoundly disturbing than the use of religious fanaticism for political ends, regardless of denomination.[45]

Rather than stress his Catholicism as a unique determinant in his decision making, Waldheim presented his moral code as the result of numerous influences and experiences. His liberalism is apparent in his belief in upholding human dignity, the importance of international law for fostering security, the value of democratic institutions, and the hope that international organizations might deter the passions of national power politics.[46] The experience of war had taught him that war promises not glory but only the pain and suffering of the innocent and victimized. Indeed, the experience of the war so dominates his reflections that one can summarize his views as follows:

1. The world must learn to avoid Europe's tragic twentieth-century history.
2. Dialogue among conflicting parties is always better than silence.
3. War never achieves its intended results.
4. Reason is to be preferred to passion.
5. Tragedies can be avoided by persistent effort.
6. Collective action is preferred over national action.
7. Any specifically religious motivation for decisions must be balanced against competing values—a pragmatic process.

Waldheim's words, life experiences, and others' comments suggest that several strands of moral values coexist in his inner code, sometimes in uneasy tension. First, of course, are the ideals of Roman Catholicism, which include the beliefs in the dignity and integrity of humanity, the ability of religion to promote a charitable spirit and to relieve human suffering, and tolerance for peoples (his understanding of the Ten Commandments), all in the context of a personal piety that endures today. The first of these religious ideals is embraced by the political liberalism that informed Waldheim's thinking and diplomatic pursuits. A secretary-general operating with these values can be expected to take an active stand on human rights issues and to uphold a vision for social justice.

Second is the pragmatism that Waldheim absorbed from his cultural heritage, the war years, and his struggle to attain personal and professional goals. Here his choices become more utilitarian, incremental, practical, result-oriented, and even self-interested. The religious value of tolerance for diverse people and acceptance of their differences, in other words, can be seen not only as Catholic idealism or liberalism but also as pluralist pragmatism.[47] As a pragmatic secretary-general, Waldheim guarded the office's neutrality, avoided ideological extremes, was more representative than innovative in the discharge of his office, viewed calculations and decisions with an eye to self-interest, tried to reduce risk, and, if he could not always advance the cause of the United Nations over other interests, at least to avoid suffering any loss of status or political prestige.

Choices are not made in a vacuum, of course, but in the context of political crises, international actors, others' decisions, and the demands of the office. As the operative mechanism in pragmatism is ongoing dialogue with the changing conditions of context, pragmatism cannot save any secretary-general from facing dilemmas along the way. But pragmatism can help an officeholder contend with the constraints of the external environment, because it requires them for making decisions.

Cases and Policy Choices

Conflicts in Cyprus and the Middle East, Namibian independence, work on a UN human rights resolution, and concerns over staffing presented Waldheim with difficult challenges, not least because he inherited them from his predecessors, but because they persisted throughout his tenure, they became signature issues for him.[48] As such, these issues allow us to examine Waldheim's actions, and to look at how his ethical framework affected his decisions, more closely.

Cyprus

Cyprus had been on the UN agenda since 1964, four years after it gained independence, making the UN Force in Cyprus (UNFICYP) one of its most long-lasting and costly peacekeeping operations. UNFICYP was created to prevent violence between the Greek and Turkish Cypriot communities and to forestall any external invasions. Financial support for troops came from the nations supplying them and the government of Cyprus, with voluntary contributions from other states. Formal dialogue between Greek and Turkish Cypriots through the Inter-Communal (IC) talks over issues of governance, violence, a constitution, and pragmatic needs broke down in 1971. Waldheim traveled to Greece, Turkey, and Cyprus in June 1972, after UN forces halted a shipment of arms from Czechoslovakia destined for Greek Cypriot forces.[49] Moving quickly and calling upon both sides to resume discussions, Waldheim appointed a special representative to continue negotiations, seeking additional funds to minimize the UNFICYP deficit and extend UNFICYP's mandate. The IC talks continued through much of 1973, but lack of progress led Waldheim to return to the region in August.[50]

If 1972–73 marked a point of stabilization in the cycles of violence and negotiation, 1974 did the reverse.[51] The IC talks were suspended on April 2, 1974, and only direct negotiation by Waldheim convinced Greek and Turkish Cypriots to resume them. In a rapid succession of events, a Greek Cypriot coup ousted Archbishop Makarios from power and forced him to flee the island on July 15 (he returned to power in December). Waldheim did not accept the credentials of the coup leaders and demanded that UNFICYP not recognize the new government.[52] War resumed in Cyprus that summer, and Turkey committed troops to Cyprus in support of Turkish Cypriots on July 19, with both sides directing their forces to the international airport in Nicosia.[53] The Security Council approved numerous resolutions (353, 354, 355, 357, 358, and 359) demanding an end to the fighting and the resumption of negotiations and expressing concern for UNFICYP's safety. Although Waldheim's conversations with Turkish, Greek, and Cypriot leaders achieved a ceasefire, the causes of the conflict persisted. Indeed, international and local conditions worsened as more than two hundred thousand Cypriots were displaced, Greece withdrew from NATO, and Turkish troops remained in Cyprus and succeeded in limiting UNFICYP actions.[54] A line of demarcation restricted activities between Greek and Turkish Cypriot communities, and postwar humanitarian emergency assistance became a primary concern for the United Nations.[55]

Waldheim returned to Cyprus in February 1975 to meet with Makarios and Denktash, the leaders of the Greek and Turkish Cypriot factions. He presented the Security Council with a report indicating that the Cypriot leaders were willing to talk; the council reciprocated by requesting that Waldheim use his good offices (Resolution 367) to bring about a solution.[56] Waldheim traveled from the region to locations in Europe to meet with the various leaders, hosting a series of shuttle diplomacy negotiations. Beginning in Vienna on April 28, Waldheim mediated five rounds of negotiations (April 28, June 5, July 31, September 8, 1975, and February 17, 1976).[57] The talks did not stop the Turkish Cypriot community from declaring independence for their side of the island, nor did they prevent an early closure of the fifth round.[58] Waldheim's call for constitutional and territorial proposals from both sides to maintain the unity of Cyprus went unheeded.[59]

Waldheim's involvement during his second term moved between breakthrough and disenchantment.[60] Waldheim achieved the first face-to-face meetings between Makarios and Denktash, developing what became known as the Makarios-Denktash principles of negotiation.[61] The IC talks resumed in the spring of 1977, but no compromise proposals for constitutional reforms were presented. By 1978 support for UNFYCIP was so low that it ran a deficit of $61 million, nearly a fifth of its annual cost.[62] Humanitarian aid for displaced persons had not stopped since the 1974 conflict, and neither had sporadic violence. Not content to wait for the parties to the conflict to present new proposals, Waldheim offered ten principles, which again received the assent of all parties.[63] Sounding a premature note of triumph that disputes could be settled through guided negotiations, Waldheim waited a year for IC talks to resume in August 1980. Disappointed by the lack of progress, Waldheim provided no further initiatives during the remainder of his term.

The Middle East

The United Nations' presence in the Middle East runs parallel to its history as an organization. The UN Truce Supervision Organization (UNTSO) has been operative since 1948.[64] Waldheim witnessed the escalation of tension, terrorism, and violence in the region, and heated General Assembly resolutions against Israel. Successful UN policies under Waldheim included maintaining peaceful borders once new conflicts abated, and some modest success as a mediator in the Geneva peace talks. Nevertheless, his efforts, coupled with the increasingly strident UN tone against Israel, left little improved at the end of his tenure.[65]

Waldheim did not travel to the region in his first year (1972), even though the dangers there spiraled beyond the need for legitimate and secure borders.[66] Israel repeatedly invaded southern Lebanon in search of Palestinians. Palestinian terrorists attacked the summer Olympic Games in Munich, killing athletes and themselves in an airport tarmac shootout.[67] The Security Council passed Resolution 316 condemning Israel's actions in Lebanon and encouraged Waldheim to use his good offices for all sides, and Egyptian president Anwar Sadat ominously called upon his people to make economic sacrifices in preparation for war.[68]

Violence between Palestinians and Israelis occurred throughout 1973, and war broke out in October when Egyptian and Syrian forces attacked Israel.[69] Jordan and Iraq assisted Syrian military forces before Israel turned back Egyptian armor and infantry and almost succeeded in taking Damascus. The Security Council passed Resolution 338 on October 21, calling for all parties to stop fighting, recognize Israel, and begin negotiating on issues that had hindered a just regional peace. Egypt and Israel (without Syria) agreed to a truce the following day, and Security Council Resolution 339 requested that Waldheim mobilize a force of observers.[70] Waldheim quickly moved nine hundred UNFICYP troops to the Middle East, and Security Council Resolution 340 provided for the organization of another peacekeeping force to the region—UN Emergency Force II (UNEF II)—to serve as a buffer between Israel and Egypt.[71]

Paralleling Waldheim's efforts were those of the U.S. secretary of state, Henry Kissinger, who secured acceptance of the peace plan, a ceasefire, and agreement for further negotiations between Israel and Egypt.[72] Both the United States and the Soviet Union recommended that Waldheim preside at the Geneva Middle East Peace Conference, which on December 21 brought them, Egypt, Israel, and Jordan together for face-to-face Arab-Israeli peace talks. Early in 1975 the former adversaries signed another treaty, also negotiated by Kissinger, to separate the forces, which prevented the use of the Suez Canal and extended the reach of UNEF II through graduated force removal.[73]

The October war had two fronts, and the next phase of UN peacekeeping operations began, five months later, to address the conflict between Syria and Israel.[74] A disengagement treaty facilitated by Waldheim was signed by Syria and Israel in Geneva and opened operations for the UN Disengagement Observer Force (UNDOF), a border patrol force of approximately fifteen hundred troops.[75] Mandates for UNEF II and UNDOF were routinely extended.[76]

Until the next major battleground took shape in southern Lebanon, the years between 1975 and 1978 saw improvements in relations between Egypt and Israel, gradual destabilization in Lebanon, and increasingly harsh rhetoric against Israel in the General Assembly.[77] Waldheim tried to reconvene the Geneva talks but failed owing to Israeli reservations about including the Palestinian Liberation Organization (PLO).[78] The General Assembly seated the PLO in discussions on the Middle East, and Security Council debates on Jerusalem and the West Bank included Palestinian observers. The General Assembly created a committee on the Exercise of the Inalienable Rights of the Palestinian People, while Israel boycotted a UN conference on the Middle East on account of the presence of the PLO.[79]

Aggravated internal fighting in Lebanon in 1975 between Christians and Muslims turned into civil war in 1976 and became the newest roadblock to peace in the Middle East. In April 1976 Waldheim addressed the Security Council on Lebanon and on how escalating destabilization might threaten global peace.[80] Syria entered Lebanon not only as a mediator but with troops, threatening to end UNDOF operations.[81] The threat was not resolved until May, and then only through direct negotiations between President Assad and Waldheim.[82]

To circumvent the 1977 impasse in the Geneva peace talks, Waldheim renewed his shuttle diplomacy with Arab and Israeli leaders to discuss the representation of Palestinians. His efforts never allayed concerns that the talks should include only equal parties (states), the previous delegations, or how far to extend Palestinian observer status beyond the Jordanian delegation.[83] Despite this, a regional breakthrough occurred in November, when Sadat came to Jerusalem to pray and to address the Israel Knesset, although it led to his condemnation in the Arab world.[84] At the end of 1977, Waldheim's address on his efforts was greeted by the General Assembly's endorsement of a PLO presence at future Geneva negotiations. Waldheim agreed to a Sadat proposal to bring Geneva representatives to Cairo and resume the moribund talks, only to remove himself from future negotiations following the objections of the Soviet Union to the Sadat plan.[85]

Israel invaded southern Lebanon in early 1978, following numerous border attacks by the PLO, prompting the Security Council to create a UN Interim Force in Lebanon (UNIFIL).[86] UNIFIL was mandated to observe the removal of Israeli armed forces, restore peace and security, and assist the government of Lebanon in addressing its concerns for providing local authority—this in a country of civil conflict penetrated by other states, militaries, the PLO, and polarized religious communities.[87] Israeli forces left the region temporarily, thus allowing UNIFIL to enter its border positions in Lebanon but be harassed on all sides.[88]

The failures at Geneva and the 1978 Camp David accords signaled that responsibility for Middle East negotiations had shifted venue, lessening the influence of the United Nations.[89] The accords opened borders between Egypt and Israel. UNEF II's mission ended in June 1979.[90] With increased incursions by Israeli ground and air forces and PLO assaults on Israel, Waldheim called Security Council meetings for new peace talks on southern Lebanon in August 1979. His call went unheeded by Israel, the Christian Lebanese, Palestinians, and Syria.

Social and Economic Affairs: Namibia

Namibia represented the last vestige of European colonialism in Africa. A German colony prior to World War I, Namibia had been governed by South Africa under a League of Nations mandate that it refused to relinquish even after the onset of the UN trusteeship system.[91] South Africa also ignored a 1950 International Court of Justice advisory opinion to the General Assembly stating that Namibia should be under UN supervision.[92] The political climate changed in the 1960s, after a decade that saw newly created independent African states, anticolonial liberation movements, and increased global hostility against apartheid.[93] The Southwest Africa People's Organization (SWAPO) began as a political opposition movement in 1960, and in 1966 it added violent struggle for liberation to its activities. The General Assembly created the UN Council for Namibia (1967), a supervisory council for Namibian affairs, while UN policy was to negotiate control away from South Africa, moving Namibia toward self-determination and national elections as quickly as possible.[94]

Waldheim believed in the growing importance of developing nations in the global order, and he was convinced that security would be enhanced by their independence and economic development. He entered the discourse over Namibian affairs almost immediately upon taking office, spurred on by a series of Security Council resolutions to initiate fact-finding missions, appoint a special representative, and begin negotiations between South Africa and Namibia.[95] Initial efforts went badly when South Africa resisted Waldheim's request to meet Namibian representatives, and his special envoy blundered in signing a document saying that regional development would lead to a successful transition to independence. The document put the United Nations temporarily on record as agreeing with South Africa's effort at extending its *Bantustan* policies into Namibia.[96] Further negotiations by Waldheim in 1973 failed to bring progress, and at the end of that year the Security Council passed Resolution 342, calling for Waldheim to end his efforts at dialogue.[97] In light of the lack of progress, the General Assembly declared SWAPO to be the legitimate representative of the Namibian people.

Violence in the region and the adversarial relations between South Africa and the United Nations intensified following Resolution 342. The United Nations approved indirect forms of support for Namibia. A Namibia trust fund with annual UN contributions for future transition expenses was established along with Namibian educational opportunities in Zambia, and the Security Council again demanded (1974) that South Africa quit its administration of Namibia.[98] The General Assembly asked Waldheim to begin radio transmissions into southern Africa announcing the UN efforts on Namibia's behalf. South Africa pushed back by inviting Namibian ethnic leaders to a gymnasium in Windhoek to discuss and sign the Turnhalle agreements, allowing South Africa to lead Namibia toward elections by the end of 1979.[99] The Security Council downplayed the legitimacy of Turnhalle by passing Resolution 385, which reminded the world that South Africa had no jurisdiction over Namibian affairs.[100] The General Assembly resolved that SWAPO was the only legitimate representative of the Namibian people and that only it could negotiate for Namibia. South African military troops entered Angola (now supported by Cuban military advisors) in search of SWAPO bases, and the General Assembly passed resolutions seeking economic sanctions and reparations from South Africa for all frontline states.[101] In an effort to alleviate the violence, Western members of the Security Council formed the Contact Group (the United States, Canada, France, Britain, and Germany) and began searching for alternatives with African leaders.[102]

Five years after Waldheim's first special representative went to the region, another was sent to report on regional tensions, issues separating the major parties, and any latent support for UN initiatives. Waldheim also traveled to the region a second time.[103] The Contact Group's involvement led to an agreed-upon set of proposals between South Africa and SWAPO that were incorporated into Security Council Resolution 435.[104] The resolution called for a UN Transition Assistance Group (UNTAG) of civilian administrators and military peacekeepers to monitor a ceasefire, support efforts toward elections by the end of 1978 or seven months following the startup of UNTAG, and the safe return of displaced Namibians to their homes.[105]

What appeared to be a breakthrough in 1978 ended in hardened positions the following year. South Africa challenged the impartiality of the United Nations, noting that SWAPO could not be monitored as it had no fixed bases.[106] South Africa stated that it would abide by election results based upon the Turnhalle Agreements,[107] while Waldheim defended Resolution 435 and was supported by the Contact Group.[108] South Africa continued its invasion of Angola, rejecting UN proposals for a ceasefire or for efforts to create a demilitarized zone in southern Angola.[109]

Although meetings occurred—including a 1981 Geneva peace conference that allowed Waldheim to bring together direct contact between adversaries—no political progress on Namibia took place in Waldheim's final years at the United Nations. The General Assembly continued to pass resolutions damning South Africa, ultimately expelling its representative to the United Nations a second time, while the UN Council on Namibia investigated the extent of South African expropriation of Namibian natural resources.[110] Four Security Council efforts to mobilize an embargo of South Africa were vetoed by the United States and France. South African incursions into Angola deepened, and fighting took place with both Angolan troops and SWAPO personnel. A new U.S. policy under the Reagan administration attempted to achieve constructive engagement, and the Contact Group changed direction by linking progress on independence with the removal of Cuban military personnel from Angola.[111]

Religious Human Rights

Support for universal human rights remains central to the work of the United Nations, and events during Waldheim's tenure provided opportunities for his engagement in this area. It was during his tenure as secretary-general that the United Nations saw the high-water mark of the call to economic rights formulated in the concepts of a New International Economic Order (NIEO), codified at the fourth UN Conference on Trade and Development (1976) in Nairobi. During the Waldheim years the United Nations oversaw the Geneva Conference Against Racism (1978) and declared the first International Year for Women. The UN Human Rights Committee began operation during the Waldheim era, and interest in religious human rights revived during his tenure.[112]

Waldheim explained his commitment for human rights using the charter's language and the constraints of international politics:

> My guideline in the defense of human rights is: the good of the people concerned. I offer my service unofficially, on a purely humanitarian basis. Whether it be a matter of intervening to unite families, protecting the rights of a national minority, or alleviating harsh sentences, I am always extremely careful to assure the government concerned that I do not intend to interfere in its internal jurisdiction. Because most governments are loath to be accused of succumbing to outside pressure, I often conduct my interventions without publicity. But I have never hesitated to make a public appeal if I believe the circumstances warrant it.[113]

Waldheim's annual reports to the General Assembly did not comment extensively on human rights, and when he did address this subject his remarks echoed the tension between issues of national sovereignty and the need to advocate for the rights of human beings against state power. For example, he wrote in one report:

> The protection of human rights is an area where the credibility of the United Nations is especially at stake. Over the past years the international community has been faced with a number of matters affecting human rights, which have posed—sometimes in a very acute form—the difficulty of reconciling the sovereign jurisdiction of Member States with the principles laid down in the Universal Declaration of Human Rights. The United Nations has been active in attempting to improve fundamental human rights and freedoms in some areas but has proved unable to act in other cases.[114]

Yet problematic conflicts need not end in stalemate, as Waldheim also emphasized how a secretary-general's behind-the-scenes efforts could produce results, even when public appeals might have been more desirable.[115] Although the impact of conflict upon human rights was important to

Waldheim, he also acknowledged the relationship between human rights and the global political economy.[116] In keeping with commentary on the conditions facing people in the developing world, Waldheim wrote that it was "increasingly clear that peace and development are necessary for the full realization of human rights. At the same time, in the absence of respect for human rights, peace and development lose much of their meaning. It is essential, therefore, that the efforts of the United Nations and its Member States to promote and protect civil and political as well as economic, social and cultural rights should be accorded the highest importance."[117] This statement mirrors Waldheim's remarks above on the bounded capacities of the office of secretary-general. Defending the important moral principle of human rights against violation is weighed within a system of sovereign states.

As in the other cases, work toward a religious human rights document preceded Waldheim's tenure as secretary-general. The United Nations first grappled with religious discrimination in 1956 through its Sub-Commission on Prevention of Discrimination and Protection of Minorities, which produced a report in 1960. Though work on a preliminary UN declaration ended in 1964, the General Assembly would again request (in 1974) that the Commission on Human Rights produce a draft declaration. The commission began in 1974 but failed to meet in 1976, and Waldheim did not mention the process in his annual reports until 1977. A draft of the *Declaration on the Elimination of All Forms of Intolerance and of Discrimination Based on Religion or Belief* finally surfaced in 1980 (the year of the pope's visit to the United Nations) and was ratified by the General Assembly in 1981.[118] Waldheim specifically referred to the work on religious rights and advocated its progress in his *Reports of the Secretary-General on the Work of the Organization,* identifying the work of the commission as one of the United Nations' most prominent and positive achievements.[119]

In sum, Waldheim's approach to human rights tried to achieve a balance between critical need and sovereign national interests. His framework for understanding and pursuing human rights was instrumental at the interpersonal and international levels of analysis, was understood through the lens of the sacredness of human life, and was seen as important for minority relations, international and civil war, and the global economy. This is somewhat ironic when paired with Waldheim's war record. Whether this irony can be attributed to Waldheim's learning from the past, to his doing what was politically prudent, or both, is difficult to determine.

Staffing Policies

Principles of international civil service suggest that UN employees should be neutral, impartial, and focused upon the work of the global organization and its charter rather than on any national interests. Although he is given credit for making difficult cost-saving decisions and financial reforms to help manage the UN budget, Waldheim was plagued during his tenure by charges of politicization in his personnel decisions.[120]

One can ask whether the politics of personnel decisions under Waldheim was purely an internal organizational problem, given the funding practices of several states both prior to and during his administration. Both the Soviet Union and France withheld payments on debt-servicing for peacekeeping operations when they disagreed with UN objectives. Although Waldheim was able to garner President Nixon's support for him and the United Nations at the beginning of his first term, his criticism of the American war in Vietnam pushed Nixon to side with those in Congress who sought to reduce U.S. commitments to the global body from about one-third of its annual budget to one-quarter.[121] Financial stress in the United Nations was perhaps never as great as in April 1972, when $11 million was needed for payroll and only $1 million was available.

Filling Secretariat positions often served institutionally strategic purposes. Although one critic softened this charge by acknowledging that Waldheim had reformed the process of selecting top UN officials, he also argued that Waldheim did nothing to curb "mediocrity and politically expedient appointments."[122] Apparently this problem was so widespread that another critic lampooned the idea that Waldheim favored one superpower over another, saying that his favors were evenly distributed.[123]

So serious were the allegations of patronage that the City University of New York undertook an unsolicited independent study, concluding in 1972 (at the beginning of Waldheim's first term) that member states' pressure to have their own people hired in Secretariat positions was increasing, that women had lost ground in the number of hires, and that competence in the job was a casualty of political pressure. Similar conclusions were reached in Waldheim's second term by the UN Staff Association, which charted a 74 percent increase in total UN personnel between 1970 and 1979 due to double-staffing to cover for incompetent political hires. Although the larger size of the Secretariat payroll might be explained in part by increased activity and expanded state membership, the General Assembly created more than one hundred positions in 1979, spurring inflationary pressures and a rise in unnecessary personnel.[124] Waldheim denied charges that his staff was incompetent and that he had politicized the Secretariat, but one senior staff official confirmed the practice, especially for positions of secondary importance.[125]

Values and Decisions

How much did religious values influence Waldheim's decision making? In addition to Waldheim, senior staff members who served with him at the United Nations were asked specifically about the public and private character of the man's religious beliefs. They were asked about the theological principles important to a Roman Catholic perspective on concerns of public order, the common good, just war, and the relationships between religion and state. Although all of those interviewed concurred that religion played an important part in Waldheim's life and that he still is a devout man, no colleague defended the position that religious principles, Roman Catholic religious beliefs, or spiritual practices contributed to his public decisions as secretary-general. No one could remember hearing Waldheim talk about just war concerns, even in cases where issues of justice (the Middle East or Namibia) might have been expected to be part of the conversation. Indeed, most of those interviewed considered the idea that conflict should be viewed through the lens of just war principles as too abstract to have played a part in Waldheim's thinking. No colleague recalled how their former boss spoke about the origins of human rights or could remember having policy discussions in which decisions would hinge upon the intrinsic dignity of human beings. All of Waldheim's colleagues agreed that religious thinking and belief did not enter into their conversations about violence in Cyprus or the Middle East.[126] (Waldheim himself spoke of the many influences on his decisions and value structure, including the Cold War, the specific proposals necessary for peace processes to continue among the conflicted parties, and the importance of quiet diplomacy.)[127] The overwhelming consistency of his colleagues' comments does not necessarily mean that religious values had no importance for Waldheim, however, or that they had no influence, perhaps subconsciously, in his policymaking. It only reveals that other influences were more apparent to those who worked with him on a daily basis.[128]

Avoiding the public demonstration of religious thoughts and beliefs was part of Waldheim's United Nations and its largely secular environment, according to his former colleagues.[129] The practice of keeping religious belief outside the public policy process applied as well in the areas of economic justice, the pursuit of independence for Namibia, and the passage of the UN Human Rights Statement on Religious Tolerance in his last month in office.[130]

It would thus be difficult to attribute Waldheim's decisions and policies in the cases discussed here to his Roman Catholicism. On the contrary, his decisions are in keeping with earlier statements about maintaining distance between religion and politics. One possible exception is Namibia, where his Roman Catholic social values may have had more play in his political and moral hopes for fairness, tolerance, and acceptance. But his comments on Namibia jibe equally well with his statements on the importance of international law and a necessary boundary between the powers of the state and individuals. It is unlikely that any sure causal relationship can be made between his religious beliefs and his policy decisions.

If not Roman Catholicism, then what of the other value pole that informed Waldheim's actions as secretary-general—that of pragmatism? "Pragmatic" was the term that those who knew him best used most often to describe Waldheim's primary values and the means by which he made decisions. When they used this term his colleagues were referring to Waldheim's political instinct for "finding a way" around or through a problem. It is what they meant when they talked about his belief in the efficacy of quiet, behind-the-scenes negotiation for the purposes of solving problems through incremental change.

In the institutional role of secretary-general, pragmatism tends to lead to activities and decisions that have the potential to increase the visibility of the United Nations and its highest office; at the very least, it tends not to harm them. Because it is a style of operation where meaning is found in practical results, consequences, and causes—indeed, in the avoidance of ideology (or theology)—pragmatism includes (1) a focus on acceptable solutions to all parties; (2) the ability to evaluate gains and losses; (3) the intent of avoiding losses that would negatively affect personal function; (4) an emphasis on incremental proposals and solutions that achieve actual results; and (5) a clear understanding of the location of authority for decisions. Pragmatic policy actions that have the potential to increase the visibility of the United Nations and its highest office include (1) the secretary-general's direct personal involvement in global crises and negotiations; (2) actions on the part of the secretary-general that exhibit statesmanlike leadership; (3) an increase in the involvement of the United Nations and its capacities in problem-solving efforts; and, after calculating the risk, (4) innovative proposals that enhance ongoing programs.

Waldheim demonstrated these qualities and adopted these approaches for the work at hand. Faced with a lack of funding and the threat of bankruptcy, Waldheim cut the budget, got commitments from major powers for additional resources, and tightened operations, and in all of these actions he was praised for his leadership and problem-solving abilities. As the General Assembly expanded with new members, so too did demands on the Secretariat to provide employment for an increasingly pluralist community. Although, as we have seen, he was accused of favoritism in staffing the Secretariat, he was not, as we have also seen, the only secretary-general to have expanded the staff to fit political objectives, and there may have been no simple solution to this problem.

The above indicators are also witnessed in Waldheim's pragmatic approach to Namibian issues, as interviews with his former colleagues confirmed. The complexity of African interests and African member states in the General Assembly, increasing general interest in Third World concerns, and antipathy toward South Africa and its regime did not readily lend themselves to solutions motivated first and foremost by concerns with justice, altruism, or other humanistic values. At some deeper level of thinking, such values—much like tenets of Roman Catholicism—may have helped to inform Waldheim's approach to Namibia, but the realities of international politics on the African continent called for calculated and incremental approaches. Indeed, if a solution was to be found, such approaches were necessary. Becoming personally engaged in negotiations and then later retracting that engagement, working with frontline African states and following the directives of the Security Council, devising principles for further negotiation while complementing the work of others present ample evidence of tactical incrementalism. Coupled with the goals of serving the interests of the United Nations and enhancing its position (or at least not harming it), pragmatism provides a more comprehensive understanding of the values supporting Waldheim's Namibian policy choices.[131]

The earlier discussion of conflict mitigation and peacekeeping on Cyprus and in the Middle East also bear out Waldheim's pragmatic approach. Indeed, incremental steps that could be supported by clear links to authority, that sought to bring conflicted parties together and that would be evaluated against a standard for improving the position of goals and parameters, and invitations to provide negotiating points or constitutional language were made to all parties. When shuttle diplomacy and ongoing negotiations between adversaries in Cyprus and the Middle East stalemated, Waldheim ceased additional direct negotiations under his auspices but maintained full support for ongoing peacekeeping efforts as a necessary and stabilizing influence.

These conflicts offer evidence of Waldheim's efforts at enhancing the role and statesmanlike character of the office of secretary-general, something that in his view had fallen through past administrations. He asserted the visibility of the United Nations, whether through direct and almost annual meetings with leaders of the conflicts or through assigned special representatives. In both settings Waldheim offered his services for conflict mediation and negotiation directly and as often as requested by either the General Assembly or the Security Council. In the Middle East Waldheim facilitated the Geneva peace talks between Israel and its adversaries encouraged by the permanent members of the Security Council. He took on the role of chief mediator between Greek and Turkish Cypriots in talks that would move between Cyprus, Vienna, Geneva, and New York, again at the request of the Security Council.[132] Waldheim was also given high marks for quickly mobilizing UNFICYP and shifting its service into Sinai with the new UNEF II, thereby helping to create an effective buffer zone between Israeli and Egyptian forces and thus speeding up the process of peacekeeping. All of these actions by Waldheim help demonstrate the above indicators of role pragmatism.

Waldheim inherited all of these problems, and he passed them on to his successors. On the surface, such a record seems undistinguished and unsuccessful. With the exception of a high point in negotiations or the low point of war in 1974, Security Council reports on Cyprus are monotonous in their repetition of breaches of the peace, fluctuating numbers of UNFICYP forces, and requests for more funds for the UNFICYP mission. A similar assessment can be made of the regularity of efforts in Namibia between 1974 and 1978. Reports from the Middle East show less continuity because of the expanding conflict around Israel's borders—seemingly a sign of UN ineffectiveness. Yet the resumption of peacekeeping operations in this area was an expansion of responsibilities for the United Nations and its secretary-general. According to James Jonah, undersecretary-general during Waldheim's tenure, the resumption of peacekeeping operations after a ten-year hiatus was one of Waldheim's successes, and helping the

Security Council develop guidelines for peacekeeping operations could be attributed to his leadership.[133]

Other UN operations were also expanded during the Waldheim years. These included two special sessions on economic development and a conference that would lay the foundation for the first and only functional operation of the UN system to be headquartered in the developing world—the UN Environmental Program (UNEP). Additional UN offices were begun in Vienna, too, primarily involving crime and drug interdiction.

Waldheim was no visionary, and it would be foolish to expect tremendous innovations from a man who believed in the incremental nature of the work of the United Nations. Even so, certain of his decisions were in fact innovative, and these occurred after he had calculated the risk between policy failure and maintaining past efforts. Waldheim provided a series of negotiating points during his mediation over Cyprus that many thought would finally break the impasse. He achieved direct negotiations between Israelis and Egyptians for the first time, as well as the first consultations between Israel and its adversaries in the Geneva peace talks. In addition, Waldheim presented a series of talking points for South Africa and SWAPO that, with the assistance of five Western countries, initially appeared to promise success. What one sees in Waldheim's decisions and policies is that his focus on enhancing the functions and securing the status of the United Nations and the position of secretary-general was more relevant and effective than pursuing any given sectarian doctrine.

A pragmatic, incremental, results-directed approach to decision making that could advance UN interests while avoiding losses is not an extraordinary achievement. But it is in keeping with Waldheim's conception of the constraints of the office and the need to balance multiple interests.[134] If this sounds like the realism of mere self-interest, this should not be a surprise. According to one colleague, Waldheim ran his executive staff much like any foreign ministry pursuing national objectives.[135]

The Enigma Revisited

Two themes emerge in this examination of Waldheim, his service to the United Nations, and the question of his moral and religious values. By comparing his sources of moral values with policy choices, it seems clear that religion was less a factor than pragmatic realism in explaining Waldheim's policy decisions.

In light of his personal history, however, the question remains: Was Waldheim a moral man?[136] Urquhart's writings notwithstanding, the answer of Waldheim's colleagues seems to have been a resounding "yes, but."[137]

Does any literature of ethics and responsibility that used World War II as a context for understanding moral choice offer any clues? After all, the belief that Austria was the first victim of the Nazi war machine provided an understanding for some of that country's wartime experiences.[138] What motivated some to take bold risks to spare a persecuted people? In the case of a Huguenot community in France, author Phillip Hallie described a convergence between strong leadership and historical empathy of one persecuted people for another (Huguenots also experienced oppression), based on the theological imperative for hospitality toward strangers, the exceptionalism of the biblical Jewish community, and an ability to identify oppression with the persecution of Jesus Christ.[139]

Similar moral questions arose as nations prepared for the 2005 commemoration of the Holocaust at Auschwitz. Simon Kuper has endeavored to understand why two national communities perceived to have similar humanistic convictions, namely, the Danes and the Dutch, could have reacted so differently to the Nazi occupation. What produced Danish defiance and Dutch complicity, Kuper asks, and concludes that the Danes, with their socially conscious form of Lutheranism, saw "no distinction" between Christian and Jew, whereas the Dutch lacked that cultural religious context.[140]

Austrian history is not so simple. Neither a Danish monoculture nor the experience of Huguenot oppression in France informed prewar Austria. However, the openness of prewar Austria to Nazi influence does at least coincide with a similar openness to Nazi persuasion on the part of French forces against rebels in Le Chambon, and on the part of the Dutch. The context for moral choices does not decide those choices; it only influences the logic for how they may be made.

Another ethicist has suggested a means of evaluating moral choices under extreme duress, interpreting the act of moral choice through his experience as a prisoner of war. The conditions he faced worked to break down any semblance of moral civility or code of conduct that might have been in effect under normal conditions. Langdon Gilkey writes:

> I was forced continually to notice, in any situation of tension and anxiety, when the being or security of the self is threatened, [that] the mind simply ceases to be the objective instrument it pictures itself as. It does not weigh the rational arguments on both sides of an issue and coolly direct

a submissive ego to adopt the "just and wise solution." Such a picture of the mind of man is a myth of the academics, accustomed to dealing with theoretical problems in the study or the laboratory rather than existential problems of life as it is lived. In life, man is a total self, interested above all in his own well-being. His mind, like his emotions, is an instrument of that self, using its intelligence to defend his status when that is threatened and to increase his security when opportunity arises.[141]

This passage suggests something about decision making and character when extreme demands are made of the self in an unsettled or harmful context. Deciding in favor of something that goes against one's personal interest is, at least, more difficult when one cannot see the ultimate outcome of those decisions. Gilkey's observation raises the question: When coerced into making choices for good or ill, is one fully responsible for one's actions? Undoubtedly there is an important difference between the conditions in which Gilkey found himself and Waldheim's situation in wartime Vienna, but the question is relevant just the same.

A final reflection comes from Bruce Birch and Larry Rasmussen, who explore the deviance of a medical doctor sworn to save life while regularly performing "special actions" of mass murder in a concentration camp, reporting them in his diary as casually as his comments about the day's meals. Birch and Rasmussen review the connection between individual character and systemic evil and, in relation to committing (or allowing) genocide, note, "Shared rage must give way to routine compliance with a steady, socially legitimated, effective authority." For this to occur, three conditions must be met: (1) there must be reciprocal reinforcing "influences of social values, social organization, and character traits"; (2) social arrangements must have the capability "to channel character," becoming "conduits" that "encourage some character traits and ignore or obstruct others"; and (3) "role morality" carries with it the ability to distinguish different moralities for different purposes and social functions. In other words, the doctor's moral culpability and character may not change, but his actions must be interpreted, in part, by his assigned role in a larger, socially constructed evil. Birch and Rasmussen similarly evaluate Waldheim's persona to show that "role morality" explains how an alleged war criminal and advocate for social justice reside in a "morally shallow individual who is all too susceptible to the pressures . . . of roles and their contexts."[142]

These moral reflections help us to interpret Waldheim's legacy. Attempting to portray Waldheim in an either-or equation—as either guilty or innocent, good or evil, the advocate or abuser of human rights—misses the mark. Waldheim has been both, many times over. His tendency to be influenced by external factors and functional roles more than by religious teleology provides some parameters for explanation. We can take Waldheim at his word when he says that Christian values were important to him, but they were embedded in the values of pragmatism and the institutional interests of a vast organization. And, finally, the competitive structures of the Cold War under which the United Nations labored during Waldheim's leadership were stronger than the pressures brought to bear on them by the moral assessments of one man, in one office, making choices.

Notes

1. For more information, the reader can consult almost any of Paul Tillich's, Mircea Eliade's, or Rudolph Otto's theological or phenomenological writings.

2. Clearly these terms are not owned only by the United States and its citizens. But they hold significant meaning for Americans, as revealed in the example of Vietnam, specifically by how many Americans continue to visit the Vietnam War Memorial in Washington, DC, or how that chapter in America's history still commands such importance in presidential politics a quarter-century later.

3. This became clear when I spoke informally with Austrians about their thoughts on Waldheim. People spoke candidly about their disappointment, their feelings that all had not been written about the man, their pride in their country and about Waldheim's place in history, and their desire for greater openness on the part of the secretary-general and less harsh judgments of him. Because of the emotional and sometimes morally ambiguous nature of observations about Waldheim, it is critical that commentators, including myself, be transparent about their reference points. We all bring our own history—in my case, a family history involved with World War II, Germany, and immigration—and our vocations and values to our analysis. Whole communities may respond differently to what Waldheim is or becomes for them. And then there is Waldheim's own perspective on the symbol that he has become. When I asked him how he integrated his various public images and what lessons he had learned from this integrative process, Waldheim responded, "Wer einen guten Teil des vergangenen Jahrhunderts mit seinen heilen und dunklen Stunden miterlebt ha—und von seinem Land und den Vereinten Nationen in so verantwortungsvolle Funktionen gewahlt wurde, der wird wohl mit der unterschidlichen Beurteilung seines Lebens und Wirkens rechnen mussen" (letter, March 30, 2005). Roughly translated, Waldheim replied

that those whose life and work span the many light and dark hours of the last century, and who serve in accountable positions for their country and the United Nations, must count on (receiving) comparative interpretations and conclusions. In such a shadowed light, enigma becomes a place of shelter.

4. I relied on UN documents, secondary sources, reports of Waldheim's military service, and popular articles in writing this chapter. I also conducted interviews with Waldheim and several senior deputies. In addition to Waldheim himself, I interviewed Rev. Dr. Paul Wee, former executive director of Lutheran World Ministries, New York (January 6, 2005, Alexandria, Virginia); Dr. Rafee Ahmed, Waldheim's former chief of staff (January 8, 2005, telephone); Mr. Samir Sambar, former liaison to the Middle East and head of the UN Information Office in Lebanon under Waldheim (January 10, 2005); Dr. Diego Cordovez, former undersecretary-general for economic affairs and a political affairs administrator under Waldheim (January 14, 2005, telephone); Dr. Albert Rohan, former staff member under Waldheim and also former assistant minister of foreign affairs for the Austrian Ministry of Foreign Affairs (January 21, 2005, Vienna); and Dr. James Jonah, former undersecretary-general for administrative affairs under Waldheim (January 29, 2005, telephone). In addition to the personal interview with Waldheim at his home in Vienna (January 21, 2005), the former secretary-general responded to questions by letter dated March 30, 2005. In addition to my areas of focus in this chapter, Waldheim counted as significant areas of his administration decolonization, strengthening the legacy of human rights, strengthening and expanding the use of peacekeeping forces, caring for refugees and victims of natural disasters, and the reduction of potential future conflicts due to inadequate international agreements.

5. For more on these events and developments, see Richard Bassett, *Waldheim and Austria* (New York: Viking Press, 1989); Barbara Jelavich, *Modern Austria, Empire and Republic, 1815–1986* (London: Cambridge University Press, 1987); Radomir Luza, *Austro-German Relations in the Anschluss Era* (Princeton, NJ: Princeton University Press, 1975); and Eric Solsten and David McGlave, eds., *Austria, a Country Study* (Washington, DC: Library of Congress Research Division, 1994).

6. Kurt Waldheim, *In the Eye of the Storm* (Bethesda, MD: Adler and Adler Publishing, 1986), 12.

7. Seymour Maxwell Finger and Arnold A. Saltzman, *Bending with the Winds: Kurt Waldheim and the United Nations* (New York: Praeger, 1990), 2; Kurt Waldheim, *The Challenge of Peace* (New York: Rawson, Wade, 1980), 12.

8. Waldheim, *Challenge of Peace*, 21.

9. Waldheim, interview by author, January 21, 2005.

10. Benedict's comments on the need for a crusade of Catholic social action came in the aftermath of World War I in his encyclical *Paterno iam diu*, November 24, 1919, on the postwar ills of people in Eastern Europe. Pius XI used the commemoration of St. Francis of Assisi in *Rita expiatis*, April 13, 1926, and later the

global economic collapse in *Nova impendet,* October 2, 1931, for similar calls for a renewed sense of Catholic good will, charity, and generosity.

11. The appeal for peace as the will of God found its way into many of the papal encyclicals of the period, even as the popes acknowledged that the old animosities and hatreds had not dissolved. Benedict XV said as much in *Quod iam diu* on December 1, 1918, and in the aftermath of the peace negotiations in *Pacem, dei munus plucherrimum* on May 23, 1920. Still prior to the onset of World War II, Pope Pius XI issued his appeals for global peace in *Ubi arcano dei concilio* on December 23, 1922, linking the pursuit of God's peace with justice for all peoples. Although his encyclicals on peace as God's will were not as clear as his predecessors', Pius XII issued a Christmas message on December 24, 1944, titled *Democracy and a Lasting Peace,* which emphasized the relationship between global peace and democratic citizenship and leadership.

12. Perhaps the most complicated and complete expression of this call to order and transform all human relationships came in Pius XI's encyclical *Quadragesimo anno,* on May 15, 1931. The concepts Pius laid out in that document were valued by the Vatican II reformers in the 1960s and the Medillin conferences on liberation theology in Latin America, as well as by the next pope, Pius XII, in his Christmas message of 1942, ironically titled *The Internal Order of States and People.* As close to a prophetic witness, perhaps, as anyone of the era, Pius wrote that in order to achieve peace in times of great darkness, the dignity of the human person, social unity, dignity for labor, the rehabilitation of a juridical order, and a Christian conception of the state were all necessary.

13. Pius XI, *Mit Brennender Sorge,* March 14, 1937, available at http://www .papalencyclicals.net/Pius11/P11BRENN.HTM.

14. Pius XII, *Democracy and a Lasting Peace,* Christmas 1944, available at http:// www.papalencyclicals.net/Pius12/P12XMAS.HTM.

15. Pragmatism often refers to the influential American philosophy popularized by Charles Sanders Pierce, William James, and John Dewey in the late nineteenth and early twentieth centuries, and in more recent times by Richard Rorty.

16. Diego Cordovez, interview by author, January 14, 2005.

17. William James, *Pragmatism,* available at http://radicalacademy.com/ adiphiloessay18.htm.

18. Nicholas Rescher, *Realistic Pragmatism: An Introduction to Pragmatic Philosophy* (Albany: State University of New York Press, 2000), 8.

19. Audrey Thompson, *Political Pragmatism and Educational Inquiry,* http:// www.ed.uiuc.edu/EPS/PES-Yearbook/96_docs/thompson.html.

20. *American Pragmatism,* http://radicalacademy.com/amphilosophy7.htm; *Pragmatism,* http://bartleby.com/65/pr/pragmatism.html; Kelly Parker, *Public Hearings/Hearing Publics: A Pragmatic Approach to Applying Ethics,* http://agora.phi .gvsu.edu/kap/Public_Hearings/ph.essay.html.

21. Thompson, *Political Pragmatism and Educational Theory*.

22. J. Donald Butler, *Four Philosophies and Their Practice in Education and Religion* (New York: Harper and Brothers, 1951), 428. One theologian goes so far as to describe a series of metaphysical propositions for the ethical pragmatist from which knowledge and value increase. These propositions hold that the world is all foreground, that it is characterized by process and change, that it is precarious, incomplete, indeterminate, and pluralistic, that it has ends within its own process, that it is not/does not include a transempirical reality, that it guarantees no progress, and that humanity is continuous with the world but is not an active cause in the world. See Butler, *Four Philosophies*, 431. Such propositions contain the basis for a highly realistic, incremental, and questioning ethic for what can be obtained by personal actions. The propositions prescribe that if anything is to be obtained for the good, actions must take place within a known quantity of information, set of communities, and social realities.

23. Rescher, *Realistic Pragmatism*, 226.

24. Butler, *Four Philosophies*, 437. Note that moral pragmatism has been recognized as possessing certain faults and challenges. Some of these challenges pertain to what appears to be too strong a reliance on individuation in a sometimes arbitrary process of finding patterns, trends, or meaning in an indeterminate universe. Ontology takes on greater negativity than it deserves in an ethic primarily defined by operationality (as opposed to "is-ness"). A further examination of weaknesses within pragmatic ethics are described in Butler, *Four Philosophies*, 476–82, and in the critical examination of pragmatism in Arthur O. Lovejoy, *The Thirteen Pragmatisms and Other Essays* (Baltimore, MD: Johns Hopkins University Press, 1963).

25. See *Pragmatism*, http://www.newadvent.org.cathen/12333b.htm; Rescher, *Realistic Pragmatism*, 4.

26. Cordovez, interview; and Rohan, interview by author, January 21, 2005. As a career UN diplomat, Cordovez cited this interest over against a reduction of respect in general for the United Nations (preceding Waldheim's tenure), and as having produced results that would benefit future holders of the office of secretary-general.

27. Waldheim, interview.

28. Finger and Saltzman, *Bending with the Winds*, 4.

29. International Commission of Historians, *The Waldheim Report, as submitted February 8, 1988 to Federal Chancellor Dr. Franz Vranitsky* (Copenhagen: Museum Tuscalanum Press, 1993), 34.

30. Waldheim, *Challenge of Peace*, 23–24.

31. James Daniel Ryan, *The United Nations Under Kurt Waldheim, 1972–1981* (Lanham, MD: Scarecrow Press, 2001), 10–12.

32. Finger and Saltzman, *Bending with the Winds*, 12–13.

33. Ryan, *United Nations Under Waldheim,* 12.

34. Neal M. Sher, *Kurt Waldheim and Nazi Wartime Atrocities: The Uncensored Justice Department Report* (Upland, PA: DIANE Publishing, 1994), 204.

35. General Assembly of Pennsylvania, House Resolution No. 257, adopted April 6, 1988.

36. International Commission of Historians, *Waldheim Report,* 210–14. The international independent investigative commission of military historians was formed after a request by President Waldheim to the Austrian government in the spring of 1987.

37. Bernard Cohen and Luc Rozenzweig, *Waldheim* (New York: Adama Books, 1987), 165–66.

38. Waldheim, *In the Eye of the Storm,* 21.

39. The chronology of Waldheim's diplomatic and political appointments are as follows: 1945—first appointment to the Austrian Foreign Ministry (Vienna); 1948—first overseas posting, Austrian Embassy in Paris; 1951—headed Foreign Ministry's Office of Personnel (Vienna); 1955—permanent observer to the United Nations, minister and later ambassador to Canada; 1960—director of the Foreign Ministry's Political Department (Vienna); 1964—permanent representative of Austria to the United Nations; 1968—federal minister of Foreign Affairs (Vienna); 1971—lost election as People's Party candidate for president; 1972—first term as UN secretary-general; 1976—second term as UN secretary-general; 1986—elected president of Austria (People's Party).

40. Kurt Waldheim, *The Austrian Example* (Vienna: Verlag Fritz Molden, 1971), 205.

41. Waldheim, *In the Eye of the Storm,* 38.

42. Brian Urquhart's preface to Waldheim's *Challenge of Peace,* viii.

43. Waldheim, *Challenge of Peace,* 1–6.

44. Waldheim, *In the Eye of the Storm,* 44.

45. Ibid., 266–67.

46. For a succinct discussion of the political philosophy of liberalism in international affairs, see Michael Doyle, "Liberalism and World Politics," *American Political Science Review* 80 (1986): 1151–69.

47. Thompson, *Political Pragmatism and Educational Theory.*

48. Waldheim's memoirs and Brian Urquhart's *A Life in Peace and War* (New York: Harper and Row, 1987) both address these issues extensively, as does Ryan's *United Nations Under Waldheim.*

49. Waldheim, *In the Eye of the Storm,* 79–80.

50. United Nations General Assembly, *Introduction to the Report of the Secretary-General on the Work of the Organization,* Supplement 1, 27th Session (New York: United Nations, 1972), 21; Waldheim, *In the Eye of the Storm,* 81.

51. In a report by the secretary-general to the Security Council documenting the events and progress in Cyprus between June 1 and December 1, 1973,

paragraph 77 of UN Document S/11137 still paraphrases the special representative to Cyprus as believing that there were no insurmountable obstacles that would prevent constitutional compromise between Greek and Turkish Cypriots.

52. Ryan, *United Nations Under Waldheim*, 210; Urquhart, *A Life in Peace and War*, 255.

53. Waldheim, *Challenge of Peace*, 66.

54. Urquhart, *A Life in Peace and War*, 257.

55. United Nations Department of Public Information, *United Nations Annual Yearbook*, vol. 28 (New York: United Nations, 1974), 17–18.

56. Waldheim, *Challenge of Peace*, 69.

57. Waldheim, *In the Eye of the Storm*, 87–88.

58. Ryan, *United Nations Under Waldheim*, 219–23.

59. Waldheim, *Challenge of Peace*, 91.

60. Urquhart, *A Life in Peace and War*, 259

61. Waldheim, *Challenge of Peace*, 73.

62. As identified by Waldheim in his report to the Security Council on December 1, 1978, document S 12946, pars. 60–66. It should be remembered that Waldheim made special appeals for funds for Cyprus in almost every one of his reports to the Security Council and the General Assembly, as well as in his annual reports.

63. Waldheim, *Challenge of Peace*, 77.

64. Robert Riggs and Jack C. Plano, *The United Nations: International Organization and World Politics*, 2d ed. (Belmont, CA: Wadsworth Publishing, 1994), 114.

65. Ryan, *United Nations Under Waldheim*, 118.

66. The first major trip to various capitals and principal leaders occurred in September 1973. Waldheim described his feelings of "foreboding" about Middle East conditions and the curious resistance of leaders to discuss issues in his second autobiographical account, *In the Eye of the Storm*, 59.

67. Ryan, *United Nations Under Waldheim*, 180, 182.

68. Urquhart, *A Life in Peace and War*, 236. Resolution 316 passed on June 26, 1972; the United States abstained. The language of the resolution was almost entirely directed at limiting Israeli actions and maintaining the sovereignty of Lebanese territory. The resolution deplored all forms of violence but did not direct any consequential activities to others involved in the Middle East conflict.

69. UN Department of Public Information, *United Nations Annual Yearbook*, vol. 28 (New York: United Nations, 1974), 3.

70. Ryan, *United Nations Under Waldheim*, 197–99.

71. Waldheim, *Challenge of Peace*, 83; Urquhart, *A Life in Peace and War*, 240.

72. Waldheim, *Challenge of Peace*, 82.

73. Ryan, *United Nations Under Waldheim*, 202, 44–45.

74. Riggs and Plano, *United Nations*, 114.

75. Urquhart, *A Life in Peace and War*, 249–51.

76. Evidence of this is found in Waldheim's biannual reports to the Security Council on the ongoing activities of the different UN peacekeeping operations.

77. Waldheim, *In the Eye of the Storm*, 187.

78. Waldheim, *Challenge of Peace*, 85.

79. Ryan, *United Nations Under Waldheim*, 233, 235.

80. Ibid., 74–75.

81. Waldheim, *In the Eye of the Storm*, 187.

82. Ryan, *United Nations Under Waldheim*, 239.

83. United Nations General Assembly, *Introduction to the Report of the Secretary-General on the Work of the Organization*, Supplement 1a, 32d Session (New York: United Nations, 1977), 3–4.

84. Ryan, *United Nations Under Waldheim*, 253.

85. Waldheim, *Challenge of Peace*, 90–92.

86. Urquhart, *A Life in Peace and War*, 289–90.

87. The difficulties brought on by the extent of this broad mandate for a peacekeeping force are reviewed in Waldheim's report to the General Assembly on October 17, 1977, his report on the implementation of Security Council Resolution 425 to the Security Council on March 19, 1978, and in Urquhart, *A Life in Peace and War*, 290. Urquhart initially lays blame on the Security Council for the lack of precision in the mandate, while Waldheim reviews the difficulties on the ground between the conflicted parties and the wider geopolitical and regional historical context.

88. Urquhart, *A Life in Peace and War*, 291.

89. Waldheim, *In the Eye of the Storm*, 75.

90. Riggs and Plano, *United Nations*, 120–21.

91. Urquhart, *A Life in Peace and War*, 308.

92. Riggs and Plano, *United Nations*, 144.

93. Waldheim, *Challenge of Peace*, 51–52.

94. Riggs and Plano, *United Nations*, 144.

95. Waldheim, *Challenge of Peace*, 53.

96. Waldheim, *In the Eye of the Storm*, 103.

97. Ryan, *United Nations Under Waldheim*, 114.

98. Ibid., 114–15.

99. Waldheim, *Challenge of Peace*, 54.

100. United Nations Department of Public Information, *United Nations Annual Yearbook*, vol. 30 (New York: United Nations, 1976), 28.

101. Ryan, *United Nations Under Waldheim*, 245, 258, 253.

102. Urquhart, *A Life in Peace and War*, 309.

103. Waldheim, *In the Eye of the Storm*, 103.

104. Urquhart, *A Life in Peace and War*, 309.

105. Riggs and Plano, *United Nations*, 145.

106. Urquhart, *A Life in Peace and War,* 309–10. These points are displayed in a series of letters between the minister of foreign affairs for South Africa on March 6 and March 15, 1979, and from Waldheim to the foreign affairs minister on January 2 and March 15, 1979. The detailed criticisms and alternative proposals even following Security Council Resolution 435 indicate how disputed was the implementation of the UN Namibia project, or, as Urquhart notes, the South African's "perennial search for new and insurmountable obstacles to progress" (*A Life in Peace and War,* 309).

107. Waldheim, *Challenge of Peace,* 56.

108. United Nations General Assembly, *Report of the Secretary-General on the Work of the Organization,* Supplement 1, 36th Session (New York: United Nations, 1982), 9.

109. Ryan, *United Nations Under Waldheim,* 266–70.

110. Ibid., 116–17.

111. Waldheim, *In the Eye of the Storm,* 107; Riggs and Plano, *United Nations,* 145.

112. Ryan, *United Nations Under Waldheim,* 85–88, 94.

113. Waldheim, *Challenge of Peace,* 44.

114. United Nations General Assembly, *Introduction to the Report of the Secretary-General on the Work of the Organization,* Supplement 1a, 28th Session (New York: United Nations, 1973), 5. In the same report Waldheim discusses the "recurring dilemma" of protecting innocent civilians during times of conflict within states.

115. See UN General Assembly, *Introduction to the Report of the Secretary-General,* Supplement 1a, 32d Session, 8.

116. Issues of the NIEO were important in the ongoing debate on the global economy during the 1970s. Writers who were relatively sympathetic to Waldheim's performance, such as Ryan in *United Nations Under Waldheim,* write about Waldheim's interest both as a conviction (as in *The Austrian Example*) and as political necessity over his lost support among Western nations.

117. United Nations General Assembly, *Report of the Secretary-General on the Work of the Organization,* Supplement 1, 36th Session (New York: United Nations, 1982), 8–9. See also an earlier report, *Introduction to the Report of the Secretary-General on the Work of the Organization,* Supplement 1a, 29th Session (New York: United Nations, 1974), 8, in which Waldheim pointed to the connection between human rights and an equitable economic system.

118. Elizabeth Odio Benito, *Elimination of All Forms of Intolerance and of Discrimination Based on Religion or Belief, a Report by the Special Rapporteur* (New York: United Nations, 1989), 1–3.

119. Waldheim's rhetoric on human rights becomes more emphatic on the relationship between human rights, security, and development, and more assertive in connection to Third World interests. In both the 1981 and 1982 *Report of*

the Secretary-General on the Work of the Organization (Sessions 36 and 37), the work of the Commission on Human Rights is set apart and applauded, while in the latter Waldheim welcomes and looks forward to advances on the *Declaration on the Elimination of All Forms of Intolerance and of Discrimination Based on Religion or Belief.*

120. Ryan, *United Nations Under Waldheim,* 21–23.

121. Ibid., 23.

122. Urquhart, *A Life in Peace and War,* 230.

123. Shirley Hazzard, *Countenance of Truth: The United Nations and the Waldheim Case* (New York: Viking Press, 1990), 93.

124. Ryan, *United Nations Under Waldheim,* 25, 159–60.

125. Cordovez, interview. The former undersecretary, who began his service under U Thant, said that the practice had become more acute during the Waldheim years than previously, but also that it had continued unabated and in fact increased dramatically since then.

126. Some of Waldheim's colleagues said that they never had any significant conversations about religion with Waldheim and suggested that the secular nature of the United Nations would naturally dampen such conversations. Some raised the question whether such ideas were necessarily relevant to the issues and decisions involved in the cases of Cyprus, the Middle East, Namibia, and even religious human rights. Cordovez, Jonah, and Ahmed, all of whom served throughout Waldheim's tenure and had his utmost confidence, agreed that Waldheim's activism typically eschewed abstract thinking.

127. Waldheim, interview.

128. When I asked him how faith or another religious value factored into his actions in peace building, Waldheim responded characteristically by identifying the commonalities of religious traditions rather than emphasizing any specific advantage or trait that makes one unique in its pursuits of justice and peace.

129. Ahmed and Cordovez, interviews.

130. The Reverend Dr. Paul Wee (former executive director of Lutheran World Ministries of the Lutheran Council of the United States) told me that Waldheim could understand and sympathize with the concerns of the independence movements in Namibia and their religious supporters. Although these movements were not religious in scope, Wee believed that Waldheim spoke with some knowledge of the church's interests in the region and specifically for the people of Namibia. Waldheim's other former colleagues did not necessarily concur. Cordovez, Ahmed, and Jonah all pointed out that the drafting of the Human Rights Statement on Religious Tolerance was already under way before Waldheim became secretary-general, and that the wider bodies of the United Nations received little direct influence from Waldheim. Waldheim's record, especially his comments to the General Assembly, cited earlier, show more directly

his understanding of the importance of this document and of human rights generally.

131. Much the same thing can be said about Waldheim and human rights. Waldheim's leadership on religious tolerance fits the pragmatic model of an external process moving at a steady pace, a pace that quickened, perhaps, following the visit of John Paul II to the UN.

132. Waldheim recounted his story of the Cyprus talks, where after a long and arduous day of stalemated negotiations, he provided a confidential meal in a secluded room of the Sacher Hotel in Vienna, providing personal "time and space" for the adversaries to become comfortable with one another. Leaving early in the belief that the negotiators were moving toward agreement, Waldheim confessed frustration and sadness when he learned the next morning that the appearance of civility and progress of the evening had evaporated.

133. Jonah, interview. Jonah spoke at great length of the importance of the regulation—not a splashy achievement but a significant one that continues to be of use.

134. In his written comments of March 30, 2005, Waldheim emphasized the ethical balance between the representational position of the United Nations, especially in relationship to human rights, and the legitimate needs and interests of the individual states in the United Nations. In response to a question on his motivation in the NIEO movement of the developing states, Waldheim cited the ecological, economic, security, and moral risks in the relationships between North and South, all of which had to be balanced carefully. Time and again Waldheim stressed the importance of risk assessment, contextual analysis, and balancing competing interests in making decisions, a process that insists on the importance (and perhaps even the primacy) of external factors.

135. Jonah, interview.

136. Waldheim rejects the charge that he was without moral courage, pointing to his record of activism and service during his tenure as secretary-general and concluding that no decision is ever made without a context and without considering the active interests of all other parties. Waldheim, letter of March 30, 2005.

137. Or, more extensively, "yes, he was a moral man and sought to do good things through the office of secretary-general, but he should have been more transparent about his past. It is perhaps a part of his cultural heritage and diplomatic training to provide information as needed and for clear purposes, hence a part of pragmatism." Some of the former colleagues I interviewed suggested that it is too soon to venture a definitive conclusion on this question, and that history will be the judge.

138. Both Waldheim and Rohan made this basic argument about Austrian victimization in my interviews with them.

139. Philip Hallie, *Lest Innocent Blood Be Shed* (New York: Harper/Colophon, 1979).

140. Simon Kuper, "Delivered from Evil," *Financial Times,* January 22, 2005.

141. Langdon Gilkey, *Shantung Compound* (San Francisco: Harper and Row, 1966), 93.

142. Bruce C. Birch and Larry L. Rasmussen, *Bible and Ethics in the Christian Life,* rev. and exp. ed. (Minneapolis: Augsburg Fortress Press, 1989), 87, 90–91, 94.

7

RELIGION, ETHICS, AND REALITY
A Study of Javier Perez de Cuellar

BARBARA ANN RIEFFER-FLANAGAN
AND DAVID P. FORSYTHE

*The Secretary-General is supposed to be a kind of a conscience of the
international community, he has to be honest enough to say what he
really believes without being moved by such considerations as whether
member countries will like or dislike his report.*

—JAVIER PEREZ DE CUELLAR [1]

This chapter analyzes the personal values of Javier Perez de Cuellar and
the extent to which his ethical framework influenced him during his tenure as UN secretary-general between 1982 and 1991. The research question at the heart of this chapter inquires whether, during these ten years as
secretary-general, Perez de Cuellar's personal values shaped his initiatives
and decisions to any great extent. Or, conversely, does the office, shaped as
it is by legal and political factors, leave little room for exercising influence
based on personal values?

Much of the relevant literature suggests that the personal qualities or
inner code of the secretary-general can sometimes count in the exercise
of influence.[2] Of course, how successful secretaries-general are in their
initiatives is an entirely different matter. Still, it is a formidable challenge
to try to separate the legal and political factors that affect the office from
the moral and religious values of the person who tries to perform "the
most impossible job in the world."

In the case of Perez de Cuellar, we first note some of the early influences on his thought (Catholicism) and the personal values he eventually
developed (an ethic of liberalism). Each of these influences contributed
to an ethical framework that stressed the equal and autonomous worth

of individuals, especially those in need, as well as a concern for peace and justice. These values also overlap with the norms of the UN charter, especially its human rights provisions.

Perez de Cuellar's public statements often accorded greater weight to the UN charter than to Catholicism or liberalism. A secretary-general may not be expected to build support or deflect criticism by stressing an inner code of right and wrong, but rather by stressing the duties of the office under public norms. One's ethical framework and public law, however, can be inextricably intertwined. For example, Perez de Cuellar's bold policies in Central America were the result of the political space provided by powerful states, as well as the norms of the UN charter; but what he did there also reflected his personal values. Dynamism in pursuit of public norms, in the context of political space provided by others, may be a product of personal values.

Despite Perez de Cuellar's personal views or the principles of the charter, however, political reality often limited his course of action. International relations and power politics being what they are, the wishes of powerful states in this Westphalian system often trumped the initiatives, not to mention the personal values, of Perez de Cuellar. Fundamentally, if the permanent members of the Security Council or the parties in a conflict are unwilling to compromise or negotiate or support the secretary-general, none of the secretary-general's initiatives, motivated by religious beliefs or otherwise, make a difference. Thus the secretary-general can do only as much as more powerful actors allow him to do.[3] As one of his colleagues said, "There is no point diving into an empty swimming pool."[4]

Given Perez de Cuellar's recognition of the weakness of his office, given his own reluctance to use the secretary-general's office for personal crusades—a function of his innate modesty—and given his fear of what he called "moral hubris," it is not surprising that his inner code was not overwhelmingly influential during this tenure.[5] He knew that there were pragmatic limits to what the secretary-general and the United Nations could achieve in international politics. Moreover, he believed that the position of the secretary-general depended upon a reputation for impartiality that necessarily limited any personal crusade.[6]

In this study we argue that the tenure of Perez de Cuellar demonstrates that his ethical orientation, more than his religious values, was part of the man who occupied the office of secretary-general. Of course, formal religious upbringing may indirectly affect personal ethics. Despite his personal values, which came into play to varying degrees, what was primary in the exercise of influence for that position was the political context—mainly the power of states to affect the desires and priorities of the secretary-general. These conclusions are drawn from the written and oral statements by Perez de Cuellar both during and after his tenure as secretary-general, as well as from interviews with him and his colleagues at the United Nations.[7]

We begin by examining the ethical framework of Perez de Cuellar. This includes his religious background—notably Catholicism—and his ethic of liberalism. We look next at the organizational and normative framework within which any secretary-general operates—namely, UN norms and international law more broadly. The following section examines the political constraints—power politics in international relations—and their impact on the UN secretary-general. The next section then discusses some of the activities of Perez de Cuellar and how political realities, more than his personal beliefs, dictated his actions. In conclusion we reflect on the limits of social science in trying to distinguish the religious, ethical, legal, and political factors in personalized public policy.

Personal Values: A Preliminary View

Javier Perez de Cuellar was born on January 19, 1920, in Lima, Peru. He describes growing up in his relatives' house as a traditional Catholic home. He received a traditional Catholic education in Roman Catholic schools in Lima. After attending law school and studying international law, Perez de Cuellar spent much of his adult life as a diplomat in various foreign cities and at the United Nations. He joined the Peruvian delegation to the Preparatory Commission of the United Nations in 1945.[8] Perez de Cuellar was Peru's ambassador to Switzerland, Poland, Venezuela, and the Soviet Union. He also represented Peru at the United Nations as ambassador in the early 1970s. After serving as secretary-general, Perez de Cuellar again represented Peru, this time as ambassador to France.

Catholicism

Catholicism, like most other major religions, is a complex body of beliefs encompassing various tenets.[9] The central aspect of Catholicism is the belief in Jesus of Nazareth as the Messiah or anointed one, who sacrificed his life to provide salvation to those who believed in him. Jesus' teachings, as recorded by his followers in the decades after his death, form the foundation of Catholicism. We discuss a few tenets of Catholicism that are most relevant to the basic norms of the UN charter, while avoiding most theological debates and complexities.

EQUAL HUMAN DIGNITY

Jesus preached that we should love one another and treat one another with respect. This principle, partially reflected in "the Golden Rule"—do unto others as you would have others do unto you—can be said to inform the UN charter and the Universal Declaration of Human Rights, which encompass the notion that all individuals have dignity and deserve respect.

OBLIGATIONS TO THE POOR

One recurring theme throughout the New Testament is Jesus' teachings on the obligations to the poor. In addition to forgiveness (turning the other cheek), an important element of the Catholic faith is the obligation to take care of others. Assisting the poor and needy through charity, to raise them to an equitable if not equal standing, is also a central aspect of this faith (which appears in a more secular form in various UN activities). Some scholars have gone as far as to say that the Catholic preaching of love and charity to the poor was the most important aspect of Jesus' teachings.[10] Jesus taught his followers to "sell what you own, and give the money to the poor, and you will have the treasure in heaven."[11] This moral lesson is repeated throughout the New Testament, as the rich were invited into the faith and encouraged to minister to the needs of the poor.[12] This increased the appeal of Catholicism by helping the homeless, impoverished, orphans and widows, and those who had fallen prey to natural disasters such as earthquakes or fires.[13] Taking care of the less fortunate and those in need is an aspect of UN work through the UN Children's Fund (UNICEF), UN Development Fund (UNDP), UN High Commissioner for Refugees (UNHCR), and so forth. And this message was repeated by Perez de Cuellar during his tenure as secretary-general.

Given that many Catholic principles fit with UN norms and principles and general activities, we searched for a clear connection (in interviews, speeches, and the literature) between Catholicism and Perez de Cuellar's diplomatic record. While we believe that Perez de Cuellar's Catholic heritage may have influenced his ethical framework, we are unable to demonstrate this with certainty. The overlap between Catholic tenets and UN principles and values is clearer than the connection between Catholicism and the secretary-general's actions.

By all accounts, the adult Perez de Cuellar was a European Catholic.[14] In terms of lifestyle he was a Francophone, fluent almost without accent in French, and very much taken with the French way of life. After his public service he retired to Paris, not Lima. Like many French, or many modern Italians for that matter, his Catholicism was almost nominal, more a matter of culture and tradition than of active church commitment. He saw himself as an ecumenical Christian, not one to emphasize the finer points of Catholic theology. Like many French and Italian Catholics, he believed in the importance of family planning, thus disregarding the church's teachings on this issue. In later years he showed some tolerance for gay people, again bucking the church's position. Unlike Kurt Waldheim, he did not attend Mass regularly or partake systematically of other Catholic rituals. No colleague we interviewed could recall a situation or event in which Perez de Cuellar reflected on his Catholic upbringing or talked about the importance of religion for his public role. He thought that public officials should put their personal religion in the freezer while serving in office. At one point he insisted that a word in a UN report be removed, because in certain languages it had a religious connotation.[15] He was more likely to read French poetry after a stressful day than selections from the New Testament.

To the extent that Perez de Cuellar can be said to be Catholic in matters of faith, it seemed to be a traditional, mainstream form of Catholicism, European style. There is no evidence that he was much affected by the "liberation theology" that was influential in parts of Latin America during his lifetime and that emphasized a more radical form of Catholicism focusing on the plight of the poor. Whereas parts of the Catholic Church in Latin America (and elsewhere for that matter) were aligned with, and defensive of, the aristocratic and other upper classes, liberation theology concentrated on the liberation of the poor and marginalized, not only in theological terms of salvation for the next life but also in terms of political and economic liberation in the here and now. As secretary-general, Perez de Cuellar sometimes spoke of the importance of development and the eradication of poverty. One of his major regrets was that he was unable as secretary-general to do more about underdevelopment in the world. But he spoke equally of the importance of state sovereignty and recognized governments, especially before his second term as secretary-general. Over time he may have identified more and more with the poor and down-trodden and victimized, but we found no evidence that this evolution stemmed from his Catholic heritage, much less from the Latin American version of liberation theology—the latter gaining some prominence only after the formative years of his youth.

It seems to have been the case that Perez de Cuellar was irritated that the Vatican would not officially recognize his second marriage, the first having ended in divorce.[16] Be that as it may, Perez de Cuellar did visit the Vatican on several occasions. He seemed to place great importance on such visits, but this was primarily for political reasons. He viewed these visits in the context of securing Vatican support for UN policies. At these meetings in Rome, religion was not discussed.

We do not deny that Perez de Cuellar's personal liberalism may have been a by-product of his Catholic upbringing. It is not uncommon for people who were raised in the Christian faith to become secular liberals, secular humanists, or secular champions of human rights and human dignity. It is likely in at least some cases that a Catholic heritage focusing on the worth of the individual in God's sight contributed to the secular liberal values that eventually characterized the adult viewpoint. But in the case of Perez de Cuellar, we could establish no definitive link between his religion and his inner code. There seems to be no major Catholic priest or educator who was instrumental in the development of his personal ethics. All we can say is that his personal ethics ran parallel to a moderately liberal but not radical interpretation of Catholicism. It might be fair to think of Perez de Cuellar as a South American version of a French Catholic who had a sense of noblesse oblige to those of misfortune or lesser rank.

One can note in passing that Perez de Cuellar's concern over the nuclear arms race and the destructive capabilities of nuclear weapons was similar to that voiced by the Catholic Church and the pope. On numerous occasions various representatives of the church condemned the buildup of conventional and nuclear weapons in the United States and the Soviet Union. Pope John Paul II urged the nations of the world to embrace disarmament. In a message to the General Assembly session on disarmament in 1982, the pope announced that the Catholic Church would continue to promote peace and "will not rest until there is a general, verifiable disarmament and the human race is committed to those choices that guarantee a lasting peace."[17] The pope saw the arms race as an ethical crisis, especially given that resources spent on nuclear and conventional weapons could be used to improve the situation of poor nations instead. While the secretary-general also saw the arms race as a moral issue, we found no evidence that either papal statements or other church pronouncements affected Perez de Cuellar. Again we see parallel value structures, but no cause-and-effect relationship.

One can likewise note the similarities between the secretary-general's call for debt relief and aid to the Third World and comments made by Pope John Paul II. The pope repeatedly requested that wealthy nations provide more economic aid to the world's poor. In his *Centisimus annus* (May 1, 1991), John Paul II argued that the West was not upholding its duties to the poor throughout the world.[18] The pope was concerned that Third World debt was taking an economic, social, and human toll and in the process bringing some nations to the brink of disaster.[19] But again, we find no definitive evidence that the secretary-general's comments about development, poverty, debt relief, and the like had a religious foundation.

In general, we find that if Perez de Cuellar's Catholicism had any important impact on his public role, it was mainly through the development of his personal—essentially secular—ethics. But any such linkage remains conjecture.

Liberalism: Respect for the Individual

Perez de Cuellar's philosophical orientation eventually came to be liberal.[20] Liberalism focuses on individuals, their dignity, and their inherent freedoms. Many liberals, although not all, have made autonomy the foundation of their political philosophy. Liberals argue that all persons are free and autonomous creatures simply because they are persons, irrespective of race, gender, or social status. This freedom entails the ability to choose and to act on one's own conception of the good life. As Will Kymlicka puts it, "The defining feature of liberalism is that it ascribes certain fundamental freedoms to each individual. In particular, it grants people a very wide freedom of choice in terms of how they lead their lives. It allows people to choose a conception of the good life, and then allows them to reconsider that decision, and adopt a new and hopefully better life plan."[21] Liberals strongly endorse human rights, especially the right to freedom of speech, conscience, religion, and association. This list, although not exhaustive, constitutes a sphere of personal autonomy.[22]

The underlying foundation of individual freedom is the assumption that all members of society possess dignity. Respecting individual dignity enhances individual well-being and provides for human potentiality.[23] By protecting and promoting individual freedom and tolerating this diversity, societies uphold and reinforce the dignity of human beings. In order to further human potential, society needs to treat individuals as autonomous beings and therefore respect the choices they make.[24] This is accomplished through a constitutional framework and through the rule of law.

Without doubt, Perez de Cuellar's personal ethics, his inner code of right and wrong, was centered on human dignity, human freedom, human rights—certainly this was the case by the time of his second term. Of course, these values are embedded in the UN charter. But eventually his interest in, and commitment to, such values was not just legalistic and pro forma but became internalized.

This was not always the case. As a Peruvian diplomat, and then in his first term as secretary-general, Perez de Cuellar was known more for his traditional respect for state sovereignty, his traditional diplomatic practice and discretion, and his going with the flow rather than rocking the boat in the name of human rights and other liberal causes. This was a major reason why he was chosen by the five permanent members of the Security Council as secretary-general; he seemed a safe choice. As undersecretary-general for political affairs during the Waldheim era, he had compiled a report on prison conditions in Uruguay that seemed to be a whitewash by comparison to a leaked report from the International Committee of the Red Cross.[25] Also, he decided not to renew the contract of the dynamic (and undiplomatically outspoken) UN director of human rights, Theo van Boven of the Netherlands, and replaced him with the much less activist and much more discrete Kurt Herndl of Austria.[26] As of the early 1980s, Perez de Cuellar was anything but a determined and committed liberal.

As will be shown below, however, he took great strides for, even great risks for, human rights in places like Central America. True, his initiatives there were well founded in charter principles. True, they were seen as necessary means to the end of peace and security. But by all accounts he was personally committed to achieving a better deal for individuals, including those who had been marginalized and exploited under previous political arrangements.

Likewise in the Iran–Iraq war, as we will show, he took initiatives regarding the use of chemical weapons, not only because such means and methods of armed conflict violated international law but because he was personally opposed to such developments on the basis of his personal sense of right and wrong. Later, when his office issued a report on that part of the world, Perez de Cuellar insisted on using the word "genocidal" to describe certain Iraqi policies toward Iraqi Kurds. His personal sense of outrage about what had been done to individuals affected this particular decision, even if it was only a matter of semantics in a UN publication.

Then there was his sense of impartiality. Some of the people who worked with the secretary-general commented repeatedly on his sense of fairness when dealing with various interlocutors. It seems to have been the case that Perez de Cuellar did not admire or respect a number of political figures with whom he dealt. But his colleagues were consistent in saying that he always gave political representatives a fair hearing. Insofar as his personal code stressed equal treatment of individuals, it can be said to be part of his liberal personal ethics.

Likewise, there was his commitment to the rule of law, another liberal value. This part of his personal code could be intertwined with his sense of fairness. For example, having worked diligently for the withdrawal of the Republic of South Africa from Namibia, on the eve of that area's independence the secretary-general found himself confronted by clear violations of the key agreement by the Southwest Africa People's Organization (SWAPO). And despite his efforts for black independence, with SWAPO as the leading organization for national liberation, the secretary-general was scathing in his criticism of SWAPO's violations of the accord. One can understand Perez de Cuellar in this episode as being committed to international law and diplomatic agreements. But one can also read him as committed to evenhanded treatment of all violators of international agreements, whether they were black nationalists or white supremacists. In this case the dividing line between commitment to the rule of law, required by his office, and commitment to basic fairness as a product of personal ethics is difficult to establish.

In summary, to this point, Perez de Cuellar's diplomatic track record reflected a strong sense of equity, fairness, and impartiality, which at times took the form of equality under law. Especially in his second term he showed great respect for human dignity and human rights, not just as a matter of legal or organizational obligation but as a matter of personal ethics. In the same way, he treated his colleagues in the Secretariat with great personal respect and great personal concern. He did indeed eventually manifest a personal ethics of liberalism centered on human dignity. His early missteps regarding Uruguay and van Boven have obscured this point for numerous observers.

Other parts of his inner code do not fit so neatly with liberalism. We are not suggesting that values like modesty contradict liberalism, only that they do not fit clearly within the definition of liberalism. In any event, by all accounts Perez de Cuellar was characterized by an absence of the kind of pride and arrogance and hauteur in his public life that was associated with his successor, Boutros Boutros-Ghali. Now, it may be that in his personal life he manifested a certain pride and vanity.[27] Be that as it may, in his public role Perez de Cuellar thought of his office as a place for team effort, team responsibility, and team credit. His view of the office of the secretary-general emphasized duty, service, and commitment, not personal achievement. When some of his colleagues told him that it was unfortunate he did not garner more recognition for his efforts in places like Iran, Iraq, Afghanistan, and Central America, he replied with apparently genuine modesty that such things were unimportant—that what counted was recognition for the organization, not for himself.[28] In the 1990s, when the prospect of a UN ceremony in New York, to which all living former secretaries-general were to be invited, raised the prospect of embarrassment for Waldheim, then on the nonentry list of the United States because of events stemming from his involvement in World War II, Perez de Cuellar let it be known that the secretaries-general should not be invited. This was done to save Waldheim embarrassment and further controversy.

Institutional Norms

Many liberal values are inherent in the UN charter and especially in the International Bill of Rights. According to one source, Woodrow Wilson's liberalism in international relations, which was the foundation not only for the League of Nations but also for the United Nations, means a commitment to peace and arms control, to human rights and democracy, and to private property and free trade.[29] It is well known that the liberal values of the charter were heavily influenced by Western thought, through the primary role of the United States.[30]

The International Bill of Rights, which is a diplomatic rather than a legal term and a composite of the 1948 Universal Declaration of Human Rights, the 1966 International Covenant on Civil and Political Rights, and the 1966 International Covenant on Economic, Social, and Cultural Rights, recognizes many individual freedoms.[31] It also recognizes the duty of states to provide for minimal socioeconomic goods and services when individual freedom and competition fail to provide them.

Whatever the liberalism required by UN norms, in the charter the foremost function of the organization is the maintenance of international peace and security. The United Nations as an institution was designed to promote peace, particularly between states. Like other secretaries-general before him, Perez de Cuellar therefore sought to develop in the international community the confidence to use the United Nations as a "brokering agency to achieve peace."[32] As expected, Perez de Cuellar stressed this role continually, but with room for morality: "But peace as envisaged by the UN Charter is a just peace: take that moral dimension away and we are back to the disorder and the injustice of power politics."[33]

Perez de Cuellar saw the charter as a moral statement:

> The expression may be somewhat old fashioned, but it is a matter of international morality. The philosophy of the Charter of the UN is perfect. We could change articles but I don't think we need to change the spirit of the Charter which means a kind of religion for the international community. The Charter contains principles which should be adhered to by all countries[,] and every transgression of the rules should be treated as immorality. It is the moral approach to all international problems that we need.[34]

Here we see the secretary-general transforming international legal norms concerning security into a moral code—almost a secular religion, if you will. In a 2002 interview, Perez de Cuellar referred to the charter as his philosophy: "I used to say that the UN Charter is my credo. I believe in the Charter."[35] Thus Perez de Cuellar did not rigidly distinguish the charter as part of international law from ethics, morality, philosophy, or indeed maybe from an informal religion. It was clear to him that the charter was not just a matter of technical, specialized legal language, but of values, justice, ethics, morality. So it is often fruitless to ask whether his motivation was ethical or legal. It was both at once. It seems that the longer he served as secretary-general, the more the liberalism inherent in the charter became a genuine inner liberalism for the man himself. If so, we have the merger of Perez de Cuellar's personal values with his formal external code in the form of charter principles.

Policy Choices

Perez de Cuellar was selected to be secretary-general primarily because he was "the least objectionable candidate," especially to the permanent members of the Security Council.[36] Waldheim had sought a third term as secretary-general, but China was opposed. That Waldheim up to that point had proved acceptable to the other P-5 members indicated that they preferred a docile and nonintrusive secretary-general, even if he manifested various character flaws and was far from dynamic. Another candidate, Salim Salim of Tanzania, had supported efforts to develop a New International Economic Order (unlike Perez de Cuellar), and had openly rejoiced at the admission of Communist China to the United Nations, and so drew the veto of the United States.

Initially the international community could not agree on a new candidate. Ultimately the P-5 thought that Perez de Cuellar was unlikely to make international waves as head of the United Nations. He seemed safe. This perception stemmed partially from his quiet personality and his modesty and humility as a public official. As one official said, "If Perez de Cuellar had to choose between going to a museum and being invited to a meeting of the G-7, he would choose the museum every time."[37] However proud and even vainglorious he might have been in private social circles, his public persona was otherwise. The widespread perception of him as a humble man fit with his track record as a traditional but reliable Peruvian diplomat. No one expected him to be a dynamic leader who would seek profound changes at the United Nations or in international relations.[38] He remained modest, but in his second term he also proved to be creative and dynamic in an understated way.

Constraints of the Office

The secretary-general is "both [the] symbol and guardian of the original vision of the organization."[39] The office is embedded with constraints. Perez de Cuellar understood the confines of his office. He continually stressed that "fidelity to the aims of the Charter" must always be paramount to any secretary-general.[40] He warned that the secretary-general could not boldly venture too far from the charter, or attempt too little:

> Anyone who has the honor to be cast as Secretary-General has to avoid the two extremes in playing his or her role. On one side is the Scylla of trying to inflate the role through too liberal a reading of the text: of succumbing, that is, to vanity and wishful thinking. On the other is the Charybdis of trying to limit the role to only those responsibilities which are explicitly conferred by the Charter and are impossible to escape: that is, succumbing to modesty, to the instinct of self-effacement, and to the desire to avoid controversy.[41]

Undertaking too much without the support of the Security Council is likely to hamper the effectiveness of the secretary-general and lead to a loss of respect for the institution and the office, thus making achievement of charter goals more difficult. Doing too little can also leave the organization impotent in areas in which it might otherwise accomplish much. Perez de Cuellar cautioned against assuming that the secretary-general was an omnipotent individual capable of single-handedly securing world peace, and he warned against succumbing to personal bias in efforts to achieve peace: "Moral concern must not become moral hubris. The Secretary-General must not allow himself to be influenced by his own judgment of the moral worth of either party's position or, for that matter, by what the leaders or media of one country glibly say about the position of the other. Subjective attitudes must not be allowed to hinder progress towards mutual understanding between the parties."[42] The conviction that it is better to be an honest broker than a moral or legal judge deeply influenced his conduct.[43]

In addition, a secretary-general is limited in the initiatives he can undertake. The restraints imposed by the charter are set out in articles 98 and 99.[44] Besides handling issues sent to him by the various organs of the organization and making annual reports, the secretary-general's political initiative lies mainly in article 99's provision to bring threats to international peace and security to the attention of the Security Council. A secretary-general must be cautious when invoking article 99, however. If a situation is brought to the attention of the Security Council and then ignored by the permanent members, it will have little chance of being addressed. And the reputation of the organization and the office of the secretary-general will suffer. Thus a secretary-general must use careful political judgment when invoking article 99.[45]

The Political Reality of International Relations

Perez de Cuellar was not a starry-eyed liberal idealist by any means. He understood that "one's expectations have to be realistic and yet not divorced from the ideals embodied in the Charter of the UN. The international environment, fraught with tensions and acute differences, will inevitably be reflected in the debates in the UN."[46]

Throughout most of his tenure as secretary-general, Perez de Cuellar had to deal with the many conflicts arising from the Cold War. The USSR and the United States often used the United Nations to disseminate propaganda points and to prevent certain initiatives that might benefit "the enemy." Neither adhered consistently to charter principles or always honored the intentions of the UN founders. An ideological "higher law," of either anticapitalism or anticommunism, trumped respect for positivistic international law found in the UN charter. To complicate matters, many of the developing countries occasionally elevated a "higher law of anticolonialism" over charter provisions. When the new secretary-general began his first term, on January 1, 1982, he did not believe that "either superpower displayed sufficient respect for an organization both found useful as a listening post, diplomatic venue, and propaganda arena."[47]

The superpowers and the five permanent members of the Security Council could thwart or ignore Perez de Cuellar's initiatives. The Falkland Islands/Islas Malvinas War was a good example of his failure to impact a situation. Perez de Cuellar realized early in April 1982 that the United Nations might be called on to address this conflict. He believed that the charter gave him a moral imperative to try to prevent the conflict between the United Kingdom and Argentina from escalating into war.[48] After U.S. secretary of state Alexander Haig was unsuccessful in his attempts to settle the dispute, the responsibility fell to the United Nations. Haig's efforts failed primarily because of the disparate positions of both countries.[49] Ultimately, Perez de Cuellar's labors in May 1982 also failed to resolve the issue, despite agreement on roughly 75 percent of the issues by the two belligerents.[50]

Events like these led the secretary-general, in his 1982 annual report, to conclude that "time after time we have seen the Organization set aside or rebuffed, for this reason or that, in situations in which it should, and could, have played an important and constructive role."[51] In general, when the superpowers or the P-5 did not want the United Nations or its secretary-general meddling in their affairs, they could ensure that Perez de Cuellar remained a spectator in the international arena. Perez de Cuellar understood this very well, commenting, "there is not much I can do if the international atmosphere of mistrust [between the superpowers] does not improve."[52]

Great Power Politics

Without doubt, the most significant event of Perez de Cuellar's tenure was the internal transformation of the Soviet Union. In March 1985, after a series of leadership changes in the USSR, Mikhail Gorbachev came to power. Perez de Cuellar recognized, during an early encounter with Gorbachev at the funeral of President Chernenko in 1985, that the United Nations had an opportunity to take a more active role in global issues. During this meeting Gorbachev expressed his support for the United Nations: "I think that the Soviet Union, from now on, will be very supportive of the UN, because we think that in the future all problems should be solved through your organization. You can rely on me."[53] Perez de Cuellar realized that Gorbachev was someone he could work with—the new Soviet leader was the "real McCoy."[54]

Gorbachev understood the weakness inherent in the Soviet political and economic system and sought to use the United Nations and multilateral cooperation as a new framework for global security. In two articles published in *Pravda* and *Isvestia* in September 1987, he argued that the United Nations was a vital institution necessary to achieve a comprehensive system of international peace and security.[55] This new attitude on the Soviet side, which prompted changes on the U.S. side as well, allowed the United Nations and the secretary-general to be more active and assertive. Either the two superpowers were to be in agreement on some issues, or they felt secure enough on other issues to allow the secretary-general room to maneuver in search of a policy not controlled by either party. The critical point remains that it was the changes in the Soviet Union and consequently the changes in the international environment that allowed the secretary-general to be more proactive and successful on some international fronts. These changes, however, did not originate from Perez de Cuellar's religious beliefs.

Policy Choice: Peace and Security

Global disarmament was a constant priority for Perez de Cuellar. Given the anarchic and insecure state of international relations, most nations are reluctant to disarm and thus forfeit any strategic advantage they might achieve through the buildup of weapons. Perez de Cuellar had two related motivations for disarmament. First, disarmament was implicit in the UN charter.[56] Just as important was the devastating impact on civilians around the world of expensive arms races and violent clashes. Early in his tenure as secretary-general Perez de Cuellar explained the importance of the issue:

> At the present stage in international affairs, there is a compelling need to make a credible and substantial advance towards arms limitation and disarmament . . . The world cannot wait for the dawn of ideal conditions before

undertaking concrete measures of disarmament. I would very much hope that the forthcoming special session will help restore the momentum of progress in this field. It will be closely followed by a growing world audience increasingly alarmed by the prospects of a nuclear holocaust. We all share a heavy responsibility to ensure its success.[57]

Perez de Cuellar felt that he and the United Nations had "the responsibility of assuring the survival of humanity and of organized society on this earth," which was imperiled by the deadly impasse of the superpowers and the potential for mutually assured destruction (MAD).[58] Yet, given the weakness of his office, Perez de Cuellar found that he could make little progress on issues of disarmament and arms control. The progress that was made occurred because of decisions made in Moscow and Washington.

CENTRAL AMERICA

Perez de Cuellar's concern over the situation in Latin America was not surprising, given his own national origins. While Latin America was hardly his only concern, as his work in Namibia, Afghanistan, and elsewhere demonstrates, he was especially vocal in his concern for his home continent.[59] In addition to his personal views, however, Central America became a Cold War battleground, so there were also political reasons to give great attention to the region.

According to Perez de Cuellar, the roots of all of the conflicts in Central America lay in the social and economic inequality throughout those societies. The unequal distribution of resources, which allowed a small segment of the population to enjoy vast wealth while the majority suffered in poverty, played a central role in the conflicts in Chile, El Salvador, Nicaragua, and Peru, to name but a few examples.[60] These economic disparities, which were enforced by the "structural violence" of the governments that benefited from them, including government-sponsored death squads, had led to armed rebellions. This situation, in turn, had led to external involvement.

A number of initiatives were undertaken to deal with these violent conflicts. The Contadora peace plan originated in January 1983 when the foreign ministers of Mexico, Panama, and Venezuela developed a strategy to encourage peace and limit foreign interference in the conflicts in Central America. The Security Council expressed its support for this initiative in Resolution 530 and requested that the secretary-general keep the council informed of developments there. Perez de Cuellar believed that he had "a moral responsibility to act in the interest of peace if there appears to be any chance of success."[61] In the early years of his first term, he simply offered UN assistance to the Organization of American States (OAS) and to the Contadora group, if they desired. He would become more involved toward the end of his term as secretary-general, as the Cold War drew to a close.

Perez de Cuellar faced a number of constraints when dealing with the conflict in Central America. For one thing, he had no mandate to act in the early 1980s from the Security Council, and Washington clearly wanted to limit UN involvement in its "backyard." In addition, the states that began the Contadora process wanted to protect their turf. They did not want another body to intervene and steal some of their thunder.[62] The OAS also wanted to keep the United Nations out of what it regarded as its diplomatic territory. Thus Perez de Cuellar had to walk a very fine diplomatic line. Initially the Contadora process failed to bring peace to Nicaragua or El Salvador, the two Central American states most wracked by violence. This was most probably a direct result of the failure of Contadora to include guerilla factions in the peace process.[63] The Arias Plan, named after President Arias of Costa Rica, was a follow-up initiative designed to end the turmoil in Central America in February and March 1987. It improved upon the earlier efforts by providing specific conditions for ceasefires, amnesties, dialogue with opposition groups, and a verification commission.[64]

Both plans probably would have failed had two events not occurred that changed American foreign policy. The first was a scandal in the United States and the second was a change in executive leadership. These provided the opening for what proved to be a critical element in the attainment of peace: the involvement of the secretary-general and the United Nations in the peace plan.

The context for these changes was the improved relationship between the USSR and the United States at the end of the Reagan era, circa 1987–88. The long Cold War was finally coming to an end, and Gorbachev's Soviet Union was expressing much less interest in Central America. This in turn diminished the extent to which Castro's Cuba could support the Sandinistas in Nicaragua or oppose the government in El Salvador.

In this context, the scandal in the United States proved optimal for the situation in Central America. The Iran-Contra affair involved Oliver North's operation to sell arms to Iran and to use the proceeds to support the Contras, who were trying to violently bring down the leftist-Sandinista government of Daniel Ortega in Nicaragua. This scandal, which came to light in November 1986, tarnished the Reagan administration and limited Reagan's ability to flex American muscle in Central America after 1986.[65] Reagan had kept the United Nations at arm's length when it came to this region, but after the Iran-Contra affair became public, he was unable to decisively influence events in the region. Given a weakened executive, the Congress, controlled by the opposition party and long opposed to Reagan's foreign policy in Central America, was able to block many of the administration's policies.

George H. Bush, elected U.S. president in 1988, was considerably more moderate in his views toward Central America and also viewed the United Nations more favorably, having been the U.S. representative there in the past. These changes in the United States, coupled with the changes in Soviet foreign policy under Gorbachev, paved the way for the active involvement of Perez de Cuellar and the United Nations.

NICARAGUA

In early 1989 the Arias Plan began to gain momentum. The government of Nicaragua scheduled elections for February of the following year. These elections would be open to all parties and would be monitored by international observers. To ensure a free and fair process, Nicaragua invited the United Nations to verify the elections. The Security Council authorized Perez de Cuellar to assist in these endeavors in Resolution 637 (July 27, 1989). In response, the secretary-general sent a team of officials to Nicaragua, with Elliot Richardson as the head of the UN Observer Mission to Verify the Election Process in Nicaragua (ONUVEN) to assist the OAS in the monitoring of elections (August 25). Thus, in ONUVEN, for the first time in cooperation with OAS, the United Nations took part in the domestic elections of a member state. This was a seminal moment in contemporary peacekeeping. The election ultimately resulted in the defeat of the Sandinista government.[66] Also crucial to the success of the electoral process was the Bush administration's unqualified support for the outcome.[67]

The United Nations' contribution to democracy in Nicaragua went beyond the electoral process. After the election the United Nations was asked to collect weapons from the rebels. The UN Observer Group in Central America (ONUCA) was established by Resolution 644 (November 7, 1989) and enlarged by Resolution 650 (March 27, 1990) to verify the voluntary demobilization of the Nicaraguan resistance. Although there were some difficulties, the United Nations, through its collection of rebel weapons, had set a precedent that could be built upon in the future.

On April 19, 1990, the Nicaraguan government and the Contras signed a ceasefire agreement.[68] By June 1990 the United Nations had successfully completed its mission. The results were quite dramatic, especially with respect to small-scale peacekeeping. A genuinely free and fair election had taken place, and the democratic results had ushered in a new government. The secretary-general was essential in this development, but the crucial factor here was that the international environment had changed.

EL SALVADOR

The United Nations also played a pivotal role in helping to end the civil war in El Salvador. The conflict, which began in 1979, had reached a stalemate by the late 1980s. This, along with the end of the Reagan administration, encouraged the government of El Salvador and the rebels to consider negotiating. Perez de Cuellar embraced the opportunity as an obligation of the secretary-general and sent Alvaro de Soto as his special representative to negotiate an end to the conflict between the Frente Farabundo Marti para la Liberacion National (FMLN) and the elected government of Alfredo Felix Cristiani.[69] De Soto's efforts led to an agreement, signed in the summer of 1990, between the two parties to respect human rights by avoiding all activities "that threaten the life, integrity, security or liberty of individuals."[70] Ultimately the UN Observer Mission in El Salvador (ONUSAL) was established to monitor the human rights situation in El Salvador. Despite this progress, a ceasefire remained elusive, and the fighting continued.

Perez de Cuellar was eventually able to bridge the gap between the government and the FMLN in eleventh-hour negotiations in New York. With the end of his tenure as secretary-general looming (December 1991), Perez de Cuellar approached the task with a sense of urgency, inviting both parties to New York for negotiations. Just before midnight on December 31, 1991, the two sides agreed to a ceasefire. As in the case of Nicaragua, Gorbachev's lack of interest in the situation and U.S. pressure for a peace agreement provided Perez de Cuellar with an opening.

The policies in both El Salvador and Nicaragua allowed a critical development in international relations—second-generation or complex peacekeeping, featuring UN field missions with broad mandates that covered a variety of human rights issues.[71] Perez de Cuellar had been bold and creative in his efforts to foster both human rights and security; the first fed into the second. It was not merely a matter of human rights or security any more than it was a matter of charter provisions versus an ethical framework or the reality of power politics. The record of the UN secretary-general in Central America was the result of all three factors at once: attention to UN norms, to liberal principles of rights and dignity, and to the acknowledged self-interest of various states and nonstate actors.

THE IRAN–IRAQ WAR

The war between Iran and Iraq (1980–88) began when Iraqi dictator Saddam Hussein attacked Iran in pursuit of territorial gains and the glory and wealth that come with them. The Iranians defended their territory as part of a religious struggle. While Iraq had superior weapons, and within the first few weeks occupied some seven thousand square kilometers of Iranian territory, Iran managed to repel the attacks.[72] Iraq's military advantage led many policymakers in Europe and the United States to expect a quick Iraqi victory. In addition, the Iranian mullahs had almost no experience with domestic or international politics.[73] For these reasons, the survival of the Islamic Republic was rather unexpected. Iran's greater population, and Iranians' willingness to fight and die for their nation, if not for religion, was Iran's advantage over Iraq. But neither Iraq's military superiority nor Iran's greater will achieved victory by either side, and so the war dragged on.

For the first four years of his term, both the Soviet Union and the United States wanted Perez de Cuellar to remain on the sidelines of the conflict. From the American perspective, consistent with its double-containment strategy, it was advantageous for Iraq and Iran to fight with each other because both would be weakened. It was only after Iran had scored a number of military successes that the United States decided that the international community should become involved. The Reagan administration feared that either Iraq would end up another Islamic republic or that the flow of oil would be interrupted. It was in this context that the United States provided Iraq with certain intelligence, and also delivered to it certain materials useful in the making of chemical and biological weapons.

Although the UN Security Council was silent on the use of chemical weapons, Perez de Cuellar undertook a number of diplomatic missions to address the issue. He was horrified by the use of chemical weapons, but his personal views were largely ignored by the conflicting parties and by the Security Council.[74] Still he persisted in making humanitarian efforts to stop the "war of the cities" and the bombing of civilian areas. Although neither side exercised restraint for very long, the secretary-general's efforts spared a number of lives.

Eventually Perez de Cuellar was able to broker a peace agreement between the parties, because each side despaired of military victory, the permanent members of the Security Council had encouraged him to "do what you think is right," and the secretary-general was viewed as an impartial player.[75] On his own initiative, Perez de Cuellar rewrote Resolution 598 in a way that eventually gained Iranian acquiescence. So the Iranians came to rely on the secretary-general, even though they believed that Iraqi aggression had not been properly condemned by the Security Council. Hostilities ultimately ended on August 20, 1988, after the secretary-general held final discussions between the foreign ministers of both countries. Perez de Cuellar took a great sense of satisfaction in this. That he had been able to bring an end to the conflict was a diplomatic surprise that helped the image of the United Nations.[76]

Yet it remained true that in the early stages of the war, the personal views and attempted diplomacy of the UN secretary-general had made little difference in the course of events. It was only after both parties recognized that they faced an endless stalemate, and the United States encouraged Iraq to be flexible, that political space opened for mediation by Perez de Cuellar.

AFGHANISTAN

Fighting between the Soviet Union and Afghanistan began when the Soviet Union invaded that country in November 1979; the war lasted for nine years. The Soviets, in spite of their superior weapons, were unable to vanquish the various Afghan coalitions. The Americans were supplying the indigenous Afghan forces with stinger missiles.[77] As in the early stages of the Iran-Iraq war, neither superpower initially wanted the United Nations to resolve the situation in Afghanistan.

Perez de Cuellar's initial involvement with the Afghan crisis began when he was appointed by Secretary-General Waldheim to be his personal representative for Afghanistan. He accepted the assignment because the fighting "had raised tensions dangerously in an already volatile region and profoundly disrupted the lives of the Afghan people." By the time Perez de Cuellar became secretary-general, more than 6 million people, about one-third of the country, had fled Afghanistan to neighboring countries.[78]

For a number of years, however, neither Perez de Cuellar's efforts nor the initiatives of others were particularly effective, as the two sides and their backers tried to control the situation through violence. The fundamentals of the situation were therefore similar to the early years of the Iran-Iraq war.

Ultimately, after years of negotiations by Perez de Cuellar, and later by Diego Cordovez, the new special representative, the United Nations was able to negotiate a settlement.[79] The Geneva Accords signed on April 14, 1988, mandated the voluntary return of refugees, the withdrawal of foreign troops, nonintervention by the two superpowers, and international guarantees by the Soviets and the Americans.[80] The United Nations was able to provide humanitarian assistance to the Afghan people though Operation Salam.[81]

As with the situation in Central America, this diplomatic success had its origins in the changes in the Soviet Union under Gorbachev. The Soviet withdrawal from Afghanistan was the result of Gorbachev's view that the USSR was overextended and was living beyond its means in foreign policy. There was also the factor of domestic fatigue in the Soviet Union, especially concerning the increasing number of body bags returning from Afghanistan. Gorbachev viewed the war as a "bleeding wound."[82] On April 3, 1986, he announced that the Soviets would leave Afghanistan, and by the end of 1988 he had fulfilled his commitment. Perez de Cuellar credits the changing climate between the superpowers for the ultimate resolution of the Afghan problem: "We therefore decided to wait until the parties expressed the desire for the resumption of UN efforts before taking further action. Fortunately, there was a very significant change! Mikhail Gorbachev came to power in Moscow."[83] Thus Perez de Cuellar credits environmental forces for the changes in Afghanistan:

> It was not the negotiating skill of the United Nations that persuaded the Soviet Union to withdraw its armed forces from Afghanistan. This was the result of the invincible resistance of the Mujahideen, the effective arms they received from the United States and the support for their struggle extended by Pakistan, Iran and Saudi Arabia. The timing of the withdrawal of the Soviet troops was settled between theAmerican and the Soviets as was the belated agreement to cut off arms deliveries to the combatants.[84]

The UN Good Offices Mission in Afghanistan and Pakistan (UNGOMAP) was a UN victory, but in this case the United Nations and its secretary-general merely facilitated what the Soviets were committed to doing. The success in ending the violence in Afghanistan during 1979–88 meant no final victory for Afghanistan as a nation, for it continued to experience the ravages of domestic violence and, eventually, another round of international war starting in late 2001.

Population Control and Family Planning

Population control was an issue that some observers predicted would put Perez de Cuellar and his Catholicism at odds with his role as secretary-general. Controlling the birth rate is a central issue in many third world countries because these nations lack the economic resources to provide for millions of citizens, and in some cases a billion or more people, within their borders. For many countries, especially a large country such as China, keeping the birth rate down by decreasing pregnancies is one key to long-term development. Various methods of family planning, including access to abortions and contraception, aid in limiting the birth rate.

These methods contradict traditional Catholic dogma, which stresses that life begins at conception and that all life is valuable. The Catholic Church "rejects contraception, sterilization, and abortion as solutions to the population problem."[85] In a letter to the secretary-general, Pope John Paul II explained the church's view:

> The children of the world cry out for greater respect for their inalienable individual dignity and for their right to life from the first moment of conception, even in the face of difficult circumstances or personal handicap. Every individual, no matter how small or how seemingly unimportant in utilitarian terms, bears the imprint of the Creator's image and likeness (Gen 1:26). Policies and actions which do not recognize that unique condition of innate dignity cannot lead to a more just and humane world, for they go against the very values which determine objective moral categories and which form the basis of rational moral judgments and right actions.[86]

The resistance to abortion was evident at the International Conference on Population held in Mexico City on August 6–14, 1984, at which the Vatican, with the help of the United States, sought to advance a resolution that rejected promoting abortion as a method of family planning.[87] The Reagan administration, which was often at odds with the Vatican on policy issues, including aid to the third world and disarmament, supported the Vatican completely on this issue. An antiabortion stance fit nicely with Reagan supporters of the religious right in the United States.

The Reagan administration thus withheld funds from the UN Fund for Population Activities (UNFPA). On July 12, 1984, the United States announced that no American funds would flow to agencies that supported population control. On September 25, 1985, the United States withheld $10 million from the UNFPA, claiming that money was going to China, which forced sterilization and abortions on women.[88]

On this issue Perez de Cuellar clearly broke with part of his Catholic heritage. Most individuals who worked with the secretary-general suggested that his religious beliefs did not influence most of his public policies, and this is most evident in this instance.[89] "I am a Catholic, of course, but I am not in agreement with the position of my church as far as birth control is concerned," he said. "I am very much against abortion, but at the same time I am very much for birth control."[90] He understood the need for population control through family planning, and he vigorously defended UNFPA from criticism from whatever quarter.[91]

UNFPA did not actively promote abortion, however, as part of its family-planning counseling. Moreover, in places like China, where there was considerable controversy about abortion, UNFPA had never advocated abortion as a means of population control. The Reagan administration's association of abortion with the UNFPA was never based firmly on fact, but it was a useful way of placating Reagan's political base in the United States. The same scenario was to play out in the George W. Bush administration two decades later: U.S. monies were withheld, even though the family-planning policies of this agency actually reduced the demand for abortions. While Perez de Cuellar believed firmly in population control through contraception, in this respect he was not different from many Catholics.

Administration and Budget

As secretary-general Perez de Cuellar faced additional problems besides the Cold War rivalry. He spent much of his time focused on the financial problems of the United Nations, especially member states' financial obligations.[92] One especially challenging issue was the payment of UN dues, in which the United States was seriously in arrears. After spasmodic congressional withholding, the United States under Reagan began a systematic reduction of its contributions to the United Nations. This was due in part to the anti-UN attitude of many in the Reagan administration. In his 1985 annual report Perez de Cuellar noted his "deep concern at the practice of certain member states selectively withholding their duly assessed contributions. This can only have a most detrimental effect on the future viability of our Organization."[93] Unfortunately, Perez de Cuellar was never able to resolve this problem fully. Later secretaries-general had to face it as well.

Certainly there were legal dimensions to this controversy.[94] But one can also ask whether U.S. policies were really moral, in that they risked the destruction of the United Nations and its agenda of peace, human rights, and development. There were no religious aspects to the matter.

One additional administrative aspect of Perez de Cuellar's tenure as secretary-general was the trust he put in his delegates. Although not connected to his religious views, Perez de Cuellar often delegated responsibility to those around him. Everyone we interviewed who worked closely with him mentioned the confidence he placed in them to carry out the objectives of the organization. As suggested earlier, such respect for his colleagues as individuals can be seen as part of his personal and secular ethics.

The Ethics of Policy Choice

The office of secretary-general involves an endless series of difficult choices, and the moral authority and record of the secretary-general take their shape from how these choices are made. Evaluating these choices is clearly a complex process: While the personal values of the secretary-general are real, if often elusive, his moral authority is subjective, amounting to different things in the eyes of different actors.

In judging whether a decision is moral or immoral, one can focus on outcomes (did a given decision have positive consequences?), or on the means used to arrive at the decision (e.g., should one pay off terrorists to secure the release of hostages?). The method one uses to analyze a specific situation will influence one's conclusion. The complexity only increases when one takes into account whether the final outcome was bad for some individuals but good for others, or whether the principles used to decide how to respond to a situation were ethical or not.

Take the fundamental tension between state sovereignty and human rights. Is it moral for the secretary-general to challenge a state assertively over human rights issues if this will lead that state to resist UN involvement while providing no further protection for individuals? Was it really moral in the long run for van Boven or Mary Robinson to speak out so strongly on human rights, if their public diplomacy caused states to retrench in defense of sovereign repression? Perez de Cuellar understood this dilemma very well.

> It is not an easy task, because there is a contradiction between the United Nations' role as a monitor of human rights and its role as an organization of governments. There are many instances when we cannot monitor the implementation of the declaration [1948 Universal Declaration] as well as we would like because many countries say we are interfering in their internal affairs. The border between interference in internal affairs and monitoring human rights is a very difficult one.[95]

Despite his belief in the importance of human rights, Perez de Cuellar often deferred to state sovereignty.[96] The Chinese government's massacre of civilians in Tiananmen Square in 1989 brought forth no bold criticism, only implied and indirect criticism, from Perez de Cuellar—primarily because it could be seen as within the domestic jurisdiction of a sovereign state. He explained:

> That [the declaration of martial law by the People's Republic of China] is a typical case of a government exerting its legitimate authority. It is an internal problem in which the United Nations has no right to interfere, because all governments have the right to apply martial law. The issue is the way in which martial law is applied. It is one thing to preserve order, and quite another to misuse the right to apply martial law. It is possible to preserve order while at the same time maintaining respect for human rights. The Chinese government has the right to apply martial law, provided it is exerted in a legal manner with full respect for the Chinese people's human rights.[97]

To take another example, should the secretary-general speak out publicly and criticize a violation of the UN charter, or remain silent and pursue quiet diplomacy instead? Perez de Cuellar also undertook what he referred to as "discretion diplomacy." When he went abroad he would sometimes quietly discuss the situation of a few political prisoners. For example, while meeting with President Najibullah of Afghanistan in September 1990 Perez de Cuellar requested and won the release of a French national working for a nongovernmental organization who had been taken prisoner in Afghanistan.[98]

Perez de Cuellar understood that this involved a difficult decision and that it was not clear which choice would yield the greatest benefit: "The

Secretary-General can quite often intervene confidentially with a regime and gain the freedom, or at least an improvement in conditions, of individual political prisoners. Yet a critical public report can jeopardize his ability to perform this useful service. A balance has to be drawn as to which course can produce the greater benefit for those suffering from a deprivation of their human rights."[99] There is also the difficulty of placing UN personnel in harm's way in order to protect civilians in danger.[100] One former UN official described a conversation with Perez de Cuellar in which the secretary-general reminded him that he needed to be concerned about his safety while negotiating the release of hostages. While Perez de Cuellar ultimately left the decision up to the individual, he was concerned with the moral dilemma of whether to put individuals in the line of fire in order to help others.

Finally, every secretary-general must struggle with the decision whether to pursue a pragmatic course of action or stand up for moral or legal principles concerning nonintervention over human rights. This was especially true with regard to Central America: "As a Latin American, I hate the idea of interference, and if I don't like interference by Latin Americans in each other's problems I dislike still more interference by powers external to the area, whether American or Soviet or even Cuban."[101]

We think it unwise to try to formulate sweeping generalizations about the moral authority of particular secretaries-general across a range of issues, given these types of complexities. A secretary-general who openly criticizes a Great Power may gain in "moral authority" with developing countries but at the same lose in "moral authority" with that particular state. Thus there is no one definite perception or reality. Different actors will have different views.

Conclusion

We have tried to show that while the personal values of the UN secretary-general do inform his public role, his ethical framework is normally quite secondary to the political factors impinging on that office. In short, the secretary-general's internal code is usually not as important as the external code, which includes not only international legal norms but also his analysis of the dominant political factors in the environment.

A clear example of this can be seen in Perez de Cuellar's evolution over the course of his tenure as UN secretary-general. The single most significant event that took place during his tenure was the internal transformation of the Soviet Union. Prior to this he felt impotent with respect to many situations throughout the world.[102] The critical point remains that it was the changes in the Soviet Union, and consequently the changes in the international environment, that allowed the secretary-general to be more proactive and successful on some international fronts. It was not simply that in his second term he became a more assertive and influential secretary-general, or was more driven by his religious or moral beliefs. The collapse of the Soviet Union and the end of the Cold War gave him more room to maneuver. Likewise, no matter how deeply Perez de Cuellar may have felt about the use of chemical weapons in the Iran-Iraq war, or about the continuation of the war itself, he proved powerless to achieve beneficial change before the belligerents themselves were ready.

We have also tried to show that sometimes the internal and external codes overlap, making it impossible to say with certainty which actions derive from personal values and which from the external demands of the office and the UN charter. We have suggested that Perez de Cuellar's dynamism and willingness to take risks in places like El Salvador were the product of his personal values, his commitment to UN norms, and his astute reading of power politics. Indeed, over time his personal values may have stemmed from, and become coterminous with, charter principles. He was, after all, the product of legal training, and he had great respect for legal principles. In this and other situations, we would do well to recall that events have multiple causes, and that internal and external codes, politics and law, morality and power politics, all can become entangled in complex ways.

While secretary-general from 1982 to 1991, Perez de Cuellar worked consistently for the maintenance and restoration of international peace and security. This goal is, of course, the primary duty of the United Nations as an organization, and it was evident in his attempts to end the conflicts in the Middle East (Afghanistan, Iran/Iraq) and Latin America (El Salvador and Nicaragua). Advancing peace is also a core tenet of both Catholicism and liberalism. Without definitive evidence as to priorities, it is impossible to completely separate internal influences and motivations from external ones.

Perez de Cuellar also demonstrated his commitment to impartiality, freedom, and promoting the well-being of the poor, disadvantaged, and vulnerable. He was especially proud of his work relating to peacekeeping and human rights: "One of the greatest successes of the United Nations is to have brought about the recognition of human rights," he told an inter-viewer.[103] Perez de Cuellar considered his efforts to help Namibians achieve independence one of his enduring accomplishments.[104] These values are consistent with the Catholic ethos in which he grew up, as well as with his commitment to liberalism. Humanitarian concerns, autonomy, and fair and impartial treatment of individuals are also standards enshrined in the UN charter and Universal Declaration of Human Rights. Once again we see parallel value structures, from within and without, making it impossible to clearly delineate between the two realms.

By all accounts, Perez de Cuellar manifested a personal trait that influenced his public role and stood him in good stead with his interlocutors: his strong sense of fairness. He tried to be equitable in performing the functions of his office. Impartiality was a key component in this. "If quiet diplomacy is to succeed, it needs the confidence of all parties," he wrote. "And that means that the Secretary-General must not only be impartial but must be perceived to be so. He must not let his independence of judgment be impaired or distorted by pressures from governments. He should have no part in any diplomatic deal or undertaking which ignores the principles of the Charter."[105] Even here, though, we see that his notions of equity, neutrality, and impartiality were linked to his respect for the norms of the charter. Perez de Cuellar might be compared to Harry Truman. Both started high office with little support and little expectation of significant accomplishment. But over time both left a record that compared well with others, certainly in historical perspective. And both left a record of strong personal conviction, even if some of their personal hopes and aspirations were defeated by political reality.

Notes

1. Javier Perez de Cuellar, "Interview with Perez de Cuellar," *Third World Quarterly* 6 (1984): 13–24.

2. See Leon Gordenker, *The UN Secretary-General and the Maintenance of Peace* (New York: Columbia University Press, 1967); Benjamin Rivlin and Leon Gordenker, eds., *The Challenging Role of the UN Secretary-General: Making "The Most Impossible Job in the World" Possible* (Westport, CT: Greenwood, 1993); Arthur W. Rovine, *The First Fifty Years: The Secretary-General in World Politics, 1920–1970* (Leyden: A. W. Sijthoff, 1970).

3. Courtney Smith, "More Secretary or General? Effective Leadership at the UN," *International Politics* 40 (2003): 145.

4. Interview by authors, December 2004, New York.

5. Javier Perez de Cuellar, "The Role of the UN Secretary-General," in *United Nations, Divided World: The UN's Roles in International Relations*, 2d ed., ed. Adam Roberts and Benedict Kingsbury (Oxford: Oxford University Press, 1994), 134.

6. Ibid.

7. We would particularly like to thank Javier Perez de Cuellar for granting an extended interview, actually a day-long discussion, in Paris during the summer of 2005.

8. Javier Perez de Cuellar, *Pilgrimage for Peace: A Secretary-General's Memoir* (New York: St Martin's Press, 1997), 20–21.

9. For some general historical works on Catholicism, see Dennis C. Duling and Norman Perrin, *The New Testament* (Fort Worth, TX: Harcourt Brace College Publishers, 1994); Birger A. Pearson, *The Emergence of the Christian Religion* (Harrisburg, PA: Trinity Press International, 1997); and Rodney Stark, *The Rise of Christianity: A Sociologist Reconsiders History* (Princeton, NJ: Princeton University Press, 1996).

10. Adolf Harnack, *The Mission and Expansion of Christianity*, trans. James Moffatt (New York: Harper Torchbooks, 1962), 147.

11. Mark 1:16–20; 2:13–14. See further J. A. McGuckin, "The Vine and the Elm Tree: The Patristic Interpretation of Jesus' Teachings on Wealth," in *The Church and Wealth*, ed. W. J. Sheils and Diana Wood (New York: Basil Blackwell, 1987). He ordered his apostles to take nothing for their missionary journeys except a staff; no bread, no bag, no money in their belts, but to wear sandals and not to put on two tunics. Mark 6:8–10; Matthew 10:9–11; Luke 9:3–4.

12. For a further discussion of charity in the Pauline tradition, see Shirley Jackson Case, *The Social Triumph of the Ancient Church* (New York: Libraries Press, 1971), 50.

13. Stark, *Rise of Christianity*, 161.

14. This section is based on interviews conducted in New York toward the end of 2004 with several colleagues who worked closely with Perez de Cuellar.

15. Interview by authors, December 2004, New York.

16. Ibid.

17. Edward J. Gratsch, *The Holy See and the United Nations: 1945–1995* (New York: Vantage Press, 1997), 186.

18. George J. Lankevich, *The United Nations Under Javier Perez de Cuellar, 1982–1991* (Lanham, MD: Scarecrow Press, 2001), 290.

19. Gratsch, *Holy See*, 76–77.

20. Perez de Cuellar, *Pilgrimage for Peace*, 25. We distinguish philosophical from political liberalism. The first focuses on general views of the individual in society, based on transcendent notions such as right, good, value, and virtue. The second focuses on public policies and factional organizations in the here and now. Philosophical liberals who champion personal freedom may identify with a wide

variety of policies and political factions or parties. In this sense Henry Kissinger was correct to regard Ronald Reagan as a philosophical liberal, in that Reagan believed in progress, the perfectibility of "man," and the values of democracy and human rights. Later we refer to a third form of liberalism, a liberal foreign policy á la Woodrow Wilson.

21. Will Kymlicka, *Multicultural Citizenship* (Oxford: Oxford University Press, 1995), 80. Kukathas has offered a similar definition of liberalism: Liberal political theories, it is widely held, assume or argue that the good society is one not governed by particular common ends or goals but provides the framework of rights or liberties or duties within which people may pursue various ends, individually or cooperatively. It is a society governed by law and as such is regulated by right principles. These are principles of justice, which do not themselves presuppose the rightness or superiority of any particular way of life. Chandran Kukathas, "Are There Any Cultural Rights?" in *The Rights of Minority Cultures,* ed. Will Kymlicka (Oxford: Oxford University Press, 1995), 228–55.

22. *Universal Declaration of Human Rights,* articles 12, 18, 19, and 20.

23. David Boaz, *Libertarianism* (New York: Free Press, 1997), 96.

24. This notion of dignity is derived from Kantian liberalism: "Kantian liberalism begins with the claim that we are separate, individual persons, each with our own aims, interests, and conceptions of the good life. It seeks a framework of rights that will enable us to realize our capacity as free moral agents, consistent with a similar liberty for others." Michael J. Sandel, *Democracy's Discontent: America in Search of a Public Philosophy* (Cambridge, MA: Harvard University Press, 1996), 11.

25. See especially Iain Guest, *Behind the Disappearances: Argentina's Dirty War Against Human Rights and the United Nations* (Philadelphia: University of Pennsylvania Press, 1990).

26. Ibid. While the weaknesses of Perez de Cuellar's report on Uruguay prisons are clear, there is much about the nonrenewal of van Boven that remains unclear. In the latter case, some of the key memos remain secret. The exact views of the secretary-general at that time, and why he held them, have not been definitively established.

27. Interviews by authors, fall and winter 2004, New York and New Haven.

28. Interviews by authors, December 2004, New York.

29. Michael Mandelbaum, *The Ideas That Conquered The World: Peace, Democracy, and Free Markets in the Twenty-First Century* (New York: Public Affairs Press, 2002).

30. On the founding of the United Nations, see especially Stephen C. Schlesinger, *Act of Creation: The Founding of the United Nations* (Boulder, CO: Westview Press, 2003).

31. An interesting conflict developed when, in the summer of 1983, UNESCO voted to limit freedom of the press. Perez de Cuellar suggested that this illiberal

move was "misguided" but admitted that the policies of UNESCO were independent of Secretariat control. "What I cannot accept is an arrangement which leads
to censorship of the press." Perez de Cuellar, "Interview with Perez de Cuellar," 24.

32. Speech at Harvard, January 1986; Lankevich, *United Nations Under Perez de Cuellar*, 55.

33. Perez de Cuellar, "Role of the UN Secretary-General," 133.

34. Quoted in Altaf Gauhar, "Breaking the Big Stick of the Superpower," *South* (October 1983): 37–39.

35. Interview with Javier Perez de Cuellar, April 4, 2002, Paris, UN Intellectual History Project (forthcoming, read by permission).

36. Lankevich, *United Nations Under Perez de Cuellar*, 2.

37. Interview by authors, December 2004, New York.

38. Kent J. Kille and Roger Scully, "Executive Heads and the Role of Intergovernmental Organizations: Expansionist Leadership in the United Nations and the European Union," *Political Psychology* 24 (2003): 175–98.

39. Brian Urquhart, "Selecting the World's CEO: Remembering the Secretaries-General," *Foreign Affairs* 74 (1995): 21–26.

40. Perez de Cuellar, "Role of the UN Secretary-General," 126. He also said, "They [member states] must honor the Charter of the UN which offers a new, philosophical and moral approach to global problems." Perez de Cuellar, "Interview with Perez de Cuellar," 19.

41. Perez de Cuellar, "Role of the UN Secretary-General," 126.

42. Ibid., 134.

43. This is a view held by other organizations that lack hard power and must rely mostly on moral authority to generate influence. It is the view, for example, of the International Committee of the Red Cross, which, in its efforts to develop and apply international humanitarian law, mostly seeks to avoid public criticism while trying to build pragmatic cooperation on the principles of independence, neutrality, and impartiality. See David P. Forsythe, *The Humanitarians: The International Committee of the Red Cross* (Cambridge: Cambridge University Press, 2005).

44. Article 98 states, "The Secretary-General shall act in that capacity in all meetings of the General Assembly, of the Security Council, of the Economic and Social Council, and of the Trusteeship Council, and shall perform such other functions as are entrusted to him by these organs. The Secretary-General shall make an annual report to the General Assembly on the work of the Organization." Article 99 reads, "The Secretary-General may bring to the attention of the Security Council any matter which in his opinion may threaten the maintenance of international peace and security."

45. Perez de Cuellar, "Role of the UN Secretary-General," 131.

46. Javier Perez de Cuellar, "To Transcend All Divisions," *Review of International Affairs* 33 (1982): 5–6.

47. "I have not got sufficient indication that governments are really interested in using the UN mechanism for solving international problems." Perez de Cuellar, "Interview with Perez de Cuellar," 15; Giandomenico Picco, *Man Without a Gun: One Diplomat's Secret Struggle to Free Hostages, Fight Terrorism, and End a War* (New York: Times Books, 1999), 28.

48. Interview by authors, December 2004, New York.

49. Perez de Cuellar, *Pilgrimage for Peace,* 362. Perez de Cuellar's own initiatives for peace were largely ignored. In this book he describes how his memoranda were sometimes met with silence from one of the parties.

50. It was also reported that Haig resented the secretary-general's efforts. If Haig was unable to mediate the situation, how could someone else do so? Perez de Cuellar was frustrated by the inability of the United Nations to fulfill its obligations and broker peace around the world. This he expressed at the Institute for East-West Security Studies on April 21, 1982, when he said that "the UN, rarely asked to arbitrate between the great powers, was clearly able and willing to assist in the settlement of regional disputes." Quoted in Lankevich, *United Nations Under Perez de Cuellar,* 8. Perez de Cuellar's faith in his ability and the organization's ability to prevent conflict might be inflated. One wonders, given the dynamics involved in the Falkland Islands War, whether any organization or individual could have prevented the conflict.

51. Javier Perez de Cuellar, *Anarchy or Order: Annual Reports, 1982–1991* (New York: United Nations Publishers, 1991), 17.

52. Perez de Cuellar, "Interview with Perez de Cuellar," 15.

53. Interview with Perez de Cuellar, April 4, 2002, Paris, UN Intellectual History Project.

54. Perez de Cuellar was very clear about the debt he owed to Gorbachev, as was made clear in our interviews in New York and Paris, December 2004 and May 2005. See also the views of Perez de Cuellar on this subject in Thomas G. Weiss, Tatiana Carayannis, Louis Emmerij, and Richard Jolly, eds., *UN Voices: The Struggle for Development and Social Justice* (Bloomington: Indiana University Press, 2005), especially 272–73.

55. Lankevich, *United Nations Under Perez de Cuellar,* 71.

56. Articles 11.1 and 26.

57. Perez de Cuellar, "To Transcend All Divisions," 6. At a press conference on December 12, 1984, Perez de Cuellar expressed his frustration: "the ideological confrontation of the superpowers and their nuclear weapons jeopardize the future of humanity." Quoted in James Feron, "UN Chief Warns Nuclear Powers," *New York Times,* December 13, 1984.

58. Perez de Cuellar, "Role of the UN Secretary-General," 139.

59. During Perez de Cuellar's first interaction with the media after being selected as secretary-general, the Peruvian noted that his selection was "an act

of justice to Latin America and the entire Third World." Quoted in Lankevich, *United Nations Under Perez de Cuellar*, 2.

60. Gauhar, "Breaking the Big Stick," 39. This concern for the poor and the negative consequences that can arise from the neglect of the poor coincides with the tenants of Catholicism discussed earlier.

61. Perez de Cuellar, *Pilgrimage for Peace*, 396, 399.

62. Ibid., 399.

63. Perez de Cuellar considered using article 99 in conjunction with the conflicts in Central America. He ultimately decided against doing so because the Reagan administration did not support UN involvement in its backyard. Perez de Cuellar, *Pilgrimage for Peace*, 398. This again suggests the limited space in which the secretary-general must operate.

64. Ibid., 402.

65. Thomas M. Magstradt, *An Empire If You Can Keep It: Power and Principle in American Foreign Policy* (Washington, DC: Congressional Quarterly Press, 2004), 118–19.

66. Perez de Cuellar agreed, despite his personal commitment to the principle of nonintervention in the internal affairs of states. Perez de Cuellar, *Pilgrimage for Peace*, 412. On March 16, 1990, Perez de Cuellar asked the Security Council to authorize the use of UN forces to oversee Contra demobilization.

67. David P. Forsythe, "The United Nations, Democracy, and the Americas," in *Beyond Sovereignty: Collectively Defending Democracy in the Americas*, ed. Tom Farer (Baltimore, MD: Johns Hopkins University Press, 1996), 134.

68. Lankevich, *United Nations Under Perez de Cuellar*, 268.

69. Forsythe, "United Nations," 119.

70. Perez de Cuellar, *Pilgrimage for Peace*, 421–22. Perez de Cuellar also indicates that the United States pressured him to drop de Soto because he was viewed as sympathetic to Salvadoran rebels, but the secretary-general refused.

71. See David P. Forsythe, "Human Rights and International Security: United Nations Field Operations Redux," in *The Role of the Nation-State in the 21st Century*, ed. Monique Castermans et al. (The Hague: Kluwer, 1998), 265–76.

72. Robin Wright, *In the Name of God* (New York: Simon and Schuster, 1989), 25; A. Taheri, *The Spirit of Allah: Khomeini and the Islamic Revolution* (London: Hutchinson Publishers, 1985), 272.

73. Wright, *In the Name of God*, 24. Iran's population was three times bigger than Iraq's.

74. Former Secretariat official, interview by authors, September 28, 2004.

75. Perez de Cuellar, *Pilgrimage for Peace*, 131; Picco, *Man Without a Gun*, 79.

76. On August 15, 1990, Iraq agreed to a final peace with Iran—a return to original borders and the exchange of prisoners—because Hussein wanted

regional support regarding Kuwait and Gulf War. Lankevich, *United Nations Under Perez de Cuellar*, 108.

77. Picco, *Man Without a Gun*, 33.

78. Perez de Cuellar, *Pilgrimage for Peace*, 184, 210.

79. Cordovez, the special representative appointed by Perez de Cuellar, proved to be something of a headache for the secretary-general. He was critical of Perez de Cuellar's leadership, especially with regard to Afghanistan. Although Cordovez was replaced in 1990, the secretary-general did not publicly express any hard feelings. One could argue that this was due to the "turn-the-other-cheek" attitude taught to him as a boy in Catholic school. Perez de Cuellar himself suggested, "I tolerated him despite his apparent disloyalty because I thought this was in the best interest of an Afghan settlement." Perez de Cuellar, *Pilgrimage for Peace*, 187.

80. Ibid., 196.

81. Lankevich, *United Nations Under Perez de Cuellar*, 88.

82. Picco, *Man Without a Gun*, 33.

83. Perez de Cuellar, *Pilgrimage for Peace*, 192.

84. Ibid., 212.

85. Gratsch, *Holy See*, 252.

86. Message of Pope John Paul II to Javier Perez de Cuellar, September 22, 1990, documented in Carl J. Mauricci, ed., *Serving the Human Family: The Holy See at the Major UN Conferences* (New York: Path to Peace Foundation, 1997).

87. Lankevich, *United Nations Under Perez de Cuellar*, 160.

88. Ibid., 159.

89. Former Secretariat officials, interviews by authors, December 2004.

90. Interview with Perez de Cuellar, April 4, 2002, Paris, UN Intellectual History Project.

91. Perez de Cuellar, *Pilgrimage for Peace*, 13.

92. Tapio Kanninen, *Leadership and Reform: The Secretary-General and the UN Financial Crisis of the Late 1980s* (Boston: Kluwer Law International, 1995).

93. Perez de Cuellar, *Anarchy or Order*, 91.

94. See further David P. Forsythe, *The Politics of International Law* (Boulder, CO: Lynne Rienner, 1990).

95. "An Interview with the Honorable Javier Perez de Cuellar, Secretary-General of the United Nations," *Fletcher Forum of World Affairs* 14 (1990): 89.

96. "If you summarize what *human rights* means, it is the right to live in peace. Peace is not only the absence of war, but well-being and economic and social justice. That is why I feel that, apart from the Charter of the United Nations, the Declaration of Human Rights is the greatest success of the organization." Ibid., 88–89.

97. Ibid., 89.

98. Perez de Cuellar, *Pilgrimage for Peace,* 206.

99. Ibid., 407.

100. "We should give them the assurance that if they [the peacekeeping force] are brushed aside they will be protected, and appropriate action will be imposed." Perez de Cuellar, "Interview with Perez de Cuellar," 16. "However, the suffering of the Afghan people required a response . . . I urged UNICEF and the UN Development Program not to evacuate their personnel." Perez de Cuellar, *Pilgrimage for Peace,* 211.

101. Perez de Cuellar, "Interview with Perez de Cuellar," 21.

102. "My first five year term I did not have a sense of accomplishment." Quoted in Lankevich, *United Nations Under Perez de Cuellar,* 11.

103. "Interview with the Honorable Perez de Cuellar," 88.

104. Perez de Cuellar, *Pilgrimage for Peace,* chapter 11.

105. Perez de Cuellar, "Role of the UN Secretary-General," 133.

8

A REALIST IN THE UTOPIAN CITY

Boutros Boutros-Ghali's Ethical Framework and Its Impact

ANTHONY F. LANG JR.

I do not claim to elevate the vision of the Utopian city called for by the Islamic thinker Al-Farabi to that of a Utopian world, for I cannot promise to go beyond what is feasible and what is possible. Despite the close ties that bind me to optimism, my ties to realism are even closer. —BOUTROS BOUTROS-GHALI[1]

Boutros Boutros-Ghali was sworn in as secretary-general of the United Nations on December 3, 1991. The first post–Cold War secretary-general was raised an Egyptian Coptic Christian and educated in France as an international lawyer. These aspects of his background contributed to an ethical framework that influenced his leadership of the United Nations at a crucial moment in its history. This ethical framework was generally consistent with the external code embodied in the UN charter and overall system. But, like all secretaries-general, Boutros-Ghali interpreted the charter in a unique context, and his initiatives and decisions pushed the United Nations as a political system in new and innovative directions.

The first section of this chapter describes Boutros-Ghali's ethical framework, derived primarily from his religious background and his education in international law.[2] That framework includes five principles:

- The importance of tolerance
- The importance of forgiveness and reconciliation
- The importance of human rights based on a classical liberal political philosophy

- The moral importance of the nation-state as the institution that can structure and protect human goodness
- The importance of democracy on the domestic and international levels

As we shall see, these five elements overlap and intersect both in their origins and in their impact on policy decisions. They are listed separately as a heuristic device, and so should not be seen as discrete moral principles to which Boutros-Ghali referred as a sort of checklist. Rather, their combined force and their interaction with one another constituted his ethical framework and led him to undertake unique and sometimes controversial initiatives.

The chapter examines how this ethical framework influenced three sets of events at the United Nations: the organization's role in Somalia and the Balkans; its role in the postconflict reconciliation and democratization process in Cambodia; and the writing of *An Agenda for Democratization,* the last and most controversial of Boutros-Ghali's three *Agenda* documents while in office. Examining these three events in light of the ethical framework described above reveals that various elements of the framework did influence some of his decisions and that at times his ethical framework was overridden by the demands of power politics. Understanding a secretary-general's ethical framework can help explain some aspects of his tenure in office, but it does not explain all of them in every context. The final section of the chapter discusses this conclusion in the context of questions about responsibility and realism in the current international order, focusing briefly on two moments when an ethical approach was badly needed but failed to materialize—the massacres in Rwanda and Srebrenica.

Boutros-Ghali's Ethical Framework

Boutros Boutros-Ghali was born on November 14, 1922, in Cairo. His family was one of the "two hundred" that practically governed Egypt prior to the socialist revolution of 1952.[3] His family had a history of involvement in Egyptian politics; his grandfather served as prime minister and his uncle as foreign minister. While his family's wealth and social status gave Boutros-Ghali unique opportunities, especially education in the best schools, his religious background as a Coptic Christian placed him in a more complicated position in Egyptian culture. The word *Copt* derives from the original Greek word for Egypt and can be used to refer to any native Egyptian Christian; indeed, some refer to three Coptic communities in Egypt, the Orthodox, the Catholic, and the Protestant. Most colloquial references to Copts, however, refer to the Orthodox Church, of which Boutros-Ghali is a member.

Boutros-Ghali's religious background as a Coptic Christian shaped his ethical framework in two important ways. First, Boutros-Ghali believed that Christians approach politics differently from other monotheistic traditions through their emphasis on forgiveness in matters of past conflict. Second, as a member of a minority religious tradition in a strongly religious society, Boutros-Ghali believed that the international community needed to help protect minorities, which led him to emphasize the importance of tolerance.

A thorough account of the theology and history of the Coptic Church is beyond the scope of this chapter; it will suffice here to provide a thumbnail sketch for purposes of context.[4] The Coptic Church is one of the few "monophysite" Christian churches, a term that refers to a theological debate about the ontological status of Jesus Christ. Within the Coptic Church, the concept of monophysitism retains some importance,[5] although it is more of a historical issue than one of centrality to Christian theology today.[6] This theological debate is less important for understanding the impact on Boutros-Ghali than is the history of the Coptic Church within Egyptian society.[7]

Christianity was the primary religion in Egypt until the Muslim armies arrived in the mid-seventh century. For Christians, this meant a diminished political status, including limits on their ability to serve in public office and the imposition of a special tax. When the British occupied Egypt in the late nineteenth century, the Christian community was faced with a dilemma. On the one hand, the existence of a Christian power in Egypt, especially one that professed to be interested in the status of minorities, held out some promise for an alleviation of discrimination. On the other hand, by aligning themselves too closely with an occupying power, the Copts would be seen as a fifth column among Egyptian nationalists.[8]

This conflicted status of Christians affected Boutros-Ghali's family directly in the assassination of his grandfather. Appointed prime minister in 1908, Boutros Ghali was assassinated in 1910, ostensibly because he lost Egypt the Sudan. But Boutros-Ghali pointed out in an interview that "the reality was that the population was happy to get rid of a Christian."[9] Indeed, that Boutros-Ghali would describe the assassination of his grandfather in this way suggests that he, and perhaps the historical memory of many Copts in Egypt, focused on the fragile status of Christians rather than any policy decisions made by the prime minister.

Boutros-Ghali describes his childhood as very religious and says that he received a "strong religious education at home."[10] His mother took her two sons to church every Sunday, and an aunt attended services every day. He notes that his family had a "special place" within the church, a place defined by the family's history and wealth. As one colleague has put it, Boutros-Ghali was "profoundly marked by the history of his family."[11] It is also interesting to note that he moved away from the Coptic Church not because of any crisis of faith or belief but, he claims, for purely "practical reasons"—namely, the demands of political work and his education.[12]

Apparently Boutros-Ghali's religious practice was more confessional than spiritually based. "I came from a noted Coptic family active in Church affairs," he has written, "but I myself had not been active in the Church."[13] Charles Hill, one of his staff members at the United Nations and the editor of his collected papers, when asked about Boutros-Ghali's religious background, noted that "he mentioned his observation of the main holiday calendar and his family's long tradition of influence and stewardship in the church, but not the faith itself."[14]

Boutros-Ghali's participation in one religious service provides some insight into his attitude toward his own religious belief and practice. He described attending a Christmas service on January 6, 1997, shortly after he returned to Cairo after failing to gain a second term as secretary-general. The service was held at the Boutrossiya, his family's church, where he visited the burial plots of his family, including his influential grandfather and uncle, before entering the church for the service, suggesting the link between his family and the church. After viewing the tombs and being depressed about their dilapidated state, he visited with the patriarch, which suggests his access to those with high authority in the church. Finally he attended the service, which, he intimated, was a bit too long for his liking. He described the visit and the service as a participation in an "ancestral ceremony," which suggests that his may not be a lived Christian faith but an action that connects him to his family and past.[15]

A secondary religious influence made an additional impression upon Boutros-Ghali. While studying in Paris in the late 1940s, he was taught Islamic law by Louis Massignon, an influential French Catholic theologian whose writings on Islamic mysticism are among the most important works of French Orientalism.[16] Boutros-Ghali called him a "guru" and later contributed a short foreword to a selection of essays on him, in which he lauds him as the embodiment of a dialogue between civilizations.[17] When asked about important figures in his life, Boutros-Ghali mentioned Massignon but added that "when one is young, one needs mentors to help with 'metaphysical problems.'"[18] In any case, Boutros-Ghali certainly respected a figure who could move between the worlds of European Christianity and Islam. The ability to appreciate different religious traditions, and to transcend them by focusing on their shared practice of mystical prayer, may have been appealing to someone whose religious background demanded an appreciation of the Other. And despite his suggestion that Massignon had been important only in his youth, a copy of a journal devoted to Massignon was sitting prominently on his desk during my interview with him.

How does this relation to the Coptic Church—what Boutros-Ghali describes as more "tribal" than anything else—constitute part of his ethical framework? For one thing, his Coptic confessional background contributed to a belief in tolerance. For Copts facing a political system oriented toward Muslims, tolerance of the Other is a central political virtue. Without it, Christians in Egypt would have no place in the political system. Tolerance is not simply grudging acceptance of the Other but a real acceptance that differences are to be accepted and celebrated. Tolerance not only is important in itself, but, according to Boutros-Ghali, it grounds core political practices like democracy and human rights. At a meeting sponsored by the UN Educational, Scientific, and Cultural Organization (UNESCO), Boutros-Ghali placed democracy and tolerance within an overall ethical framework:

> These basic democratic principles constitute a fundamental source of common values that can be described as the common heritage of humankind. . . . But the recognition of universal values does not mean that a veil should be drawn over the specific historical, religious, and cultural characteristics that make up the genius peculiar to each society and each nation state. For general principles of democracy can be embodied in different ways, depending on the context.[19]

Another principle central to Boutros-Ghali, and one that he himself identifies as resulting from his Christian beliefs, is the importance of forgiveness and reconciliation in postconflict situations. In reflecting upon his contribution to various attempts at postconflict reconciliation—a focus of much of his tenure as secretary-general—Boutros-Ghali stated that "forgiveness is often more important than justice."[20] He gave the examples of South Africa and El Salvador as places where truth commissions had demonstrated that reconciliation was more important than "punishing criminals."

In reflecting upon the importance of reconciliation, Boutros-Ghali argued that the pursuit of peace required reconciliation, even if this sometimes meant sacrificing justice. "The pursuit of justice can create new conflicts," he said, and concluded that reconciliation must be part of any peacemaking process. He also emphasized, however, that each community engages in the process of reconciliation in different ways. Citing his involvement in El Salvador, Boutros-Ghali noted that every community needs to find the proper balance between reconciliation, peace, and justice.[21]

Two principles thus emerge from Boutros-Ghali's religious background: tolerance and its relationship to democracy, and forgiveness and reconciliation. Boutros-Ghali was not a man who drew directly upon his faith or prayer in making decisions, but his religious background most certainly contributed to his ethical framework. As he put it in an interview, "I was not a man who said 'let us pray' and hoped God will help me make a decision; but certainly my Christian background was a very important element in the way I thought about reconciliation."[22]

International Law

A second important influence on Boutros-Ghali's ethical worldview derives from his education and work as an international lawyer. Boutros-Ghali received his PhD in international law from the Sorbonne in 1949. He then returned to Cairo, where he taught law at Cairo University. After a year as a visiting Fulbright Fellow at Columbia University in New York, he returned to Cairo, where he headed the Department of Political Science. He held visiting positions at the University of Paris, University of Kuwait, and University of Khartoum. He also served in numerous capacities in the world of international jurists, including on the International Law Commission and the International Commission of Jurists.[23] His legal writings are extensive and reflect a wide range of interests and influences. His first publication focused on the role of regional organizations in the pursuit of peace in the international system.[24] Other publications explore the League of Arab States, diplomatic practice, the equality of states and international organizations in the international system, and Arab foreign policies.[25] His identity as a scholar of international law has persisted throughout his career. When asked how he wanted to be remembered as secretary-general, he noted that he was the only one to have been a scholar.[26]

The study of international law and politics led Boutros-Ghali to a belief in the importance of law, rights, and democracy. He has said that "studying international law and human rights makes one a liberal, whether that is in Paris or Cairo."[27] What specifically about studying international law contributed to Boutros-Ghali's ethical views? The most general, yet perhaps the most important, element is a belief in the inherent goodness of human beings. Liberalism in this account assumes that humans are not inherently evil—the position of some Christian worldviews and of classical realism—but that humanity has the potential for cooperation and resolution of conflict. International jurists, however, are not the liberal idealists that E. H. Carr castigated in his famous account of the inter-war period; rather, they understand that while people can formulate laws and design systems to protect rights, these views often come into conflict with self-interested behavior.[28] Boutros-Ghali's profession as an international jurist led him to a chastened liberalism, one aware of the foibles of humanity but hopeful about its potential. This view is embodied in a note he sent to a friend while serving as secretary-general:

> Descartes is not saying that man "behaves in a reasonable way" but rather that the ability to distinguish truth from falsity is a characteristic shared by all mankind. In other words, regardless of social class, education, or national or ethnic background, everyone shares what Descartes calls "good sense" and can distinguish good from evil. I do not think this implies optimism or pessimism about the future of the human race. Indeed, the fact that man acts unreasonably—and is often ruled by his heart, his stomach, or by fear—means that he knows what he is doing is not right. Those who are guilty of cruelty in war, for example, may be obeying their passions but in their heart of hearts they know they are wrong or not obeying "common sense." That thought, indeed, is a rather optimistic one in that it leaves some ground for hope about the human condition. . . . I would rather see fear replaced by confidence in institutions established to ensure fairness in international relations, just as I would see "reason" as able to triumph over irrationality in human and international relations generally.[29]

In an interview with David Frost, he made a similar point: "We [humanity] are both [good and bad]. From time to time you find that human nature is very bad and from other times you find such a wonderful reaction that you feel, again, very optimistic."[30] These statements reflect Boutros-Ghali's belief in a shared "common sense" that shapes ideas of right and wrong, even when those concepts of right and wrong are violated. The idea of a shared human nature that arises from the right use of reason mirrors a belief in the perfectibility of human nature, even in moments when people act in manifestly evil ways, as they did repeatedly, of course, during his watch as UN secretary-general.

One way to connect general philosophical views on ethics and the law is through a philosophy of international law. The two predominant traditions here are natural law and positivism. Boutros-Ghali drew on both in his understanding of international law. When asked about his philosophy of international law, he described it as something about which he did not concern himself much, but he did offer that he saw international law as nothing more than the history of international affairs.[31] This is the answer of a positivist, someone who sees legal rules as derived from social practices in a specific context.[32] Jean-Marc Coicaud, one of his speechwriters, described his approach to international law as focused mainly on the UN charter, though on occasion he sought the advice of international law colleagues from his days as a professor.[33] His approach to the charter and its evolution displays positivist elements. At one point he suggested that the charter should be open to interpretation because it can "hold fast to principle but also adapt to new conditions."[34]

This positivist orientation gives rise to one of the most important elements of Boutros-Ghali's ethical framework: his belief that the sovereign state is the central institution in international politics and law. Boutros-Ghali's position on this question is often misunderstood, certainly in the American political context, where he is seen as the representative of a globalizing elite seeking to overthrow the sovereignty of nation-states. In fact, however, he is a firm believer in the importance of the state as the site of both political participation and protection of the weak from the strong. Some of his early writing in international law demonstrates a concern with protecting sovereignty as the means to keep the state system egalitarian.[35] In a speech he delivered in Vienna on June 11, 1993, he emphasized the importance of the nation-state as central to the identity of human beings: "Between the isolated individual and the world, there must be an intermediate element, an organized community that enables the individual to participate in the life of the world. This element is national sovereignty. . . . The individual finds identity in the nation. And nations are the building blocks of universalism. There is no international community if there are no nations."[36]

In an article in the *New York Times* Boutros-Ghali argued that the United Nations must be oriented toward preserving the nation-state as globalization proceeds: "Between ultra and micro-nationalism, the United Nations seeks to preserve the nation-state as the very foundation of international life and to bring states together in an enlightened multilateralism that can enhance their specific interests while advancing the common cause."[37] For Boutros-Ghali, the importance of the state was a moral principle. In meeting Pope John Paul II, he noted that the pope supported his view that "the rights of nations, like human rights, are derived from a universal moral law."[38]

For Boutros-Ghali, then, the state was a central institution for understanding politics. This principle can be considered part of his ethical framework, for it is the framework in which people can fulfil themselves through political participation and protection of rights. At the same time, however, Boutros-Ghali also draws upon a natural law tradition in his understanding of international law, a source that prevents him from privileging the sovereign state above all else. Hill has suggested that while Boutros-Ghali approached legal issues in a positivist vein, "he personally believed in natural law."[39] In one article written during his tenure as secretary-general, Boutros-Ghali used Hugo Grotius, a central figure in the natural law tradition, as a framing device to discuss the role the United Nations could play in constructing an international order that reflected the law.[40] Boutros-Ghali's reference to Grotius suggests that he sees international law as derived in part from natural law philosophy rather than solely from the positivism that predominates in today's international system. Rather than look to the Security Council for authority, Boutros-Ghali suggests that law arises from the rational reflections of people who live in community. That this article focuses on the role that international legal tribunals can play in creating a more law-governed world—rather than the powers of the Security Council—points toward a law derived from the judge and not the executive.

The combination of positivism and natural law approaches to international law, along with his chastened liberalism, results in two further important values of Boutros-Ghali's ethical framework: human rights and democracy. Neither of these two ideals can be identified too closely with the positivism of the nineteenth- and twentieth-century traditions of international law. The assumptions of the international legal community concerning democracy were that promoting and encouraging it in sovereign states was not the responsibility of outside actors, including the United Nations. It thus came as a shock to some when Boutros-Ghali concluded his tenure at the United Nations with his *Agenda for Democratization*. As discussed below, his emphasis on democracy in this statement, and his efforts to promote democracy in Cambodia, demonstrated an extraordinary shift for the United Nations, one that arose in part from Boutros-Ghali himself.

Human rights had not been an important part of international law, despite the various human rights instruments that appeared during the early years of the post–World War II era. At the moment when the United Nations could become the institution it had been designed to be, the question of whether to intervene in state affairs for purposes of protecting human rights became a central issue. While it was less a part of the debate in Somalia, certainly the intervention in the Balkans and the United Nations' role in that intervention was grounded upon protecting the human rights of minority populations. For Boutros-Ghali, despite the importance he placed on the state and its sovereignty, protecting human rights was an important principle. As he stated in one speech, "Human rights are, by definition, the ultimate norm of all politics."[41]

From his international law background, then, Boutros-Ghali drew three important elements of his ethical framework: the importance of human rights; the centrality of the sovereign state for giving persons meaning and for protecting human rights; and the importance of supporting democracy. We have seen how his religious background produced two other dimensions of his ethical framework: tolerance and reconciliation. Together, these five elements constitute the core of Boutros-Ghali's ethical framework. The question remains, however, whether this framework affected any of his initiatives as secretary-general.

Boutros-Ghali as Secretary-General

Let us look now at three areas in which Boutros-Ghali initiated policies or interpreted mandates in ways that demonstrated some independence from UN member states and the Security Council: (1) the evolution of the United Nations from strictly peacekeeping to peace-enforcement actions in Somalia and Bosnia-Hercegovina; (2) the promotion of and support for postconflict reconciliation as part of the democratization process in Cambodia; and (3) the writing of his *Agenda on Democratization*.

In each case, the overall mandate or mission came originally from the member states, usually through the Security Council. But in each area Boutros-Ghali pushed the mandate and, in his execution of it, certain ideas and policies that do not seem to have been intended by the member states. As a result, each of these issue areas demonstrates both the constraints and the opportunities of the office. Even more important, each area demonstrates the influence of Boutros-Ghali's ethical framework in different ways. The conclusion examines how various elements of that framework occasionally conflicted with each other, or conflicted with the various demands and constraints of the office.

From Peacekeeping to Peace Making

Boutros-Ghali is perhaps most closely associated with the rapid change in peacekeeping operations that took place during his tenure. His *Agenda for Peace,* the result of a request by the Security Council, set out a wider range of options for UN forces when it came to intervention. Boutros-Ghali initiated certain key changes in peacekeeping and peace enforcement in both Somalia and the Balkans. In both cases the decision to commit forces to a postconflict or ongoing conflict situation arose from the Security Council. But in both cases Boutros-Ghali's recommendations, made in reports to the council, along with certain strategic and tactical decisions made by the UN forces and authorized by Boutros-Ghali, did change the mission in important ways. It is important to emphasize that neither Boutros-Ghali alone nor even the UN bureaucracy was solely responsible for the entire course of these interventions. Let us focus on those instances where Boutros-Ghali's role made a difference.

SOMALIA

The intervention in Somalia launched what was to become a new and controversial form of UN military action. As Boutros-Ghali noted, "There was no model for the United Nations to follow in its efforts to bring humanitarian assistance and peace to the people of Somalia."[42] What began as a military operation undertaken primarily by the United States to protect food supplies was rapidly turned into a "nation-building" operation that sought to ensure reconciliation and new political institutions among Somalis. Two instances in the intervention are the focus here: Boutros-Ghali's efforts to persuade the United States and the Security Council to turn the focus of the intervention to peacekeeping, culminating in a new mission mandate in March 1993; and his efforts to pursue Mohammed Aideed after an attack on a group of UN peacekeepers in June 1993, which eventually resulted in the October 1993 firefight that led to the end of the mission.

The Somalia operation began in April 1992 with a small peacekeeping force sent to observe a tentative ceasefire between the warring factions, later known as the UN Operation in Somalia (UNOSOM I).[43] As the situation deteriorated, the United Nations authorized the United States to send in a large force to ensure the delivery of food aid, what became known as the Unified Task Force (UNITAF), which began in December 1992. As the famine that had prompted the intervention waned, the United Nations and the newly arrived Clinton administration began to consider ways of bringing about political reconciliation and new institutional structures. In March 1993 UNOSOM II was created by Security Council Resolution 814 and launched with a more expansive mandate, including the dismantling of weapons supplies of the warring factions.

It was this new mandate that resulted in part from the efforts of Boutros-Ghali. While it must be emphasized that the Clinton administration fully supported this enlarged mandate and saw it as part of a more muscular multilateralism, Boutros-Ghali's reports and personal diplomacy helped create this expanded mandate.[44] Boutros-Ghali believed that without political reconciliation, the entire project in Somalia would fail; he accordingly convened a meeting of the various factions, along with regional organizations, in Addis Ababa in January 1993, which resulted in a series of agreements that sought to end the fighting and create new institutions.[45] This meeting, along with a meeting in March 1993, was designed to allow the Somalis themselves to rebuild their political institutions, even as the international community was engaged in a massive intervention. As Boutros-Ghali stated at the opening of the conference, "The crisis in Somalia can only be resolved by the Somali people themselves, through a process of national reconciliation."[46] Many of his public, and also his private, statements on Somalia emphasized the importance of national reconciliation as the means of resolving the conflict.[47]

But it was his belief that UNITAF was ill conceived on one other point that brought about the most important changes in the mandate. Boutros-Ghali argued that unless the warring factions were disarmed, by force if need be, no new political structures could be built.[48] Boutros-Ghali also initiated other aspects of what became UNOSOM II, such as the expansion of the mandate to include the entire country (UNITAF had focused primarily on Mogadishu, the capital). But it was the disarmament elements of the mandate that were so controversial, especially to the faction leaders. Although they agreed in principle to disarmament in the various meetings of national reconciliation they attended, many believed that this was an effort to weaken their power in any future political settlement.

Boutros-Ghali saw in this initiative a part of the larger project of peace enforcement, which he had articulated in the *Agenda for Peace*. He also saw it as necessary for the work of reconciliation to take place, a project he believed could not succeed if warlords continued to operate with impunity.[49] Of course, the Security Council ultimately authorized the expanded mandate, and the U.S. government was a strong supporter (initially, at least) of this revised mandate. But it is important to emphasize that the report issued by Boutros-Ghali gave concrete form to the new mandate. Many of the themes that found their way into the report reflected the views Boutros-Ghali expressed both in his *Agenda for Peace* and in his earlier negotiations with the Bush administration in convincing the United States to undertake UNITAF. One can, then, conclude with some certainty that Boutros-Ghali's own views, views that were strongly informed by the principle of national reconciliation, played an important role in bringing about the change to UNOSOM II.

The disarmament provisions led to a conflict that shaped the course of the intervention. On June 5, 1993, a group of Pakistani peacekeepers engaged in exactly the type of disarmament mission envisioned in Boutros-Ghali's report were attacked by followers of Mohammed Aideed, one of the leading warlords. The weapons depot they attacked also included the premises of Radio Mogadishu, run by Aideed supporters and a major source of hostile reporting on the United Nations and United States. The attack resulted in twenty-four deaths and fifty-six casualties. According to a UN report issued later, this attack had been planned for some time; when Aideed found out that UN peacekeepers were going to start forcefully disarming his militia, he began preparing for a military response.[50] The attack led to the passage of Security Council Resolution 837 the very next day, which authorized the secretary-general to take "all measures necessary against those responsible for the attacks."

Resolution 837 did not state precisely what the UN forces should do, but by using the phrase "all measures necessary" it gave them a wide ambit. On June 12 UNOSOM forces undertook air and ground actions against the Aideed faction, including the radio station. Boutros-Ghali said of these attacks:

> The actions undertaken by UNOSOM II should be seen in the context of the international community's commitment to the national disarmament programme endorsed by all Somali parties. . . . The United Nations is determined to continue working with responsible Somali leaders and factions to eliminate the heavy weapons which have been used to terrorize the Somali people for so long. Today's action was also undertaken to facilitate the restoration of law and order by neutralizing a radio broadcasting system that has contributed to violence in Mogadishu. . . . The intent of the actions taken by UNOSOM II today is to stabilize a volatile situation and to enable steps to be taken towards the initiation of serious disarmament. Now that this task has been begun, the political reconciliation process and the rehabilitation of Somalia can move rapidly ahead.[51]

The UNOSOM II attack generated considerable controversy. Boutros-Ghali replied to expressions of concern from the presidents of Djibouti, Eritrea, Ethiopia, and Kenya, justifying the attacks as an attempt to ensure law and order and as part of the reconciliation process.[52] The military efforts against Aideed continued, culminating in attempts to capture him by U.S. military units that were serving alongside the UNOSOM II force.

The October attacks were largely a U.S. effort, and their failure resulted in part from the confused command structure under which they were initiated. But many involved claimed that they were only part of the larger effort to punish Aideed for his refusal to cooperate with the reconciliation process. Significantly, Boutros-Ghali also believed in the importance of capturing Aideed. While he believed that he was bound by Resolution 837 to undertake this sort of action, he notes in his memoirs that he agreed with the Security Council on this point.[53] It is also important to emphasize that the first military response by UNOSOM II, the June 12 attacks, were authorized and defended by Boutros-Ghali.

Do these two initiatives on the part of Boutros-Ghali in the context of Somalia relate to or, more important, result from his ethical framework? The overriding principle for Boutros-Ghali in Somalia appeared to be national reconciliation—and, moreover, reconciliation that could be facilitated by the international community but had to come from the factions themselves. This belief motivated him to convene reconciliation conferences in January and March 1993, an important part of his push to expand the UNOSOM mandate to include disarmament and geographic expansion. This goal appeared in almost all of his statements on Somalia, including those in which he authorized attacks on the Aideed faction and its radio station. This emphasis on reconciliation, of course, arises in part from his Christian influence but is also part of the UN external code. Given Boutros-Ghali's ethical framework, however, that external code produced a strong orientation toward reconciliation.

Yet Boutros-Ghali also made a clear decision to use military force in ways that most certainly did not lead to reconciliation. By excluding the Aideed faction from the political process when he decreed the method by which he should be arrested and tried, Boutros-Ghali placed other values before the need for reconciliation. It is difficult to see how this decision would fit into Boutros-Ghali's ethical framework, unless perhaps as part of his international law background, which emphasized the human rights that the Aideed faction had been violating. It might be safer to conclude, however, that Boutros-Ghali's decision to target Aideed, a decision supported by the United States, was the product of his more realist inclinations. His liberalism, as we have seen, was a chastened one and reflected his belief that at times force was necessary to bring order. It can be argued that the use of force in this way constitutes an ethical position, although this argument is not made here.[54] Boutros-Ghali's ethical framework certainly informed some of his decisions in the context of the intervention in Somalia, especially in the expansion of UNOSOM II. At the same time, though, it cannot completely explain his decisions and initiatives in Somalia, which necessitated policies that undercut the overriding ethical goal of reconciliation.

THE BALKANS

The conflict in the Balkans occupied a great deal of Boutros-Ghali's attention during his tenure as secretary-general. We can take it that he would have preferred otherwise, judging from his remark that the war in Bosnia-Hercegovina was generating so much interest because it was a "white man's war," whereas African conflicts enjoyed no such international spotlight.[55] Indeed, during his first year in office Boutros-Ghali argued against sending UN peacekeepers into the region, given the failure of the Security Council to commit funds or real enforcement powers to UN troops there.

But, despite his initial concerns, Boutros-Ghali devoted a great deal of effort to the war in the Balkans. As in many other cases, it is not entirely clear how much of the UN action in Bosnia stemmed from Boutros-Ghali's own initiative and how much can be attributed to the Security Council or to powerful member states. But it is possible to discern certain operations and decisions that can be closely associated with the secretary-general, among them Boutros-Ghali's view that Yugoslavia should not be split into different regions but should remain a single state in which minorities were protected. This idea, which ran counter to the efforts of the Europeans, never bore fruit; nevertheless, the advice he gave to the Security Council and wider international community does show his ethical framework at work.

The United Nations began its formal intervention in Bosnia with Security Council Resolution 743, which created the UN Protection Force (UNPROFOR) in February 1992.[56] The mandate in this intervention was strictly peacekeeping, organized around facilitating the ceasefire that had been agreed to by the parties in the fall of 1991. Soon, however, it became clear that this force was incapable of preventing violence and violations of human rights. In response to these developments, the Security Council authorized an enlarged mandate with the passage of Security Council Resolution 770, in August 1992, what later became known as UNPROFOR II. This mission was authorized to protect relief supplies throughout the country and ensure the safety of UN personnel working in Bosnia.

In the interim between these two resolutions, however, Boutros-Ghali expressed frustration in a number of quarters that his advice was not being heeded. He argued that the Security Council and the European Community had authorized an increased mandate without considering how it would be funded or what powers it ought to have. His anger was directed in particular at Lord Carrington, a British diplomat who was serving as the EC representative.[57] He also did not hesitate to communicate his displeasure to the Security Council. In a letter dated July 20, 1992, Boutros-Ghali did not mince words in expressing his anger at statements made by the president of the council, Jose Luis Jesus, concerning the Security Council's wish that UNPROFOR would help with disarmament:

> I must express my considered opinion that it would have been preferable if the Security Council, as has been the usual practice heretofore, had requested and awaited a technically grounded opinion by UNPROFOR and by me, given our responsibility for the operation of UNPROFOR, before taking such a position. . . . I am, of course, at the service of the Security Council. At the same time, however, I would hope that my views would be ascertained in areas which are clearly within my competence. Otherwise,

an unfortunate gap may arise between political desiderata and the technical realities on the ground.[58]

In the same letter he expressed concern that the Security Council was acting on measures that were really arising from recommendations within the European Community.[59] Boutros-Ghali believed that these new demands would make UNPROFOR seem more partisan in its operations, that it would be moved from a peacekeeping mission to a peace-enforcement mission. This was reflected in the text of Resolution 770, which called for the use of "all means necessary," a code for using force if need be.

This tension between Boutros-Ghali and the members of the Security Council and EC came out at the London conference, held in late August 1992. He reminded the conference that the demands being made of UNPROFOR were not being matched by the resources given it. In the closing day of the conference, he asked how the increasingly large mission was to be funded, only to be met by silence.[60] He demanded that the member states "face reality," something he believed they had not up to that point been able to do.

His opening statement at the London conference also reveals how Boutros-Ghali viewed the conflict in relation to his ethical framework. He argued that this conflict could only be dealt with by means of the central institution of the international system—the state. While recognizing that Yugoslavia no longer existed, he insisted that the new states must "possess all the rights and duties held by their fellow-states in the international community."[61] He argued that each ethnic group within Bosnia-Hercegovina should not be allowed to create its own nation-state, for this would result in endless fragmentation. Instead, returning to his experience as a Copt, he argued for the importance of protecting minority rights:

> One requirement for solutions to these problems lies in commitment to human rights with a special sensitivity to those of minorities, whether ethnic, religious, social, or linguistic. The General Assembly will soon have before it a declaration on the rights of minorities. That instrument, together with the increasingly effective machinery of the United Nations dealing with human rights, should enhance the situation of minorities as well as the stability of States. One approach to the solution of this crisis should include a special appeal to the leaders of all religious denominations. In them is enshrined the moral and spiritual responsibility to defend and uphold the dignity and life of each human life regardless of creed.[62]

The international community ultimately failed to act on Boutros-Ghali's attempt to orient the conference toward a regime that would focus on the protection of minorities. Instead, Bosnia was broken into "entities" that have not been able to resolve their differences to this day.

This is not to argue that Boutros-Ghali's position, as expressed at the London conference, was one that he himself stuck to throughout his tenure. Rather, his statements there clearly expressed the concerns he felt at that moment, concerns he did not believe the Security Council was taking seriously. This is also not to argue that his position led to any specific initiatives; indeed, his position was not adopted at all. The point is that his attempts to lead the international community away from a breakup of the multiethnic status of Bosnia-Hercegovina were partly inspired by his ethical framework. His proposal combined the importance of the sovereign state—a principle drawn from his career as an international lawyer—with the protection of minorities within a state context—a principle drawn from his experience as a Coptic Christian in Egypt. For Boutros-Ghali, allowing each group to create its own state, rather than learn to coexist within already existing state structures, threatened the stability of the international system as a whole, as the wars in the Balkans amply demonstrate. This perspective led him to be highly critical of the approaches advocated by various powerful states in the European Community and the Security Council. Whether adopting his views would have changed the outcome of the conflict in the Balkans is impossible to know; suffice it to say that Boutros-Ghali did not hesitate to communicate his views to those whom he was serving.

Postconflict Reconciliation and Democratization

Next to Somalia and the Balkans, the UN intervention in Cambodia was probably the most important peacekeeping operation undertaken by the institution during Boutros-Ghali's tenure. The mission followed upon the 1991 Cambodian settlement agreements, signed in Paris by the Supreme National Council, which represented the major players in the country at the time, along with eighteen interested state parties, and witnessed by Boutros-Ghali's predecessor, Javier Perez de Cuellar.[63] As part of those agreements, the United Nations was asked to play a substantial role in governing Cambodia as it made the transition to a new governance structure. As a result, the Security Council passed Resolution 718 on October 31, 1991, creating the UN Transitional Authority in Cambodia (UNTAC).[64]

This mission differed from others, however, in that its primary focus was the creation of a new political structure after years of devastating civil war. The foremost element of that new political structure, one in which the United Nations played a major role, was the implementation of elections to create a new Cambodian legislature and constitution. Boutros-Ghali came to office after the Paris agreements had been signed and the role of the United Nations had already been approved. He was thus confronted with a situation in which he had to both develop and implement a radically new peacekeeping structure with only a few months' experience. Two actions can be attributed directly to Boutros-Ghali here: (1) emphasizing elections as the central component of UNTAC's mandate, both in the original implementation plan and even as the Khmer Rouge engaged in harassment of voters and UN personnel, and (2) the use of the secretary-general's "good offices" in his assiduous courting of Prince Norodom Sihanouk throughout the process.

The relationship between UNTAC and the various Cambodian factions was fraught with complications, especially in the overlapping spheres of authority.[65] This structure meant that political campaigning and organizing an election was extremely complicated. Boutros-Ghali's insistence on sticking to the election path was thus constantly being challenged. Pushing through the elections did reflect the external code of the United Nations, whose mandate was to help countries move toward peace and stability, and also Boutros-Ghali's own internal code, drawing upon his views on the importance of democracy in protecting human rights and creating peace.

On February 19, 1992, Boutros-Ghali delivered to the Security Council his report on the creation of a mission for achieving the ends stipulated in the Paris agreements.[66] That document spelled out in concrete detail the various elements of UNTAC's mission, ranging from protecting human rights to promoting economic rehabilitation to disarmament. Underlying many of these elements was the overarching goal of ensuring a safe and secure environment for elections: "The election is the focal point of the comprehensive settlement" (par. 49). The document also relates many of the other components of the mission to the elections, including the military component (par. 64) and police component (par. 113). The appendices to the report include a calendar oriented toward the elections, which were scheduled for late May 1993.

One might ask whether the report of February 19 can be attributed to Boutros-Ghali alone. Indeed, it is obvious that the report is based largely on information compiled by UNAMIC, the advance mission undertaken by the United Nations prior to UNTAC's deployment. At the same time, Boutros-Ghali's description of the plan in his memoirs suggests that it did not accord with the standard UN procedure and indicates that it may have come from his own perspective rather than the UN bureaucracy: "On February 19, 1992, I proposed a UN force . . . estimated to cost more than $1.7 billion, a far larger undertaking than any previous UN operation, and far beyond the concept of traditional UN peacekeeping. The UN was not prepared for it; deployment would be agonizingly slow, and many mistakes marked the effort to get the operation under way."[67] While one can never be sure in reading memoirs the extent to which authors distort the record, one can surmise that the drafting of the *Agenda for Peace,* which was occurring simultaneously, may have influenced Boutros-Ghali's efforts here, efforts that ran counter to "traditional UN peacekeeping."

In a number of postmortems on UNTAC, a persistent critique is that the timetable for elections was too rushed. For instance, one commentator argued that the environment for elections was not secured by the military and police.[68] Another claimed that the timeline for elections was simply "unrealistic from the outset."[69] On top of the logistical difficulties of registering voters in a country where records did not exist, the security situation was perilous. During April 1993, when the election campaign officially took place, attacks on civilians and members of UNTAC's military command persisted. Seven UNTAC peacekeepers were killed and fifteen wounded in April alone.[70] In early 1993 Boutros-Ghali was being advised to postpone the elections. He was also asked to withdraw all UN personnel and was warned of growing dangers to the mission during this period. He concluded, however, that the success of the mission required that "the United Nations had to risk going forward with the voting as scheduled."[71]

The elections were held between May 23 and 28 and were considered by most to be a resounding success. Despite the intimidation by Khmer forces, more than 80 percent of eligible voters cast a ballot, confirming the efforts of UNTAC and Boutros-Ghali. Indeed, many were surprised at the success of the vote, as the violence preceding it had raised expectations that it might have a limited turnout or even fail to take place. Although the post-UNTAC period can certainly not be characterized as one of peace and democracy, the task of holding elections, the "focal point" of the mission, was a success.

A final dimension of the Cambodian mission of relevance to this discussion concerns Boutros-Ghali's role in courting Prince Sihanouk and his use of the office of secretary-general to push forward the mandate. During UNTAC's operation, Boutros-Ghali made two trips to Cambodia and spent most of his time meeting with Sihanouk. Most accounts of the Cambodian leader describe him as "mercurial," and some question not only his temperament but his moral judgments as well.[72] These judgments reflect, first and foremost, Sihanouk's alliance with the Khmer Rouge during the early 1970s. When Khmer forces took over the country in 1975, Sihanouk was installed as president. During the reign of the Khmer Rouge, Sihanouk was practically a prisoner in his palace in Phnom Penh, and a number of his children were killed during the genocide. Although he clearly dissociated himself from the Khmer Rouge during this period, he was also instrumental in bringing them to the table in the Paris talks that eventually led to the signing of the Paris agreements.

Boutros-Ghali worked hard to keep Sihanouk part of the process. His first trip to Cambodia, in April 1992, was designed to highlight the importance of UNTAC and support its activities. It also included sessions with Sihanouk during which the prince sought to convince Boutros-Ghali that the United Nations needed to remain engaged in Cambodia. The next trip, one year later, took place in much more precarious circumstances. UNTAC forces were under attack and the mission stood on the verge of collapse. As he sought to counter pessimism among the UN staff, Boutros-Ghali also worked to persuade Sihanouk not to give up hope.[73]

While working on Sihanouk, Boutros-Ghali also worked on both the political factions and Cambodian public opinion. He met with the factions in the throne room and urged them to work together in the election process. This was in the context of direct attacks by the Khmer faction on the party of Sihanouk's son, Norodom Ranarriddh. In what was certainly a bluff, he even threatened UN military action against those parties that would not cooperate.[74] He also gave a presentation on the UN radio station to the Cambodian people, imploring them to stay involved in the process of democratization.[75]

Boutros-Ghali was instrumental in making elections the central focus of UNTAC and in promoting reconciliation among the warring parties as the election date approached. Both in writing up the implementation plan and in refusing to postpone the election, he made decisions that had a direct impact on the future of Cambodia. It appears that his ethical framework played an important part in this process. Pushing through a democratic election as violence and intimidation flourished and in the context of a society that had never known such processes does not indicate that principle was sacrificed for politics. More interestingly, Boutros-Ghali's insistence on democracy and elections, while a newly emerging idea in the international system, was not necessarily part of the United Nations external code at that moment. Unlike the reconciliation process in which he used his good offices, democratization had not traditionally been part of the UN culture, especially in the context of a Cold War that made democracy a weapon of the United States and its allies. One may conclude that Boutros-Ghali helped push the institution toward a greater focus on the promotion of and support for democracy as part of its mandate.

Changing the Culture of the United Nations: An Agenda for Democratization

In addition to managing the various UN peacekeeping and democratization missions, Boutros-Ghali also sought to provide a theoretical foundation for the changing role of the United Nations. Along with various speeches and statements, his most influential contributions to this new conception of the United Nations (and, as a result, to a new conception of international relations) were his three *Agenda* documents. The first document, *An Agenda for Peace,* was requested by the special meeting of the Security Council at the level of heads of state. It provided a new framework for peacekeeping and helped develop the newer, more radical idea of peace building and peace enforcement. The course of peacekeeping throughout the 1990s, however, resulted in the United Nations as an institution drawing back from Boutros-Ghali's ideas, particularly being hesitant to pursue peacemaking operations.[76]

The second *Agenda* document was requested by the General Assembly in 1992, perhaps at the suggestion of Boutros-Ghali himself.[77] While he may have suggested it, the creation of this document would not have been possible without the General Assembly's request. Boutros-Ghali's arguments in this document were important as well, for he tried to change the thinking about development from something imposed on the developing world to a process in which leaders and activists were more involved. This resulted in part from Boutros-Ghali's previous role as a diplomat from Egypt, a country that receives large amounts of development aid from the international community but is also fiercely proud of its heritage and often chafes at the condescending manner in which aid is distributed.[78] The *Agenda* also sought to move development debates out of a Cold War context, which had structured development as a weapon used by the United States and Soviet Union.

While these two *Agenda* documents were important and resulted from Boutros-Ghali's own ideas, organs within the United Nations also requested them. His last *Agenda,* however, came from him alone at his own initiative. Indeed, as Boutros-Ghali admits, there was strong resistance to publishing the document even within the UN bureaucracy:

> My senior political advisor, Rosario Green, an impressive Mexican woman with whom I had worked closely, sent me a memo declaring my draft to be "pontificating and paternalistic" and urging me to reconsider. Other senior UN officials lectured me that my case for democratization of the international system was "weak and inchoate." The United Nations had no authority to do anything in the field of democratization beyond what member states requested it to do. Some had asked for electoral assistance; none had asked for anything like what I had written in my report, so "the idea for an Agenda for Democratization should not be encouraged."[79]

Despite these warnings, Boutros-Ghali persisted in writing a document that he believed "tied the other two together."

The drafting of this agenda is explored in greater depth in an article by the speechwriter who collaborated most closely with Boutros-Ghali on this document. Caroline Lombardo served as one of Boutros-Ghali's speechwriters, a group who also served as a policy-planning unit for the secretary-general.[80] She traces the evolution of the *Agenda* document through various speeches and pronouncements up to its issuance as a UN publication and report to the General Assembly. Lombardo provides two important insights into the document. First, she reveals the resistance to it from within the United Nations. The official drafting of the *Agenda* began when a group of democratizing states that had met in Managua requested a catalogue of UN activities in support of democracy. Boutros-Ghali took this as a chance to draft a theoretical justification for democracy, which was not what the states had suggested. This process, led by the same Rosario Green who condemned the final *Agenda*, revealed a UN bureaucracy competing for influence and resources and then disparaging the final report for going beyond not just the Managua request but the UN mission as a whole.[81]

Lombardo's second point links this document to Boutros-Ghali's ethical framework. His ideas about democracy had been germinating throughout his tenure as secretary-general. Under his leadership the United Nations had been actively involved in democratization processes in Cambodia, El Salvador, and Mozambique. Alongside these missions, Boutros-Ghali gave various speeches and talks on democracy in which he emphasized its importance for both peace and development.[82] He made two central arguments in the *Agenda*. The first was that democracy is essential to the achievement of peace and development. While he acknowledged the problem of "prioritising" democracy before development, he argued that the two must remain tied together.[83] Second, and more innovatively, he argued that democracy is not just important at the domestic level but must also become part of the international system. He argued that the international system currently allows the most powerful to dominate it, and that only by giving voice to other agents in the system can this problem be rectified. His picture of international democracy was not simply a state one, however, nor did he necessarily advocate a world parliament. Rather, he suggested that agents, ranging from states to private corporations and other nongovernmental organizations (NGOs), should become a more active part of the international decision-making process. He gave as a possible model something that came from the series of global conferences he had chaired on issues ranging from population, to women's issues, to human rights. Boutros-Ghali saw in those conferences a potential model by which a wide range of actors in the international system could play a role in debating and formulating solutions to the most pressing problems in the international system.[84]

The focus on international democracy led him to a discussion of the structure of the United Nations. He emphasized that, although it is an intergovernmental organization, the United Nations needs to be open to "forces from civil society," primarily NGOs, which should play a greater role in forums like the Economic and Social Council.[85] Interestingly, he also focused on the role of the International Court of Justice and the growth of international criminal tribunals as potential pathways to greater democracy at the global level. His argument here is based on the idea that ensuring the rule of law supports democracy.[86]

Lombardo notes that Boutros-Ghali's justification for democracy, at both the national and international levels, arose from a combination of normative and practical arguments. Indeed, emphasizing the two "levels" of democracy resulted both from a "Kantian" sense that peace could not exist without democracy and also from a pragmatic sense that the developing world will not support democracy initiatives unless they are linked to an attempt to democratize the international system.[87]

Finally, Lombardo points out that Boutros-Ghali believed that his role (and that of the UN Secretariat) was not only to undertake the mandates of the Security Council and General Assembly but to help shape international law and the structure of the international system: "Boutros-Ghali saw a strong resemblance between the way a legal scholar participates in the making of international law and the way a UN Secretary-General participates in the making of international policy. Each could be understood as the man in the middle. . . . In short, Boutros-Ghali saw international lawyers and Secretaries-General as builders of conceptual "foundations"—for effecting change and consolidating it."[88] This understanding of his role, and his conception of democracy as connected to the rule of law, arises from his background as an international lawyer. His ideas about democratization and how to make it part of the international system arose in large part from his education as an international lawyer.[89] This central part of his ethical framework did not correspond with the external code of the UN system, as demonstrated by the resistance to his proposals from within the bureaucracy. At the same time, his innovation on this score played an important role in making democracy a more formal part of the international system. Coupled with his promotion of democratic initiatives in Cambodia, El Salvador, and elsewhere, Boutros-Ghali helped to change the thinking of the international community concerning democracy and its role in global governance.

Conclusion

Boutros Boutros-Ghali served as secretary-general of the United Nations at a moment that was both full of promise and rife with danger. His attempts to rethink peacekeeping, development, and democracy, while also accommodating the most powerful state in the system, led to initiatives that drew on his ethical framework yet also tended to contradict his moral values at times. Some of the initiatives identified in this chapter reflect his ethical framework; others do not. Table 8.1 suggests a possible conceptualization of how the five principles with which this chapter began might have played a role in the various initiatives discussed here. This table vastly oversimplifies the conclusions that can be drawn from these

Table 8.1 Boutros-Ghali's Principles and Initiatives

Principles/Initiatives	Tolerance	Reconciliation	Human rights	Centrality of the state	Democracy
Somalia reconciliation	Yes	Yes	No	Yes	No
Somalia capture of Aideed	No	No	Yes	Yes	No
Bosnia multiethnic statehood	Yes	Yes	Yes	Yes	No
Cambodia elections	Yes	Yes	Yes	Yes	Yes
Cambodia meetings with Sihanouk	Yes	Yes	No	Yes	No
Agenda for Democratization	Yes	No	Yes	No	Yes

different initiatives and their relation to Boutros-Ghali's ethical framework, but it does provide a basic overview, one that others may wish to investigate in more depth.

This analysis has supported the hypothesis that ethical frameworks do influence the role of the secretary-general in the conduct of his office. A potential objection to this conclusion arises from the two events in the tenure of Boutros-Ghali where "ethics" seem glaringly absent: the 1994 Rwandan genocide and the 1995 massacre of Bosnian men and boys at Srebrenica. I have dealt with the question of responsibility in Srebrenica elsewhere, so I will address only the case of Rwanda briefly here.[90] The details of the Rwandan genocide are generally well known. Tensions between the Tutsi and Hutu, the two largest ethnic groups in Rwanda, had been simmering for years. Tutsis, anointed by European colonial administrators as the political leadership of the country, were in the minority by the 1990s. Various political formulas had been attempted to bring the two groups together, but extremists on both sides had exacerbated tensions for their own political purposes. An agreement facilitated by the United Nations created a tentative peace in 1993, which included a small peacekeeping force. In January 1994 the leader of that force sent a telegram to UN headquarters forcefully stating his fears of an impending genocide. That cable was buried in the UN bureaucracy and never reached the Security Council. When the plane carrying the Rwandan president, a moderate Hutu, was shot down in April 1994, extremists in the Hutu majority undertook a large-scale extermination program, killing both Tutsis and moderate Hutus.

Some have argued that it is not the Great Powers alone that bear responsibility for the Rwandan tragedy, but the United Nations itself. And while it is true that the UN bureaucracy may have failed to heed the warnings of its peacekeepers, the U.S. government refused even to call the massacre genocide and failed to engage itself in the unfolding trauma, as did most other powerful states (France eventually sent a small peacekeeping force).[91] The question of who is responsible for the bloody massacre of more than half a million people over the course of a mere four weeks continues to be debated. Kofi Annan commissioned a report soon after coming to office that placed the blame on a wide array of actors, including the UN system and the office that Annan himself headed, the Department of Peacekeeping Operations.[92] Boutros Boutros-Ghali has stated that he most definitely felt responsible—not for a failure to respond but for his failure to convince the Great Powers, particularly the United States, that they should act quickly.[93] That Boutros-Ghali saw his job as one of convincing the Great Powers of the urgency of the situation can be seen either as an abdication of responsibility or as evidence that he understood that the United Nations will not work without the United States and other Great Powers. The question of how a secretary-general can or cannot influence events must take into account the constraints placed upon him by the international system. At the same time, as this chapter has sought to demonstrate, those constraints are not ironclad. There are arenas in the UN system in which leaders can assert a certain amount of "moral authority." In so doing, however, they take on a certain amount of moral responsibility for their acts or failures to act.

As the role of the secretary-general has evolved, questions about his (and perhaps someday her) responsibility will evolve as well. We may no longer ask simply that the secretary-general bring matters to the attention of the world or wield his moral authority more effectively. It may be that, over time, secretaries-general will be asked to perform more roles. If the office is to change, however, we must be cautious about the responsibilities we place upon one individual. As Boutros-Ghali pointed out in his acceptance speech, while we may want a Utopian City, we must remain realists in our expectations about what can be accomplished. Boutros-Ghali struggled with this tension throughout his tenure, as will future secretaries-general.

Notes

1. "Oath of Office," December 3, 1991, reprinted in Charles Hill, ed., *The Papers of United Nations Secretary-General Boutros Boutros-Ghali*, 3 vols. (New Haven, CT: Yale University Press) (hereafter *Papers of Boutros-Ghali*), 1:1 See also his reference to this speech in his memoirs, Boutros Boutros-Ghali, *Unvanquished: A UN-US Saga* (New York: Random House, 1999), 12.

2. Two other elements of his personal background influenced his ethical framework: his nationality as an Egyptian and his role as a diplomat. In a full biography of Boutros-Ghali, these dimensions of his background would need to be examined in more depth, but space limitations prevent this here.

3. Boutros Boutros-Ghali, *Egypt's Road to Jerusalem: A Diplomat's Story of the Struggle for Peace in the Middle East* (New York: Random House, 1997), 4–5.

4. A good description of both the theology and practices of the Coptic Church can be found in Otto Meinardus, *Christian Egypt: Faith and Life* (Cairo: American University in Cairo Press, 1970). English-language information on the Coptic

Church can also be found on various Coptic Church websites. An extensive site run by the Coptic Centre in Stevenage, UK, provides links to a number of organizations and text documents (www.copticcentre.com). Two from the United States are quite extensive, including statements by the current Coptic patriarch, Pope Shenouda III. See St. Mark's Parish in New Jersey (http://saintmark .com/), which also hosts a site devoted to explaining the Coptic Church in general (www.copticchurch.net), and St. Mark's Coptic Church in Cleveland, Ohio (www.stmarkcoccleveland.org/). I have no way of ascertaining the accuracy of the information posted on these sites, but they seem in communion with the general tenets of the Coptic Church in Egypt, as they are founded by Egyptian immigrants to the United States. The official website of the Coptic Church in Egypt—www.copticpope.org/—contains more Arabic than English.

5. See Pope Shenouda III, *The Nature of Christ* (1999), available at www .copticchurch.net/topics/theology/nature_of_christ.pdf.

6. For details of this theological controversy, see Henry Chadwick, *The Early Church,* rev. ed. (London: Penguin Books, 1993), 194–205; and E. Glenn Hinson, *The Early Church: Origins to the Dawn of the Middle Ages* (Nashville: Abingdon Press, 1996), 310–25.

7. In fact, when Boutros-Ghali himself read through an earlier version of this chapter, he suggested deleting much of the material on theology, noting, "I don't even remember these distinctions, and they have had no impact on me." Boutros Boutros-Ghali, interview by author, April 22, 2005, Paris. I would like to thank Boutros Boutros-Ghali for his time in both responding to questions and reading a draft version of this chapter.

8. A good treatment of the Coptic reaction to this conflicted political situation is B. L. Carter, *The Copts in Egyptian Politics* (London: Croom Held, 1986).

9. Ibid., 12–13; Boutros-Ghali, interview.

10. Boutros-Ghali, interview.

11. Alioune Londin Beye, "Boutros Boutros-Ghali: Un Homme de Paix," in *Boutros Boutros-Ghali: Amicorum Discipulorumque Liber,* vol. 1, *Peace, Development, Democracy* (Brussels: Bruylant, 1998), 9.

12. In addition to these practical reasons, Coptic services are held on Sundays and usually last all day. But in Egypt Sunday is the first day of the work week, whereas Friday is the holy day of Muslims and Saturday is typically a day of rest. As a result, some Copts must choose between going to work that day and attending services.

13. Boutros-Ghali, *Egypt's Road to Jerusalem,* 10.

14. Charles Hill, e-mail to author, January 16, 2005.

15. Boutros Boutros-Ghali, *En attendant la prochaine lune: Carnets 1997–2002* (Paris: Fayard, 2004), 19; see also Boutros-Ghali, *Unvanquished,* 193, 259.

16. For an interpretation of Massignon's thought, see Pierre Rocalve, *Louis Massignon et l'Islam* (Damascus: Institut Francais de Damas, 1993).

17. Boutros-Ghali, *Egypt's Road to Jerusalem*, 130; Boutros Boutros-Ghali, *Emancipier la francophonie* (Paris: L'Harmattan, 2002), 271.

18. Boutros-Ghali, interview.

19. Boutros Boutros-Ghali, ed., *The Interaction Between Democracy and Development* (Paris: UNESCO Publications, 2002), 10.

20. Boutros-Ghali, interview.

21. Boutros Boutros-Ghali, telephone interview by author, January 30, 2006.

22. Boutros-Ghali, interview, April 22, 2005.

23. See Alain Plantey, "Boutros Boutros-Ghali," in *Boutros-Ghali: Amicorum Discipulorumque Liber*, 1:51–58, for some insights into his education in France.

24. Boutros Boutros-Ghali, *Contribution à l'etude des ententes régionales* (Paris: Editions A. Pedone, 1949).

25. For a full bibliography, see Boutros-Ghali's curriculum vita, available at www.southcentre.org/introduction/bbgcv.pdf.

26. Boutros-Ghali, interview, April 22, 2005.

27. Ibid.

28. E. H. Carr, *The Twenty Years' Crisis*, ed. Michael Cox (London: Palgrave Publishers, 2001 [1939]).

29. *Papers of Boutros-Ghali*, 1:402–3.

30. Ibid., 1:592.

31. Boutros-Ghali, interview, April 22, 2005.

32. Terry Nardin, "Legal Positivism as a Theory of International Society," in *International Society: Diverse Ethical Perspectives*, ed. David R. Mapel and Terry Nardin (Princeton, NJ: Princeton University Press, 1998), 18.

33. Jean-Marc Coicaud, telephone interview by author, January 12, 2005.

34. *Papers of Boutros-Ghali*, 1:540.

35. See, for example, Boutros Boutros-Ghali, *Le principe d'egalite des etats et les organisations internationales* (Paris: Leydes, 1960), in which he argues that the international legal system is premised on protecting the de jure equality of states, especially through their participation in international organizations.

36. *Papers of Boutros-Ghali*, 1:665–66.

37. Boutros Boutros-Ghali, "Don't Make the UN's Head Job Harder" *New York Times*, August 20, 1993, reprinted in *Papers of Boutros-Ghali*, 1:744.

38. Boutros-Ghali, *Unvanquished*, 253.

39. Charles Hill, e-mail.

40. Boutros Boutros-Ghali, "A Grotian Moment," *Fordham International Law Journal* 18 (1995), reprinted in *Papers of Boutros-Ghali*, 3:1536–43. Caroline Lombardo, who drafted this article for Boutros-Ghali, pointed out in an e-mail communication that Boutros-Ghali's intention here was not to develop new ideas about the sources of international law, but rather to build upon the particular moment to promote international peace and security. Although this may be the case, I would argue that the use of Grotius and the very idea that innovations can be made

to international law that might correspond with moral ideas rather than state practice suggests the point being made. Lombardo read through a draft of this chapter and made extensive comments that were quite helpful.

41. *Papers of Boutros-Ghali,* 1:674.

42. Boutros Boutros-Ghali, "Introduction," in *The United Nations and Somalia, 1992–1996,* United Nations Blue Book Series, vol. 7 (New York: UN Publications, 1996), 5.

43. I rely here on Anthony F. Lang Jr., *Agency and Ethics: The Politics of Military Intervention* (Albany: State University of New York Press, 2002), 155–86.

44. A case can even be made that the Bush administration that initially authorized UNITAF had in mind an expanded intervention in the later stages; see ibid., 170–71.

45. Boutros-Ghali, "Introduction," in *United Nations and Somalia,* 38–39.

46. Statement to a preparatory meeting on national reconciliation, January 4, 1993, reprinted in *Papers of Boutros-Ghali,* 1:435.

47. See Boutros-Ghali to Mary Robinson, president of the Irish Republic, January 18, 1993, reprinted in ibid., 450–51.

48. S/25354, March 3, 1993, "Further Report of Secretary-General submitted in pursuance of paragraphs 18 and 19 of Resolution 794," reprinted in *United Nations and Somalia,* 251.

49. Boutros-Ghali, *Unvanquished,* 92–94.

50. S/26351, August 24, 1993, executive summary of a report by Professor Tom Farer on the June 5, 1993, attacks, reprinted in *United Nations and Somalia,* 299–300.

51. Statement by the secretary-general in Vienna, June 12, 1993, reprinted in ibid., 268–69.

52. See ibid., 270–72.

53. Boutros-Ghali, *Unvanquished,* 96.

54. For an argument that realism can be considered an ethical tradition, see Steven Forde, "Classical Realism," in *Traditions of International Ethics,* ed. Terry Nardin and David R. Mapel (Cambridge: Cambridge University Press, 1992), 62–84.

55. Boutros-Ghali, *Unvanquished,* 44.

56. Spyros Economides and Michael Leifer, "Former Yugoslavia," in *The New Interventionism, 1991–1994: United Nations Experience in Cambodia, Former Yugoslavia, and Somalia,* ed. James Mayall (Cambridge: Cambridge University Press, 1996), 66.

57. See Boutros-Ghali, *Unvanquished,* 44; and Boutros-Ghali to Lord Peter Carrington, August 7, 1992, reprinted in *Papers of Boutros-Ghali,* 1:202.

58. Ibid., 177.

59. Economides and Leifer, "Former Yugoslavia," 75.

60. Boutros-Ghali, *Unvanquished,* 48–49.

61. Address to the International Conference on the Former Socialist Federal Republic of Yugoslavia, London, August 26, 1992, reprinted in *Papers of Boutros-Ghali,* 1:230–31.

62. Ibid., 231.

63. Nishkala Suntharalingam, "The Cambodian Settlement Agreements," in *Keeping the Peace: Multinational UN Operations in Cambodia and El Salvador,* ed. Michael Doyle et al. (Cambridge: Cambridge University Press, 1997).

64. For a basic description of UNTAC's mandate, see *The Blue Helmets: A Review of United Nations Peace-Keeping,* 3d ed. (New York: United Nations Department of Public Information, 1996), 447–84. For a fuller documentary record, see *The United Nations and Cambodia, 1991–1995,* United Nations Blue Book Series, vol. 2 (New York: United Nations Department of Public Information, 1995).

65. For a critical assessment of many of these authority and governance problems, see Mats Berdal and Michael Leifer, "Cambodia," in Mayall, *New Interventionism,* 25–58.

66. Report of the secretary-general on Cambodia, S/23613 and Add. 1, obtained from the UN Documentation Centre, http://documents.un.org.

67. Boutros-Ghali, *Unvanquished,* 32.

68. Suntharalingam, "Cambodian Settlement Agreements," 105.

69. Cherly M. Lee Kim and Mark Metrikas, "Holding a Fragile Peace: The Military and Civilian Components of UNTAC," in Doyle, *Keeping the Peace,* 126.

70. *Blue Helmets,* 469–70.

71. Boutros-Ghali, *Unvanquished,* 81.

72. One book about him is Milton Osborne's *Sihanouk: Prince of Light, Prince of Darkness* (London: Allen and Unwin, 1994).

73. Boutros-Ghali, *Unvanquished,* 78.

74. Ibid., 80.

75. See *Papers of Boutros-Ghali,* 1:558.

76. Perhaps the clearest indication of this shift is the Brahimi report, published in 2000 largely in response to the two special reports on Srebrenica and Rwanda, both of which Kofi Annan requested. The Brahimi report can be obtained at www.un.org/peace/reports/peace_operations/.

77. Boutros-Ghali, *Unvanquished,* 158.

78. For example, the United States gives both Israel and Egypt large amounts of foreign aid. In the case of Israel, that aid is granted without conditions and without stipulations; in the case of Egypt, the aid is given with very specific provisions about how it should be spent and is usually tied to USAID projects.

79. Boutros-Ghali, *Unvanquished,* 320.

80. Caroline Lombardo, "The Making of an Agenda for Democratization: A Speechwriter's View" *Chicago Journal of International Law* 2 (2001): 254.

81. Ibid., 262–63.

82. See the Gauer Distinguished Lecture in Law and Public Policy, October 18, 1994, *Papers of Boutros-Ghali,* 2:1298–1306.

83. *Agenda for Democratization,* reprinted in ibid., 3:2051 (par. 121).

84. Ibid., 2030–46 (pars. 61–103).

85. Ibid., 2047 (par. 107).

86. Ibid., 2047–48 (pars. 114–15).

87. Lombardo, "Making of an Agenda for Democratization," 258.

88. Ibid., 259–60.

89. His practical experience as part of the Egyptian diplomatic service also contributed to this sensibility, as he was involved with development projects in Africa that linked good governance with aid.

90. Anthony F. Lang Jr., "The United Nations and the Fall of Srebrenica: Meaningful Responsibility and International Society," in *Can Institutions Have Responsibilities? Collective Moral Agency and International Relations,* ed. Toni Erskine (Houndsmills, Basingstoke, UK: Palgrave Macmillian, 2003), 183–206. For a good treatment of the role of the French in the Rwandan genocide, see Daniela Kroslak, "The Responsibility of Collective External Bystanders in Cases of Genocide: The French in Rwanda," ibid., 159–82.

91. Michael Barnett and Martha Finnemore, *Rules for the World: International Organizations in World Politics* (Ithaca, NY: Cornell University Press, 2004), 121–54.

92. Report of the Independent Inquiry into the Actions of the United Nations During the 1994 Genocide in Rwanda, December 15, 1999, available at www .un.org/News/ossg/rwanda_report.htm.

93. Boutros-Ghali, interview, April 22, 2005.

9

POLITICS AND VALUES
AT THE UNITED NATIONS
Kofi Annan's Balancing Act

COURTNEY B. SMITH

The day after his appointment as the seventh secretary-general of the United Nations, on December 17, 1996, Kofi Annan was asked during a press conference how he would define his new job. He responded that "the Secretary-General's role is multifaceted. Some have referred to it as an administrator and manager. That is an essential part of the work. But he also has a political and diplomatic role, and above all, a moral voice which should be heard periodically when necessary."[1] Nearly eight years later, in response to a similar question, Annan replied, "In jobs like these, it's important to be able to keep your balance."[2] These responses raise the question that lies at the heart of this chapter: How did Annan seek to balance these various roles, especially when they seemed to push him in different directions? And to what extent did Annan's own values influence the manner in which he managed this balance, in particular with regard to harnessing the moral voice afforded to both the office of secretary-general and the individual who occupies it?

During his first six years as secretary-general, Annan's behavior and policy choices were widely praised as representing an effective balance between his various responsibilities. For example, in announcing its decision to award the 2001 Nobel Peace Prize to Annan and the United Nations, the Norwegian Nobel Committee observed that:

> Kofi Annan has devoted almost his entire working life to the U.N. As Secretary-General, he has been pre-eminent in bringing new life to the organization. While clearly underlining the U.N.'s traditional responsibility for peace and security, he has also emphasized its obligations with regard to human rights. He has risen to such new challenges as HIV/AIDS and

international terrorism, and brought about more efficient utilization of the U.N.'s modest resources. In an organization that can hardly become more than its members permit, he has made clear that sovereignty can not be a shield behind which member states conceal their violations.[3]

More colorful descriptions of Annan's leadership at the time were similarly positive. Richard Holbrooke, a former U.S. ambassador to the United Nations, called Annan the "international rock star of diplomacy."[4] CNN founder Ted Turner similarly observed that Annan "has the toughest job in the world and everybody loves him."[5]

Despite these glowing assessments, Annan experienced his share of disappointments as secretary-general as well as earlier in his career. Key events in this regard are the genocide in Rwanda and the fall of Srebrenica, both of which occurred in the mid-1990s, when Annan was the under-secretary-general in charge of UN peacekeeping. While his reputation was able to survive these failures owing to the fact that there was plenty of blame to go around, and also to his very frank apology, these events affected who Annan is and what he tried to do as secretary-general.[6] More disappointments occurred in the final four years of his tenure, a difficult period for Annan. The U.S. war in Iraq, begun in March 2003, the subsequent deaths of twenty-two UN staff members in a terrorist bombing in Baghdad in August 2003, the revelation of his son's role in the oil-for-food scandal in 2004, and ongoing investigations into sexual improprieties within the UN peacekeeping mission in the Congo and by the former UN High Commissioner for Refugees all took their toll on the typically steady, confident, and charismatic secretary-general.[7] While these difficulties did not diminish Annan's stature in the eyes of some supporters, they certainly shaped his behavior as secretary-general.

Annan, like his predecessors, found that his behavior and policy choices as secretary-general required that he carefully reconcile what he would like to see happen with the political realities of each situation he faced while in office. Some incumbents have erred on the side of caution, choosing not to "rock the boat" by provoking the ire of powerful member states; others, however, including Annan, have sought to push the organization to act whenever events require it, not just when political considerations allow it.[8] Such behavior is generally, though not universally, viewed in a positive light. Mark Malloch Brown, the former head of the UN Development Programme who also served as the secretary-general's chief of staff, favorably compared Annan with Dag Hammarskjöld with respect to this type of proactive behavior: "We've had a series of Secretaries-General since Hammarskjöld who were more secretaries than generals. This is the first time since then we have a Secretary-General who dwarfs his institution."[9]

This willingness to pursue policies that may run counter to the interests of UN members does not come easily for those in the office of secretary-general. As noted previously in this volume, according to its first occupant, Trygve Lie, the secretary-generalship is "the most impossible job in the world."[10] While not all observers, or even all of Lie's successors, would share his characterization, many would agree that the "often conflicting responsibilities of the Secretary-General make the post one of the most demanding imaginable."[11] One of the main reasons for this difficulty is the diverse range of administrative, diplomatic, political, and moral responsibilities that incumbents face. This reality led one journalist who profiled Annan to describe the position as "one of the world's oddest jobs, half moral witness and half C.E.O."[12] It is not just the range of tasks, however, that contributes to the difficulties facing the secretary-general; it is also the fact that these tasks must be performed without sufficient resources or authority, while 192 member states watch the secretary-general's every move to make sure that their individual conceptualizations of the office are being realized. The specific nature of this predicament as it confronted Annan when he embarked on this "job from hell" has been vividly described: "a good and uncommon man invested with the hopes and moral authority of the world, charged to deal with evil, and at the same time buffeted and limited in that task by the world's principalities and powers."[13]

The following pages explore in detail Annan's efforts to balance the religious and moral values that anchored his inner code with the political pressures on the office, referred to here as the external code.[14] The chapter begins with an examination of the personal values that inform his ethical framework and considers briefly how Annan's personal attributes effectively complemented his values. The next part of the chapter builds on the discussions of the office of secretary-general and its political environment found in the introductory chapters of this volume to explore the particular constraints Annan faced while in office. The third section explores how Annan balanced the requirements of his inner and external codes with respect to certain key policy choices he faced in the areas of peace and security, humanitarian assistance, economic development, and organizational reform.

Handling each of these policy choices involved a careful balancing act of both external and internal pressures, and each one also required a different ethical tradeoff, given Annan's personal values and the limits of the office. This study finds that his moral compass certainly influenced how he approached his job, but that its influence on his behavior was joined with the political realities of various crises the United Nations was asked to address.[15] Support for the argument advanced here is based in part on personal interviews of a number of current and former high-ranking UN officials who worked closely with Annan during his time as secretary-general.[16]

Annan's Ethical Framework

Exploring Annan's ethical framework is a formidable task, in that secretaries-general tend to treat their personal values as a private matter so as not to jeopardize their impartiality in the eyes of member states. This is especially true in the case of Annan, who, according to Elisabeth Lindenmayer, Annan's longtime special assistant, is "warm and remembers the name of your child, but he's difficult to know. There is a large part of him we don't have access to."[17] Nonetheless, it is clear that Annan was guided by certain values and principles that were important weapons in his arsenal throughout his tenure.[18]

Religious Beliefs

Annan is a private man who frequently deflects questions about himself; when one reporter asked him about religion, a highly personal matter, he looked "truly horrified."[19] However, his reluctance to discuss his religious beliefs has not stopped others from identifying him as an individual with "spiritual status."[20] This status is reflected in the religious or quasi-religious images that have been used to describe his stature in the eyes of his staff and the international community. For example, longtime adviser Shashi Tharoor dubbed him a "yogi,"[21] and author William Shawcross called him "the world's secular pope," a characterization repeated by at least two other journalists who have profiled Annan.[22]

Annan may be viewed by some through a religious lens, but the real issue for this study is the degree to which Annan himself seems to be guided by any religious beliefs. Growing up in Ghana, both sides of his family were rooted in the country's diverse tribal and ethnic cultures: his mother was Fante and his father was half-Fante and half-Ashanti. Although Annan could have been a chief for either of these tribes, and was in fact asked in the early 1990s to consider serving as the paramount chief of the Akwamu region (he declined),[23] Annan has said that he grew up "atribal in a tribal world."[24] Instead of adhering to one of the many tribal faiths found in Africa, Annan became a "practicing Christian," and is the product of Ghana's most influential and prestigious secondary school, a Christian boarding school called Mfantsipim that was founded by the Methodist Church under British colonial rule.[25] As noted in chapter 1, a report by Religion Counts on the role of religion at the United Nations has further identified Annan as a member of the Anglican Church and described him as someone who has "religious sensitivities, if not exclusively spiritual motivations."[26] However, the report never explores the central question of this study: Was Annan merely sensitive to religious values as UN secretary-general, or was he in fact guided by them?

A definitive answer to this question is not easily given, but several of the UN officials interviewed for this project were adamant in their view that Annan is extremely sensitive to the religious values of others. As secretary-general, he visited and was visited by numerous religious leaders representing the full spectrum of faiths. He was involved in outreach to religious groups in other ways, such as through meetings with interfaith nongovernmental organizations. One person recalled a gift from an interfaith organization that he valued very highly, a framed poster that had versions of the Golden Rule or equivalent statements of faith from fifteen different religious traditions. Annan also supported the meeting of religious leaders at UN headquarters in advance of the Millennium Summit in 2000 and the United Nations Year of Dialogue Among Civilizations in 2001. Another colleague interviewed for this project attributed Annan's openness to different religions to his African roots, as it is not uncommon for members of the same family to be of different faiths, as was true for Annan himself. This staff member recalls Annan commenting on several occasions that "the problem is not with the faith but with the faithful." Journalist Philip Gourevitch echoes this emphasis on tolerance in describing Annan's view of his African heritage as a "deliberative approach to life, marked always by a breadth of mind and generosity of spirit."[27]

Members of Annan's senior staff reported that he "does not wear his own religious beliefs on his sleeve." In fact, he was quite careful as secretary-general to avoid any appearance of favoring one religion over another, and even politely declined my request for an interview on the subject of

his religious beliefs. Despite this careful behavior, staff members I interviewed indicated that they were under the impression that Annan attends
church somewhere in between "occasionally" and "regularly," even if
they could not identify exactly which church, or in some cases even what
denomination. Respecting the religious beliefs of others and attending
church does illustrate, as the Religion Counts report observes, that Annan
is sensitive to religious values. Yet it tells us little about the extent to which
these values guide his behavior and actions.

The UN staff I interviewed were reluctant, and in some cases unwilling, to offer any specific observations on this point. Several journalists,
however, have been able to probe Annan gently about the role of religion,
God, prayer, and faith in his life and in his decisions. In a conversation with
Shawcross, Annan confided, "I was not particularly religious. I'm still a
believer, but I'm not the sort of person you will see quoting the Bible. But
it's there to fall back on when you need it. And the sense that you are not
alone in whatever situation."[28] In this and other encounters Annan conveyed that he does see a role for God in his life, most clearly in the manner
in which his entire career unfolded at the United Nations rather than back
in Ghana as he originally planned growing up. Annan answered a question
from Melinda Henneberger about the role of religion in his life in much
the same way: "Not in a sanctimonious way" was he a person of faith, he
said, "but yes, I am a believer."[29] Henneberger's question was prompted by
a conversation Annan had with an unnamed person regarding the power
of prayer. This very issue is at the heart of Joshua Cooper Ramo's exploration of Annan's virtues, in particular his faith. Annan told Ramo that he
prayed in the morning after waking and said, "Sometimes I ask questions
in my prayers. The world is so cruel. How can people be so cruel? What
can one do?" He went on to confide, "I am still struggling with evil. I still
don't understand how there can be so much evil, and I'm not sure that I
ever will understand."[30]

Annan expressed this same "astonishment at the existence of evil" in
interviews with other journalists.[31] At the same time, he wrestled with
labeling specific individuals as evil, no matter how cruel or hideous their
actions might be. His internal struggle to reconcile evil and forgiveness
was most apparent in a speech he made at the National Conference of the
Trinity Institute in May 2004:

> I don't even think that the word "evil" is a regular part of my vocabulary.
> There is something about the word, when we apply it to another human

being—and more especially to a group of human beings—that makes me uncomfortable. It is too absolute. It seems to cut off any possibility of redemption, of dialogue, or even coexistence. It is the moral equivalent of declaring war. . . . I think it may be helpful if we resolve, when we use the word "evil" as an adjective, to apply it to actions rather than to people. Of course, it is tempting, when someone commits many evil acts, to say that that person is evil in himself or herself. But I am not sure that it is right. [32]

Near the end of this speech Annan connected his reluctance to name specific individuals as evil to his religious faith: "Personally I do not feel—either as a Christian, or even as a simple human being—that I have the right to make such an absolute judgment about any of my fellow human beings, however evil the acts they may have committed."

Annan's struggle to comprehend cruelty and evil is one of the reasons why Brian Urquhart, a former undersecretary-general, observed during Annan's tenure that he "has taken seriously the idea of being a conscience for the international community. He's used the office to push some very important ideas that are not immediately popular."[33] Although it was not possible for any of his senior staff interviewed for this project to judge the extent to which these ideas stem solely from his Christian faith, Annan's difficulty in reconciling evil and forgiveness is a recurring challenge for Christians throughout history. It is clear to those around Annan that he has been a "committed globalist" since his college days and that, as secretary-general, he advanced a vision of what some have called a "moral world order."[34] There appear to be two important moral values at the heart of his vision, both of which are consistent with the Golden Rule, which lies at the heart of his Christian faith: a concern for the dignity of every human being and a deep commitment to the peaceful resolution of conflict.

Moral Values

The first of these values, human dignity, is what Urquhart had in mind when he described some of Annan's ideas as unpopular. The most controversial part of Annan's thinking on human dignity was laid out in his annual address to the General Assembly on September 20, 1999.[35] In this speech he argued that the international community must be willing to disregard state sovereignty and intervene to protect individual human beings from those who abuse them. This effort to place individual sovereignty above state sovereignty became known in some circles as the Kofi Doctrine.[36] It was immediately criticized by a varied group of delegates, policymakers, journalists, and academics as setting a dangerous precedent for unending humanitarian wars, but because of Annan's stature, he "got away" with this direct challenge to the status quo.[37]

One important source of Annan's concern for human dignity, and arguably the reason why he feels so strongly about this value, lies in the UN's failures during the mid-1990s in Rwanda, Bosnia, and Somalia.[38] According to those who worked for him, Annan has indicated that these failures are among the worst experiences of his life. He feels to some extent personally responsible (as the head of UN peacekeeping at the time) for the inability of the international community to appreciate the magnitude of these events as they unfolded and the failure to mobilize the political will to respond in an appropriate manner. But those close to Annan have concluded that his concern with human dignity was present long before his service as undersecretary-general in the early 1990s. For example, one adviser interviewed for this project observed that the civil rights movement in the United States was important to Annan while he was a student at Macalester College in the early 1960s. Although Annan was not deeply involved in issues of racial equality at the time, he did learn important lessons about being in the minority. Stories from this period describe how he narrowly avoided being assaulted for walking with a white girl, was denied service in restaurants and barbershops, and was subjected to verbal insults.[39] But Annan's most important memories from these years are an apology from the mayor, that his American friends got more upset than he did, and that those who denied him service seemed to be more embarrassed by it than he was.

These early events spurred Annan's thinking about human rights and equality, firmly establishing in his mind that individuals have claims and obligations toward each other regardless of race, religion, ethnicity, or any other characteristic. They also helped cultivate in Annan a great compassion for the well-being of others, including strangers. While Annan was dating his current wife, Nane, long before he became secretary-general, the couple came upon a man crying, hunched over in a phone booth on Roosevelt Island in New York City.[40] While most people would not have noticed, or at least pretended not to, Nane recalls how Kofi talked to the man and listened to his problems. For some time thereafter, the man would come by and visit with the future secretary-general. This willingness to engage with people in distress, to listen to their concerns, has remained an important part of who Annan is. Examples of this are seemingly endless: a man in East Timor who burst into tears while recounting the violence he had experienced; a hundred-year-old woman in Kosovo who could only keep asking how this could happen to her at her age; refugees in Darfur who described how they had walked for seven days with everything they owned in order to escape ethnic killing; and victims of torture who were still haunted by their pain.[41] In all of these situations Annan maintained a deep commitment to the most vulnerable victims of human tragedy.

Annan did more than meet privately with victims of abuse in his effort to pursue human dignity. According to those who worked closely with him, he saw it as part of his responsibility as secretary-general to represent the interests and needs of innocent victims who lacked a voice of their own. In fact, some consider that human rights were one of the hallmarks of his policy priorities as secretary-general.[42] The colleagues I interviewed mentioned his focus on "bread-and-butter" human rights issues like oppression, genocide, political freedom, and the promotion of democracy. They were quick to add that his view of human rights also encompassed the right to overcome poverty, HIV/AIDS, pollution, gender discrimination, and any other conditions that limit human well-being.[43] This more expansive view of human dignity was clearly articulated in his Nobel Peace Prize acceptance speech in 2001: "Throughout my term as Secretary-General, I have sought to place human beings at the centre of everything we do—from conflict prevention to development to human rights. Securing real and lasting improvement in the lives of individual men and women is the measure of all we do at the United Nations."[44] This address also indicates that, at least in Annan's judgment, his concern for human dignity has been directly reflected in his behavior and policy choices while in office.

Annan's second moral value, the peaceful resolution of conflict, is similar to the first in that it represents a marriage between who he is as a person, the teachings of his religious faith, and the principles of the organization he led. In a speech to the Council on Foreign Relations in 1999, Annan said, "By precedent, by principle, by charter and by duty, I am bound to seek [my] ends through peaceful diplomacy."[45] This desire was as much personal as organizational; during his 1998 mission to Iraq, Annan told Saddam Hussein, "I feel that I have a sacred duty to do whatever I can to avoid the bloodshed and tragedy, and you have to help me make that possible."[46] This willingness to negotiate with apparently any individual in any situation led some diplomats to conclude that Annan was conflict-averse to the point that it could have created "a danger of allowing things to slide because they may involve conflict."[47] Along similar lines, journalist David

Rieff has concluded that Annan was "in principle and practice, committed to the peaceful resolution of conflicts at almost any price."[48] To his credit, however, Annan also understood that at times diplomacy may need to be backed by force if it is to succeed; but he felt that his role remained the same even in these situations.[49] Again with regard to Iraq, Annan argued that "member states or the [Security] Council can play tough. I'm not in a position to do that. They have to let me do it my way. They should not encourage me to be a Rambo—because I can never be a Rambo or use language that is not mine."[50]

UN officials who worked with Annan have frequently commented on his commitment to negotiation and conflict resolution. Tharoor has said that Annan "believes rather passionately in peaceful resolution . . . it is bred into his bones."[51] Likewise, Richard Butler, the former head of the UN Special Commission investigating Iraqi disarmament, has observed that "Kofi takes immensely seriously his role as the person in charge of the maintenance of international peace and security. That goes with the turf. It's the nature of his office that while others consider the use of war, the world should have a voice extolling the virtues of peace. He's admirably suited to that and feels it deeply."[52] Those who have had to negotiate with Annan have reached a similar conclusion. Madeline Albright, while she was U.S. secretary of state, said of Annan, "He feels his responsibility is to make sure always that there's peace, that you can work things out."[53]

Annan's commitment to diplomacy and negotiation stems from his college and boarding school years. One American friend from college, Susan Linnee, has described Annan as above all "'a facilitator,' someone who sought the common ground among people and tried to bring them together."[54] Even earlier, at Mfantsipim, Annan successfully led a hunger strike to protest the quality of the food and, according to one classmate, also "had his way of talking to the seniors without antagonizing them" such that "he could calm them down and persuade them not to punish him" for infractions of the school code.[55]

Several of the UN staff members interviewed for this research also suggested the cultural roots of this moral value. They attribute Annan's commitment to consensus building in nearly all situations to the African sense of the world as a community or village where people do things together. Whether he was negotiating with dictators or simply running a meeting of his staff, Annan preferred to push for consensus on the best course of action, not just a quick agreement on whatever it was politically expedient to do. Annan's tendency toward consensus building can be seen even in the face of clear indications that particular member states or other actors preferred that he adopt different behavior and policy choices. Several people recalled situations in which Annan's reaction to initial opposition was to push for consensus. "What are we here for if not this?" he would ask. They also observed that his preference for negotiation and consensus building translated well into the settings of multilateral diplomacy; nearly all the people I interviewed recalled at least one instance in which Annan diffused a tough negotiation by bringing everybody along in the search for widespread agreement.

Nearly every person interviewed for this project argued that Annan cares deeply about human dignity and the peaceful resolution of conflict. One used a line from the movie *The Blues Brothers* to describe how seriously Annan viewed his responsibilities as secretary-general, calling him a "man on a mission from God." Others said that they saw examples of these moral considerations in Annan's decision making "on a daily basis."

Annan's Personal Attributes

Annan's personal attributes merit brief attention here for two reasons. First, existing literature on the UN secretary-general has long understood that the personality and character of the incumbent can play an important role in determining the specific policies and actions that will be pursued while in office.[56] This is especially true in the case of the political and diplomatic functions of the secretary-general, a point made by Leland Goodrich nearly forty years ago when he concluded that Hammarskjöld's success in expanding the scope of the office was due in part to his diplomatic skill, intelligence, and moral integrity.[57] Second, every person interviewed for this study argued that Annan's personal attributes were almost perfectly matched with his moral values, and that they made it easier for him to see his values reflected in the conduct and policy choices he pursued in office.

One of the characteristics most often attributed to Annan, and one well suited to the values discussed above, is his remarkable presence in all social settings.[58] While he is not a man of great physical stature, he is often seen as possessing great personal dignity. Some have described Annan with language usually reserved for royalty, saying that he has "an elegance that comes less from dress than from equipoise" and "a more gracious, divine-right-of-kings feel" about him.[59] His wife, Nane, has linked his presence and dignity to his sense of compassion, using a Swedish word that means "cast whole" to describe him.[60] Journalist David Usborne concluded a profile of Annan by saying that he "above all emanates humanity. It is a quality that is at the core of his personality."[61] A final reflection of the significance of Annan's presence and dignity is that people have noticed when this quality was absent, as after the United States invaded Iraq in March 2003 without Security Council authorization. During this period Annan seemed "surprisingly shaky . . . uncharacteristically unsure of himself, and oddly distracted."[62] Likewise, revelations of his son's unsavory financial dealings as part of the oil-for-food investigation in late 2004, and the fact that Kojo hid this from his father for so long, severely dented Annan's morale and left him shaken and depressed.[63]

Regardless of how one describes it, this sense of presence and dignity enables Annan to enjoy "slightly mysterious powers of persuasion," an attribute that has served him well in his efforts to pursue negotiation and diplomacy over force.[64] Holbrooke commented that he "has a nearly magical ability to move people through his personal charm and gentle strength."[65] Kieran Pendergrast, a former undersecretary-general for political affairs, and Georges Abi-Saab, a friend of Annan's from graduate school, both indicated that this ability even extends to very difficult people, because Annan seems to be on good terms with everybody.[66] A number of interpersonal skills contribute to Annan's powers of persuasion; the two most often mentioned are charisma and charm.[67] In addition, Annan is often credited with an "exquisite" sense of tact joined with the courage to remain firm in even the most difficult situations.[68] Annan's courage is enhanced by his deep sense of loyalty to his word, to his principles, and to his staff, even in the face of opposition. It is also buttressed by the fact that Annan is "an exceedingly patient man" who does not require symbolic victories to stay engaged in an issue.[69] Annan himself has indicated that this patience is due in part to the African culture in which he was raised.[70]

Intelligence and efficiency are also personal attributes that enhance Annan's leadership. Although Annan is no doubt intelligent, a number of people have suggested that Annan is "not an intellectually formidable figure" or "an intellectual heavyweight."[71] They suggest, instead, that his intelligence stems from his "preternatural instinct for saying and doing precisely the right thing."[72] Annan is typically very careful with the words and language he uses.[73] According to Iqbal Riza, who served as Annan's chief of staff until December 2004, Annan's effectiveness in language is based more on his "instinct and intuition than on calculation."[74] The importance of instinct and intuition can also be seen in Annan's decision-making style. Nane has described her husband as being very efficient, so much so that he "refuses to touch a piece of paper more than once."[75] Some have attributed Annan's efficiency to the fact that his highest degree is in management, which Stanley Meisler has described as training "in getting things done."[76] Lindenmayer, by contrast, attributes his efficiency to his "African style" of decision making: "He asks us what we think, listens, is silent and thinks, and then he announces clear decisions."[77] His intelligence and decision-making style are buttressed by a very pragmatic and practical orientation toward each situation he faces.[78] One frequently cited example of this from Annan's college days recalls his initial reluctance to wear "unsightly" earmuffs until the cold Minnesota winters at Macalester College caused him to rethink this decision; the lesson he took from this was to "never think that you know more than the natives do."[79]

Nearly every discussion of Annan's personal attributes highlights his calm and reserved manner. One of the most remarkable aspects of this "innate" aspect of his personality is that Annan actually becomes calmer the more dangerous the situation.[80] This calmness has been linked to one apparent paradox in his character: that his soft-spoken manner masks a strong sense of self-possession and self-restraint.[81] Nearly all the writers who have profiled Annan have indicated that they have rarely if ever seen him angry.[82] Some exceptions are usually mentioned, such as during long trips or conversations about personal and organizational failures, but these often seem oriented toward disrupting the "UN legend" regarding his calmness to show that he, like everyone else, "is perfectly capable of everyday pique."[83] Even on the rare occasions when he did become angry during his tenure as secretary-general, the effects were not always very noticeable. Jeremy Greenstock, the former British ambassador to the United Nations, has said, "When [Annan] is displeased or angry, there is just the flicker of the eyes, or he just looks down briefly."[84] Annan of course has been asked on multiple occasions why anger seems to be so alien to him, to which he has replied that anger is "a negative energy . . . so to be rancoring and let it linger, and be grumpy, and bear grudges, and all this—it's something that has never been part of me, because I find not only is it not necessary, but it takes a lot out of you, it distracts."[85]

Annan is also widely known for his modesty, yet another trait that facilitated policy choices consistent with his values of human dignity and peaceful resolution of conflict. One of Annan's former advisers, John

Ruggie, says, "He's the least ego-driven person I've met. It's almost as if he removes himself from the mess and says, 'This is not about me.' It comes from a deep sense of personal security from knowing who he is."[86] According to Lindenmayer, his modesty stems from his days as a track athlete in college, where he learned how to lose gracefully.[87] Some have indicated that this absence of ego was one of the reasons why the United States favored Annan for the position of secretary-general in the first place: It was thought that his modesty would make him malleable to U.S. interests.[88] Rather than being a negative trait, however, Annan's lack of ego served him well because it was understood that he was not advancing an agenda of his own.[89] This perception was further reinforced by the fact that Annan was nearly always "a model of equanimity;" his face and body language hid nothing, and yet they also gave nothing away. Even close aides were known to say, "We're trying to read his body language. That means we have no idea."[90]

Annan's personal attributes are all consistent with his view of effective leadership at the United Nations. During an interview in December 2004 he said:

> I have learned from experience and observation [that] there are two schools of thought. There is the school of engineers: those who take assertive action, they grab the iron while it's hot, bend it, shape it, and if it doesn't suit them they throw it away. This works in the short term. And then there is the school of the farmers: those who plant a tree and know that the tree will need air, water, and sunlight. They prune the tree, take care of it, get it to grow, and they create an environment for it that encourages growth. This works in the long term.[91]

The interviewer then asked Annan whether U.S. president George Bush was the engineer and he the farmer. Annan chose not to respond, but his personal attributes as discussed above show clearly that he is perfectly suited to the role of a farmer. This approach to leadership is complemented by the fact that Annan possesses a "keen sense of the possible" and a "near mystical faith in positive outcomes."[92]

External Context

The opening chapters in this volume by Kent Kille and Dorothy Jones indicate that officeholders' freedom to act is limited by the political environment they face and the historical evolution of the norms of the office they inhabit. Each secretary-general faces a particular external code given the environmental and role constraints (and opportunities). Articles 97 through 101 of the UN charter outline the rights and duties of the secretary-general, but these articles also allow for some uncertainty in regard to what the position was intended to be.[93] As a result, the nature and scope of the job have evolved over time as each secretary-general has endeavored to make the office his own.[94] This is especially true in the case of "internationally active Secretaries General" who, according to Malloch Brown, "have succeeded by convincing genuinely important individuals, heads of government and so on, that they can be helpful."[95]

This process of evolution and expansion of the office is of central significance for this study because the UN charter "charges the Secretary-General with conflicting responsibilities" to both act independently and do the bidding of the organization's members.[96] The limitations and opportunities associated with these dual roles "dictate that [the secretary-general], like others with broad political responsibilities, cannot be everything to everybody on all occasions."[97] As a result, it is important to explore the political environment Annan faced as secretary-general and the manner in which he interpreted the responsibilities of his office.

The Environment

Given that international governmental organizations are composed of member states, the general patterns of cooperation and conflict in world politics have a direct bearing on the activities of these organizations.[98] The UN's objectives, the resources it has to pursue them, and the obstacles it faces along the way are all products of the external environment in which it operates. The international political environment does more than just influence the organization as a whole, however; it also affects the work of the secretaries-general by "establishing the parameters of their behavior" and by "compound[ing] the difficulties of the office."[99] In the case of Annan, two aspects of the environment had the greatest influence on his time in office: the growing demand for the services of the organization and his office, particularly in the developing world, and the on-again, off-again relationship between the United Nations and the United States.

The end of the Cold War led to enlarged expectations for the United Nations in the management of a wide range of transnational problems. This created many challenges for the organization and for the office of secretary-general.[100] Benjamin Rivlin has observed that "the changed international political climate has greatly increased the demands for the services of the Secretary-General as mediator, conciliator, peacekeeper, peacemaker, election supervisor, dispenser of emergency assistance, and implementer of unprecedented Security Council decisions."[101] Unfortunately for Annan, as Rivlin points out, these new responsibilities did not carry with them additional powers or resources. As a result, it is increasingly important yet increasingly difficult for the secretary-general to address the needs of those individuals living in regions of conflict or poverty. There is some irony for Annan in this development. On the one hand, his rapid advancement at the organization in the early 1990s was the result of both his capabilities and the need for experienced staff to move quickly into new and uncharted territory in the face of new demands on the United Nations.[102] On the other hand, according to Tharoor, the reason why the secretary-general and his staff want to serve the United Nations is that they have "grown up in societies which need the international system to work well."[103] As a result, the growing needs of the developing world created external pressures on Annan to be a more activist secretary-general.

A second important environmental impact on the office of secretary-general has to do with the organization's membership. Gordenker has called the member states "an unavoidable environmental presence for the Secretary-General" that must be managed carefully, especially when they are pulling in different directions.[104] While all member states represent potential "bosses" for the secretary-general given their collective control of the organization, it is really the relationship with the five permanent members of the Security Council that an officeholder must closely cultivate, given that these powers "have a major voice in all UN actions, including the selection and reappointment of the Secretary-General."[105] During Annan's tenure, one permanent member more than any other provided the greatest environmental constraints: the United States. One of the primary reasons for this is the uneven and sporadic relationship between that country and the organization itself. In the years since the end of the Cold War, the level of U.S. engagement at the United Nations has fluctuated between close cooperation, outright hostility, and everything in between.[106]

Annan's personal relationship with the U.S. government included a number of incongruities that made his balancing act as secretary-general more challenging. First and foremost, the United States, more than any other country, engineered his rise to the position of secretary-general. Annan's first political missions for the United Nations came immediately before and after the first Gulf War, when he was sent to Baghdad to secure the release of nine hundred members of the organization's international staff and nearly half a million other foreign workers.[107] His success led his predecessor, Boutros Boutros-Ghali, to appoint him the second-ranking official in the new Department of Peacekeeping Operations in 1992. From that point forward, however, his rise was due to U.S. support. In 1993 the United States pushed to have Annan replace Marrack Goulding as the undersecretary-general in charge of peacekeeping, thinking that he would be "more flexible" toward U.S. interests.[108] This view was confirmed in 1995 when Annan authorized NATO bombing in the former Yugoslavia while Boutros-Ghali was out of contact with UN headquarters on a flight to China.[109] After the Dayton Accords were completed, Boutros-Ghali sent Annan to be his special representative in Zagreb, which some viewed as a means of sidelining Annan as a potential rival for the position of secretary-general.[110] Whatever Boutros-Ghali's motive, Annan performed well in the eyes of the Americans, and he became their preferred candidate for secretary-general once they made the decision to deny Boutros-Ghali a second term.

Despite initial opposition from France,[111] nearly all of the member states liked Annan as a successor to Boutros-Ghali.[112] Because of strong American support for his appointment, however, and because Annan had spent much of his adult life in the United States, some continued to believe, well into his first term, that he was "as much the first American Secretary-General as the first from sub-Saharan Africa."[113] These views persisted in the case of some member states, which perceived Annan as the most pro-American secretary-general in history, even after the Security Council failed to authorize the U.S. invasion of Iraq in March 2003.[114] But there were also signs that Washington got more than it bargained for when it championed Annan, even during the relatively multilateral years of the Clinton administration.[115] This caused some observers, including Sergei Lavrov, then the Russian ambassador to the United Nations, to conclude that Annan appeared "to be everybody's Secretary-General."[116] This point was further reinforced by the accelerating attacks on Annan by conservative members of the U.S. Congress in the months after Annan labeled the war in Iraq "illegal" and the investigations into the oil-for-food scandal intensified.[117] Despite these difficulties, it was widely known that Annan enjoyed a close relationship with Colin Powell while Powell was U.S. secretary of state; they spoke several times a week and considered each other close friends.[118] Powell has said of Annan, "He is open, he listens, he doesn't roll over, and he always tries to do what's right. In the toughest of times he is always there to give us a sanity check."[119] Unfortunately, Annan's relationship was not as close with Condoleezza Rice, which toughened the nature of the environmental constraints that Annan faced late in his term, after Rice replaced Powell as secretary of state.[120]

The Office and Its Moral Authority

In their opening chapters to this volume, both Kille and Jones discuss how the job of secretary-general involves administrative and managerial functions as well as political and diplomatic ones. Annan, like other incumbents, was keenly aware of these dual roles, as his press conference response, quoted at the beginning of this chapter, illustrates. As a result, the "double-barreled title" of secretary-general,[121] while both awkward and confusing, actually makes a great deal of sense: The job encompasses the role of a secretary focusing on administrative and managerial matters, and the role of a general dealing with political and diplomatic issues.[122] Shawcross has observed that these roles can be viewed as incompatible: "The old conceit was that the holder of the job could try to be either a secretary or a general, but would hardly be able to combine both tasks."[123] In practice, however, every secretary-general has favored a mix of the administrative and political functions of the office, with the exact balance varying from one incumbent to the next and even within the tenure of a single individual, based on their own understanding of the office and the situations they faced.[124]

The Americans favored Annan in 1996 precisely because he "promised to be more secretary than general," as they expected that he "would work better as a manager of the institution and not as a maker of diplomatic waves."[125] But it is equally clear that the developing world, and in particular Africa, saw Annan as one of their own and therefore wanted him to be a general who would advocate for them vis-à-vis the major powers.[126] To his credit, Annan was acutely aware of these divergent expectations and the realities of his office: "There are times when I have to be a secretary," he said, "and there are times when I have to be a general and show leadership."[127]

One thing that helped Annan balance his own moral values and the responsibilities of the office was that his desire to see the organization pursue human dignity and the peaceful resolution of conflict was perfectly consistent with the norms and principles of the office. It is thus often difficult to determine whether secretaries-general have adopted a particular behavior or selected a particular policy choice because of their own ethical frameworks or because of the nature of the office. This is a common question in any study of leadership: Is it the office that makes the person or the person who makes the office? In the case of Annan, two considerations suggest that his own values, rather than those of the office, lay at the heart of his behavior and policy choices. First, as we have seen, Annan's commitment to human dignity and the peaceful resolution of conflict predate his tenure as secretary-general. Second, nearly every staff member interviewed for this chapter indicated that, in the words of one of them, "Kofi was made long before he became secretary-general" and that he "raised the stature of the office beyond what it is traditionally afforded due to the person he is."

There is an added dimension to the office of secretary-general that is not captured in the secretary-versus-general distinction but is nonetheless relevant to this study: the extent to which the position provides its occupant with "moral authority" in the eyes of the international community. The character of the incumbents can have a significant impact on the degree to which they are perceived as enjoying moral authority, even while at least some of that moral authority derives from the nature of the position itself.[128] Whereas some writers have conveyed a sense of surprise that the United Nations or the secretary-general enjoys a "moral role,"[129] many have observed that, in certain situations, the only power an incumbent may possess is the "moral authority" that stems from the principles of the charter and the impartiality of the office.[130]

Annan has been compared to Hammarskjöld because of his understanding that both the office and the organization enjoy this moral authority.[131] This assertion is based on an oft-quoted comment Annan made at the Council on Foreign Relations in 1999, where he said that the secretary-general "is invested only with the power that a united Security Council may wish to bestow, and the moral authority entrusted to him by the Charter."[132] Annan used high-profile reports produced by his office, such as the Millennium Development Report, to convey the "self-conscious and unusually keen sense he [had] of the normative role of the UN"[133] as an organization with "the avowed purpose of transforming relations among states, and the methods by which the world's affairs are managed."[134] In a more recent report, "In Larger Freedom," Annan wrote, "In preparing the present report, I have drawn on my eight years' experience as Secretary-General, on my own conscience and convictions, and on my understanding of the Charter of the United Nations whose principles and purposes it is my duty to promote."[135] Such comments explicitly convey that Annan saw both his own ethical framework and the moral authority of the office as two important and interrelated influences on his policy priorities.

The office of secretary-general, then, is endowed with a certain degree of moral authority, but the personal values and attributes of the incumbent can enhance or diminish that authority. In the case of Annan, some observers assert that he diminished or even squandered it altogether. Gourevitch has argued that Annan's tenure was "tainted from the beginning" because of his role in Rwanda and Bosnia in the mid-1990s. "Those world leaders who later hailed him as a moral exemplar at best ignored that history, at worst regarded it as a kind of credential: since Annan was a compromised figure, they did not have to fear his censure."[136] Rieff mounted an even stronger attack, arguing that "moral judgments are not part of what he sees as his role" and that "his gift is not for moral candor or moral leadership."[137]

Fortunately for Annan, these negative assessments of his moral standing are in the minority. Meisler cites fellow journalist Shawcross when he observes, in reference to Annan and Nelson Mandela, that "there are only two people with great moral stature in the world today, and both are Africans with gray hair."[138] In his own writing, Shawcross has been even stronger in advocating the view that Annan's personal attributes and values have enhanced the moral authority of the office. Annan has told Shawcross that he "fervently believes in the ideals of the UN," to the extent that Shawcross concludes that Annan has an almost "quasi-religious belief in the institution." Furthermore, Shawcross argues that Annan came "to personify more than any other international official in decades" both "the United Nations and its ideals" and "the spirit of the international community, with all its hopes, heroism, and disappointments."[139]

The Ethics of Policy Choice

The chapters in this volume share two broad and ambitious goals: first, to uncover the religious and moral values that make up the ethical framework of each secretary-general; and second, to explore whether these values had an impact on the behavior and policy choices of each secretary-general given the external constraints he faced. In the case of Annan, this second step must be a tentative one, given that he only recently concluded his term of office. Furthermore, each of the policy choices examined below—Iraq, Darfur, the Millennium Development Goals, and organizational reform—are ongoing issues that will require attention well into his successor's term. These policy choices span major areas of UN activity regarding peace and security, human rights, development, and administration. These particular areas of policy, however, represent situations where Annan appears to have adopted behavior or made choices that are not politically expedient given the pressures he faced. I argue that Annan decided to do what he felt was necessary rather than what was easy in each of these cases because he was guided by his ethical framework.

In all four of these areas Annan faced a number of situations in which he had to choose between two competing values, either of which would have been a compelling choice given the realities of the situation. In chapter 1 of this volume, Kille identifies four such ethical dilemmas that might be identified in the tenures of all the secretaries-general: "taking a normative stand versus seeking support from states, speaking out strongly versus protecting the office, taking a principled stand versus operating on a pragmatic basis, and accomplishing a mission versus staff security." The case studies that follow demonstrate that Annan faced each of these ethical dilemmas while in office.

Iraq

No issue dominated the UN security agenda during Annan's tenure more than Iraq. Many of the profiles of Annan that were used in the preceding discussion were written with a focus on Iraq. Furthermore, many of the UN staff members interviewed for this project identified Iraq as a situation in which Annan faced a series of tradeoffs between what he wanted to see happen and what the constraints of the situation seemed to allow. Several of Annan's specific actions and policy choices regarding Iraq merit attention when exploring the impact of his ethical framework: his 1998 trip to Baghdad in the face of initial opposition by the Security Council, his decision not to support the war in 2003 and his subsequent labeling of the war as illegal, his letter that sought to avoid the offensive in Falluja in November 2004, and his reluctance to commit UN personnel to Iraq, both before and after the terrorist bombing in August 2003.

By early 1998 the United Nations and Iraq had reached an impasse regarding the disarmament inspections that were required as part of the ceasefire agreement from the first Gulf War. The crux of the dispute related to the access of inspectors from the UN Special Commission (UNSCOM) to certain areas that Iraq had labeled "presidential sites" and declared off limits. Annan found himself the target of intense pressure, both from the Americans (and to a lesser extent the British), who were preparing to bomb Iraq into accepting a hard-line policy, and from the Russians, the French, the nonaligned, and the Vatican, who all wanted Annan to undertake a diplomatic mission to Iraq in the hope of resolving the crisis and avoiding war. Despite opposition from members of the Security Council, including some permanent members, Annan wanted to make the trip, but he was "determined not to go until [he] had all the elements in place."[140] But exactly what "elements" needed to be in place created an ethical dilemma for Annan: Should he wait for consensus among council members, or should he go without a mandate from the council?

As events unfolded, Annan was able to use his persuasiveness and patience, as well as to capitalize on widespread public opposition to a possible bombing campaign, in order to develop a unified council position supporting his trip during a series of February meetings.[141] As a result, he was able to avoid one of the ethical dilemmas discussed in this volume: seeking the support of states versus taking a normative stand. Given the extensive coverage of these events in the press, it is nonetheless possible to speculate on the choice Annan would have made had he not been able to resolve this ethical tradeoff. Annan has said in interviews that he would have gone even without the backing of a unified council: "I had a constitutional duty to avert this kind of tragedy if I can."[142] Apparently Annan made this known to Albright and it had an impact on the U.S. decision to shape the mandate of Annan's trip rather than withhold support for it entirely.[143]

One senior UN official interviewed for this research indicated that Annan's willingness to devote so much of his time, energy, and negotiating skill to securing council support for his trip, or to lay the groundwork for a possible trip without council support, was due to his commitment to the peaceful resolution of conflict and the depth of his personal courage. Another senior adviser, however, does not think Annan would have gone without council support, regardless of his moral priorities, because such a trip would have been "politically disastrous." While these conflicting accounts make it impossible to know which tradeoff Annan would have made, they do share a common theme: that Annan's commitment to the peaceful resolution of conflict, based on his own values and charter ideals, influenced his behavior and policy choices during this crisis.

Annan faced a similar ethical dilemma in regard to Iraq beginning in September 2002. As had been the case four years before, the United States and Britain were becoming increasingly frustrated with Iraqi noncompliance, the Security Council was divided on the best course of action, and Annan was convinced that force should be used only once all possible avenues of conflict resolution had failed.[144] At first it appeared that Annan might be able to avoid a direct tradeoff between taking a normative stand and seeking the support of states, as he had in 1998. Annan supported the U.S.-led effort to draft Security Council Resolution 1441 in November 2002, which established a more robust inspections regime, and also helped secure its unanimous approval by personally lobbying the president of Syria for his support.[145] Unfortunately, the months that followed this success were a trying time for the United Nations and for Annan himself, as weeks of diplomatic maneuvering were unable to prevent the use of force.[146] According to Henneberger, "the advent of war caught Annan by far greater surprise than it should have," and clearly left him weary and disappointed.[147]

As much as Annan sought to avoid the war, Henneberger observes that he was surprisingly quiet in his condemnation of the war once it started.[148] Had he decided that taking a normative stand in opposition to the war was not worth the political costs the secretary-general and the United Nations would suffer by further alienating the United States? However, Annan's behavior during this period is more appropriately understood as reflecting another ethical dilemma mentioned above: speaking out strongly versus protecting the office. For more than a year Annan's standard response to questions about his view of the U.S. invasion of Iraq was that "it was not in conformity with the Charter."[149] This careful language allowed Annan to avoid making the ethical tradeoff by both speaking out (conveying his view that the war was not the appropriate course of action) and protecting the office (not directly stating that the U.S. decision was wrong).

This ambiguity, however, was difficult to sustain, and in September 2004 Annan was finally pushed in an interview to label the U.S. invasion "illegal."[150] This comment had immediate negative consequences for Annan within the U.S. government. To make matters worse, Annan faced the same ethical dilemma just two months later, in November, when the United States and Britain prepared to mount an offensive in Falluja, Iraq. Annan knew that any effort to prevent the use of force in favor of diplomacy was likely to be viewed as an attempt to influence the U.S. presidential election, just a few days away, which would of course invite further attacks against him and his office. Annan decided to speak out anyway, by sending a letter to President Bush and British prime minister Tony Blair, portions of which were leaked to the media. While Annan's behavior during this period can be viewed as too little too late in terms of justifiable criticism of the United States, one senior UN official argued that Annan's decision to "say what should be said, not what is easy" in these situations required both courage and "moral stuffing."[151]

Annan's policy choices regarding Iraq forced him to address one additional ethical dilemma mentioned above: accomplishing a mission versus staff security. Not long after the American and British invasion swept through Iraq, Annan began to face heavy pressure from these countries to send an envoy and other UN staff to Iraq. At first Annan resisted, as it was not at all clear what UN personnel would be doing there and whether their safety could be assured. This was a difficult choice for Annan, especially given his commitment to human dignity and his desire to ease the suffering of the Iraqi people, but he also understood that the United Nations could not enter Iraq merely to act as a rubber stamp for coalition policies.[152] Annan's opposition to sending personnel changed after the UN's role in postwar Iraq was enhanced in Security Council Resolution 1483, passed in May 2003. A team of UN officials headed by Sergio Vieira de Mello was stationed in Iraq shortly thereafter. Tragically, Annan's initial concerns about staff safety proved to be well founded when a terrorist bomb destroyed the UN's Baghdad headquarters on August 19, 2003, killing twenty-two people, including Vieira de Mello. Annan's policy choices regarding this ethical dilemma were profoundly changed by these events. More than a year after the bombing, Annan was asked in an interview if he would send more UN personnel to Iraq, to which he responded, "I will do that, but for security reasons I can't say how many and when."[153]

The impact of Annan's ethical framework on his behavior and policy choices can be seen throughout his handling of Iraq. Each tradeoff he made was influenced by his moral values of peaceful resolution of conflict and human dignity. That Annan's values figure prominently in his handling of Iraq is significant given the salience of this ongoing crisis to the majority of UN members. On several occasions he made politically difficult choices rather than do the easy thing. The case was no different in another crisis he faced: the human tragedy unfolding in Darfur.

POLITICS AND VALUES AT THE UNITED NATIONS   323

Darfur

The United Nations confronted many cases of humanitarian assistance during Annan's tenure, but the one selected for discussion here is the situation in Darfur, a region in the Sudan. Several of the staff members interviewed for this project indicated that Annan's commitment to keeping this issue on the international and Security Council agenda, his multiple trips to the region, and his appointment of an international commission to investigate the events in Darfur all demonstrate that, as one of them put it, he was "driving the issue behind the scenes like nobody's business." Furthermore, they argue that his commitment to the people in Darfur was based on his own values and compassion, not on political calculations.

The Sudan has been locked in a civil war for all but eleven of the years since the country gained independence in 1956.[154] This war between the North and the South over religion and resources may finally be coming to an end, with a comprehensive peace agreement signed by the government and the main rebel group in January 2005. Unfortunately, the end of one conflict in the Sudan gave way to the emergence of another in early 2003, when rebels in the region of Darfur mounted an armed attack against government forces. Fighting in Darfur has been intense, with both the government and its allied militia, the Janjaweed, attempting to crush the rebels. Security Council Resolutions 1556 (July 2004) and 1564 (September 2004) expanded the mandate of the existing UN Advance Mission in the Sudan (UNAMIS) to include limited monitoring of the situation in Darfur, but at the time the Security Council declined to take any further action regarding the fighting and human rights abuses in the region. As a result, Annan's desire to have the United Nations and the Security Council mount a more robust response to the situation in Darfur presented him with two ethical dilemmas.[155]

The first was the choice between taking a principled stand and acting pragmatically. According to three of Annan's advisers interviewed for this research, Annan began to push the Security Council to act in Darfur as soon as the scope of the killings and other human rights abuses came to light. For Annan, the need to act was directly linked to his personal concern for human dignity, as well as to the memory that the United Nations had failed to act in support of human dignity in Rwanda and Srebrenica. Although Annan was not explicit on this point, one senior UN official observed that his thinking on Darfur appeared to be heavily influenced by the *Responsibility to Protect* report that was released in December 2001.[156]

Despite this personal commitment to Darfur, Annan was confronted with a Security Council that could not agree about what course of action to take, and Annan had to decide how best to prod the council to action. His close advisers indicated that Annan could have adopted an uncompromising stand and "screamed" at the council to act, even by invoking article 99 of the UN charter if necessary. Instead, with his patience, presence, and reserved personality, Annan chose to work behind the scenes by repeatedly pushing council members to overcome their differences and design an effective response.

Annan knew that council members were divided in terms of how they viewed events in Darfur: Some saw a clear case of genocide, but others did not.[157] At this point Annan became more pragmatic in his approach and asked the council to let him appoint a commission of inquiry to investigate the reports of humanitarian and human rights violations. According to his aides, Annan saw the commission as a way to narrow the differences among council members such that more robust action, in line with charter principles and his own moral values, would be possible. Unfortunately, Annan's pragmatism did not achieve his goal: The commission did not label the violations in Darfur genocide, and the differences among council members persisted, so that the Security Council did not approve more robust UN action in Darfur until August 2006.[158] Furthermore, even once this more robust approach was approved, it remained inoperable in the following months because of the objections of the Sudanese government and the unwillingness of some council members to push for action without the government's consent.[159] This continued difficulty starkly illustrates the limits of pragmatism, but the individuals interviewed for this project felt strongly that this strategy allowed Annan to make more headway on Darfur than would have been possible through a more confrontational and uncompromising approach.

The depth of Annan's commitment to resolving the situation in Darfur presented him with another ethical dilemma: accomplishing a mission versus staff security. In this case the mission did not involve providing services on the ground but prodding the Security Council to adopt a more robust response. As his aides told me, Annan knew that one of the ways to keep Darfur on the international agenda was to travel to the region himself, which he did on several occasions as the situation worsened. He visited refugee camps in neighboring countries, chaired donor conferences in the region, and made trips to Darfur itself. The visits to Darfur were especially risky for the secretary-general, and at least one such trip in spring 2005 was strongly opposed by Annan's security personnel.[160] Annan decided that the merits and objectives of the trip outweighed these concerns, and he drew upon his own personal courage to proceed as planned. Two of Annan's aides interviewed for this project recalled situations in which Annan was asked if Darfur was worth it, in terms of both the time he was spending on it and the personal risk he was assuming. Annan's response was linked directly to his concern for human dignity: "If we do not help these people, who else will mobilize on their behalf?"

The Millennium Development Goals

While security and humanitarian issues dominate many headlines about the United Nations, 75 percent of what the organization does (in terms of staff and resources) is devoted to development.[161] One of the staff members interviewed for this project discussed an interesting paradox regarding the secretary-general and development issues. Since security and humanitarian issues are more salient to member states, the secretary-general enjoys more room to maneuver with respect to development issues. But officeholders are also more limited in terms of the impact they can have, simply because the organization they head has a smaller effect on addressing world poverty than do the major international financial institutions. In spite of this limitation, three individuals interviewed for this research remarked that Annan launched one of his important development initiatives, the Millennium Development Goals (MDGs), because of his personal commitment to human dignity rather than political calculations. His work on the MDGs involved two of the ethical dilemmas mentioned above: taking a principled stand versus operating on a pragmatic basis, and taking a normative stand versus seeking support from states.

As we have seen, Annan's conception of human dignity encompassed, among other things, freedom from poverty, discrimination, and other forms of human misery. According to two of his aides, these issues were of special concern to Annan because of his roots in a region that faces obstacles to development on a daily basis. Annan thus began his first term as secretary-general committed to designing a more effective UN role for the promotion of development. One obstacle that he and the United Nations faced was the sheer complexity of the organization's activities in this area. One adviser suggested that Annan's most efficient strategy would have been to consolidate and otherwise streamline the many agencies, programs, and funds dealing with development issues. This strategy was attractive because it also happened to be consistent with Annan's early reform agenda, which included an effort to add "sunset provisions" to UN mandates that would terminate programs that had outlived their usefulness. But Annan chose to pursue a less efficient but more pragmatic approach to development in the face of resistance from those UN members who feared that their "pet" programs and agencies might be the target of the sunset provisions. The MDGs became the centerpiece of this new pragmatic approach, in that they were designed to coordinate and focus the UN's development work without provoking the level of resistance that eliminating existing programs would have done.

Promoting the MDGs may have been a pragmatic decision for Annan, but it was also one based on a keen understanding of the normative role of the United Nations.[162] Annan's Millennium Report, which was released in March 2000 and provided the early basis for the MDGs, indicated that the United Nations had a key role to play in development given the shared values of the organization's membership: "It is our job to ensure that globalization provides benefits, not just for some, but for all . . . that opportunities exist, not merely for the privileged, but for every human being everywhere."[163] Annan identified a number of broad and ambitious goals, with concrete targets, for consideration by member states at the Millennium Summit in September 2000. The Millennium Assembly adopted nearly all of these goals by consensus in its Millennium Declaration, and eight of the goals were subsequently identified as those that would receive priority across the United Nations system.[164] Thus, in the aftermath of the Millennium Summit, Annan seemed to have used a pragmatic approach to effectively reconcile his normative desire for the United Nations to be more focused on development issues with the need to seek broad support from the organization's members.

Annan's effort to balance his normative stand on the MDGs with securing the support of states was shaken in August 2005, when the new U.S. ambassador to the United Nations, John Bolton, conveyed his country's opposition to including any references to the MDGs in the outcome document of the World Summit in honor of the UN's sixtieth anniversary.[165] Because Annan felt that the MDGs were seen by most countries (and himself) as defining the UN's mission, he cut short a vacation in Africa so that he could participate in the negotiations leading up to the September 2005 summit. Despite the lack of U.S. support, Annan continued to push for the inclusion of the MDGs in the outcome document: "I don't think anyone can remove them from the general public's perception of how we are moving ahead with development," he said; "I'm not sure the other member states would want to see the millennium development goals dropped, or worse, expunged from the document."[166] In the intense negotiations that followed, Annan used his persuasiveness and the backlash against the United States among other member states to push Bolton to soften the U.S. position.[167] Thanks to these efforts, Annan was able to reconfirm his normative support for the MDGs while still securing the broad support of member states; the final outcome document contains multiple references to the MDGs.[168]

Organizational Reform

Annan made UN reform a central and recurring theme of his tenure as secretary-general.[169] He advanced proposals dealing with key areas of the organization's legitimacy, such as Security Council expansion and the replacement of the UN Commission on Human Rights with a more effective Human Rights Council.[170] As contentious as these issues were among member states, much of Annan's personal effort on UN reform centered on organizational management, including efficiency, accountability, and staff conduct. Management reforms were so important to Annan because his long UN career made him familiar with the organization's weaknesses from the inside out and instilled in him a desire to improve its performance; because these issues more naturally fell under his purview as the organization's chief administrative officer; and because the organization's leading member, the United States, considered these issues especially salient.

During Annan's second term, the United Nations was rocked by a series of ethical scandals involving its staff, including accusations of sexual harassment by the UN High Commissioner for Refugees, Ruud Lubbers, and the UN peacekeeping troops deployed in the Congo. According to three of Annan's advisers whom I interviewed for this project, these accusations created great tension between Annan's commitment to human dignity and his deep loyalty to his staff and colleagues. Annan was torn between speaking out against the alleged abusers and protecting the organization by remaining loyal to its staff until an investigation could be completed. One of these advisers also indicated that Annan's perceived "foot dragging" with respect to removing Lubbers from office may also have reflected his reluctance to create a conflict before he had sufficient grounds to dismiss Lubbers.

More far-reaching in its scope and impact was the oil-for-food scandal, in which Saddam Hussein skimmed nearly $11 billion in illegal profits from the $64 billion program.[171] The scandal created an ethical cloud over the secretary-general because a yearlong investigation headed by Paul Volcker raised questions about Annan's personal involvement through the activities of his son, Kojo. The final report of Volcker's committee found that Annan "failed to curb corruption and mismanagement at the United Nations, but it did not find evidence to support charges that he improperly influenced the . . . program."[172] Specifically, the report faulted Annan for conducting only a cursory investigation when presented with information regarding the employment and lobbying activities of his son. Annan's misplaced trust in and loyalty to his son, and his penchant for efficiency, may have overridden his typically cautious nature in this case. The findings of the report were not as bad for the secretary-general as his supporters feared, and critics' calls for his resignation abated in the months that followed.[173] The findings were troubling nonetheless, and they hampered Annan's effectiveness as secretary-general for the remainder of his term.[174]

Conclusion

Although definitive conclusions on the impact of Annan's ethical framework on his actions in office await further analysis and reflection, it seems safe to say that Annan's personal values of human dignity and the peaceful resolution of conflict influenced his behavior and policy choices during his time in office. At the same time, it is clear that Annan's ethical framework was coupled with, and sometimes overshadowed by, the political realities of the crises the United Nations faced during his tenure. At times Annan was able to design a strategy that reconciled, or at least balanced, the ethical tradeoffs he faced. But this was not possible in all situations, and Annan, like his predecessors, experienced his share of frustration in cases where the vicissitudes of international politics permitted human suffering and conflict to persist.

Unfortunately, the final years of his second term were a difficult time for Annan. In his end-of-the-year press conference in 2005, Annan cited the tsunami in Southeast Asia, Lebanon, Darfur, and the oil-for-food scandal, among other things, when he observed: "It was both a difficult year for the world and, obviously, for me and the Organization."[175] Author

Simon Chesterman challenged Annan's once-vaulted status as a "secular pope": "Stalin famously underestimated the power of the pope by asking how many military divisions he commanded. The Secretary-General, Nobel Peace Prize notwithstanding, knows that he commands no divisions. The problem, as the UN celebrates a grim 60th birthday, is that he now also lacks a congregation."[176] Furthermore, these difficulties weakened the moral authority of the secretary-general in the eyes of some UN observers. At the same press conference, a reporter ventured, "One of the most important things that the Office of the Secretary-General has, the most sacred thing, is high moral authority. The Office of the Secretary-General has taken a lot of beating in the last year. What is it that you can do and ask your advisors to do in order to elevate it back to the position so that your moral voice is heard across the world?"[177] Annan did not dispute the reporter's assessment of his diminished moral authority but replied, "Obviously we need to press ahead and do the important work that is ahead of us, and speak out when we have to." At the end of this press conference, Annan indicated that he was "raring to go next year." It remains to future historians to judge whether he was able to get his congregation back.

Notes

1. UN Press Release GA/9212, December 18, 1996.

2. Klaus Brinkbäumer, "The Campaign Against Kofi," *Spiegel Online,* December 7, 2004, available at www.spiegel.de/international/spiegel/0,1518,331280,00 .html.

3. Norwegian Nobel Committee, "The Nobel Peace Prize 2001," October 12, 2001, available at http://nobelprize.org/peace/laureates/2001/press.html.

4. Quoted in Gregory A. Maniatis, "On Top of the World," *New York Magazine,* November 19, 2001, 44.

5. Quoted in Stanley Meisler, "Man in the Middle: Travels with Kofi Annan," *Smithsonian,* January 2003, 35.

6. The legacies of these events will be explored in more detail below. They have been covered extensively in the media. For example, see Maniatis, "On Top of the World"; Meisler, "Man in the Middle"; Philip Gourevitch, "The Optimist: Kofi Annan's U.N. Has Never Been More Important or More Imperiled," *New Yorker,* March 3, 2003; David Usborne, "The Forceful Peacemaker: Kofi Annan, United Nations Secretary-General," *Independent,* December 19, 1998; James Traub, "Kofi Annan's Next Test," *New York Times Magazine,* March 29, 1998; David

Rieff, "Up the Organization: The Successful Failures of Kofi Annan," *New Republic,* February 1, 1999.

7. The impact of these events will also be explored in more detail below. Media coverage includes Melinda Henneberger, "Weight of the World," *Newsweek,* May 26, 2003; and Meryl Gordon, "No Peace for Kofi: A Father's Burden," *New York Magazine,* May 2, 2005.

8. Courtney B. Smith, "More Secretary or General? Effective Leadership at the United Nations," *International Politics* 40 (2003): 141–47.

9. Quoted in Linda Fasulo, *An Insider's Guide to the UN* (New Haven, CT: Yale University Press, 2004), 17.

10. Quoted in Benjamin Rivlin, "The Changing International Political Climate and the Secretary-General," in *The Challenging Role of the UN Secretary-General: Making "The Most Impossible Job in the World" Possible,* ed. Benjamin Rivlin and Leon Gordenker (Westport, CT: Praeger, 1993), 3.

11. Fasulo, *Insider's Guide,* 19–20.

12. Maniatis, "On Top of the World," 46.

13. William Shawcross, *Deliver Us from Evil: Peacekeepers, Warlords and a World of Endless Conflict* (New York: Simon and Schuster, 2000), 26.

14. For a discussion of the concepts of inner code and external code as applied to the secretary-general, see the first two chapters in this volume.

15. Drawn from Joshua Cooper Ramo, "The Five Virtues of Kofi Annan," *Time,* September 4, 2000, 42. His use of the term "moral compass" seems to be very consistent with the definition of "ethical framework" used in this volume.

16. These interviews were conducted in New York City in May and June 2005. The following individuals agreed to be thanked in a footnote: Michael Doyle, former assistant secretary-general and special advisor for strategic planning; Kieran Prendergast, undersecretary-general for political affairs; Robert Orr, assistant secretary-general for policy planning; Lamin Sise, director for legal affairs and human rights in the executive office of the secretary-general; Gillian Sorensen, former assistant secretary-general for external relations; and Patrick Hayford, director for African affairs in the executive office of the secretary-general. I am grateful for their contribution to this research, although none of them bears responsibility for my conclusions.

17. Quoted in Henneberger, "Weight of the World," 35.

18. Brinkbäumer, "Campaign Against Kofi."

19. Henneberger, "Weight of the World," 35.

20. Traub, "Kofi Annan's Next Test," 44.

21. Maniatis, "On Top of the World," 45; Traub, "Kofi Annan's Next Test," 50.

22. See Shawcross, *Deliver Us from Evil,* 32, 250; the comment is repeated in both Ramo, "Five Virtues," 39, and Henneberger, "Weight of the World," 37.

23. Shawcross, *Deliver Us from Evil,* 218; Meisler, "Man in the Middle," 37; Traub, "Kofi Annan's Next Test," 49.

24. Traub, "Kofi Annan's Next Test," 49.

25. See Shawcross, *Deliver Us from Evil,* 34, 218, 250, for the description of Annan; see Gourevitch, "Optimist," 58, for the description of the school.

26. Religion Counts, *Religion and Public Policy at the UN* (Washington, DC: Religion Counts, 2002), 36; Annan is also identified as Anglican in Gordon, "No Peace for Kofi," 42, and in two of the interviews conducted for this study.

27. Gourevitch, "Optimist," 58.

28. Shawcross, *Deliver Us from Evil,* 218–19.

29. Henneberger, "Weight of the World," 35.

30. Ramo, "Five Virtues," 42.

31. Gourevitch, "Optimist," 52.

32. UN Press Release SG/SM/9286, May 3, 2004.

33. Quoted in Ian Williams, "Kofi Annan: A 'Moral Voice,'" *The Nation,* June 19, 2000, 20.

34. Ramo, "Five Virtues," 36, 39.

35. UN Press Release SG/SM/7136 and GA/9596, September 20, 1999.

36. Ramo, "Five Virtues," 37; Ian Johnstone, "The Role of the UN Secretary-General: The Power of Persuasion Based on Law," *Global Governance* 9 (2003): 450.

37. Williams, "Kofi Annan," 20; see also Shawcross, *Deliver Us from Evil,* 411–14.

38. See for example Gourevitch, "Optimist," and Williams, "Kofi Annan." Several of the UN officials interviewed for this report also discussed the impact of these events in relation to Kofi Annan's commitment to human dignity.

39. See, for example, Gourevitch, "Optimist," 61; and Traub, "Kofi Annan's Next Test," 49.

40. Ramo, "Five Virtues," 40.

41. These specific examples are drawn from ibid.; interviews by author, 2005.

42. Johnstone, "Role of the UN Secretary-General," 449.

43. See also Shawcross, *Deliver Us from Evil,* and Gourevitch, "Optimist."

44. Kofi Annan, "Nobel Lecture," December 10, 2001, available at http://nobelprize.org/peace/laureates/2001/annan-lecture.html.

45. Quoted in Shawcross, *Deliver Us from Evil,* 34.

46. Ibid., 269.

47. Traub, "Kofi Annan's Next Test," 47.

48. Rieff, "Up the Organization," 20.

49. Gourevitch, "Optimist," and interview by author, 2005. See also UN Press Release SG/SM/9286, May 3, 2004.

50. Quoted in Shawcross, *Deliver Us from Evil,* 321.

51. Quoted in Usborne, "Forceful Peacemaker," 5.

52. Quoted in Shawcross, *Deliver Us from Evil,* 275–76.

53. Quoted in Ramo, "Five Virtues," 38.

54. Gourevitch, "Optimist," 61.

55. Quoted in Meisler, "Man in the Middle," 36.

56. For a recent review of this vast literature, see Kent J. Kille and Roger M. Scully, "Executive Heads and the Role of Intergovernmental Organizations: Expansionist Leadership in the United Nations and the European Union," *Political Psychology* 24 (2003): 175–98.

57. Leland M. Goodrich, "The Political Role of the Secretary-General," in *The United Nations Political System,* ed. David A. Kay (New York: John Wiley & Sons, 1967), 136–37.

58. Shawcross, *Deliver Us from Evil,* 217, 250; Fasulo, *Insider's Guide,* 19; Ramo, "Five Virtues," 37.

59. Traub, "Kofi Annan's Next Test," 48; Gourevitch, "Optimist," 50.

60. Ramo, "Five Virtues," 40.

61. Usborne, "Forceful Peacemaker," 5.

62. Henneberger, "Weight of the World," 33.

63. Gordon, "No Peace for Kofi," 47.

64. Traub, "Kofi Annan's Next Test," 47.

65. Quoted in Maniatis, "On Top of the World," 44.

66. Ibid. (Pendergrast); Gourevitch, "Optimist," 70 (Abi-Saab).

67. Henneberger, "Weight of the World," 37; and Williams, "Kofi Annan," 22.

68. See, for example, Traub, "Kofi Annan's Next Test," 47; Fasulo, *Insider's Guide,* 28; Williams, "Kofi Annan," 21.

69. Henneberger, "Weight of the World," 34.

70. Gourevitch, "Optimist," 58.

71. Traub, "Kofi Annan's Next Test," 49–50; Maniatis, "On Top of the World," 45.

72. Maniatis, "On Top of the World," 45.

73. Meisler, "Man in the Middle," 36; Maniatis, "On Top of the World," 47.

74. Quoted in Traub, "Kofi Annan's Next Test," 50.

75. Quoted in Henneberger, "Weight of the World," 36–37.

76. Meisler, "Man in the Middle," 33.

77. Quoted in Brinkbäumer, "The Campaign Against Kofi."

78. See Gourevitch, "Optimist;" Henneberger, "Weight of the World;" Brinkbäumer, "Campaign Against Kofi."

79. Quoted in Meisler, "Man in the Middle," 37. The story also appears in Shawcross, *Deliver Us from Evil,* 218.

80. Ramo, "Five Virtues," 39; Shawcross, *Deliver Us from Evil,* 217.

81. Traub, "Kofi Annan's Next Test," 48, 50.

82. For example, see Brinkbäumer, "The Campaign Against Kofi"; and Ramo, "Five Virtues," 42.

83. Henneberger, "Weight of the World," 34. Additional examples of situations in which his calm nature was breached can be found in Meisler, "Man in the

Middle," 38; Traub, "Kofi Annan's Next Test," 81; and Shawcross, *Deliver Us from Evil*, 273.

84. Quoted in Maniatis, "On Top of the World," 45.

85. Gourevitch, "Optimist," 60. See Usborne, "Forceful Peacemaker," 5, for a similar statement.

86. Quoted in Maniatis, "On Top of the World," 45; see also Gourevitch, "Optimist," 66.

87. Gourevitch, "Optimist," 66.

88. Henneberger, "Weight of the World," 35.

89. Shawcross, *Deliver Us from Evil*, 292.

90. Gourevitch, "Optimist," 50.

91. Brinkbäumer, "The Campaign Against Kofi."

92. Henneberger, "Weight of the World," 35; Traub, "Kofi Annan's Next Test," 49.

93. Shawcross, *Deliver Us from Evil*, 223; Fasulo, *Insider's Guide*, 20.

94. For a detailed discussion of the charter articles and how successive secretaries-general have sought to expand them, see chapter 1 in this volume.

95. Quoted in Fasulo, *Insider's Guide*, 21.

96. Rivlin, "Changing International Political Climate," 17.

97. Leon Gordenker, "The UN Secretary-Generalship: Limits, Potentials, and Leadership," in Rivlin and Gordenker, *Challenging Role of the UN Secretary-General*, 277.

98. Robert W. Cox and Harold K. Jacobson, "The Framework for Inquiry," in *The Anatomy of Influence: Decisionmaking in International Organization*, ed. Robert W. Cox and Harold K. Jacobson (New Haven, CT: Yale University Press, 1973), 25–34.

99. Rivlin, "Changing International Political Climate," 6, 13.

100. For example, see the introduction to Thomas G. Weiss, David P. Forsythe, and Roger A. Coate, *The United Nations and Changing World Politics* (Boulder, CO: Westview Press, 2001), 1–18.

101. Rivlin, "Changing International Political Climate," 17.

102. Shawcross, *Deliver Us from Evil*, 220; Gourevitch, "Optimist."

103. Quoted in Gourevitch, "Optimist," 64.

104. Gordenker, "UN Secretary-Generalship," 266.

105. Smith, "More Secretary or General," 145.

106. For an overview of this relationship, see Courtney B. Smith, "The Politics of U.S.-UN Reengagement: Achieving Gains in a Hostile Environment," *International Studies Perspectives* 5 (2004): 197–215.

107. Shawcross, *Deliver Us from Evil*, 220.

108. Meisler, "Man in the Middle," 37.

109. Shawcross, *Deliver Us from Evil*, 182.

110. Ibid., 189, 222–23, 238.

111. Shawcross, *Deliver Us from Evil*, 237–40; Usborne, "Forceful Peacemaker," 5.

112. Traub, "Kofi Annan's Next Test," 47.

113. Rieff, "Up the Organization," 20.

114. Henneberger, "Weight of the World," 35.

115. Usborne, "Forceful Peacemaker," 5.

116. Quoted in Gourevitch, "Optimist," 54.

117. Brinkbäumer, "The Campaign Against Kofi."

118. Maniatis, "On Top of the World," 44; Fasulo, *Insider's Guide*, 29.

119. Quoted in Gourevitch, "Optimist," 56.

120. Maniatis, "On Top of the World," 44–45.

121. Gourevitch, "Optimist," 53.

122. Smith, "More Secretary or General," 142.

123. Shawcross, *Deliver Us from Evil*, 223.

124. Smith, "More Secretary or General," 142.

125. Usborne, "Forceful Peacemaker," 5; a similar argument is found in Traub, "Kofi Annan's Next Test," 47.

126. For example, see Brinkbäumer, "The Campaign Against Kofi;" interviews by author, 2005.

127. Maniatis, "On Top of the World," 45.

128. C. V. Narasimhan, *The United Nations: An Inside View* (New Delhi: Vikas Publishing House, 1988), 274.

129. Williams, "Kofi Annan," 20.

130. Traub, "Kofi Annan's Next Test," 44; Maniatis, "On Top of the World," 45; Shawcross, *Deliver Us from Evil*, 35.

131. Meisler, "Man in the Middle," 34.

132. Quoted in both Shawcross, *Deliver Us from Evil*, 34, and Gourevitch, "Optimist," 52.

133. Johnstone, "Role of the UN Secretary-General," 452.

134. "We the Peoples: The Role of the United Nations in the Twenty-First Century," Report of the Secretary-General to the Millennium Assembly, UN Document A/54/2000, March 27, 2000, par. 9.

135. "In Larger Freedom: Towards Development, Security, and Human Rights for All," Report of the Secretary-General for Consideration by Member States, UN Document A/59/2005, March 21, 2005, par. 4.

136. Philip Gourevitch, "Power Plays," *New Yorker*, December 13, 2004, 35.

137. Rieff, "Up the Organization," 21–22.

138. Meisler, "Man in the Middle," 38.

139. Shawcross, *Deliver Us from Evil*, 328, 34, 26, 411.

140. For an overview of the events leading up to the impasse, see Shawcross, *Deliver Us from Evil*, 259–65.

141. Traub, "Kofi Annan's Next Test," 48–49; Shawcross, *Deliver Us from Evil*, 264–66.

142. Quoted in Traub, "Kofi Annan's Next Test," 49.

143. Shawcross, *Deliver Us from Evil*, 264; Traub, "Kofi Annan's Next Test," 48–49.

144. See Gourevitch, "Optimist," for an overview of the period before the invasion of Iraq in March 2003.

145. Meisler, "Man in the Middle," 35.

146. For an overview of this period, see James Traub, "The Next Resolution," *New York Times Magazine*, April 13, 2005, 50–53.

147. Henneberger, "Weight of the World," 36.

148. Ibid., 33.

149. Brinkbäumer, "The Campaign Against Kofi."

150. Ibid.

151. Interview by author, 2005.

152. Henneberger, "Weight of the World," 34.

153. Brinkbäumer, "The Campaign Against Kofi."

154. Background information on the conflict in the Sudan and Darfur can be found at the website for the United Nations Mission in the Sudan (UNMIS), www.un.org/Depts/dpko/missions/unmis/background.html.

155. Annan's desire to see the United Nations do more in regard to Darfur was a central theme in four of the personal interviews conducted as part of this project.

156. International Commission on Intervention and State Sovereignty, *The Responsibility to Protect* (Ottawa, Canada: International Development Research Centre, 2001).

157. For this and the preceding insights, I am indebted to my interviews with former UN staffers, conducted in 2005.

158. The report of the Commission of Inquiry is contained in UN Document S/2005/60, February 1, 2005; see also UN Security Council Resolution 1706, adopted on August 31, 2006.

159. See the Security Council Report, *Monthly Report for October 2006*, September 28, 2006, 3–5. This report is also available at www.securitycouncilreport.org.

160. Two UN officials told me about the internal debates concerning Annan's travel to the region. One mentioned that the fate of Dag Hammarskjöld, who died in a plane crash while traveling in the Congo in 1961, was in the back of everyone's minds.

161. A. Leroy Bennett and James K. Oliver, *International Organizations: Principles and Issues* (Upper Saddle River, NJ: Prentice-Hall, 2002), 297.

162. Johnstone, "Role of the UN Secretary-General," 452.

163. "We the Peoples," par. 45.

164. UN Document A/RES/55/2, September 18, 2000.

165. Barbara Slavin, "Bolton Dives Right in to Effort to the Change U.N." *USA Today*, September 12, 2005.

166. Warren Hoge, "Bolton Makes His Case at U.N. for a New Focus for Aid Projects," *New York Times,* September 1, 2005.

167. Information on this backlash can be found in "Crunch Time for UN Reform," *Economist,* August 31, 2005; and Evelyn Leopold, "U.S. Offers Compromise Language on UN Summit Goals," Reuters, September 6, 2005.

168. The World Summit Final Outcome Document is UN Document A/RES/60/1, October 24, 2005.

169. Major reports on reform released during Annan's tenure include "Renewing the United Nations: A Programme for Reform," Report of the Secretary-General, UN Document A/51/950, July 14, 1997; "We the Peoples"; "Strengthening the United Nations: An Agenda for Further Change," Report of the Secretary-General, UN Document A/57/387, September 9, 2002; "In Larger Freedom."

170. "In Larger Freedom."

171. For an overview of the oil-for-food program and the findings of the investigative committee headed by Paul Volker, see Warren Hoge, "Annan Failed to Curb Corruption in Iraq's Oil-for-Food Program, Investigators Report," *New York Times,* September 7, 2005.

172. Ibid.

173. Warren Hoge, "Some Question Annan's Viability at U.N." *New York Times,* March 31, 2005.

174. See, for example, Annan's end-of-the-year press conference for 2005, contained in UN Document SG/SM/10280, December 21, 2005.

175. Ibid.

176. Simon Chesterman, "Duty Pulls Annan in Two Directions," *International Herald Tribune,* September 9, 2005.

177. UN Document SG/SM/10280, December 21, 2005.

10

THE SECULAR POPE

Insights on the UN Secretary-General and
Moral Authority

KENT J. KILLE

This concluding chapter provides a comparative analysis of the secretaries-general. The chapter looks back across the individual case studies to examine the components of the officeholders' ethical frameworks and whether, in conjunction with external contextual considerations, the role played by the secretaries-general was shaped accordingly. This comparison demonstrates the variation that exists across the officeholders in terms of the core personal values that they possess, how these values combine to create the overarching ethical framework, and the degree to which mapping these frameworks leads to a better understanding of their tenures. The chapter concludes with an evaluation of the ethical framework model and the implications for the moral authority of the secretary-general, as well as the study of religious and ethical dimensions of leadership in international affairs more broadly.

Comparing the Ethical Frameworks of the Secretaries-General

Each case study chapter in this volume examines the ethical framework of a secretary-general and the implications for that officeholder's handling of the job. In comparing these case studies, it is useful to revisit the dimensions of the proposed analytical approach (as summarized in figure 1.1) in order to address a series of related questions. What inner code of religious and moral values made up each secretary-general's ethical framework? What environmental and experiential factors informed the development of this ethical framework? How decisive were the personal religious and moral values in terms of the decisions made in office? To what degree did the interaction between ethical framework and external context shape the decision-making process? How did these ethical frameworks change, if at all, over the term of office? In carrying out such a review, the stage is set for considering how well the approach provides a useful analytical roadmap for exploring important variation across the officeholders and generating insights on the secretary-general as a moral authority.

The Inner Code of Religious and Moral Values

As noted in chapter 1, previous analyses have indicated that there should be an interesting degree of variation among the religious beliefs of the secretaries-general. The case studies here bear out this presupposition. Although all but one of the secretaries-general—the Buddhist U Thant—adhered to the Christian faith, the particular denominations varied from Lutherans Trygve Lie and Dag Hammarskjöld, Catholics Kurt Waldheim and Javier Perez de Cuellar, the Coptic Boutros Boutros-Ghali, and the Anglican Kofi Annan.

As we have seen, however, mere religious labels do not necessarily determine any given officeholder's religious values. Although Lie and Hammarskjöld grew up in neighboring Norway and Sweden, their Lutheranism differed in significant ways. Likewise, as Hammarskjöld's interest in medieval mysticism and other spiritual influences demonstrates, the personal values of individual officeholders often came from religious influences outside their formal faith traditions. A similar pattern is noted in the case of Thant, who was attracted to the work of a range of spiritual thinkers, and in Boutros-Ghali's connection with the teachings of Louis Massignon. Boutros-Ghali's Coptic Christian minority status in Egypt also demonstrates the potential broader implications of religion within a particular cultural context, while the discussion of Annan's religious values raises intriguing questions about his exposure to tribal influences in Ghana and the ways in which they may have interacted with his Christian beliefs.

The case studies also make it apparent that analysis should be extended beyond religion to consider the broader moral values of the secretaries-general. The seven occupants of the office examined here varied according to how important religion was to their lives, and in several cases other moral values were more central to their ethical frameworks. The most "devout" secretaries-general appear to be Hammarskjöld, Thant, and Annan, a conclusion that reinforces previous work on these men. Yet the analysis of Waldheim also emphasizes the importance of his Catholic beliefs.

As the example of Waldheim illustrates, however, even if religion is important on a personal level, conscious efforts can be made to separate religious values from political considerations. Rieffer-Flanagan and Forsythe note for Perez de Cuellar that, "unlike Kurt Waldheim, he did not attend Mass regularly or partake systematically of other Catholic rituals," yet, interestingly, both men shared a proclivity for separating personal religious beliefs from the public political realm. Rieffer-Flanagan and Forsythe conclude that religion was not of central importance to Perez de Cuellar in the way that it was to Waldheim. This is also the case with Lie and Boutros-Ghali—although none of these men repudiated their religious upbringing. Rather, the analyses indicate that religious tradition was not as crucial for them in comparison to other officeholders. Boutros-Ghali retained some important connections to the Coptic Church and, as Lang notes, he did not suffer from "any crisis of faith or belief." For "practical reasons," however, among them the pressure of other duties, he did not make religious practice a central focus of his life.

Religious and moral values were at times perceived as closely connected. Some of the authors argue that it was difficult to separate the moral and religious dimensions of an officeholder's overall ethical framework. For example, Smith's analysis of Annan centers on two values—concern for human dignity and commitment to the peaceful resolution of conflict—which, he argues, can be derived from both Annan's spiritual grounding and his moral stance. Other cases tell a more complex tale, such as the three-part structure of Hammarskjöld's values mapped out by Lyon (see figure 4.1), which combines religious and moral considerations.

In the case of other secretaries-general, the line between religious and moral categories is clearer. Boutros-Ghali's belief in tolerance and the importance of forgiveness and reconciliation are viewed as connected to his Coptic standing in Egyptian society, while an emphasis on human rights, the centrality of the state, and democracy are broader moral considerations derived from other sources. Even for Lie and Perez de Cuellar, religious thought may have translated into broader moral values. Lie's religious values apparently remained intact in his personal life, and according to Muldoon probably "gave him a moral vocabulary that he could and would employ throughout his life, personally and professionally"—but they were largely "subsumed" under his secular moral values in relation to the political realm. Similarly, Perez de Cuellar's "essentially secular" personal values may still be a "by-product" of his religious roots, although this conclusion must remain at the level of conjecture.

Clearly there are both similarities and differences between the ethical frameworks of the various secretaries-general. A concern for justice is part of the ethical frameworks of Lie, Hammarskjöld, and Perez de Cuellar. Thant's "humility" and Perez de Cuellar's "modesty" appear to be similar, while the two also share personal values that are often related to a secretary-general's moral standing: Thant's integrity and Perez de Cuellar's impartiality. The latter's sense of equity, fairness, and equality is echoed in Lie's fairness and equality and in Hammarskjöld's neutrality and equality. Lie and Perez de Cuellar, along with Boutros-Ghali, also valued human rights deeply (although Perez de Cuellar's devotion to this value evolved and was strengthened during his time in office) and shared a commitment to and respect for law. Boutros-Ghali extended this legal commitment into specific support for the centrality of the state and democracy. The two core values of Annan, human dignity and peaceful resolution of conflict, were shared by Lie (dignity) and Hammarskjöld and Perez de Cuellar (peace). Hammarskjöld's self-sacrifice and service and Perez de Cuellar's commitment to service and duty over personal achievement, along with Thant's "service over self," are also related concepts, while Lie also drew from his mother "an appreciation for hard work, self-sacrifice, and service to others." Finally, although not as central to either analysis, Hammarskjöld's support of economic opportunity resonates well with Perez de Cuellar's promotion of the well-being of the poor and disadvantaged.

Moral value dimensions that appear as more distinct among the officeholders include Thant's equanimity, along with his simplicity and detachment, which in part relate to his Buddhist ideals. Although not so far removed from the humanitarian concerns of other secretaries-general, Boutros-Ghali's particular emphasis on tolerance and reconciliation, which relates to his Coptic Christian minority experience, also stands out. The degree of Waldheim's "pragmatism" seems to be distinct among the seven men.[1] Kuchinsky considers additional potential values as part of Waldheim's ethical framework that resonate with the other secretaries-general —including a focus on dignity, a desire to relieve human suffering, and tolerance for other peoples—but his findings emphasize the pragmatic aspect.

The Development of a Secretary-General's Ethical Framework

The initial research framework proposed a range of potential factors that could influence the development of a secretary-general's personal values: environmental factors—including religious tradition, education, culture, and family upbringing—and personal history and experience. All of the secretaries-general grew up in a particular religious tradition, but the lasting impact of this tradition was a more important part of some ethical frameworks than of others. In addition, the religious tradition dimension was sometimes connected to cultural considerations and family upbringing and how these imparted religious values.

Other aspects of culture and family shed additional light on the personal values of the secretaries-general. The case studies note distinctive aspects of culture across countries that had a lasting impact on the ethical framework. For example, Hammarskjöld's commitment to neutrality is linked in part to his Swedish upbringing, and the notion of "making the way" is connected to Waldheim's "Austrian-ness." At the same time, growing up within a particular country and culture did not guide the development of all the secretaries-general. Notable in this respect is Perez de Cuellar, who was oriented toward French culture and a traditional, European-style Catholic perspective, regardless of his South American roots in Peru, which could have influenced him toward a liberation theology approach.

The impact of family upbringing was clear for most of the secretaries-general, with the analyses of Lie and Hammarskjöld placing a particular emphasis on this dimension and Boutros-Ghali's very name demonstrating the lasting legacy of his family. An interesting extension of this concerns the approach to family that the secretaries-general themselves took. Comparing the early officeholders is revealing in this regard, as Lie was shown to be a devoted family man, while Thant was committed to an intensive work schedule despite his wife's apparent isolation, and Hammarskjöld took the emphasis on work to the extreme, remaining a lifelong bachelor and focusing solely on his professional duties.

As Jones notes in chapter 2, the secretaries-general share a high level of educational achievement; five of the seven possessed law degrees. This legal training dimension was touched on in some of these cases, but the clearest link was seen in the analysis of Boutros-Ghali—where Lang argued that, along with Coptic Christian minority status, the study of law was a core influence on the development of Boutros-Ghali's personal values. Given that Boutros-Ghali himself claimed that "studying international law and human rights makes one a liberal, whether that is in Paris or Cairo," and that liberal thinking was held by many of the officeholders, it could be important to investigate this dimension more closely to determine whether it had a greater impact on him than it did on the other

secretaries-general. Particular educational experiences are also emphasized, such as Annan's time in a Christian boarding school in Ghana and
his time completing an undergraduate degree in the United States, which
Smith connects to Annan's commitment to diplomacy and negotiation.

Experiential factors also played a part in shaping the ethical frameworks of the different secretaries-general. To begin with, generational
experiences can be considered. Jones suggests in chapter 2 that Lie,
Hammarskjöld, Thant, and Waldheim were all affected by their experience of living and working through World War II. In his study of Lie,
Muldoon certainly emphasizes Lie's diplomatic experiences during the
war. Waldheim's questionable record in relation to the Nazis is another
potential focus, but Kuchinsky also moves beyond this to consider the
broader impact that the war had on Waldheim's development. In the cases
of Hammarskjöld and Thant, however, the war does not seem to have
played such a formative role.[2] In addition, a common set of generational
experiences does not appear to bind together the other secretaries-general
from the postwar era.

On an individual level, the case studies display a range of personal history and experiences that influenced the shape of officeholders' ethical
frameworks. The political careers and engagements of the individuals,
including early political experiences, are a common theme. For example,
Lie's development in the "rough and tumble of local Norwegian politics"
can be contrasted with Hammarskjöld's elite political family background.
At times ethical dimensions were reinforced by experiences that occurred
before ascending to the secretary-generalship. For instance, Smith notes
that Annan's focus on human dignity can be related to the terrible failures
of UN peacekeeping in the 1990s, but he also observes that this focus may
have been shaped by Annan's experience with the American civil rights
movement in the 1960s.

Impact on the Role Played by the Secretary-General

With the research question central to this study—does the ethical framework of an individual officeholder impact the role played by a secretary-
general of the United Nations?—in mind, it is necessary to move beyond
considering variation in personal values and the development of officeholders' ethical frameworks and examine the impact demonstrated in the
case studies. Reviewing the analyses of the different officeholders reveals a
variety of interpretations in this regard. At times, specific personal values

and their influence are targeted—the most explicit effort in this respect is Lang's discussion of the principles that informed Boutros-Ghali's initiatives (see table 8.1). More generally, the analyses differ in their conclusions over the centrality of an officeholder's ethical framework for understanding how the individual handled the office. Rieffer-Flanagan and Forsythe argue most directly that they cannot draw clear connections between Perez de Cuellar's ethical framework and his approach as secretary-general. This stands in stark contrast to claims such as Lyon's that her study "confirms several places where Hammarskjöld drew on his ethical framework and found moral mandates for his actions, his policy agenda, and even his relations with UN member states."

However, Lyon is at pains to acknowledge, as are the other contributors, that drawing a direct link between an officeholder's ethical framework and the role he played as secretary-general is an arduous task. While this distinction will be considered further below, overall the case studies present an intriguing indication that understanding officeholders' religious and moral values often does provide important insights into their time as secretary-general. Lie's ethical framework helped give him the strength to handle difficult situations and guided his activities, and the precedents he put into place for his successors, while in office. Thant provides an example of "Buddhism in action," along with the related dimensions of his ethical framework, across his tenure. The Waldheim "enigma" is clarified through the lens of pragmatic moral consideration. By employing Boutros-Ghali's personal values in an analysis of his time in office, we get a better understanding of when and where different dimensions come into play. Annan's balancing act is guided to a great degree by his personal values. Even in the case of Perez de Cuellar, the consideration of external context is more closely revealed in conjunction with his inner code.

The cases also demonstrate that similar findings regarding the overall importance of a secretary-general's ethical framework hold across a range of issue areas, including security, economic, social, and administrative concerns. However, it is also important to note the more nuanced distinctions regarding the type of problem being addressed, as several of the analyses do. This is the approach taken in considering Boutros-Ghali's tenure. The impact of different levels of his ethical framework are traced for Hammarskjöld, as well, and a series of pragmatism indicators are tracked in the Waldheim case. Such distinctions indicate that particular ethical framework dimensions may matter more in relation to some areas than others.

A core theme of this volume is how officeholders handle the ethical dilemmas with which they are faced. In chapter 1 a series of dilemmas were noted—taking a normative stand versus seeking support from states, speaking out strongly versus protecting the office, taking a principled stand versus operating on a pragmatic basis, and accomplishing a mission versus staff security—in order to illustrate such potential areas. The analysis of Annan directly notes the definite presence and need to act in relation to all four of these dilemmas. These dilemmas were also revealed to be prevalent considerations across the tenures of the different secretaries-general. Dorn's analysis, built around seven dilemmas Thant faced, includes these four categories and extends the analysis further in directions that are apparent in other cases as well. In particular, the dilemma of the competing views of the proper role of the secretary-general—which Dorn captures as independent versus dependent office—is highlighted across the officeholders' tenures. This dimension is also stressed by Jones in a section of chapter 2 titled "Whose Servants?" and is a central consideration in the Lie case study, as Lie was the first secretary-general to face this "core dilemma." In Hammarskjöld's case, the acceptance of the office itself was perceived as a difficult dilemma.

Interaction with External Context

A further concern of this volume is how a secretary-general's ethical framework might interact with external context to guide decision making. Given the focus on moral authority, three particular dimensions were incorporated into the model: UN charter principles, the external code presented in the international realm, and role expectations for the secretary-general. One cannot consider an ethical framework in isolation and arrive at a full understanding of the decisions made by a secretary-general. In fact, a strong emphasis on the interaction between ethical framework and external context for understanding the role played by the secretary-general emerges across the cases. For a secretary-general guided by pragmatism, such as Waldheim, external cues are inherently useful for understanding his performance as secretary-general, but even officeholders who brought a stronger personal ethical vision to the office found themselves balancing their perspective with contextual pressures or expectations.

UN charter principles were drawn upon by all of the secretaries-general in conjunction with their personal values. For some, the connection between the charter and personal values was a vital consideration.

Rieffer-Flanagan and Forsythe point to the difficulty of differentiating between Perez de Cuellar's personal values and the norms contained in the charter because of the overlap between the two. Yet there does appear to be an interaction between the two, as the "moral statement" that Perez de Cuellar perceived in the charter informed and reinforced his personal inner code. This process is explicitly drawn out in chapter 4, where Lyon argues that the charter values served as an important basis for Hammarskjöld's ethical framework in conjunction with preexisting religious and moral influences (see the overlap illustrated in figure 4.2). Similarly, Smith argues that Annan's personal values connect well with the charter, thereby supporting the balance that Annan felt between his internal code and the external code presented by UN principles, and Muldoon observes that Lie's personal values and the charter ideals were "entwined." This overlap is not restricted to the six Christian secretaries-general, as Dorn also maps how well charter provisions mesh with Buddhist concepts (see table 5.1). At the same time, we might raise the question of whether the personal values of future officeholders from non-Christian backgrounds will fit so well with the orientation of the United Nations and the organization's charter.

Apart from the United Nations and its charter, secretaries-general can also draw upon the more general external code present in the international community. While these principles can provide further guidance to a secretary-general, many of the case analyses note that the underlying reality of power politics cannot be ignored. Jones's historical treatment in chapter 2 demonstrates how concerns of power and interest shaped the existing principles and guided the affairs of international organization, and this dimension has continued to be prevalent throughout the first six decades of UN leadership. As Lang phrases it in his study of Boutros-Ghali, "at times his ethical framework was overridden by the demands of power politics." For Annan this meant a particular emphasis on the relationship between the secretary-general and the powerful United States, while other cases identified a broader range of considerations for this dimension. The chapter on Perez de Cuellar, for example, emphasizes the dominant role of Great Power politics and discusses Cold War dynamics and the change in context brought about by the end of the Cold War.

All of the secretaries-general took into account what role they were expected to play. But because the role expectations are not spelled out exactly, each secretary-general has been able to bring his personal values to bear in interpreting these expectations. Hammarskjöld, for example, appeared to bring his own personal values to the role quite forcefully, whereas Waldheim accepted what Kuchinsky refers to as "the constraining environment of public service," and Annan endeavored to balance competing expectations in conjunction with his personal values.

A final consideration is whether the interaction between ethical framework and external context while a secretary-general formulated decisions provided feedback that altered his ethical framework. The case results do not provide a consistent answer to this question. The analysis of Hammarskjöld details the dynamic nature of his ethical framework, in particular as it developed in conjunction with UN principles after he took office. Similarly, Rieffer-Flanagan and Forsythe suggest that the longer Perez de Cuellar served as secretary-general, the more he internalized the liberalism inherent in the charter. Yet Lie pointed in his resignation speech, quoted in chapter 3, to the potential need for a new secretary-general "who could enter the work fresh and with fewer fixed ideas," indicating a lack of dynamic change on his own part. The Annan case study emphasizes how the personal values that informed his activities as secretary-general were in place long before he took office and remained consistent throughout his tenure. Boutros-Ghali's and Thant's ethical frameworks remained grounded solely on their preexisting values and showed little change over the course of their time in office. While Waldheim's pragmatism led him to take into account contextual cues for his decision making, this did not call for an adjustment of his personal values. In chapter 1 it was also suggested that actions undertaken by officeholders based on their ethical frameworks might in turn alter the external code in the international arena. While several of the secretaries-general did encourage reforms in how their office and the larger organization operate, we can show no unmistakable evidence of this broader effect.

Implications for the Secretary-General and Moral Authority

The analytical approach developed for this study provides a helpful roadmap for exploring variations between the secretaries-general regarding their personal values and related differences in the handling of the office. As such, this study holds important implications for examining the moral authority of the secretary-general. At the same time, one must be cautious about tracing a direct connection between an ethical framework and specific decisions made by a secretary-general. In part this is due to the difficult nature of clearly establishing when and how secretaries-general draw upon personal values. As Dorn notes in his analysis of Thant, the "precise influence of religion in specific situations is sometimes difficult to discern," because Thant, like other secretaries-general, "did not explain his official decisions using religious reasoning." Even a deeply spiritual thinker like Thant was very hesitant to express these views in a public forum. The same is true when it comes to moral values and the explicit use of moral reasoning. After all, the secretary-general operates in a secular organization composed of countries with a wide array of religious and cultural mores, and wants to be viewed as impartial on this score.

This separation is on display in Annan's reluctance to be questioned regarding his personal values—he declined Smith's request and generally sought to avoid the subject in other interviews—while still in office, whereas all other living secretaries-general willingly discussed their beliefs and principles with the authors. The related complexity of portraying Annan's values is captured by the difficulty encountered in unambiguously identifying the exact religious practices to which Annan adheres. Imagine attempting to study the impact of Hammarskjöld's personal values while he was still in office, without the benefit of the perspective afforded by the published personal accounts of those close to him and, especially, access to his inner thoughts as expressed in *Markings*.[3] With officeholders' personal values largely kept private, the subsequent effects are correspondingly difficult to track. Thus, for the latest secretary-general, Ban Ki-moon, establishing the dimensions of his ethical framework and the impact on his handling of the office will require very careful probing and analysis.

In fact, as has been stressed throughout this volume, establishing a direct link between a secretary-general's personal values and his conduct in office is an inherently difficult task. As Jones indicated with respect to President Carter, "When analysis turns outward to action instead of inward to belief, the connection between the two eludes easy explanation." The contributors to this volume have done their best to be objective in relating religious and moral values to decision making, but we must acknowledge the degree of subjective interpretation inherent in any such undertaking. As Muldoon put it in a contributors' planning meeting, each contributor had to make a certain "leap of faith" in this regard, and the tone of the chapters often reflects this. Given such complexities, as Rieffer-Flanagan and Forsythe put it, "We think it unwise to try to formulate sweeping generalizations about the moral authority of particular secretaries-general."

A further consideration in evaluating the impact of religious and moral values is the influence of context. This is a key part of Rieffer-Flanagan and Forsythe's hesitance regarding the relevance of Perez de Cuellar's ethical framework, and they therefore conclude that personal values are secondary to external political considerations in understanding his tenure. Even in cases where a more robust argument is made for the importance of personal values, there is also a caveat regarding the relative importance of political considerations, such as Smith's finding that "Annan's ethical framework was coupled with, and sometimes overshadowed by, the political realities of the crises the United Nations faced during his tenure."

As Smith suggests, however, it is often the interaction of an ethical framework with external context, rather than the influence of external factors alone, that counts. Jones conveys this in her conception of the inner code held by officeholders as a "kind of spiritual filter" that helps to guide their interpretation of the context in which they are operating. For example, Perez de Cuellar's understanding of the confines of his office was not necessarily the same as Thant's understanding, which was different again from Waldheim's, and so on.

Overall, the studies in this volume conclude that religion and morality do play a part in shaping the secretaries-general and how they handle the office. The connection is more explicit in some cases than in others. However, as a potentially important component of understanding a secretary-general's time in office, it is worth tracing the ethical framework components and how these developed. What conclusions can be drawn from this volume regarding the personal value dimensions that analysts should consider for future officeholders?

In regard to religious values, no nonreligious individual has yet held the office, but even when officeholders have possessed a strong faith, religion is not always connected to decision-making tendencies. However, there is a noted inclination in this direction, with Waldheim the only exception among the religiously oriented officeholders. For Boutros-Ghali, religion did play an important role in developing his personal values, but more from the experience of being a religious minority than from the tenets of his religion itself. Religion does not appear as centrally in the ethical frameworks of Lie or Perez de Cuellar. While neither man repudiated his religious upbringing, and in both cases there was a potential connection between religion and ethical framework, their lives did not closely incorporate religious pursuits. In the end, the argument that religion would greatly affect leadership for all secretaries-general does not hold true. Finally, although all seven officeholders had different religious values despite the common link of Christianity (with the exception of Thant), this could change in the future if the secretary-general is an individual possessing a strong adherence to a different spiritual tradition. This might have taken place with Annan's successor, when the rotation of the office returned to Asia for the first time since Thant. With the selection of the South Korean Ban, however, reports indicate that he "describes himself as a 'non-denominational Christian.'"[4]

Although many of the moral values discussed in this volume were shared by the secretaries-general, we found no distinctive pattern of shared values between particular officeholders. Instead, these values were combined in different ways to underpin the overall ethical framework. There were relatively few moral values that were held by only one secretary-general. In the case of the Buddhist Thant and the Coptic Christian minority Boutros-Ghali, the distinctive aspects of their ethical frameworks may be related to their unique beliefs and experiences in comparison to the other officeholders.

In tracing the development of the different ethical frameworks, no specific pattern was uncovered. All of the proposed influences were on display, but the exact mix of factors varied in each case. Even when secretaries-general had similar values, they often did not emanate from the same source. This suggests that it is important to explore all of these dimensions carefully when considering a secretary-general's personal values, but not to expect each factor to affect their development equally. Similarly, while it is possible to observe a feedback loop for some officeholders that altered their ethical frameworks over the course of their tenure, this was not an important consideration for all of the secretaries-general.

Did any of the case studies reveal potential lessons that might be useful in considering other secretaries-general? Many of the officeholders shared a background in law, but, as we have seen, this seemed to have a decisive influence only on the development of Boutros-Ghali's personal values. Is this an equally critical consideration for the other secretaries-general, only for Boutros-Ghali because of his particular training or personal predilection, or has this dimension been artificially overemphasized for Boutros-Ghali? A closer comparison of the officeholders in this respect could provide greater insight into this question.

When considering the place of religious and moral values in guiding decisions on issues of peace and security, it is not surprising to see discussions of just war arise in several of the analyses. However, it appears that the Buddhist Thant hewed closely to just war ideals in his handling of the Congo, while Waldheim does not seem to have taken just war considerations into account. Given the importance of the just war dimension, extending such analyses to the other officeholders could reveal important insights. In addition, the different personal value dimensions of their ethical frameworks referenced by secretaries-general in relation to the particular problem area being addressed indicates the potential need for greater nuance in the analysis along these lines across the officeholders. As Lang indicates, given space constraints he is only able to provide a "basic overview" along these lines and encourages such dimensions to be "investigate[d] in more depth," and a similar call appears to be applicable for both those cases that undertook such an initial analysis and those that did not provide such explicit consideration in this area.

Finally, the contributors to this volume were instructed to explore the potential impact of a secretary-general's ethical framework, but not to evaluate or pass judgment on the decisions taken or potential ethical lapses. The end of the Waldheim chapter glances into this realm, but a broader examination of the ethical leadership of UN secretaries-general should consider more directly the question of unethical activities. As stressed in chapter 1, officeholders cannot be expected to be "angels" at all times, so a fuller exploration of the office would incorporate a more normatively evaluative dimension.

Returning to the overarching theme of the UN secretary-general as a moral authority, let us consider two key issues: the relation of personal values to the handling of the office and the expectation that the UN secretary-general should provide moral leadership in an international arena built on power relations and national interest. Personal values affected many of the decisions secretaries-general have made and they have all taken into account the potential moral authority of the office, but the manner in which they approached this role differed according to their personal viewpoint. How each officeholder responded to the call for moral leadership has likewise differed. The interaction between ethical framework and external expectations often provides the most traction when gauging the approach to moral authority taken by each officeholder. As Smith comments in chapter 9, "Annan saw both his own ethical framework and the moral authority of the office as two important and interrelated influences on his policy priorities."

This discussion has broader implications for the expectations of how a secretary-general should serve as a moral authority. It is apparent from this study that any effort by the secretary-general to stand forth as a moral voice in the international community is a complicated and difficult undertaking. The promotion of a global ethic must be considered in conjunction with the range of ethical dilemmas that officeholders invariably face. Their choices are rarely straightforward, and the tension inherent in the dilemmas they face underlines the difficulty of developing an encompassing global ethic. Such impediments have not kept some of the secretaries-general from promoting a particular global ethic; indeed, Thant wished to write a book on the subject. However, the more likely scenario is that secretaries-general will simply continue to do the best they can to interpret and address ethical dilemmas. Because they often rely on their own individual interpretations in this, we return full circle to considering how officeholders rely on their personal values to guide their decisions.

Clearly the chapters in this volume are united by the core theme that all secretaries-general must endeavor to balance competing ethical demands. Lang discusses Boutros-Ghali's desire for utopia versus what can realistically be accomplished. Smith's chapter is titled "Kofi Annan's Balancing Act," which sums up Annan's consistent attempts to balance what he wanted to achieve with political reality. Jones's chapter is similarly titled "Seeking Balance." Comparable ideas emerge in the discussion of Thant's handling of idealism versus realism, with Thant seeking the "middle path" between "noble ideals and human reality." Waldheim focuses on "making the way," while Muldoon points out that Lie, by his own admission, was no utopian, and also attempted a "middle way."

While a secretary-general may try to use the moral authority of the office in this balancing process, such efforts will at times be overwhelmed by power politics. At the same time, however, an officeholder's ethical framework often provided the strength and guidance in relation to pressing for a return to greater emphasis on independent efforts based on moral authority. Along with independence, the importance of integrity, and especially impartiality, was reinforced across the case study chapters. In several cases a secretary-general made an important distinction between impartiality and neutrality. "Thant strove for 'impartiality' but rejected 'neutrality.'. . . He felt that on moral issues it was impossible and immoral to be neutral because neutrality implied a lack of concern," writes Dorn. Lie likewise wrote, "The Secretary-General is not to be 'neutral' above all else, 'for neutrality implies political abstinence, not political action.'" Hammarskjöld as well attempted to practice "neutral integrity" as a way to capture his commitment to avoiding "moral disinterest."

The ideals of independence and integrity are well grounded in the UN charter. Indeed, one of the common findings across the analyses of the secretaries-general was the deep connection officeholders felt with the charter. They often engaged the charter with an almost religious reverence as a sacred text and perceived themselves as the embodiment of the charter and its ethical code.[5] Individual officeholders may have interpreted the exact dictates of the charter in light of their own ethical framework, as seen, for example, in their different approaches to article 99 prerogatives. Yet, in many ways, from the perspective of the secretaries-general the charter already provides a "global ethic" for the international community, and they have done their best to uphold the document accordingly.

Religious and Ethical Leadership on the International Stage

The research carried out in this volume shows that the study of religion and politics is rightfully undergoing a "return from exile" in international relations scholarship, and we hope that our contribution demonstrates the value of analyzing leaders and the effect of their religious values. Clearly, the lack of study of religious factors in the United Nations is unfortunate and deserves further attention. At the same time, scholars should not overestimate the impact of religious values on the job performance of any given UN secretary-general.

This study also provides support for the growing examination of ethics in international affairs. The experiences of the seven UN secretaries-general demonstrate that power and national interest concerns endure, but they are not the only considerations in the international arena. As Nolan has suggested, leaders can operate as a "conduit" for raising ethical concerns in international affairs, and the UN secretaries-general have often played such a role. The claim that ethics have a place in diplomacy is amply supported by the history of the office of the UN secretary-general. Not only have officeholders faced a range of ethical dilemmas as part of their diplomatic work, but their personal ethical frameworks have often informed the handling of these dilemmas. The ideals of just war, and the degree to which they are taken into consideration by leaders entrusted with maintaining international peace and security, also need further consideration. Research could also move beyond descriptive ethics to consider normative ethics more deeply.

In the end, this study supports the contention that religion and ethics have an important place in the study of international leadership. While all individuals, and therefore all leaders, have an ethical framework of some kind, we have tried to demonstrate the ways in which this framework can vary in terms of the personal values that each person brings to a position and how those values evolve over time. While this study has focused on the UN secretary-general, a similar analytical framework could be employed for evaluating different types of leaders in international affairs. The specific operating context might vary, but both external context and personal values would play a role, and would interact, in ways similar to what we have seen in the case of the UN secretaries-general.

The secretary-general has often been referred to as the world's secular pope. This term at once captures the sense of moral authority expected of the position—including its religious overtones—and asserts the United Nations' essentially secular nature. The weighty moral expectations of the office stand in contrast to the difficult ethical dilemmas with which every secretary-general must wrestle. The job of secretary-general is never an easy one, but occupants of the office are likely to continue to rely on their personal ethics and religion and do their best to provide the moral authority the international community so sorely needs.

Notes

1. The pragmatism of other secretaries-general also plays a role in the analyses of Lie, Perez de Cuellar, and Annan. Unlike the case of Waldheim, however, it does not seem to be as central to their ethical frameworks, although Muldoon does point to Lie's "strategic pragmatism."

2. This is not to argue that World War II had no impact on these two men, but Lyon focuses more on the negative repercussions that World War I had on the political career of Hammarskjöld's father, as well as the neutral stance taken by Sweden during that war, and the possible early shaping influence these factors had on Hammarskjöld. The analysis of Thant does briefly discuss his time under Japanese occupation during the war, but Dorn indicates that it was the Karen insurgency, which came on the heels of the war, that had "a major influence on his thinking and, quite possibly, his later actions as UN secretary-general."

3. The reluctance of secretaries-general to discuss such personal values while in office is further demonstrated by Ban Ki-moon. Following his election in October 2006, the secretary-general-designate responded at a press conference to the

question "Do you believe in God? And to what degree does God or that religious belief inform your decisions?" by stating, "Now, as Secretary-General, it will not be appropriate at this time to talk about my own belief in any particular religion or God." UN Document SG/2117, October 14, 2006.

4. Olivia Ward, "Next UN Boss a Quiet Workaholic," *Toronto Star,* October 8, 2006. Another report further clarifies that Ban is "a member of the 'Non-church Movement' (Mugyohoe), which spread to Korea from Japan in the 1920s. Its members, mostly intellectuals, make the Gospel a source of inspiration for their private and public life." Aura Sabadus, "It's Asia's Turn, as UN Makes South Korean Next Leader," *Scotsman,* October 14, 2006. However, it should be noted that an *Economist* report that echoed this information subsequently printed a retraction that stated in part, "Mr. Ban does not belong to any church or religious group, believing that faith is an individual matter. We apologise for our error." "Mission Impossible?" *Economist,* January 6, 2007. Further demonstrating the perceived importance of religion and the secretary-general, Ward also notes that Ban's background is "to the annoyance of some Islamic countries, since there has never been a Muslim secretary general." However, she also observes, "But the Confucian virtues of benevolence, righteousness, propriety, and wisdom appear to be his ruling principles," which indicates that analysis of Ban's religious values, as with several of the other secretaries-general, will require broader consideration of spiritual influences. The potential deeper spiritual linkages are also evident in reports from Ban's home village, which is being visited by those seeking its *feng shui* good fortune, with his election touted by local residents as an "affirmation" of "old beliefs" and "as the fulfillment of a prophecy." In addition, Ban's mother, identified as a Buddhist, indicates that Ban "succeeded because of hard work and good karma built up by a lifetime of generosity." Martin Fackler, "On His Ancestors' Wings, a Korean Soars to the U.N.," *New York Times,* December 22, 2006.

5. Secretary-General Ban's swearing-in ceremony reinforces this view, for he requested to take the oath of office with his hand on the charter, which he said would "illustrate my faith in the Charter." UN Document SG/2119 and GA/10558, December 14, 2006.

CONTRIBUTORS

A. Walter Dorn is associate professor of defense studies at the Royal Military College of Canada and cochair of the Department of Security Studies at the RMC-affiliated Canadian Forces College. He is a scientist by training (PhD in chemistry, University of Toronto) whose doctoral research was aimed at chemical sensing for arms control. He assisted with the negotiation, ratification, and implementation of the 1993 Chemical Weapons Convention. His interests are now broader, covering both international and human security, especially peacekeeping and the United Nations. He has published works on the secretary-general, focusing on fact finding, early warning, and the use of article 99. He is also interested in the religious dimensions of international relations, and is the author of "Lotus on the Lake: How Eastern Spirituality Contributes to the Vision of World Peace" and "The United Nations as a Spiritual Institution" and the editor of *World Order for the New Millennium: Political, Cultural, and Spiritual Approaches to Building Peace* (St. Martin's Press, 1999). He also has experience in UN field missions in conflict areas. In 1999 he served as district electoral officer with the UN mission in East Timor. He has taught peacekeepers in Guatemala as well as at the Pearson Peacekeeping Centre. He served with the United Nations in Ethiopia (UNDP project) and at UN headquarters as a training adviser with the UN's Department of Peacekeeping Operations. He recently completed a report for the General Assembly's Special Committee on Peacekeeping, focusing on monitoring technologies to enhance the safety and effectiveness of UN personnel.

David P. Forsythe is university professor and Charles J. Mach Distinguished Professor of Political Science at the University of Nebraska–Lincoln. Educated at Wake Forest (BA) and Princeton (MA, PhD), he joined the faculty at UNL in 1973, serving as department chair from 1993 to 1998. He has held postdoctoral fellowships at Princeton and Yale and visiting professorships at universities in Denmark, Ireland, The Netherlands, and Switzerland. He has been a consultant to the International Red Cross and Red Crescent

Movement, and to the United Nations Office of the High Commissioner for Refugees. He served as president of the Human Rights Committee of the International Political Science Association, as vice president of the International Studies Association, and as a member of the Committee on Scientific Freedom and Responsibility of the American Association for the Advancement of Science. He has written more than seventy-five publications on different aspects of international relations, including *Human Rights in International Relations* (Cambridge University Press, 2000; translated into Chinese, Turkish, Korean, and Bulgarian), *Human Rights and Comparative Foreign Policy* (United Nations University Press, 2000) (editor), *The United States and Human Rights* (University of Nebraska Press, 2000) (editor), *The United Nations and Changing World Politics*, with Thomas Weiss, Roger Coate, and Kelly-Kate Pease, 5th ed. (Westview Press, 2007), *Human Rights and Diversity: Area Studies Revisited* (University of Nebraska Press, 2004) (coeditor with Patrice McMahon), and *The Humanitarians: The International Committee of the Red Cross* (Cambridge University Press, 2005). In the fall of 2003 the Midwest section of the International Studies Association presented him with the Quincy Wright Distinguished Scholar Award in honor of his lifetime professional achievements.

Dorothy V. Jones is a scholar-in-residence at the Newberry Library, Chicago. At the University of Chicago, where she received her PhD, she studied with the international historian Akira Iriye. A two-year MacArthur Foundation postdoctoral fellowship allowed her to pursue the study of ethics and international affairs, as did service on the board of trustees of the Carnegie Council on Ethics and International Affairs and on the editorial advisory board of the council's scholarly journal, *Ethics and International Affairs*. She has also been an associate professor in the History Department of Northwestern University. Her book *Toward a Just World* (University of Chicago Press, 2002) won the Jervis-Schroeder Prize of the history and politics section of the American Political Science Association. Her writing on the UN secretary-general includes a 1994 article titled "The Example of Dag Hammarskjöld: Style and Effectiveness at the UN" and chapters in *Ethics and Statecraft: The Moral Dimension of International Affairs* (Praeger, 2004) and *The Adventure of Peace: Dag Hammarskjöld and the Future of the UN* (Palgrave Macmillan, 2005). Her current projects include a study of restraints on the use of force, and research for two entries in *The Dictionary of Transnational History*, to be published by Palgrave Macmillan.

Kent J. Kille is an associate professor in the Department of Political Science and the chair of the International Relations Program at The College of Wooster. He has teaching and research interests in international organization, political leadership, peace studies, national identity, and active learning. He is the author of *From Manager to Visionary: The Secretary-General of the United Nations* (Palgrave Macmillan, 2006) and has written articles for *International Studies Perspectives, International Studies Review,* and *Political Psychology.* He is an associate editor of the *International Journal of Peace Studies* and served as special editor of the autumn / winter 2004 issue, "Putting the Peace Tools to Work: Essays in Honor of Chadwick F. Alger."

Michael T. Kuchinsky is an assistant professor at Gardner-Webb University. He received his BA from Wittenberg University with a double major in political science and religion. He received his MDiv from the Lutheran School of Theology in Chicago, his MA in political science from University of Richmond, and his PhD in government and international studies from the University of South Carolina. He has served as chaplain for Newberry College, project coordinator for the Africa Food Security Project at the Bread for the World Institute, and as vice president of the Luther Institute. He has also taught at Columbia College, George Washington University, Goucher College, Hood College, and Newberry College.

Anthony F. Lang Jr. is a senior lecturer in the School of International Relations at the University of St. Andrews. He has taught at the American University in Cairo, Yale University, Bard College, and Albright College, and served as a program officer at the Carnegie Council on Ethics and International Affairs. He currently serves on the editorial board of the journal *Ethics and International Affairs.* His research and teaching focus on international political theory, with particular attention to the use of military force, humanitarian intervention, and U.S. foreign policy. He has written one book, *Agency and Ethics: The Politics of Military Intervention* (State University of New York Press, 2002), edited or coedited four other books, written several book chapters—including "Conflicting Narratives, Conflicting Moralities: The United Nations and the Failure of Humanitarian Intervention" and "The United Nations and the Fall of Srebrenica: Meaningful Responsibility and International Society"—and published articles in *PS: Politics and Political Science, European Journal of International Relations, Cambridge Review of International Affairs,* and *International Relations.* His current work focuses on punishment and justice at the global level.

Alynna J. Lyon is an assistant professor in the Department of Political Science at the University of New Hampshire. She received her PhD from the University of South Carolina in 1999. Her research focuses on ethnic identity, conflict, peacekeeping, and international organizations. Her recent articles include "Revisiting the Lessons of Multilateral Peacekeeping: A Critical Analysis of UNAMIR and KFOR" in *Global Society*, "International Influences on the Mobilization of Violence in Kosovo and Macedonia" in the *Journal of International Relations and Development,* and "Policing After Ethnic Conflict" in *Policing: An International Journal of Police Strategies and Management.*

James P. Muldoon Jr. is a senior fellow at the Center for Global Change and Governance of Rutgers University–Newark, conducting research on international diplomacy and international organizations. Prior to joining the center, he was a senior research fellow at the Carnegie Council on Ethics and International Affairs (1999–2000), visiting scholar at the Shanghai Academy of Social Sciences in China (1996–99), and director of education programs with the United Nations Association of the United States of America (1986–96). His publications include the edited *Multilateral Diplomacy and the United Nations Today,* 2d ed. (Westview Press, 2005) and *The Architecture of Global Governance: An Introduction to the Study of International Organizations* (Westview Press, 2004). He lectures on diplomacy and international affairs around the world and has contributed to major newspapers and academic journals on contemporary international relations and global issues. He holds a BA from St. Louis University and an MA in political science from Miami University (Ohio).

Barbara Ann Rieffer-Flanagan is an assistant professor at Central Washington University. Her research and teaching interests revolve around religion, democracy, and human rights. She has written on the relationship between religion and nationalism and the human rights violations that result from this connection in international relations. She has also published articles on the promotion of democracy and American foreign policy. She is currently working on a book on the International Committee of the Red Cross.

Courtney B. Smith is an associate professor at the John C. Whitehead School of Diplomacy and International Relations at Seton Hall University, where he also serves as associate dean of academic affairs and director of the United Nations Intensive Summer Study Program. His teaching and research interests center on international organizations, specifically the United Nations. He has published articles on global consensus building, Security Council reform, the UN secretary-general, peacekeeping, the relationship between the United States and the United Nations, the UN Year of Dialogue Among Civilizations, and teaching about the United Nations. His book *Politics and Process at the United Nations: The Global Dance* was published by Lynne Rienner in 2005.

INDEX

influence of personal values on secretary-generalship, 229, 230, 236–37, 255–57, 343; Iran–Iraq War and, 248–49; liberal values, 235–37, 346; management style, 253; perception of office of secretary-general, 229, 230–31, 240–41; personal qualities, 237–38, 257; political constraints on decisions and actions, 230–31, 240–44; professional development, 231, 236; religious values, 232–35, 252, 339; UN budget problems, 252–53; on UN Charter, 239; UN population control and family planning initiatives, 251–52

personal qualities: significance of, in performance of secretaries-general, 61–62; as source of moral authority, 1; variation among secretaries-general, 56–57. *see also* ethical framework; moral values; religious values

pietism, 3, 70, 103n10
Pius XI, Pope, 190, 220nn11–12
Pius XII, Pope, 191, 220nn11–12
population control, 251–52
positivism, 272
Powell, Colin, 315–16
power relations among states: Lie's perception, 76; Waldheim's conceptualization, 196
pragmatism, 172–73, 353n1; Annan's, 323, 324; characteristics of, 212; moral, 192, 221n22, 221n24; vs. moral advocacy, 255; Waldheim's, 4, 188, 189–90, 200, 212–15, 340
Protitch, Dragon, 91

racial discrimination, 165; U.S. civil rights movement, 306
Radhakrishnan, Sarvepalli, 153, 156
Ramo, Joshua Cooper, 304
Ranarriddh, Norodom, 285
Rasmussen, Larry, 217
Rau, Benegal, 91
Reagan administration, 245–46, 247, 248; withholding of UN funds, 251–52
reconciliation. *see* forgiveness/reconciliation
Religion and Public Policy at the UN, 13, 14, 17
Religion Counts, 17
religious human rights, 188, 209

religious values: Annan's, 14, 302–5; Boutros-Ghali's, 14, 266–70; in ethical framework, 20–21, 36n89, 341; Hammarskjöld's, 14, 58, 113, 116–18, 121, 134–35; international affairs scholarship, 18, 32n58, 352; in international relations, 15–17; Lie's, 70–71; moral values and, 339; Perez de Cuellar's, 232–35, 252, 339; political leadership and, 16; public action and, 57, 58–60, 117–20, 121, 132, 176–77, 190, 211; religious upbringing and, 20–21; of secretaries-general, 13–14, 338, 348–49; significance of, in political science, 31–32n55; as source of conflict, 16; Thant's, 59, 143–44, 151–57, 171, 174–75, 176–77, 178–79, 185n147; Waldheim's, 211–12; in workings of United Nations, 16–18, 33n68, 71, 132–33, 175–76. *see also specific religion*
Rengger, Nicholas, 19
Rhodesia, 165
Rice, Condaleeza, 316
Richardson, Eliot, 246
Rieff, David, 307–8, 318
Rieffer-Flanagan, Barbara Ann, 4–5
Rivlin, Benjamin, 11, 17–18, 313–14
Riza, Iqbal, 310–11
role expectations, 4, 21, 345–46
Rosenau, James, 24
Rovine, Arthur, 11, 24
Ruggie, John, 311–12
Rusk, Dean, 42, 171
Rwanda, 266, 291–92, 300, 306, 318

Sacred and the Sovereign: Religion and International Politics (Carlson, Owens), 16
Sadat, Anwar, 203, 204–5
Salim Salim, 240
Schweitzer, Albert, 114, 154
secession, 162
secretary-general of United Nations, office of: annual report, 8, 81, 172–73, 208, 241; authorities and responsibilities, 7–9, 11, 39–40, 41, 49–56, 64n22, 80–81, 164, 313; characteristics of officeholders, 46–48, 56–57; commitment to peace, 61; conflicting responsibilities in, 301; employment practices, 188, 210–11;